The Possibility of Popular Justice

Law, Meaning, and Violence

The scope of Law, Meaning, and Violence is defined by the wide-ranging scholarly debates signaled by each of the words in the title. Those debates have taken place among and between lawyers, anthropologists, political theorists, sociologists, and historians, as well as literary and cultural critics. This series is intended to recognize the importance of such ongoing conversations about law, meaning, and violence as well as to encourage and further them.

Series Editors:

Martha Minow, Harvard Law School
Michael Ryan, Northeastern University
Austin Sarat, Amherst College

The Possibility of Popular Justice: A Case Study of Community Mediation in the United States

Edited by

Sally Engle Merry and Neal Milner

Ann Arbor

THE UNIVERSITY OF MICHIGAN PRESS

First paperback edition 1995
Copyright © by the University of Michigan 1993
All rights reserved
Published in the United States of America by
The University of Michigan Press
Manufactured in the United States of America

1998   1997   1996   1995   4   3   2   1

A CIP catalogue record for this book is available from the British Library.

Library of Congress Cataloging-in-Publication Data

The possibility of popular justice : a case study of community
  mediation in the United States / edited by Sally Engle Merry and
  Neal Milner.
      p.   cm. — (Law, meaning, and violence)
  Includes bibliographical references and index.
  ISBN 0-472-10426-8 (alk. paper)
  1. Neighborhood justice centers—California—San Francisco.
2. Evaluation research (Social action programs)—California—San
Francisco. I. Merry, Sally Engle, 1944-   . II. Milner, Neal A.
III. Series.
  KFX2353.2.P67   1993
  347.73′09—dc20
  [347.3079]   93-24588
      ISBN 0-472-1-08344-9 (pbk. : alk. paper)   CIP

In Memory of

Fred DuBow

Acknowledgments

The preparation of this book was supported by a generous grant from the Fund for Research in Dispute Resolution. The William and Flora Hewlett Foundation also provided a grant that enabled the authors to meet and discuss drafts of their chapters. These chapters are based in part on an earlier study of the San Francisco Community Boards program, sponsored primarily by a grant from the William and Flora Hewlett Foundation with additional funding provided by the Ford Foundation, the Burden Foundation, and the Fund for Research in Dispute Resolution.

Foreword

Robert L. Kidder

Projects such as the one that led to the production of this volume sometimes seem to take on a life of their own. They spread, they become linked with various other research and career agendas, and they manifest the many complex linkages between its core subject and the "rest of the world." So it is appropriate, on the occasion of this publication, to reflect on beginnings, the people and ideas involved in starting the ball rolling.

Any such reflection is in some ways arbitrary, our research traditions being perhaps more continuous than episodic. But for me it is impossible to hear the words "Community Boards" without immediately thinking of Fred DuBow. Fred was not alone in his interest or work in this area, but he stood out as a kind of prime mover because of his rare capacity to integrate vision, practical administration, appreciation of methodological criteria, and a constant search for theoretical meaning. The Reactions to Crime project at Northwestern's Center for Urban Studies was the part of Fred's work with which I was most closely associated. It was obvious day after day how tirelessly Fred worked at building research networks and the support for them, how the work always found its focus in his seemingly instinctive attempts to maintain theoretical perspective. It was obvious, also, that this was no idle academic exercise for him, that he was intensely committed to doing something that would apply our theories and the fruits of our research to the search for ways to help people. A fundamentally humane core oriented all of Fred's work and led, in our field work, to research dilemmas nobody had warned us about in our graduate school methods classes. Because we were conducting field work on a large scale, we regularly faced the contradiction between coping with large numbers and responding to the local and personal particulars of the communities and people we were studying. Others might have papered these contradictions over with reams of computer output. But for our Fred, the contradictions were a resource for better knowing.

Many others since then have taken different pieces of that research and linked them with other initiatives, producing a wealth of additional material on the San Francisco Community Boards that were so important to Fred. The chapters in this volume represent some of the best of that work. This is not Fred's book—but then in a way it is. If Fred had not been there, the history of this field would have been different. How different, we'll never know. But it is worth taking time to look back before moving on.

Contents

Part 1
Defining Popular Justice

Introduction

Sally Engle Merry and Neal Milner

How possible is popular justice? We can imagine a genuinely popular justice as one that is locally controlled, nonprofessional, and procedurally informal and that envisages a renewed community and decisions made according to community norms. This image of justice arises as an ideal only in societies that already have state law. Here, popular justice is promoted as an alternative to the violence and coercion of state law. According to its advocates, it provides a more consensual and nonviolent process for settling disputes. But is popular justice within state law possible? Or do the ambiguities of authority, procedure, ideology, and practice inherent in constructing an oppositional justice within a state-dominated legal system make popular justice a practical impossibility?[1] Further, popular justice relies for its authority and normativity on a social order distinct from the state. Do the kinds of communities (localized or nonlocalized) that could serve as the locus for an alternative justice exist in societies with state law? Do they occur despite cultural diversity? And do they exist in cities as well as in small towns and villages?

To consider these questions, this volume presents a case study of one experiment in popular justice, the San Francisco Community Boards. This program has made an explicit claim to create an alternative justice, or "new justice," in the midst of a society ordered by state law. The contributors to this volume explore the history and experience of the program and compare it to other versions of popular justice in the United States, Europe, and the Third World. They discuss the multiple and contested meanings of such key terms as

---

1. We take this question from Peter Fitzpatrick's chapter in this volume.

community, justice, and empowerment within American community mediation and other forms of popular justice. The case study serves as a springboard for wider theoretical discussions about the linkages among popular justice, community ordering, and state law and about the possibility of a popular justice in the context of state law.

Although popular justice is difficult to define precisely, its characteristics typically include popular sovereignty, direct governance and control by the people, the capacity of judges to exercise social power autonomously, a minimum level of institutionalization and bureaucratization, nonprofessionalized handling of disputes, and little specialization (Santos 1982:253–54).[2] Popular justice refers to systems for handling cases that are less bureaucratic rather than more, less closely connected to the state rather than more, less reliant on legal experts and more on lay people, less inclined to rely on legal forms of discourse and more on the discourses of the world outside the legal system, and less focused on rules and consistency (Abel 1982).[3]

Analytically, popular justice is located on the boundary between state law and local or community ordering, distinct from both but linked to each. Situated on this boundary, popular justice constructs its own, semiautonomous forms of discourse and order (Moore 1973). But it contains contradictions. Advocates of popular justice claim that it is the antithesis of state law: natural, collaborative, and personal in contrast to the artificial, combative, and impersonal world of state law. Unlike the adversarial and coercive procedures of law, it promises nonviolent resolution of conflicts based on the creation of mutual agreements. Popular justice is conceptualized as more

---

2. In his two-volume study of informal justice, Richard Abel notes that the boundaries of the phenomenon of informal justice must remain fluid but defines its general tendencies as follows:

> We are concerned here with *legal* phenomena, i.e., with institutions that declare, modify, and apply norms in the process of controlling conduct and handling conflict. Such institutions are informal to the extent that they are nonbureaucratic in structure and relatively undifferentiated from the larger society, minimize the use of professionals, and eschew official law in favor of substantive and procedural norms that are vague, unwritten, commonsensical, flexible, ad hoc, and particularistic. Every instance of informal justice will exhibit some of these characteristics to some degree, though in none will all of them be fully developed. (1982:2)

3. Not all of these tendencies cohere: a system of handling cases can be relatively unbureaucratic but closely connected to the state; it can use lay people who see their task as consistently imposing rules; it can use the discourses of everyday life but operate closely tied to the legal system.

closely connected to an authentic community and as more conciliatory and consensual than state law.[4]

Yet, many of the procedures, symbols, rituals, and forms of language used in popular justice derive from state law.[5] Even tribunals ideologically opposed to state law and founded on a critique of its failures still borrow its forms: the table, the book of rules, and the third party removed from the dispute. Versions of popular justice that express ideologies of resistance and self-government, such as the neighborhood courts in Chile during the Allende period (Spence 1978) and the English cooperatives Henry describes (1983) nonetheless imitate the forms of state law. Can a tribunal mimic the procedures and practices of state law and still produce less violent and more consensual justice? Can such a tribunal retain its ideological critique of state law?

Not only does popular justice mimic state law, but state law tends to colonize popular justice. For example, Galanter shows in his study of the Indian *panchayat* of the 1950s how a reform intended to produce community forums for petty cases without lawyers gradually became the bottom rung of the state legal system (1989:43). Over time, these tribunals began to make decisions by majority vote rather than by consensus, to apply statutory law, and to win government support in the execution of decrees. Similarly, Auerbach contends that dispute-resolution institutions in American society have generally become legalized over time through the gradual infiltration of legal concepts, actors, and symbols into nonlegal fields (1983). In Auerbach's description of this process, the takeover is not direct or obvious but a gradual shift in the structure of the enterprise's systems of meaning. Yet other studies document patterns of resistance to this colonization. Instead of focusing only on the extent to which the state co-opts and legalizes informal justice, this work suggests that there are ways in which formal law is itself changed through the challenge of the informal (Henry 1985; Cain 1985; Fitzpatrick 1988). The presence of informal alternatives may reshape the formal itself (Henry 1985).

---

4. Popular-justice tribunals are frequently named after indigenous systems, thus emphasizing continuities between these institutions and the community. American community mediation, for example, is often called "neighborhood justice."

5. Examples include the Knights of Labor courts in the United States in the late nineteenth century (Garlock 1982) or the law of the squatter settlements of Brazil (Santos 1977).

Popular Justice and Violence

In some ways, popular justice provides a stark contrast to the violence and coercion of law. The ideology of popular justice typically opposes violence and promises peaceful resolutions of conflict by drawing on the authority of an allegedly harmonious community. Law, on the other hand, is violent. It depends on an extensive organization of police, courts, and prisons to implement this violence. Law provides a vehicle for legitimating state-imposed coercion, pain, and death. "Legal interpretation depends on the social practice of violence for its effectiveness" (Cover 1986:1613). At times, violence and coercion are not needed to implement law. Instead, people comply voluntarily, and the law enforcers, law interpreters, and parties to the law may share its meaning. But at its base, law always lacks such voluntariness. For the most part, law is associated with coercive solutions to conflicts of interest—solutions in which the parties involved have little say. The experience of those who dispense pain (judges, other court officials, law enforcement officers) are totally different from those who must endure it. The paradigmatic situation here is the judge ordering a recalcitrant party to do something against his or her interests or to risk pain and deprivation. As Cover says, "Most prisoners walk into prison because they know they will be dragged and beaten into prison if they do not walk" (1986:1607).

Popular-justice tribunals typically lack the onerous apparatus of coercion that accompanies law. Even if the people involved in a dispute inflict some pain on one other, it is very different from the sort doled out by law. First, it is somewhat more subject to choice. Since the appearance before popular-justice tribunals is at least theoretically voluntary, neither party has to agree to accept any pain that is beyond what he or she wishes to bear. If it is accepted voluntarily, it may be viewed as a useful sacrifice that brings the recipient closer to others in the community. Second, these tribunals make no sharp distinctions between those who dispense and those who receive pain. Since the experience of the pain giver and the pain receiver is shared, there is, again at least in theory, likely to be less alienation.

There is another side, however. Since popular justice operates inside the state rather than outside of it, it can become another tool at the state's disposal, a way to exercise state control concealed by the mask of informality (Abel 1982).[6] The forms of popular justice are often vulnerable to state control. When the state has no further use for such informal resolution of disputes, it subsumes or destroys popular justice. It may refuse to refer cases or may outlaw popular-justice tribunals. If popular justice appears useful, it may be appropriated and colonized. Then the rhetoric and appearance of popular justice will mask the violence that exists within that setting. When the covert violence of law is part of the process, people are required to participate under threat of legal penalties. Under these conditions, the ideologies that emphasize shared meaning and shared experience conceal the fact that one party can inflict pain on another who has virtually no choice but to accept both the forum and the pain.

Moreover, to locate popular justice under the authority of the community rather than the state does not necessarily produce a non-violent justice. Even in the absence of state violence, community order is not necessarily peaceful or harmonious. Domestic battering, brawls, vandalism, feuds, and vigilante attacks illustrate the violence that is often part of community conflict. Although the community may be portrayed as a haven from state control, a place that encourages voluntary resolution of conflicts based on common experiences and shared meanings, it is rarely free of violence. Thus, popular justice operates between the violence of state law and the violence of community self-help, not in a harmonious community outside state law.

When popular justice embodies the violence of community self-help, as has occurred historically with vigilante and lynch-mob justice and more recently in South African townships,[7] the state may or may not be implicated. The pain may be inflicted beyond the state's gaze or as part of a resistance movement. The distinction does not matter to the recipient of popular justice's pain. Arbitrariness, dominance, and coercion are the darker sides of popular justice. To understand

---

6. Abel and others have argued that informal justice in the United States represents simply an expansion of the state in nonstate forms into community ordering (1982). Harrington demonstrates this expansion in her study of a program based on the justice system (1985).

7. Burman and Schaerf's study of popular justice in the African townships of South Africa in the mid-1980s illustrates that in an environment of extreme political turmoil and violence, people's courts imposed progressively harsher punishments, including severe floggings (1990).

the possibilities of a genuinely popular justice, it is necessary to investigate both of its sides.

The ambiguities of popular justice shape community-mediation programs in the United States as well. They also replicate the model of a court, despite a discourse of opposition: one or more third parties occupy a place above and outside the conflict. Sometimes American mediation programs claim the authority of state law to manage the disputes they hear, and in some circumstances they rely on the force of the state legal system or the threat of invoking it in order to press parties to reach "voluntary" agreements.[8] On the other hand, community-mediation programs represent a form of resistance to state law, with their commitment to uncovering and enhancing nonstate forms of ordering. They endeavor to resolve disputes nonviolently, although in many situations they rely covertly on law's violence.

Popular Justice and Social Transformation

Popular justice typically promises a new form of community as well as nonviolent justice. It commonly offers subordinate groups greater access to justice or greater control over its administration. In addition, it frequently promises tribunals more permeated by the values and rules of local communities and more under the control of local people. Popular-justice tribunals can be used by national political leaders to reshape society and to reeducate the populace. For example, the neighborhood-mediation programs created in China in the 1950s were part of a strategy for reeducating the populace into the new social order promoted by the Chinese revolution (Li 1978; Leng 1977). Salas similarly describes the political benefits to the Cuban government in the early postrevolutionary years of a public theater of local justice, carried out on the streets with a clear articulation of the new moral order (1983). Santos analyzes the importance of popular justice in furthering social transformation in Portugal after the 1974 revolution (1982). And Soviet Comrade's Courts were sites for reeducating the public into a socialist legality and social order (Henry 1983).

American promoters of community mediation of the 1970s and

---

8. Silbey and Merry observed some American mediators who relied on their connection to the courts as a source of authority over the parties (1986).

1980s similarly sought to reshape society and to give greater power over the handling of their conflicts to relatively powerless people. Many of the U.S. experiments in community mediation traced their ancestry to Soviet, Cuban, and Chinese examples. Socialist traditions from the Soviet Union, Cuba, and China were widely discussed in the legal and judicial literature of the period (e.g., Lubman 1967; Cohen 1966, 1973; Garbus 1977; Li 1978; Crockett and Gleicher 1978; Berman 1969; Cantor 1974). On the other hand, the American version of popular justice had a characteristically American flair: an emphasis on helping individuals achieve full personhood and a stress on the expression of feelings as a way of resolving conflicts.

Yet, popular justice rarely puts a previously disempowered group in control of its own conflicts or provides a setting in which a community exercises autonomous authority and makes independent, locally determined judgments. Nor does it typically challenge the hegemony of state law. Unless it establishes a base of power outside the state legal system, popular justice is more likely to entrench and reinforce social changes already occurring in other segments of society or to consolidate changes accomplished through other forms of political transformation. A significant shift in relations of power and a substantially empowered local community seem beyond the possibilities of popular justice.

Thus, there are many ways in which the ambiguities of a popular justice situated on the boundary between state law and indigenous ordering reduce its possibility. Its location produces a form of law expressive of community norms and power that is at the same time dependent on the authority of the state. It creates a nonadversarial mode of settlement that uses the forms and rituals of state law. It constructs a consensual form of justice backed by state coercion. Yet, this location also creates new possibilities. Popular justice subverts state law by constructing a cultural space—an alternative justice that is more responsive to community desires—even if this alternative is phrased within the language and structure of state law itself. It creates an oppositional discourse within state law that insists on the possibility of managing conflict without violence and asserts a model of community ordering. By constructing a vision of an alternative justice, it confronts the legal system with a persistent critique.

This volume explores the possibilities of popular justice through an intensive examination of one of the most prominent and well-funded community-mediation programs in the United States, the San Francisco Community Boards (SFCB). It uses this case study to consider the implications of community mediation for theorizing popular justice and its ambiguous relationship to state law. It examines the meanings of community mediation and its relationship to community ordering in the United States from an historical and comparative perspective.

Community Mediation in the United States

A form of popular justice labeled community mediation mushroomed in the United States in the 1970s and 1980s. It aspired to build a justice system under the authority and normative order of the community rather than that of the state. Demands for community mediation grew out of community organizing and legal-reform efforts in the early 1970s and crystallized into community-mediation programs by the late 1970s and early 1980s. Community-mediation programs often sprang from neighborhood policing and neighborhood watch efforts and from criminal-justice reform movements such as bail reform and prisoner self-governance. At the core of this movement was the hope that handling local problems in community-run forums independent of the legal system would strengthen local self-governance and rejuvenate the self-reliant communities of the past. Community-run forums promised to empower ordinary people by giving them control over their own conflicts. Community mediation hoped to replace the dominance of the legal profession and the courts in the lives of ordinary citizens with the control of neighbors and peers.

At the same time, the community-mediation movement aspired to create a system free from what it identified as major flaws in the legal system. Advocates of community mediation characterized the law as adversarial and suffused with win or lose outcomes artificially imposed by judges. Community mediation was the opposite: informal, participatory, nonprofessional, and reflective of the norms of local communities. Instead of the violence of imposed, coerced settlements, it followed consensual, conciliatory, and compromise-oriented procedures. Agreements required mutual consent.

Interest in community mediation also reflected growing disappointment with the inability of rights-oriented law-reform strategies to eliminate racial and economic inequality and to improve the quality of community life. For many, the loss of community became a more fundamental social problem than inequality. Law, with its adversarial, coercive characteristics, was reinterpreted as a problem rather than a means of reform. Replacing the state legal system with community legal processes and building the capacity of communities to manage conflicts promised to restore this sense of community.

But exactly what *community* meant remained elusive. For some, community was defined by a mythic construction of a harmonious society in which local groups settled their problems without the intrusion of state law. This was the vision most extensively mobilized by advocates of community mediation in the 1970s. Leading anthropologists were called upon to present accounts of small-scale societies in which conflict was handled consensually, and conferences were held to discuss the possibilities of transplanting these approaches to the United States (see Nader 1969 and this volume). Such conferences typically brought together academics, legal elites, and highly placed government officials.[9]

The San Francisco Community Boards was one of the most prominent examples of a form of community mediation deeply rooted in community life. Its ideology focused on the capacity of popular justice to embody community power and to express community values. This vision captured the attention of idealistic program developers, foundations, government policymakers, and countless eager volunteers. It has inspired numerous programs and training models. SFCB continues to stand for a grass-roots vision of mediation when other wings of the field are becoming more technocratic, more closely annexed to courts, and more involved with large-scale, routinized processing of cases. It still espouses neighborhood organization, empowerment, and self-government, although it also has shifted to a greater emphasis on service delivery. Its ideology is powerful, its founder charismatic.[10]

---

9. One of the most important of these conferences was the Pound Conference of 1976, at which the attorney general, Griffin Bell, and the chief justice, Warren Burger, promoted the concept of neighborhood justice centers and Professor Frank Sander presented his proposal for dispute-resolution systems tailored to the nature of the problem. See Sander 1976 for a summary of the discussion. Nader in this volume provides a discussion of the Pound Conference.

10. Raymond Shonholtz served both as the articulator of the Community Boards ideology and as the indefatigable organizer, fund-raiser, and emissary of the program from its inception until he retired from his position as executive director in 1987.

SFCB is similar to most community-mediation programs in that it endeavors to apply conciliatory procedures to a range of family and neighborhood problems as an alternative to the courts. Unlike most other mediation programs, however, it has historically eschewed all contact with the legal system and endeavored to be a self-standing entity rooted in local communities. It claims that the creation of local judicial forums under the management of the community frees individuals from dependence on the state and its alienating, disruptive, and adversarial legal system.[11] Most other community-mediation programs in the United States claim to deliver a better judicial service, to reduce court congestion, or to help people understand themselves better; SFCB, along with closely related programs, attempts to strengthen and rebuild community as well.[12]

Since its inception in 1977, the program has spawned a large number of derivatives, attracted a great deal of private-foundation funding, created a nationwide center for policy and training, and developed a nationwide organization, the National Association for Community Justice, dedicated to spreading its version of community mediation (see Shonholtz in this volume). The program operated until the mid-1980s entirely on foundation funding, sustaining a budget

---

11. In several published articles (1984, 1987) Shonholtz has articulated his vision of the transformative possibilities of a neighborhood-based form of dispute resolution, which he calls a new justice system. The following quote describes these broad goals:

> A neighborhood justice system, where all the system's functions are performed by trained volunteers, can be effective in reducing conflict, alleviating residents' fear of crime, lowering intra-community tensions, and building community cohesion and understanding. Decentralized neighborhood justice systems have the capacity to reach into a community and engage conflicts before they escalate into violence. The effort to empower neighborhoods to resolve their day-to-day conflicts is complementary to but separate from the traditional justice system. The primary task of the neighborhood delivery system is to reach cases before they enter the traditional justice system. (1984:16–17)

12. The creation of a new justice system would, in Shonholtz's vision, create or recreate a more responsible form of community, one reminiscent of civic communities of previous centuries.

> By building a system of community justice forums, community boards demonstrate that neighborhoods have important civic functions to perform. Certainly, local residents perform civic functions when they are directly engaged in the resolution of conflicts. This civic activity is an attempt by neighborhoods to manage themselves and their own conflicts. . . . Community justice forums are embryonic democratic activity and institutions in the urban neighborhood. Since this democratic responsibility and assertion of neighborhood self-governance is not based on state authority, it cannot be imposed. (1984:14–15)

of almost five hundred thousand dollars a year (see DuBow and McEwen in this volume). For a program in a poorly funded field, this represented an enormous pool of resources.

SFCB has had a profound ideological impact on the subsequent development of the alternative dispute-resolution movement. The SFCB ideology provided legitimacy for a community focus during the early years of the alternative dispute-resolution movement (see Harrington and Merry 1988; Adler in this volume). Long after many other community-mediation programs in the United States down-played aspirations toward broader social change, SFCB continued to claim that it provided better conflict-resolution services as well as contributing to a regeneration of civic responsibility and neighborly helpfulness in American community life, although, as Thomson and DuBow show (in this volume), the current SFCB mood has shifted to service delivery. SFCB also offers a distinctive vision of mediation, one that encourages the expression of feelings. It is founded on a paradigm of communication in which problems of interest or right are transformed into issues of feelings and relationships (Silbey and Sarat 1989; see Rothschild in this volume).

Provocative and inspirational, California-hot-tub in its feel, grass-roots as well as empire-building in style, self-governing and autocratic, ideologically charged yet apolitical, SFCB is an institution full of paradoxes. It offers a vision of neighborhood, community, and helping, yet it alienates many of those most dedicated to those ideals as they become frustrated with its centralized control and with the lack of social change achieved through mediation. Sometimes the process provides cathartic breakthroughs, but at other times it is manipulative and formalistic. Despite the widespread appeal of its offer to handle problems through talking and neighborhood care, it draws few cases away from the courts. Promising to concentrate on the problems of people involved in ongoing relationships, it more often deals with problems between strangers. Rather than restoring and repairing relations, it often helps to sever them. Yet, through its massive training programs and neighborhood outreach, it has promoted and implemented a fundamentally different and potentially transformative style of thinking about conflict, where communication and the expression of feelings replace force and violence. By examining this American exemplar of popular justice, the chapters in this volume explore the possibilities for popular justice in the United States.

American cities are not mosaics of small, self-governing neighborhoods, nor have they probably ever been. Is a form of popular justice rooted in the power of local communities possible here? Are people willing to submit their problems to their neighbors for consideration? Is there a community system of values by which these problems can be managed? Can a program of community mediation continue to function outside the legal system, separate from its coercive power? SFCB attracts volunteers in an era when volunteerism seems to be on the wane; it appeals to people who are single, recently arrived in the city, and more often than not, women. Why do they join, and what does the vision of community that SFCB constructs mean to them? As the chapters in this volume explore the extent to which SFCB was able to create a new justice system outside of state law, they examine how state law colonized and reshaped the new justice system and how that system resisted this colonization.

Many of the recurrent debates within the community-mediation field stem from these contradictions of popular justice. How much legal pressure should be exerted to bring plaintiffs and defendants to the table? Should mediation be a specialized mechanism for handling certain kinds of cases referred by the court or a new form of authority outside the court altogether (see Adler in this volume)?[13] Should mediators define the authority they exercise as derived from the court through, for example, "oaths of confidentiality" administered by a judge or as derived from a self-governing community (see Silbey and

---

13. The issue of the nature and extent of authority exercised by the mediator and its relationship to the authority of the state pervades popular justice in Third World countries as well. In some contexts, popular justice appears to support state power and in others to resist it. For example, Spence describes a 1971 proposal to establish neighborhood courts in Chile promoted by Allende's recently elected party, designed to establish a nationwide system of elected, neighborhood, lay-staffed courts, framed in the critique that the poor had no access to the existing legal system and that the professional judiciary was part of the legal order that discriminated against the poor (1978:143). The opposition fought the bill, proposing instead that regular judges hold court sessions without lawyers in poor and working-class neighborhoods for family, neighbor, and property conflicts. These courts retained the same professional judge but made him more accessible. The first proposal, on the other hand, advocated an alternative judicial system designed according to socialist principles to train political participation, demand making, and public involvement. These courts constituted a separate sense of legality, deciding, for example, whether or not to allow speakeasies in the community, even though they were illegal according to state law. But these courts developed within the particular context of Allende's Chile, which allowed them to flourish.

Merry 1986)? Some forms of community mediation incorporate the discourse and symbols of law, while others endeavor to rely on that of the community, of therapy, or of relationships (McGillis 1986:43–48; Wahrhaftig 1982; McEwen 1988; see further Merry 1990). SFCB is important in this debate because it has in the past deliberately resisted any contact with state law. The essays in the book stress the limits of the SFCB's autonomy as well as some important areas of resistance to the formal legal system.

Contested Terms

Several key terms are central to the SFCB and to other community mediation programs: community, justice, empowerment, and "the popular." The community-mediation movement's claim that it has created community-based tribunals that empower local people depends upon how it defines these terms. The concept of community, in particular, has been central to the elaboration of the ideology of American community mediation.

SFCB, for example, has developed an elaborate discourse of community, a set of terms and ways of talking about conflict resolution and conflict resolvers widely shared by volunteers and staff workers. Volunteer mediators are called *community members,* the process is labeled *conciliation,* sessions are *hearings,* mediators are *panelists,* conflict resolution is *civic work,* and time spent running the program is *governance work.* The volunteers, members of this internal community, spend extensive time in training and governance and relatively little in mediation, although they continue to place primary value on the task of mediation. Yet, relatively low rates of voluntary participation by clients suggest that SFCB may not be widely perceived as a center of community activity within local neighborhoods. The essays in this volume indicate that through its elaborate training programs, internal governance structure, and specialized language, SFCB has been more effective in creating community for those who volunteer to work within it than for those who use it (see Yngvesson in this volume).[14]

14. Joel Handler has developed a model of a dialogic community, one in which the client and the service provider speak to and hear one another in a form of genuine communication, a communication that empowers the client rather than forces him or her into dependency (1987). In this kind of communication, the client becomes a subject, not an object of the social-welfare state. This model comes close to the vision

Justice is defined in the community-mediation movement in terms of process. A just resolution is one achieved through a nonviolent and consensual negotiation in which the means of reaching an agreement are more important than the content of the agreement itself (Harrington and Merry 1988). The term *popular* refers primarily to nonprofessionalism in staff, procedures, and office space.

Empowerment suggests an enhanced self-reliance and a greater control over one's life. Through training and the participation of disputants, community mediation claims to empower both mediators and disputants by enhancing their capacity to manage their own conflicts. Disputants are expected to experience this empowerment when they solve their problems in a relaxed setting that allows them to tell their stories and to reach their own agreements without having a settlement imposed upon them. Ideally, they discover that they can manage their conflicts without violence. But the impact on those who handle problems seems to be greater than on those whose problems are handled.

The Research Study

Because of its substantial funding by Foundations, the pressure to do a careful study of SFCB's accomplishments mounted during the early 1980s. In 1980, the Hewlett Foundation, joined by the Ford Foundation, initiated an intensive two-year study of the San Francisco Community Boards. The research study combined an extensive quantitative study of caseloads, types of cases, characteristics of volunteers and comparison of cases referred to mediation and those handled by the police with a qualitative study of the way cases are processed, the organization of the program, and its overarching philosophy. The multiple approaches provide a detailed account of the operation of the San Francisco Community Boards program and a history of its development from the initial days in 1977 to 1983. Carried out between 1981 and 1983, the study examined the program at the pinnacle of its financial success and at the peak of its commitment to community process.[15] Although it traces later developments, the

of the founders of SFCB, suggesting another location for the creation of such a dialogic community.

15. In subsequent years, it has shifted to a narrower vision of its purpose, one more focused on providing services to resolve disputes and less committed to reshaping communities. This change, which has been very significant in the development of

case study presented in this volume focuses on the period in which the influence of the program on the mushrooming alternative dispute-resolution field was most palpable and its vision of a community-based form of popular justice most compelling.

This book presents the findings of the research study and discusses its implications from a comparative and theoretical perspective.[16] Fredric L. DuBow was responsible for the overall direction of the study, and Nancy Hanawi, Oscar Goodman, and Judy Rothschild did a substantial part of the data collection and ethnographic research under his supervision. Although the research was finished by 1985, DuBow died in 1987 before the report was completed. He did prepare a monograph-length preliminary draft of his findings, based in part on earlier drafts prepared by Hanawi and Goodman (DuBow et al. 1985). The preliminary draft Fred put together incorporated insights from all three members of the research team. The chapters in this book draw heavily on this preliminary draft. All of the contributors to the present volume studied DuBow's preliminary report, which served as the basis, in one way or another, for their chapters. The co-authored chapters draw particularly heavily on his work. Some of the contributors to this volume also worked with Fred on the original study. Because the authors are working with an unpublished body of data, the intent is to mine this data, to be evocative and provocative, rather than to provide a full description of the program itself.

The research study included several data sets: the tabulation of 1,576 cases drawn from program records from 1977 to 1982, descriptive reports and interviews of 40 cases studied intensively through interviews and observations over time with an eye to their transformations, a community survey of the quality of life and program

---

the program, is discussed in detail in DuBow and Thomson and in DuBow and McEwen, in this volume.

16. The contributors to this volume all took part in a three-day conference in which each person presented a rough draft of his or her chapter and heard the comments of the other contributors. The purpose was to enable those less familiar with the research study of San Francisco Community Boards to learn more about the study and for those who had greater familiarity with it to share their knowledge with other participants who had worked on questions about popular justice, social transformation, and community more broadly. Held in April 1989 in Honolulu, the conference provided lively discussion of these issues. Contributors subsequently revised their papers on the basis of the conference discussions. Boaventura de Sousa Santos contributed in very significant ways to the discussion at the conference.

recognition in key SFCB neighborhoods, questionnaires and interviews with eighty-two volunteers before training and ninety-one after
training, a survey of the kinds of interpersonal cases taken to one
police station in a SFCB neighborhood in 1983, observations of training, an ethnography of the program and its internal structure, and
interviews with key leaders in the neighborhoods to determine community impact. Several chapters in the first half of the book come
directly out of the DuBow study.[17]

In the past, analysis of community mediation has followed a
fairly well-worn track, focusing on assessments of the quality of
justice that mediation provides, its contributions to the efficiency of
courts, and its ability to satisfy clients.[18] But, despite the wealth of
data evaluating community mediation, there is little agreement about
its overall contribution to social justice, its relation to the state, and
its meaning in the context of contemporary American communities.
We are beginning to recognize the wide range of variation in community mediation programs (see McGillis 1986) but have not examined why they express such diverse ideologies about community
despite the common techniques they employ (but see Adler, Lovaas,
and Milner 1988; Harrington and Merry 1988) nor how to assess a
reform that is also a multivocalic social movement (Adler, Lovaas,
and Milner 1986).

The chapters in this book ask instead about the ways in which
SFCB, as an example of popular justice in the United States, produces
a genuinely popular form of justice, one that challenges state law.
They explore how it is co-opted by state law and how it resists this
co-optation. The chapters suggest that a popular justice premised on
an alternative legality can flourish in the United States, but at the
same time they expose the powerful pressures to accomodate this

17. The chapter by Douglas Thomson and Fredric L. DuBow provides an historical account of the development of the program and its characteristics as an
organization. Judy Rothschild, who was part of the original research team, writes
about the processes used by the SFCB and the ways they sought to transform disputes.
The chapter by Fred DuBow and Craig McEwen provides an excellent overview of
the program and reports many of the key findings about caseload, volunteer participation, and program functioning, contrasting with other mediation programs that
handle similar cases. Fred DuBow and Eliott Currie describe the police handling of
family and neighborhood problems in the SFCB areas.

18. Despite a general recognition of the limitations of client satisfaction as a
measure of effectiveness, much of the assessment has focused on this standard (Harrington 1985).

legality to state law either by marginalizing the caseload or by asserting authority over its disposition of cases. The authors take various approaches to the materials, from quantitative studies of caseload, characteristics of disputants, and settlement rates to more qualitative, ethnographic accounts of process and of program history and ideology. Whether the chapters are comparative or engage in thick description of SFCB itself, however, all contribute to assessing the possibilities of popular justice.

Overview of the Book

Part 1: Defining Popular Justice

The first chapter in this section, by Sally Engle Merry, examines from a global perspective the conditions under which popular justice flourishes or languishes. The comparative examination of popular justice in the United States, Asia, and Oceania highlights the ambiguous and variable relationship among community order, popular justice, and state law and the ways in which these orders reshape one another over time. The chapter develops a model of popular justice in relation to state law and indigenous ordering in order to analyze these interactions. It describes four major cultural traditions of popular justice and locates SFCB in one labeled *communitarian*.

Peter S. Adler examines the range of forms of popular justice in the United States that are called alternative dispute resolution and describes the place of the San Francisco Community Boards within this context. His chapter is comparative, emphasizing the distinctive features of SFCB and the general shape of American community mediation in the late twentieth century. This chapter demonstrates the range of forms community mediation has assumed in the United States as it has adapted to state law.

The chapter by Kem Lowry highlights the problematic nature of describing and evaluating a phenomenon such as community mediation. Lowry examines various approaches to assessment used in studies of community mediation, pointing out which questions are asked and which are not, what behavior is measured and what behavior ignored. He notes the narrow range of questions typically raised about these programs and the limited set of standards by which they have been judged. Yet the way community mediation is understood depends on the standards against which it is judged. Whether popular justice is possible depends in part on who is making the assessment and by what standards.

Part 2: San Francisco Community Boards and the
Meaning of Community Mediation

The chapters in Part 2 of the book focus on the history and development of the San Francisco Community Boards program and on a close examination of two areas of practice: 1) volunteer recruitment and training and 2) case processing and disputant characteristics. Fredric L. DuBow and Craig McEwen provide a valuable description and analysis of the operation of the program and the major conclusions of DuBow's research. The chapter examines the recruitment and training of volunteers, types of cases and disputants, and the kinds of neighborhoods in which SFCB functioned. It provides an overview of caseload during the first six years of the program, noting that the caseload was relatively small and fairly stable over time. The discussion of volunteers indicates that some of the individuals who work with SFCB experienced significant changes, becoming deeply involved in the program, learning new skills that they passed on to others, and feeling some sense of personal growth and increased capacity. Volunteers were likely to bring their friends to SFCB as disputants, and in turn some disputants became volunteer mediators. Although the impact on social change at the community and societal level is limited, it is clear that the impact of SFCB participation on the personal growth of many of the volunteers is great. DuBow and McEwen's research suggests that SFCB and other community-mediation programs are developing a new consciousness of nonviolent dispute management in the United States.

Douglas R. Thomson and Fredric L. DuBow provide a more organizational and historical perspective on SFCB, describing the internal governance system and the discourses created within SFCB. They show how the program shifted from its initial commitment to developing a new justice system based on community capacity for governance to the delivery of dispute-resolution services in association with the courts. Raymond Shonholtz, the founder of San Francisco Community Boards, describes his vision of a new justice system, articulating the aspirations for neighborhood governance and civic action that inspired the enormous output of energy and funding of the early years of the program. His chapter is a statement of the original SFCB ideology and his own account of how he came to develop it and translate it into other spheres of action. It contrasts with the previous two chapters, which focus on the patterns of development, expansion, and retrenchment and on the day-to-day practices of a program inspired by this ideology as carried out in San Francisco neighborhoods of the 1970s and 1980s.

The next three chapters compare SFCB to other programs, considering broader issues of popular justice, such as the ways disputes are transformed in different judicial processes and alternative modes of handling domestic violence. Vicki Shook and Neal Milner take up the theme of ideology presented in Shonholtz's chapter, comparing the ideologies of several programs to show how they shape the way problems are handled. They use the training materials developed by SFCB to compare its assumptions about who can be trained and serve as a mediator with those of three other forms of popular justice. They show how three contemporary North American community-justice programs, including SFCB, assume that mediation skills require the mastery of techniques that must be explicitly taught. This assumption is based on cultural values that stress classroom teaching and consider knowledge of techniques more important than knowledge about the parties. In contrast, in Polynesian Hawaiian society, where close relationships with the parties are paramount and skills in resolving conflict are assumed to be part of everyday life, mediation is not seen as something to be taught. Nor do many other cultures share the SFCB preoccupation with the expression of feelings as a mode of settling disputes. This comparative study shows clearly that the culture surrounding a mediation program structures the kind of justice it provides and demonstrates how extensively North American culture shapes American community mediation in general and SFCB in particular.

Judy H. Rothschild describes case processing in detail, emphasizing the distinctive SFCB concerns with empowerment and the importance of expressing feelings in resolving conflicts rather than eliciting facts and bargaining over issues. Through a careful ethnographic examination of the entire process of case intake, hearing, and follow-up in a single case, Rothschild argues that in the SFCB process, conflicts of interest are transformed into problems of communication. The case she describes is analyzed in the context of the neighborhood in which it emerges. Her study indicates the ways in which the SFCB process contrasts with legal processes as well as the significance of the legal context to neighborhood conflicts. Since she examines only one case in detail, one that failed to reach a settlement, it cannot be considered typical of SFCB cases, the vast majority of which do settle. Nevertheless, she provides a rich description of SFCB modes of case processing, illustrating underlying assumptions about the nature of conflict and the importance of neighborliness, and clearly demonstrating the processes by which the meaning of a dispute is transformed by the intervention of third parties.

Fredric L. DuBow and Eliott Currie examine which interpersonal cases are referred to the police from one SFCB neighborhood. Their analysis reveals significant differences between cases handled by the police and by SFCB. The typical interpersonal case referred to the police concerns domestic violence and has a female plaintiff, while the typical SFCB case concerns neighborhood quarrels. Thus, their chapter shows that SFCB does not handle an important category of violent interpersonal cases. The police do not refer these cases to SFCB, and plaintiffs do not choose to take them there on their own initiative. Since cases involving violence are routinely referred to other community-mediation programs more closely connected to the courts, it appears that because of the oppositional stance of SFCB, it has been marginalized in its caseload, restricted to a small number of cases involving relatively little violence. On the other hand, one could also argue that SFCB is able to adopt a nonviolent process for handling conflicts only because it does not deal with problems involving serious violence.

These chapters provide a way of thinking about the possibilities of SFCB. They demonstrate that SFCB defined a new form of justice, using distinct terms, procedures, and an ideology linked to goals of social transformation, as Shonholtz delineates in his chapter. It endeavored to provide consensual justice outside the realm of state law. Yet they also show the ways in which these aspirations were thwarted. Thomson and DuBow's organizational history indicates that autonomy depended on lavish generosity from private funders that rather quickly dissipated, forcing SFCB to come to terms with the state and to moderate its claims of autonomous popular justice in favor of delivery of dispute-resolution services. DuBow and

McEwen indicate that the program had a substantial impact on volunteers, yet both their chapter and DuBow and Currie's show that the caseload has remained small and limited largely to neighborhood cases, suggesting a marginalization of the program. And even in the process of case handling, as Rothschild's example illustrates, the parties could not escape the implications of state law for their agreement. Shook and Milner's chapter shows how SFCB training practices imitate the formal legal system despite its firm opposition to state law.

These chapters, along with those in part 1, also show how problematic are both the evaluation of the program's practices and the measuring of its contributions to social justice. Since a key feature of popular justice is its ideology of social change, arguments about popular justice often turn not only on the ability of one or another social reform to achieve that transformation but also on the desirability of the social change itself. Indeed, any description of the extent to which popular justice has achieved one or another form of social transformation incorporates a political stance toward the desirability of that change.[19]

Part 3: Contested Words: *Community, Justice, Empowerment,* and *Popular*

The chapters in part 3 explore the diverse meanings of *community, justice, empowerment,* and the *popular* from historical and comparative perspectives. The concept of community is the most fundamental and contested of these terms. Its meaning in one context often differs from its meaning in another.

John Paul Lederach and Ron Kraybill compare practices of mediation in Mennonite communities with SFCB procedures. In so doing

---

19. Understanding SFCB is problematic not just because it is difficult to assess to what extent it has achieved its objectives but, more profoundly, because there are different political meanings to these objectives themselves. Assessments of mediation programs that focus on productivity or outcome but that do not acknowledge the political agenda of the evaluators conceal this ever-present political dimension. The more honest approach is not to talk about efficiency and caseload as if these were devoid of politics but to put one's politics on the table and then begin to fight over the extent to which any social phenomenon promotes these politics. No matter how detailed our knowledge of the SFCB, no matter how many evaluation studies we have, assessment is a political choice, an interpretation of selected numbers and measures framed in a particular argument.

they contrast two very different types of community, an urban neighborhood and a religious congregation. The latter seems more amenable to popular justice than the former. They delineate two different models of mediation: a trust-based model and a neutrality-based model. Mennonite congregations, communities based on shared experience and culture, follow the trust-based model. Elsewhere, where community life is more diverse and less historically grounded, there are pressures to follow the neutrality-based model. Neutrality-based mediation is much closer to the SFCB approach than trust-based mediation, despite the SFCB desire to ground its processes in communities. Lederach and Kraybill describe the tensions produced by professionalization and the gradual adoption of a neutrality-based mediation practice when this model is applied to work within Mennonite congregations.

The chapter suggests that popular justice is possible within Mennonite congregations. Here, a consensual resolution of disputes grows out of shared values and experiences. However, as DuBow and McEwen indicate, the Mission district in San Francisco, where SFCB is located, is a very diverse kind of community, a far different place from even the most contentious Mennon.... congregation. Rothschild's account of a dispute similarly portrays a neighborhood in which distance and difference rather than familiarity and similarity prevail.

Barbara Yngvesson analyzes some of the multiple and coexistent meanings of the term *community*, pointing to the ways in which meanings elide from one to another. She argues that the practices of SFCB privilege an internal form of community over an external one, subtly emphasizing the community of volunteers (those in the internal community) over the community of neighbors (the external one). Thus, Yngvesson suggests that SFCB does not grow out of the community, but instead endeavors to build a program located in a community. Her analysis suggests that the kind of community upon which popular justice is premised does not exist in San Francisco but must be constructed by the program itself. Only for the internal community is popular justice possible.

Christine B. Harrington analyzes SFCB as a form of community organizing, contrasting its structure and ideology with other forms of community organizing in American history: neighborhood patrols, community governance, and direct action such as Alinksy-style organizing. Antagonism to the state and its law, the centerpiece of the SFCB ideology, was fundamental to many earlier efforts at community organizing as well. But Harrington finds that these other efforts to strengthen community identity adopted advocacy and political activism rather than the neutrality and conflict-resolution services favored by SFCB. Nor do they foreground nonviolence. Thus, her chapter describes, from a historical perspective, different forms of justice that claim to represent conceptions of *community* and *popular.*

In her commentary on the alternative dispute-resolution movement, Laura Nader explores the political significance of SFCB and other forms of alternative dispute resolution. She argues that the community-mediation movement in the United States suppresses conflict and prevents the open expression of interests under the guise of a therapeutic consciousness and commitment to harmony. She sees a clear link between elites' fear of the expression of rights in the United States and the emergence of alternative dispute resolution. The ideology of harmony of the alternative dispute-resolution movement downplays basic conflicts of interest and reduces the access to law of powerless people. From the perspective of the plaintiff's need for access to remedies, the alternative dispute-resolution movement is generally not a progressive political force but instead a conservative move to cool the fervor for litigation following the rights expansion of the 1960s and 1970s. Thus, Nader argues that these forms of popular justice cannot be described as either popular or just. Instead, community advocacy groups come closer to producing what she views as popular justice.

Peter Fitzpatrick concludes the volume with his argument that popular justice is an impossibility. He emphasizes the similarities between state law and popular justice. He suggests that popular justice is homologous with state law rather than fundamentally different, sharing the same mythic figures of the responsible, self-realizing individual and the authentic, natural community, figures which are not empirical descriptions of the world but formed historical constructs. As it adopts these constructs, mediation constitutes a new site of power in modern society. Using the expression of feelings as a way of dealing with conflict recognizes the full personhood of the individual as someone with feelings as well as interests and at the same time calls upon that person to reveal himself or herself more fully to an antagonistic opponent and an unknown audience. As Fitzpatrick argues, the revealed self is a site of power, in which other authorities can deconstruct this self and reconstruct it according to new disciplinary forms. On the other hand, Fitzpatrick raises the possibility that community mediation could represent an opportunity to seize the law on the basis of the legalities embedded in the consciousness and social lives of ordinary people.

Conclusions

What are the implications of this analysis for SFCB? That it failed to achieve a form of justice under the exclusive control of local communities seems hardly surprising. SFCB's inability to create a new civic sense and to increase neighborhood self-governance says less about the details of the program's operation and administration than about the extensive involvement of the institutions of the state, including the legal system, in the ordering of these neighborhoods. It is apparent that the residents of these San Francisco neighborhoods continued to choose law as a way of handling problems, particularly for situations involving violence. Popular justice in the sense of a new system that eschews the violence of law has not been possible. On the other hand, in some important ways SFCB has maintained autonomy from state control, although the price has been small caseloads and avoidance of many cases involving violence, particularly in domestic relations. Moreover, it has consistently championed and disseminated a vision of conflict management without the violence of law.

The chapters in this book, taken together, suggest the difficulty of achieving popular justice within the context of state law. Despite the appropriation of the symbols of community ordering signaled by the use of names such as neighborhood justice and references to community ways of handling conflict, SFCB and other American programs of community mediation tend to replicate the procedures and forms of state law more than those of local communities. The SFCB, like other programs, is neutral, not an advocate, in imitation of the legal form. In hearings, mediators sit behind a table, above and outside the conflict, representing a larger authority and taking a stand only in the interests of that authority. They expect a rational discussion of interests even as they allow space for the release of feelings. Indeed, the comparative examination of popular justice suggests that it typically replicates the forms of the legal system to which it is supposed to be an alternative. Moreover, many community-mediation programs (although this is less true of the SFCB) rely on the violence of state law, despite describing their programs as consensual and rooted in communities. They rely on the power of the law to coerce participation and to enforce agreements.

However, some programs that remain resolutely outside state law are relegated to the management of trivial problems and to those that do not involve significant violence. SFCB, which began as a genuinely oppositional program linked to local places rather than to the state, was marginalized by legal officials, who referred only cases they regarded as relatively nonviolent and trivial. This pattern was particularly marked in its early years, when it was most committed to a genuinely oppositional discourse and distinctive practice. Plaintiffs themselves were reluctant to use a nonviolent forum for problems involving significant violence. Over the years SFCB has tempered its critique of state law and forged referral links with the legal system. It has gradually merged with the bottom tier of state law, colonized through processes of funding, case referral, demands for oversight of referred cases, and requirements of supervision and reporting of work. The desire to embody community order has weakened in the face of the powerful language and ritual of state law familiar to mediators and to disputants. This colonization was harder to resist because SFCB neighborhoods lacked the political structures that could provide support and authority outside the state.

The chapters also suggest some important possibilities for popular justice. They document the emergence of an ideology of nonviolent resolution of differences and of a consensual process that operates outside the violence of the law. Community mediation represents a challenge to the hegemony of state law in its critique of law's adversarial stance and reliance on violence and in its claim to provide a different way of achieving agreements. Popular justice creates an ideological space for forums that draw authority and norms from community ordering rather than state law. The discourse of community forums challenges the authority of the state and talks about returning power to local communities or groups. Popular tribunals distant from the state and difficult to supervise permit local practices that reflect community norms rather than the standards of state law. Community mediation raises the possibility of popular seizing of the forms of law—its procedures, categories, and modes of operation—in a forum not under the control of the state, an appropriation of the ideological and symbolic power of law by non-professionals. The law they implement grows out of their everyday understandings. This is a form of resistance to the state's authority to determine law. Although there are examples of this in other settings where it is more effective, such as popular use of the law by urban squatters in Brazil (Santos 1982); nevertheless, American community mediation also represents a place in which popular understandings of law are mobilized by ordinary people to take control of law (see also Brigham 1987).

Contemporary popular justice movements in the United States such as the SFCB have had an impact on changing individuals, even when they have not restructured communities. SFCB is facilitating the turn to a more therapeutic and less adversarial way of conceiving of and handling conflict. SFCB produces volunteers who adopt therapeutic approaches for neighborhood problems and, in their use of consensual justice, see themselves as resisting state law. When a group of people become committed to an ideology that counterposes law's violence, the result is unclear. While SFCB has changed the discourse of community legal politics, it is also clear that the possibility for popular justice is much more limited than its advocates in the United States have envisioned.

REFERENCES

Abel, Richard L. 1982. "Introduction." In *The Politics of Informal Justice,* ed. Abel, 1:1–16. New York: Academic Press.
Adler, Peter, Karen Lovaas, and Neal Milner. 1986. "The Ideologies of Mediation: The Movement's Own Story." Paper presented at annual meeting of the Law and Society Association, Chicago.
Adler, Peter, Neal Milner, and Karen Lovaas. 1988. "The Ideology of Mediation." *Law and Policy* 10:317–39.
Auerbach, Jerold S. 1983. *Justice without Law? Resolving Disputes without Lawyers.* New York: Oxford University Press.
Berman, Jesse. 1969. "The Cuban Popular Tribunals." *Columbia Law Review* 69:1317–54.
Burman, Sandra, and Wilfried Schaerf. 1990. "Creating People's Justice: Street Committees and People's Courts in a South African City." *Law and Society Review* 24:693–745.
Cain, Maureen. 1985. "Beyond Informal Justice," 9 *Contemporary Crisis* 335–73.

Cantor, R. 1974. "Law without Lawyers: Cuba's Popular Tribunals." *Juris Doctor* 4:24–27.

Cohen, Jerome Alan. 1966. "Chinese Mediation on the Eve of Modernization." *California Law Review* 54:1201–26.

Cover, Robert. 1986. "Violence and the Word." *Yale Law Journal* 95:1601–29.

Crockett, George W., and Morris Gleicher. 1978. "Teaching Criminals a Lesson: A Report on Justice in China." *Judicature* 61:278–88.

DuBow, Fredric L., Oscar Goodman, and Nancy Hanawi. 1985. Preliminary Report of the Study of the San Francisco Community Boards Program.

Fitzpatrick, Peter. 1988. "The Rise and Rise of Informalism." In *Informal Justice*, ed. Roger Matthews, 178–98. London: Sage.

Galanter, Marc. 1989. *Law and Society in Modern India.* Ed. Rajeev Dhavan. Delhi: Oxford University Press.

Garbus, Martin. 1977. "Justice without Courts: A Report on China Today." *Judicature* 60:395–402.

Garlock, Jonathan. 1992. "The Knights of Labor Courts: A Case Study of Popular Justice." In *The Politics of Informal Justice*, ed. Richard L. Abel, 1:17–34. New York: Academic Press.

Handler, Joel F. 1987. *Dependent People, the State, and the Modern/Postmodern Search for the Dialogic Community.* Disputes Processing Research Program special publications, no. 19, Institute for Legal Studies, University of Wisconsin/Madison Law School.

Harrington, Christine. 1985. *Shadow Justice: The Ideology and Institutionalization of Alternatives to Court.* Westport, Conn.: Greenwood Press.

Harrington, Christine, and Sally Engle Merry. 1988. "Ideological Production: The Making of Community Mediation." *Law and Society Review* 22:709–37.

Henry, Stuart. 1983. *Private Justice.* Boston: Routledge and Kegan Paul.

Henry, Stuart. 1985. "Community Justice, Capitalist Society, and Human Agency: The Dialectics of Collective Law in the Cooperative." *Law and Society Review* 19:303–27.

Leng, Shao-Chaun. 1977. "The Role of Law in the People's Republic of China as Reflecting Mao Tse-Tung's Influence." *Journal of Criminal Law and Criminology* 68:356–73.

Li, Victor H. 1978. *Law without Lawyers: A Comparative View of Law in China and the United States.* Boulder, Colo.: Westview Press.

Lubman, Stanley. 1967. "Mao and Mediation: Politics and Dispute Resolution in Communist China." *California Law Review* 55:1284–1359.

McEwen, Craig. 1987. "Differing Visions of Alternative Dispute Resolution and Formal Law: A Review Essay." *Justice System Journal*, 12:247–59.

McGillis, Daniel. 1986. *Community Dispute Resolution Programs and Public Policy.* Washington, D.C.: National Institute of Justice, U.S. Department of Justice.

Merry, Sally Engle. 1990. *Getting Justice and Getting Even: Legal Consciousness among Working-Class Americans.* Chicago: University of Chicago Press.

Moore, Sally Falk. 1973. "Law and Social Change: The Semi-Autonomous Social Field as an Appropriate Subject of Study." *Law and Society Review* 7:719–46.

Nader, Laura. 1969. "Styles of Court Procedure: To Make the Balance." In *Law in Culture and Society,* ed. Nader, 69–91. Chicago: Aldine.

Salas, Louis. 1983. "The Emergence and Decline of the Cuban Popular Tribunals." *Law and Society Review* 17:587–613.

Sander, Frank. 1976. "Varieties of Dispute Processing." *Federal Rules Decisions* 70:111–34.

Santos, Boaventura de Sousa. 1977. "The Law of the Oppressed: The Construction and Reproduction of Legality in Pasagarda." *Law and Society Review* 12:5–126.

Santos, Boaventura de Sousa. 1982. "Law and Revolution in Portugal: The Experiences of Popular Justice in Portugal after the 25th of April, 1974." In *The Politics of Informal Justice,* ed., Richard L. Abel, 2:251–81. New York: Academic Press.

Shonholtz, Raymond. 1984. "Neighborhood Justice Systems: Work, Structure, and Guiding Principles." *Mediation Quarterly* 5:3–30.

Shonholtz, Raymond. 1987. "The Citizen's Role in Justice: Building a Primary Justice and Prevention System at the Neighborhood Level." *Annals of the American Academy of Political and Social Science* 494:42–52.

Silbey, Susan S., and Austin Sarat. 1989. "Dispute Processing in Law and Legal Scholarship: From Institutional Critique to the Reconstruction of the Juridical Subject." *Denver University Law Review* 66:437–99.

Silbey, Susan S., and Sally Engle Merry. 1986. "Mediator Settlement Strategies." *Law and Policy* 3:7–32.

Silliman, G. Sidney. 1985. "A Political Analysis of the Philippines' Katarungang Pambarangay System of Informal Justice through Mediation." *Law and Society Review* 19:279–303.

Spence, Jack. 1978. "Institutionalizing Neighborhood Courts: Two Chilean Experiences." *Law and Society Review* 13:139–82.

Wahrhaftig, Paul. 1982. "An Overview of Community-Oriented Citizen Dispute Resolution Programs in the United States." In *The Politics of Informal Justice,* ed. Richard L. Abel, 1:75–99. New York: Academic Press.

Sorting Out Popular Justice

Sally Engle Merry

Popular justice has appeared in a wide array of forms and in highly diverse locations throughout the world: in revolutionary socialist states, in fascist states, in capitalist welfare states, and in postcolonial socialist states. It is sometimes part of a government strategy to promote "law and order" by extending state authority to regions or social fields previously unregulated by state law. Pursuing this strategy, a government may create attractive, accessible courts in order to encourage its citizens to participate more fully in state institutions and to control local fighting and feuding. On the other hand, it is sometimes part of a protest against the state and its legal system by subordinate, disadvantaged, or marginalized groups. These groups may construct a counterlegal order or engage in spontaneous acts of collective judging and violence.

Popular justice has a basic temporality, a historically formed and changing quality. In this respect, it differs from the formal legal system, which typically has far greater continuity and stability. Although a particular manifestation of popular justice may be short-lived, new forms continually emerge. Some are initiated by the state, some by more or less distinct social groups endeavoring to assert some autonomy from the state, and some by dissident groups protesting the power of the state. Popular justice established in opposition

I am grateful to all the other contributors to the volume for helpful comments during and after the 1989 conference of chapter authors. Although all provided valuable comments, I am in particular indebted to Jane Collier, Peter Fitzpatrick, Rhoda Halperin, Christine Harrington, and Neal Milner for their careful reading of earlier drafts of my paper and for their insightful suggestions. Portions of this paper appeared in *Social and Legal Studies* 1 (1992): 161–76.

to the state tends to die out or be colonized by state law, while popular justice established by the state itself gradually becomes formalized and incorporated into state law.

In order to analyze the cultural diversity and temporality of popular justice, I will analyze it as a judicial institution located on the boundary between local ordering and state law with ambiguous and shifting relations to each. After describing this analytic frame, this chapter delineates four distinct traditions of popular justice that have emerged during the past century, situating SFCB within one, and then examines the temporal dimension of popular justice.

It is impossible to define popular justice tightly, but there are certain features that are characteristic of those legal institutions labeled popular justice.[1] Popular justice is a process for making decisions and compelling compliance to a set of rules that is *relatively* informal in ritual and decorum, nonprofessional in language and personnel, local in scope, and limited in jurisdiction.[2] It typically applies local standards and rules and commonsense forms of reasoning rather than state laws. Dress, demeanor, physical surroundings, and modes of talk are similar to those of the surrounding community. Proceedings are held in the local language. Popular justice forums are local in orientation and organization and nonbureaucratic in modes of taking in and considering cases, keeping records, and using forms. The staff is relatively unstratified and unspecialized. Third parties are typically lay people, usually with a small amount of training but without long periods of higher education. They are often unpaid. Decisions are produced in a relatively conciliatory, consensual manner

---

1. In his two-volume study of informal justice, Richard Abel notes that the boundaries of the phenomenon of informal justice must remain fluid but defines its general tendencies as follows:

> We are concerned here with *legal* phenomema, i.e., with institutions that declare, modify, and apply norms in the process of controlling conduct and handling conflict. Such institutions are informal to the extent that they are nonbureaucratic in structure and relatively undifferentiated from the larger society, minimize the use of professionals, and eschew official law in favor of substantive and procedural norms that are vague, unwritten, commonsensical, flexible, ad hoc, and particularlistic. Every instance of informal justice will exhibit some of these characteristics to some degree, though in none will all of them be fully developed. (1982b:2)

2. Santos defines popular justice as characterized by popular sovereignty, direct government by the people, the capacity of judges autonomously to exercise social power, a minimum level of institutionalization and bureaucratization, nonprofessionalized justice, and little specialization (Santos 1982:253–54).

rather than imposed. The proceedings are accessible to the ordinary person. There are usually no high user fees nor any need to hire a specialist such as a lawyer. Popular-justice tribunals are typically close to home and inexpensive to get to for the average person. The scheduling and duration of case handling is usually designed to accommodate the rhythm of work and family life of the clients and the officials of these forums.[3]

Popular justice forums tend to deal with problems involving small sums of money, interpersonal injuries short of murder, and most aspects of relationships between husbands, wives, and other family members. They tend to serve the lower ranks of society and the less powerful; the urban poor, rural peasants, the working class, minorities, women. Popular justice is rarely used by elites, who tend to employ the formal legal system instead.[4] The magistrates or third parties in popular-justice tribunals tend to be higher in social status than those who come to the tribunals. They are often the village leaders, generally more educated, wealthier, older, and better connected with the political system than the average person in the local community. They are typically men rather than women. The magistrates are local elites, not national elites. As Abel points out, since help tends to be extended downward and the personnel of informal institutions are of relatively low status, they help those below them (1982b:6). Popular justice typically functions as the bottom tier of

---

3. Maureen Cain emphasizes the importance of a class standpoint as she develops a typology of informal justice (1985). She defines collective justice as that which serves the interests of the working class as a collectivity through explicit identification of its class interests, through considering its clients as collective subjects with shared problems, through its focus on the long-term working-class interests, and through efforts to make the process accountable to the working class (1985:342–48). She contrasts this type with two others: professionalized justice, based on the interests and power of the professional classes, and incorporated justice, a form of adjudication taken over by an agency of capital or an agency of the state and based on its power (1985:348–60). A fourth type, populist justice, develops in fascist states. It is a form of justice not based in any particular class since there is a disjunction in these societies between monopoly capital and its functionaries (1985:361). I have provided only a brief summary of a complex and detailed argument. Its fundamental point, however, is that forms of informal justice should be categorized according to the classes whose interests they represent and that constitute the basis of their power.

4. Richard Abel argues that the reason informal justice tends to serve this clientele is because informal justice is a mechanism by which the state extends its control in order to promote capital accumulation and counter the resistance this process engenders (1982b:6).

state law, but although some students of popular justice restrict its meaning to state-sponsored tribunals, most define it more broadly.[5] Given this definition, most of American community mediation qualifies as popular justice (see further Abel 1982b).

Each manifestation of popular justice embodies and expresses a distinctive ideology, a vision of the just relations between individual, community, and state. These ideologies are part of broader political traditions of revolution and reform. Political leaders at the national level often use popular justice tribunals to reshape society. The neighborhood-mediation programs in China were an essential part of the socialization strategy by means of which the Chinese revolution proceeded and the reeducation of the populace took place (Li 1978; Leng 1977). Salas similarly describes the political benefits to the Cuban government in the early postrevolutionary years of a public theater of local justice, carried out on the streets with a clear articulation of the new moral order (1983). Santos describes the importance of popular justice in furthering social transformation in Portugal after the 1974 revolution (1982). Soviet Comrade's Courts were also sites for the reeducation of the public into a socialist legality and social order (Henry 1983).

Thus, the relations between popular justice and the state are complex and subtle, running the gamut from those popular-justice institutions that have close ties of referral and supervision by state law to those with more tenuous links, in which the state initiates the program then virtually disappears, providing minimal funding and very little supervision of procedures and outcomes. Some popular-justice institutions even resist the authority of the state but still draw upon the symbols, ritual, and language of state law, such as the Knights of Labor courts in the United States in the late nineteenth century (Garlock 1982) or the law of the squatter settlements of Brazil (Santos 1977). Even forms of popular justice that express ideologies of resistance and self-government sometimes borrow the forms of state law, such as the neighborhood courts in Chile during the Allende period (Spence 1978) and the English cooperatives Henry describes (1983; see also Collier 1977).

---

5. Tiruchelvam, for example, defines popular tribunals as state institutionalized mechanisms for conflict resolution and law enforcement that are staffed primarily by persons who lack a specialized training in law (1984:1). He excludes informal processes that are not set up by the state. He also restricts the term to societies that perceive themselves to be socialist in development strategy or political ideology.

The Structure of Popular Justice

I argue that popular justice is best conceived as a legal institution located on the boundary between state law and indigenous or local law. It can be thought of as intermediate, distinct from both sides but linked to each. In cultural terms it is conceptualized as similar to indigenous law and opposite to state law. In practice, its procedures and sources of authority are similar to those of state law and different from those of indigenous law. Peter Fitzpatrick suggests (in this volume) that popular justice and state law are not opposites but are in some senses homologous. Here, I build on his insight to develop an analytic framework for examining the cultural traditions of popular justice and its temporal variability.

Popular justice intersects on one side with the state legal system and on the other with indigenous or local legal systems. Intersections with state law consist generally of supervision by government officials, some minimal financial contributions from the state, rights to impose fines or imprison (although usually in a very circumscribed way), government involvement in the appointment of magistrates, and rights of appeal from popular-justice forums to higher courts. Intersections with nonstate modes of regulating social life include the influence of mechanisms of social control and conflict management existing within the family, village, and neighborhood and the reinterpretive influence of local cultural categories. I call these modes of legal ordering *local* or *indigenous* but acknowledge that indigenous systems are neither static nor separate from the influence of state law (Wolf 1982).

Since state law, popular justice, and indigenous ordering coexist in any society, they constitute a single social field. Problems, people, and rules cross the boundaries between them, as do possibilities of appeal, of informal networks of influence, and knowledge of identities and histories of persons and problems. Each part of the field exerts some influence on the others, although their power is unequal. These parts of the whole field coexist and mutually determine one another.

The folk conception of popular justice, as presented in the rhetoric of its proponents, differs from this three-part scheme. Popular justice is culturally constructed as similar to indigenous legal ordering and as opposite to state law. It stands between state law, culturally defined as its opposite, and indigenous ordering, culturally defined as its twin. Advocates describe institutions of popular justice as genuine, collaborative, and personal in contrast to artificial, combative, and impersonal state law. Popular justice is conceptualized as more "natural" than state law. Popular-justice reforms are typically described as recreating indigenous law rather than creating new institutions of state law. The tribunals are frequently named after indigenous systems, thus emphasizing cultural continuities with past institutions. Many of these past institutions are now defunct or no longer operate the same way, but the rhetorical flourish of the name contributes to a legitimating narrative that ties the contemporary popular-justice institutions to an indigenous past.

In the United States, for example, mediation is justified as providing a more personal and amicable way of dealing with differences than that offered by the law. This distinction is gendered as well. Talking over problems and reaching consensual settlements is culturally equated with "soft," more feminine ways of handling differences, while arguing, fighting, and going to court are the more adversarial, culturally masculine modes of dealing with differences. Indeed, many of the leaders and participants in the community-mediation movement in the United States have been women, while the legal profession has historically been defined as masculine and has continued to promote and reward men differentially. These distinctions refer not to the practices of popular justice, of course, but to the cultural categories by which it is understood. As modes of conceptualization, these categories both romanticize popular justice by locating it close to the natural community of emotions and relationships and at the same time dismiss it as relatively remote from the exercise of public power and authority.

Popular justice forums are portrayed as more distinct from state power than they really are. Despite the language of local sovereignty and control, they tend to provide a form of law that replicates the law of the state rather than the law of the community. Even tribunals ideologically antithetical to state law and founded on a critique of its failures borrow the forms and symbols of state law: the table, the book of rules, and the judge. Their procedures replicate the model of a court, with third parties who occupy a place above and outside the conflict and who represent a broader set of interests beyond the disputants.

Because popular justice is conceptualized as the antithesis of state law, its cultural definition varies with the nature of state law with which it is contrasted.[6] In countries with Anglo-American legal systems, popular justice is described as the opposite to an adversarial, rights-based, act-oriented legal system. In societies with socialist law, popular justice is presented as the expression of popular consciousness and authority, opposed to the control of the central elite. Many Third World countries equipped with colonial Anglo-American legal systems are developing customary-law forms of popular justice to reclaim a law suppressed during the colonial era. Procedures are conciliatory rather than adversarial, the characteristics of the Anglo-American legal system.[7]

In its early years, the San Francisco Community Boards drew particularly heavily on the connection between community mediation and indigenous neighborhood ordering. Shonholtz claimed that SFCB would recreate the system of civic responsibility and local self-governance characteristic of an earlier era in the United States (1987). He emphasized the role of the community in providing dispute-resolution services separate from the authority of the state, describing the SFCB process as the opposite of state law. Indeed, he deliberately built on the hostility to state law expressed by many Americans in proposing a system of justice connected to a historic vision of community. Other forms of American community mediation made fewer explicit references to the rebuilding of community and the implementation of self-governance. As Christine Harrington and I argue, SFCB succeeded in linking *consensus* with *community*, in harnessing the powerful symbol of the romanticized community of the past to consensual modes of dispute settlement (Harrington and Merry 1988). Yet, in most of its manifestations, community mediation has far closer ties to state law than to indigenous ordering. As the American community-mediation movement has developed, links to government

---

6. I am grateful to Rhoda Halperin for suggesting this point in her work on informal economies. She suggests that the nature of an informal economy changes depending on the formal economy within which it is embedded, whether capitalist or socialist, for example (Halperin and Sturdevant 1989).

7. The notion of popular justice as a form of law opposed to state law may be as old as state law itself. For example, a collection of essays on dispute settlement in early modern Europe argues that there has been an historic pattern of advocating other ways of settling family and neighborhood problems based on love rather than law (Bossy 1983). Auerbach describes a similar pattern dating to the colonial period in the United States (1983).

sponsorship, supervision, and referral have become increasingly strong.

In other countries, popular justice is also justified as growing out of or recreating indigenous ordering. For example, the Philippine system of *barangay* justice, implemented in 1978, is justified with the claim that the new reform builds on precolonial traditions of amicable dispute settlement (Pe and Tadiar 1979).[8] Similarly, popular justice reforms in Sri Lanka, initially promoted in 1949, were modeled after local councils that had existed before the colonial period (Tiruchelvam 1984:76–77). And in China, the new forms of socialist legality claimed to build upon long-existing systems of mediation.

Cultural Traditions of Popular Justice

At least since the emergence of the world economic system, various forms of popular justice have emerged and spread from one place to another, from the core to the periphery and sometimes back to the core. For example, Cuban leaders turned to the Soviet Comrade's Courts for inspiration after the 1959 revolution (Salas 1983); the Chinese looked to the same model in the early 1950s. Sri Lanka implemented local conciliation courts modeled on India's experiments in village councils (Tiruchelvam 1984). The American community-mediation movement was inspired in part by accounts of Chinese mediation, Soviet Comrade's Courts, and Ghanian moots, while representatives from Asia and Africa have recently come to the United States asking advice on establishing mediation programs.[9] It appears

8. When the chief justice of the supreme court, Fred Ruiz Castro, first advocated the creation of such "neighborhood para-legal committees" in 1976, he described the reasons for this choice of forum as an "intended throwback to Pre-Hispanic times. . . . [I]t is inspired by the realization that in spite of the intrusions into the Filipino psyche of the isms of alien civilization, the Filipino has retained an admiral degree of honor and respect for his elders" (quoted in Tan and Pulido 1981:427). On the other hand, Silliman argues that these new forms of justice are an extension of the formal legal system itself (1981–82; 1965).

9. The American movement, particularly in its early years, drew heavily on examples of consensual village mediation in Mexico (Nader 1969), West Africa (Gibbs 1963; Lowy 1978) and China (Lubman 1967; Cohen 1966, 1973; Garbus 1977; Li 1978; Crockett and Gleicher 1978) and from popular tribunals in Cuba (Berman 1969; Cantor 1974), translated into terms appropriate for the American scene (Danzig 1973; Fisher 1975; Nader and Singer 1976; Cratsley 1978). This literature focused on romantic images of amicable village dispute settlement and appeared primarily in legal, judicial, and bar association journals. Despite some warnings from social scientists that things might not be the same in the United States (e.g., Felstiner 1974; Merry

that there is now a globalization of alternative dispute resolution, as it spreads from the United States to Europe, Australia, and back to some parts of Asia and Africa.[10]

1982), this literature provided an important intellectual impetus to the alternative dispute-resolution movement.

10. I studied the American alternative dispute-resolution movement for a decade, assuming, along with many others in the field, that it is a largely American preoccupation that has awakened some interest in Europe and Australia but not much beyond these regions. But at a 1987 conference at the University of Hawaii on cultural aspects of mediation, I realized that the movement is a global phenomemon. Most of the participants were members of the Asian-Pacific Organization of Mediation (APOM), a loose collection of representatives from a number of Asian countries interested in promoting the use of mediation in their countries. At the time, APOM was spearheaded by representatives from the Philippines, a nation that had developed an extensive system of neighborhood justice, or *katarungang pambarangay*, over the last decade. The members of APOM were generally national judicial elites or legal scholars. Many of the participants came from societies in which indigenous, extrastate forms of dispute settlement are common, such as Bangladesh, Thailand, Micronesia, Nepal, Papua New Guinea, and Japan. It is to societies such as these that Americans have looked for their models of alternatives to formal law.

These nations, however, are now turning to the United States for models of mediation and neighborhood justice, citing similar problems of court congestion, overload, delay, and overemphasis on adversarial processes. In 1984, for example, the newsletter of the American Bar Association Committee on Dispute Resolution reported the visit of two lawyers from Ghana interested in learning more about American community mediation. In another example, the Philippine neighborhood-justice reform was promoted by leaders of the judiciary and government as a solution to problems of backlog and delay in the courts (Pe and Tadiar 1979; but see Silliman 1985). In his rationale for the reform, Alfredo Tadiar, who helped to draft the law, refers to the work of Lon Fuller and to discussions held at the Harvard Law School in the late 1970s, a time of ferment and enthusiasm for alternative dispute resolution (Pe and Tadiar 1979). The conference representative from Micronesia, Nikontro Johnny, reported that in his country, federal judicial leaders agree that nonadversarial forms of justice are superior for people living on small islands who have ongoing relationships with each other, but that they are unable to persuade the leaders of the state courts, who handle the kinds of land and other local problems for which alternatives would be most appropriate, to take an interest in the idea (Johnny 1987). Mr. Johnny, as national justice ombudsman of the supreme court of the Federated States of Micronesia, said that he and his colleagues in the federal system have made considerable efforts to explain this idea, have held seminars, and have even invited someone from the University of Hawaii to come and explain the procedures, but that the state courts have not adopted the idea. The representative from Sri Lanka was interested in American training to revive the system of popular justice which had operated in his country for two decades before becoming mired in local politics and falling into disfavor. Alternative dispute resolution appears to be another part of American culture that is achieving popularity in the Third World. Questions about the extent to which this spread is being actively promoted by the United States and why it is doing so, while critically important, are beyond the scope of this essay.

It is possible to distinguish four traditions of popular justice that have developed during the twentieth century, some of which have nineteenth-century roots. Each tradition contains a distinct vision of the contribution popular justice will make to the social and political transformation of society. The first two traditions, the reformist and the socialist, promote institutions of popular justice closely connected to and controlled by state law. The second two, the communitarian and the anarchic, promote institutions more closely connected to and controlled by indigenous ordering.

Reformist

The reformist tradition developed within liberal democratic states and capitalist economies. This type of popular justice endeavors to increase the efficiency of the formal legal system by streamlining it and increasing its accessibility. The goal is to improve its capacity to solve a wide range of problems. In this tradition, popular justice endeavors to make the system work better, not to change its principles. It does not critique the fundamental organization of the legal order or seek to alter relationships of power. Reformist popular justice is culturally constructed as the opposite to an inefficient rather than an unjust system of state law. Failures in the judicial system are attributed to the burdens on the legal system rather than to the underlying structures of capitalism or the law. State law is criticized for its inaccessibility for a variety of problems such as consumer grievances (Nader 1980) and interpersonal problems. The reformist tradition promises to change society by increasing participation in modern legal institutions and by revising procedures.

Popular justice in the reformist tradition promises to develop appropriate procedures for the diverse problems the legal system handles. This tradition creates specialized forums tailored to particular kinds of problems. As some prominent advocates of American alternative dispute resolution describe this approach, it is one of "letting the forum fit the fuss" (Goldberg, Green, and Sander 1985). Since certain problems are viewed as appropriate to certain forums, reformist popular justice introduces new processes tailored to particular problems.

This tradition of reformist popular justice stretches back at least to the late nineteenth century in the United States. Christine Harrington describes the judicial reorganization movement, beginning in the late 1880s, during which decentralized (and I presume uncontrolled) local justices of the peace were replaced with a new unified and specialized court system (1985). In the Progressive Era in the early twentieth century, legal reforms were similarly dedicated to improving access to justice and to efficiency, thus applying to the legal system the concepts of scientific management popular at the same time in the development of factory production and the assembly line (Harrington 1982). One reform was the municipal court, with special branches for juveniles, small claims, domestic problems, and other types of problems. The informal procedures in these new courts made them more accessible to the common person.

In postcolonial societies, the reformist tradition is an aspect of the interest in modernization. Popular justice is promoted as a way of increasing popular participation in the institutions of modern society and familiarizing village people with the workings of a centralized judicial system. For example, in India, one group of proponents of the *nyaya panchayat* reforms expected that they would increase the participation of villagers in the national legal system, educate them about the law, and teach them about participating in the institutions of modern society (Meschievitz and Galanter 1982). The initial enthusiasm for popular-justice reforms in Sri Lanka similarly came from a minister of justice who wished to make the legal system more available to villagers and to increase their involvement in the nation state (Tiruchelvam 1984).

People who hold this vision of popular justice strive to develop courts that are similar to local communities in form and language and easy for ordinary people to get to and use. Yet, these tribunals often become more formalized in an effort to enhance their legitimacy and power. Over time, they begin to adopt the language, rituals, and rules of the formal legal system. The new tribunals may become so formal that a cry for a new, more informal and accessible fringe to the existing institutions emerges. Jerold Auerbach traces this process in the United States, noting the gradual legalization of alternatives to law and the emergence of new alternatives (1983). Separate legal systems are continually absorbed by the formal legal system in Auerbach's historical study, not in the sense of a direct and obvious takeover but through the introduction of codes, standards, formal procedures, and management by lawyers and judges. Commercial arbitration, for example, was originally an informal reform but was gradually taken over by judges and lawyers and absorbed into the dominant legal categories of American society (Auerbach 1983:95–115). Similarly, the juvenile courts, which in the early twentieth century were informal reforms designed to promote accessibility and to provide a more appropriate forum, are now being supplemented by mediation for some juvenile cases. Mediation now offers an informal alternative to juvenile courts, which reformers criticize for being too formal and legalistic (Merry and Rocheleau 1985).

Contemporary American community mediation seems to be becoming more legalistic as well. As Susan Silbey and I observed, by the 1980s American community mediators working within a court mediation program tended to emphasize their connections to the court and its authority (1986). Perhaps, as Spitzer suggests, there is a long-term oscillation between formality and informality, as each new informal reform gradually becomes more formalized (1982). Westermark (1986), Paliwala (1982), and Gordon and Meggitt (1985) describe the increasing formality of the village courts in various regions of Papua New Guinea as village magistrates clamor for uniforms, handcuffs, and even jails to buttress their authority. In sum, reformist popular justice typically appears in countries with liberal legal orders and promises social transformation through improvements in procedure, accessibility, and the appropriateness of forums. Control over these forums rests squarely within state law.

Socialist

The socialist tradition of popular justice springs from Marxist-Leninist theories about the potential of popular tribunals to empower the masses to deal with rule breaking and to educate them in the forms of a new socialist society. The initial inspiration for popular tribunals was Lenin's philosophy, expressed in 1919, that workers should participate in the management of all state and communal affairs, including the administration of justice (Henry 1983). Socialist popular justice promises to transform relations of power from the domination of the bourgeoisie to that of the proletariat. It seeks to bring new groups into the position of determining justice and expresses the nascent will of the masses (Santos 1979). Endeavoring to eliminate the class that owns the means of production and seeks to justify surplus value through law, socialist popular justice tries to replace it with a government of workers.

Soviet Comrade's Courts, Yugoslav Labor Courts (Hayden 1984), and East German Konflictskommissionen are examples of socialist popular justice in European countries. The socialist tradition of popular justice has also spread to many Third World countries, particularly Cuba, Chile, and China. In these countries, popular justice was harnessed to the task of reshaping society according to a new, revolutionary vision. After the Chinese Revolution in 1949, Mao Zedong turned to the Soviet Comrade's Courts for inspiration. After a fairly legalistic period during the 1950s, he dismantled the early courts in favor of a more radical, popularly based form of justice centered in neighborhood and factory mediation. The Maoist conception of popular justice combines the Leninist view of revolutionary popular justice with that of traditional Chinese mediation, producing a distinct version of popular justice in which local forums serve to reeducate the masses in the new social order, eliminate "feudal" thinking, and strengthen the masses (Leng 1977; Garbus 1977; Cohen 1977; Hsia 1978).

In the tumultuous, politically charged years of the Allende government in Chile, popular justice was also used to increase social justice. Spence describes a 1971 proposal pushed by Allende's recently elected party that established a nationwide system of elected, neighborhood, lay-staffed courts (1978:143). Proponents argued that under the previous system, the poor had no access to the legal system, which was structured to discriminate against them (1978:143). The opposition fought the bill and developed an alternative judicial reform: regular judges would hold court sessions without lawyers in poor and working-class neighborhoods for family, neighbor, and property conflicts. These courts retained the same professional judges, but made them more accessible. The courts established by Allende's party constituted a separate sense of legality, "a legality distinct from and partially independent of the dominant and official legality of the state" (1978:178). These courts decided, for example, whether or not to allow speakeasies in the community, even though they were illegal according to state law. Thus, Allende's party advocated socialist popular justice, hoping to train political participation, demand making, and public involvement. The opposition party advocated reformist popular justice intended to provide greater access to the formal legal system.

In Cuba, Castro introduced popular tribunals in 1962 as a teaching tool and as a way to incorporate rural people into the revolutionary new society (Berman 1969; Salas 1983). At first, popular tribunals had popularly-elected lay judges, public discussion and critique of offenders, and great discretion for judges. Magistrates were guided by a small book of principles and their own judgment. To encourage broad participation, the tribunals met at night. Their goals were to reconcile parties or to rehabilitate offenders rather than to punish. These tribunals were intended to promote the education of the public into the new social order (Berman 1969; Salas 1983). By 1977, however, as revolutionary fervor was replaced by a concern with planning and order, popular tribunals in the old mold disappeared. They were replaced by more sedate, professionalized, bureaucratized, and formalized courts holding hearings in courtrooms rather than in the streets, in the daytime rather than the evening, and supervised by judges wearing judicial robes, not work clothes (Salas 1983:596, 610). The popular tribunals gradually fell into disuse as the legal profession resisted lay judges and plaintiffs were attracted to competing traditional courts. However, even these more traditional courts were influenced by the popular tribunals. They still have some lay judges and still aspire to many of the goals of the popular tribunals, such as the legal education of the public (Salas 1983:610).

In the Soviet Union as well, popular tribunals gradually assumed a more preservative than revolutionary role and became more closely connected to state law. After popular tribunals were reintroduced into the Soviet Union between 1959 and 1962, they became an integral part of the state system of social control, intended to educate the public into the rules of the socialist society, to encourage public involvement in the social order through widespread participation, and to provide a way to rehabilitate offenders and return them to society as useful members (Henry 1983:42–43). Despite the hope that socialist courts would increase worker control, in practice they were often attached to state authority and educated the public about the rules of socialist society (Henry 1983:42–43).

Similarly, in China the local mediation centers became places for enunciating and applying state policy rather than undermining state authority. In order to resist this and other more conservative developments, Mao created a new revolution, the Cultural Revolution, which again implemented more socially transformative versions of popular justice. As the post-1978 reforms in China dedicated to modernization proceeded during the 1980s, however, it seemed likely that socialist popular justice in China would again assume a less revolutionary, mass-based form. With the death of Mao, the purge of the Gang of Four, and the beginning of a new era of modernization in 1978, it appeared that China was moving toward a renewed interest in formal legality and an emphasis on rights as a way of strengthening the socialist legal system and promoting an orderly society (Hsia 1978). In the 1980s, government efforts were increasingly going into training lawyers, codifying law, and developing a formal court system.

In sum, socialist popular justice tends to reinforce existing systems of power, just as reformist popular justice does. Despite revolutionary beginnings, socialist popular justice becomes more closely tied to state power and expresses state policies. It tends to replicate the power base of which it is a part. Socialist as well as reformist traditions of popular justice form tribunals that are more closely tied to state law than to indigenous law.

Communitarian

The communitarian tradition of popular justice is much closer to indigenous ordering than to state law. Popular justice in this tradition seeks to operate entirely outside the state and its institutions. Communitarian popular justice is sometimes part of a withdrawal from secular society, an attempt to create a new religious or utopian social order. Communitarian popular justice tribunals typically develop in small communities that are explicitly dedicated to maintaining a separate social order and moral code. The Amish represent one such group, as do the kibbutzim discussed by Schwartz (1954), some utopian movements in American history (Auerbach 1983), immigrant-based legal systems, such as the Jewish conciliation courts (Yaffee 1972), Chinese family-association courts (Loo 1973), and Mennonite congregations (Lederach and Kraybill, in this volume). The Knights of Labor courts, a nonreligous version of communitarian popular justice, were created as part of a movement of workingmen's associations in the late nineteenth century in the United States (Garlock 1982). The leaders of the workingmen's associations, claiming that the state legal machinery was corrupt and run by powerful economic interests, promulgated their own rules of conduct and enforced them without appeal to the courts. The movement, attacked by the goverment, survived only twenty-five years. In the contemporary United States, some versions of communitarian popular justice simply aspire to form local social associations that are more interdependent and sharing than those characteristic of modern urban America.

This tradition of popular justice emphasizes decentralization: replacing centralized bureaucracy with small, local forums on a more human scale. Community norms rather than the legal rules of the center govern. Lay people are in charge. Those who judge are not people who have training in the core legal ideology of the society but people who know the local norms of the community in which they work. Communitarian popular justice advocates indigenous law as a means of humanizing an impersonal society and its alienating and indifferent legal system. It is postmodern in its focus on small-scale, locally derived systems of order.

In general, this type of popular justice exists only as long as the community that created it continues to exist as a more or less autonomous social group. These communities constantly struggle for autonomy from the larger society, which generally penetrates them in various ways. State law generally challenges these groups' claims to sovereignty. Without strenuous efforts to establish and maintain boundaries, as the Amish have made, these communities are unable to maintain closure and local sovereignty.

In postcolonial countries, tribunals dedicated to reviving customary law and recreating traditional communities can be considered communitarian popular justice. These reforms build on a critique of colonialism and the imposed foreign legal order. Some of the proponents of the Indian village councils (Meschievitz and Galanter 1982), the Sri Lankan Conciliation Boards (Tiruchelvam 1984) and the Papua New Guinea Village Courts (Paliwala 1982) envisaged this role for popular justice. Reviving precolonial law is difficult, however. The customary law of the colonial period is a construct of the colonial era, formed in the interaction between European law and indigenous ways of handling differences (Snyder 1981; Fitzpatrick 1981; Chanock 1985; Ranger 1983). Reintroducing precolonial law into the vastly different social conditions of postcolonial countries is problematic. Many postcolonial countries, caught in the pattern of dependent development, are pressured by the economically dominant countries of the core to retain their Western legal systems. Postcolonial countries can rarely afford an extensive commitment to this endeavor, despite the political popularity of eliminating hated alien laws, which were frequently used to control the indigenous peoples for the benefit of colonial economic development (Fitzpatrick 1982; Chanock 1985).

In the United States, communitarian popular justice emphasizes the continuities between mediation in industrialized societies and village moots in the Third World. It conforms to contemporary therapeutic consciousness with its focus on feelings and individual expression (see Bellah et al. 1985). Third parties are conceptualized as humane, responsive, and attentive to feelings rather than interests. In my opinion, San Francisco Community Boards embodies this tradition.

Anarchic

Anarchic popular justice takes the form of mass uprisings in which ad hoc groups assume the power to judge and punish outside the state legal system. In this form of popular justice, ordinary people employ the forms and language of state law to oppose it. It is often described as the actions of the masses against the enemy. Maureen Cain refers to this form of popular justice as "wildcat popular justice" (1985). I call it anarchic because it threatens the established social hierarchy and state authority. It is completely separate from state law in its authority, although it often mimics the forms of state law. But it is often closer to indigenous ordering in its source of power. Unlike the first two traditions, anarchic popular justice is rarely if ever sponsored by the state.

When Foucault defines popular justice as an action carried out by the masses against their immediate enemy, identified as such in response to some specific injury (1980:30), he is describing what I call anarchic popular justice. He argues that popular justice occurs between the masses and their enemies. When the masses decide to punish or reeducate their enemies, they do not rely on an abstract idea of justice, but only on their own experience and on the injuries they have suffered. The decision is not an authoritative one that is backed up by a state apparatus with the power to enforce the decision. Instead, the people simply carry it out themselves.

Anarchic popular justice is fundamentally opposed to the judicial system itself, which it takes to be its enemy. Foucault argues that acts of justice by the people cannot take the form of a court, since the historical function of the court toward popular justice is to "ensnare it, to control it, and to strangle it by reinscribing it within institutions which are typical of a state apparatus" (1980:1). All the great uprisings since the fourteenth century in France have attacked judicial officials, prisons, judges, and others who exercise power, such as tax collectors (1980:6). However, Foucault argues that any effort to construct a court for the expression of popular justice inevitably constrains and controls it. The form of the court itself—the table, the chairman, the magistrates, the claim that the third parties sitting behind the table are neutral with respect to each litigant and that their decision is based on what the two parties say rather than any advance decision, that this third party can determine a truth and ideas concerning what is just and unjust, plus the implication that these third parties have some authority to enforce their decision— these forms are foreign to the very idea of popular justice. Instead, they represent the beginning of the state apparatus.

Anarchic popular justice is associated with popular uprisings against the state and the existing social order, of which the French Revolution is a prime example. Santos describes several instances of this form of popular justice after the revolution in Portugal in 1974: in one, a mass trial of a man accused of killing his oppressive landlord resulted in an acquittal, and in another, a woman accused of illegally occupying a house was allowed to remain in her house by a mass jury (1982:256–62). Some argue that popular justice of this form accompanied the Chinese Revolution of 1949 and was encouraged by Mao Ze-dong during the Cultural Revolution from 1966 to 1969 (Leng 1977). Foucault, on the other hand, talking with Maoists at the height of the Cultural Revolution, was skeptical about the claims of French Maoists that China had achieved a popular justice (as he defines it above) enforced by the Red Army and expressing the class interests of the masses (1980).

Anarchic popular justice is often fleeting, an expression of popular unrest and anger, disruptive and potentially dangerous to the state and to social classes in power. It is frequently suppressed quickly by these groups. Consequently, except in periods of extensive chaos and upheaval, this form of popular justice does not last long. It is quelled by the state or brought under the control of the formal legal system. Not only is anarchic popular justice outside the state, but it is also often outside the control of local communities.

The Temporality of Popular Justice

Popular justice is not only culturally diverse, it is also subject to change over time. In order to demonstrate the fluidity of particular manifestations of popular justice, I will describe the experiences of China, Sri Lanka, and Papua New Guinea with popular justice over the last several decades. I recognize that each of these situations is highly complex and that I am not a specialist in any of them. Here I will provide a brief look at each to show how my typology helps to understand popular justice and its changes over time.

China has a long history of conciliatory forms of justice rooted in clans and villages, the prevailing way of settling differences for centuries. Until recent years, the state legal system was remote and rarely used by ordinary people. After the revolution of 1949, the government of the People's Republic of China implemented extrajudicial forums for family and neighborhood problems, small civil problems, and minor criminal offenses. These forums used many of the same procedures and terminology as the traditional system, such as mediation and social pressure (Li 1978).

The leaders of the PRC view law as an instrument for transforming Chinese society according to a revolutionary ideology. Leng observes that this perspective on law has two roots: the Marxist-Leninist theory that law is a political tool to implement Party policy, and the Maoist idea of "uninterrupted revolution" that calls for continuous efforts to reshape human nature (1977:366). Both formal and informal courts are generally seen as tools of political socialization to inculcate the new socialist morality and to increase popular participation in enforcement of rules and reform of offenders. The educational function of the courts is of paramount importance (Leng 1977:366).

The Maoist conception of law has a strong class orientation. In his famous 1957 speech, "On the Correct Handling of Contradictions among the People," Mao argued that all contradictions (disputes) should be divided into two categories: those arising among the people themselves and those between the people and their enemies (Garbus 1977:396; Leng 1977:364). The first should be resolved by a democratic process involving criticism, self-criticism, self-education, and social and political rehabilitation, and the second by compulsion and severe restraints. Mao defined the people as those who favor, support, and work for the socialist revolution and the enemies as those who oppose it. Thus, any judicial procedure has to take into account the class standing and political background of the people involved. The enemies of the people are identified as the "five black elements": landlords, rich peasants, counterrevolutionaries, rightists, and other "bad elements."

Most civil disputes and minor criminal matters are handled by extrajudicial units at the grass-roots level, such as mediating committees located in neighborhoods and factories and under the supervision of the street revolutionary committees in the cities and the people's communes in the countryside, the primary levels of government (Leng 1977:362; Cohen 1977; Li 1978). Extrajudicial units settle the overwhelming majority of interpersonal disputes and impose sanctions against people whose behavior is not serious enough for the formal courts (Cohen 1977:42). These committees are under the overall direction of the party, with the chief of the street revolutionary committee also serving as the first secretary of the party for the area (Cohen 1977:44). Although the officials of the street committee are paid, those of the subordinate committees, such as the mediation committees, usually are not, but work at other jobs as well or are homemakers or retired (Li 1978:362).

When a conflict arises, an informal resolution process is carried out by party cadres, friends, relatives, neighbors, and coworkers of the people involved. The first step is to determine if the case is an example of the first or the second kind of contradiction. If it is a dispute between two people, the approach is mediation and persuasion by individuals or a small group using familiar techniques of group pressure, criticism, and social ostracism but with the intention of indoctrinating the population with the legal and moral norms of the new society (Cohen 1977). This is the approach generally taken for problems between neighbors and spouses. If the dispute is with an enemy of the people, it requires struggle, criticism, and self-criticism before a group or, in more serious cases, detention and supervised or compulsory labor imposed by public security organs (Leng 1977:362).

The relative importance of these informal popular courts in comparison with the formal legal system has shifted along with the political swings in China (Leng 1977). During the 1950s, China adopted rather formalized Comrade's Courts modeled after the Soviet System. At the same time, there was some interest in developing a codified law. However, in the late 1950s China turned away from this legalistic trend and placed more emphasis on the extrajudicial institutions of neighborhood and factory. With the Cultural Revolution, beginning in 1966, Mao led a strong assault on formal law, promoting lawlessness as the road to justice and calling for the abolition of public security organs, the procuracy, and the court (Leng 1977; Hsia 1978). Even after the waning of the Cultural Revolution in 1969, these extrajudicial forums and the class orientation to justice remained. The 1975 constitution included Mao's two forms of contradiction, a class-based orientation to justice.

However, with the death of Mao, the purge of the Gang of Four, and the beginning of a new era of modernization in 1978, China has moved toward a renewed interest in formal legality and rights as a way of strengthening the socialist legal system and promoting an orderly society (Hsia 1978). Government efforts are currently going into training lawyers, codifying law, and developing a formal court system.

This very brief overview of socialist popular justice in the People's Republic of China suggests that it has been seen as a powerful tool for transforming society and teaching the political ideology of the revolutionary state. Yet, over time, popular justice in China tended to become entrenched in existing relations of power. In order to continue the social transformation Mao envisaged, he carried out a continuing assault on the formal legal system and encouraged judicial forms based on other sources of power. Without this continuing revolution, even socialist popular justice tends to return to a position of reinforcing an existing social order rather than transforming it.

The history of popular justice in Sri Lanka suggests a somewhat different pattern of development, but also one in which the nature of popular justice shifted with changing political currents. I rely here on the thorough account of the development of Conciliation Boards by Neelan Tiruchelvam (1984). Sri Lanka introduced Conciliation

Boards in 1949 as part of a rural development program. They were to handle local problems through conciliation, compromise, and informal procedures (1984:76–77). The boards consisted of three or four officers from the rural development societies—the new, educated elite—and the village headmen. In 1958, under the leadership of a minister of justice concerned about the limited access to justice for the poor and the need for legal aid and more responsive courts, a government statute was enacted that established the boards nationwide. In his memorandum to the cabinet in 1957, this minister of justice, M. W. H. de Silva, argued "the need for legislation to provide an inexpensive and speedy means of promoting harmony among persons estranged by evil disputes and compounding the offenses arising out of these breaches" (quoted in Tiruchelvam 1984:90). His objective was to provide a way of resolving differences quickly and satisfactorily without invoking a court of law in the first instance.

Citizens were required to submit their problems to the boards before they could go to court. The boards were empowered to impose sanctions on people who disregarded their summons to attend inquiries and to produce documents, or who were in any way disrespectful of the boards (1984:91–92). Thus, the boards indirectly acquired powers to fine and punish for disobedience although they could not impose penalties directly. Furthermore, although use of the boards was voluntary and their authority to bring about settlements depended on the consent of the parties, between 1963 and 1965 the government moved to recognize the settlements as enforceable in local courts of law. Special procedures were adopted to prosecute those who acted in contempt of the courts.

Meanwhile, the ideological meanings of the boards continued to change. During the 1950s and early 1960s, the boards continued, under reformist policies, to be viewed as a way of providing justice for those who could afford to go to court. However, under the conservative government of 1965–70, the boards were viewed as ways of reviving traditional customs. Their traditional qualities and continuities with precolonial village councils and courts were emphasized (1984:108). With the election of a more radical socialist government in 1970, the boards took on a new complexion as a mode of introducing socialist legality. They were seen as ways of raising the social consciousness of the people, embarking on a planned socialist development program, and undertaking fundamental economic and social transformation by increasing popular participation in the organization and management of society. Thus, the boards shifted in political significance with each change of administration (1984:183).

The magistrates on the Conciliation Boards were the rural educated elite, not the working classes or the peasants. Relatively educated and affluent men in their middle years, they were above the village population in age, education, occupational status, and income (1984:157). The chairman, in particular, was much more educated than the rest of the village, holding a level of education shared by only 20 percent of the national population (1984:137). The boards were originally designed to be staffed by popularly elected magistrates. However, during the 1960s, local members of parliament took an increasingly large role in the selection of magistrates, nominating their supporters and sympathizers. By 1972, the local member of parliament appointed the magistrates directly (1984:133). Litigants who belonged to opposition political parties sometimes complained to the government agency supervising these courts that they did not receive justice.

Thus, instead of fulfilling the socially transformative goals of the socialists, the boards became relatively conservative institutions that reinforced local relations of power based on party and wealth. The boards expressed the interests of the village elite connected with the ruling party. They tended to enunciate traditional norms rather than socialist ones. Nor were their procedures very conciliatory. The Conciliation Boards tended to make decisions, then pressure the parties to accept them using arguments about the weakness of the case, ridicule, predictions about the low likelihood of getting help from the courts, and the inevitable long delays in court (1984:175–76). If the parties came from the same village, the board magistrates lectured them on the need to live together in peace. If a person were deemed acting badly, he or she was condemned and criticized for his or her behavior. Tiruchelvam argues that through these processes, an adjudicatory determination was transformed into a conciliatory settlement (1984).

Similar to other experiments in popular justice, the Conciliation Boards were closely tied to the formal legal system in operation, although they were culturally constructed as its opposite. Rather than challenging prevailing social attitudes and disrupting existing social arrangements, the Conciliation Boards tended to confirm and consolidate them (Tiruchelvam 1984:186–87). They became part of the project of modernizing the countryside by providing political and legal experience for educated, wealthy elites.[11]

The experience with popular justice in Papua New Guinea is similar. In 1975, after a century of colonial rule by the Germans, the British, and the Australians, Papua New Guinea became independent. There was at that time an interest among some Papuan lawyers in developing a new legal system on the basis of what was called the underlying law, the customary law (Norokobi 1982). One of the schemes for reviving customary law was the creation of a system of local courts by the Village Courts Act of 1974, passed on the eve of independence by the new government with the acquiescence of the Australian colonial government. These courts were intended to handle local problems according to customary law and to follow informal procedures directed toward conciliation and settlement, but they were a part of the state legal system (Scaglion 1981; Paliwala 1982; Weisbrot 1982; Ottley and Zorn 1983). The Constitutional Planning Committee, working just before independence, generally pressed for the "Papua New Guinea way of doing things" and advocated, in its final report in 1973, "We must rebuild our society, not on the scattered good soil the tidal wave of colonization has deposited, but on the solid foundations of our ancestral lands" (Final Report 1973, chap. 2, par. 98, cited in Paliwala 1982:195). Although not permitted to imprison directly, the village courts could incarcerate for disobedience to the orders of the court or for failure to appear (Paliwala 1982:198).

These courts were inspired in part by a renewed outbreak of tribal fighting in the highlands and a concern about crime on the coast. Both of these law-and-order concerns strengthened the position of those who wanted strong local courts and weakened the position of those who advocated local control of judicial institutions and the implementation of customary law, since customary law would presumably allow tribal fighting as well as revenge killings and sorcery killings (Paliwala 1982:196–97; Fitzpatrick 1982:51; Ottley and Zorn 1983). Some hoped the new courts would bring the traditional machinery of social control under the authority of the state (Paliwala 1982:196–97).

---

11. Meschievitz's study of the history of panchayats in India from the early nineteenth century to the twentieth century reveals a similar pattern of co-optation by traditional power arrangements in the villages and patterns of disuse by the public (1987).

The Village Courts Act provided for both village magistrates and the implementation of customary law and procedure (Paliwala 1982). But the Village Courts did little to revive and strengthen customary law. The expatriate Australians at the higher levels of the court system overturned decisions made on the basis of customary law, while the foreign economic interests in the country resisted the return to customary law with its acceptance of practices such as sorcery killings and revenge (or payback) killings, in which a kinsman of a murdered person would kill any member of the lineage of the murderer in retaliation, even if he did not commit the murder himself (Fitzpatrick 1982). Many members of the government regarded the customary legal system as a threat to its authority and legitimacy (Ottley and Zorn 1983:254).

Moreover, in various regions of the country, the magistrates themselves clamored for more authority and endeavored to draw on the symbols of state law: the flag, the handbook of the Village Courts Act, the uniform, and the handcuffs (Paliwala 1982; Westermark 1986; Gordon and Meggitt 1985:230-31). The magistrates saw themselves as imposing government law, not people's law. They were typically the dominant class in the countryside, members of the rich peasantry, although not usually the very richest in a village (Paliwala 1982; Fitzpatrick 1982). The courts were often used by local "middle peasants" to enhance their power within their immediate area (Fitzpatrick 1981, 1982). The magistrates were typically male, between thirty-five and fifty, important in the local clan, and people who had links with institutions outside the village, such as councilors, policemen, medical orderlies, cooperative officers, or even church officials (Paliwala 1982:202). Moreover, in 1978 the courts came under the control of local *kiaps,* local government officials who, since the colonial period, exercised a variety of policing, judicial, and governing functions in the local areas (Paliwala 1982:199). Indeed, the implementation of Village Courts took place at the same time as the previously more self-sufficient, isolated communities were changing as wage labor, cash cropping, and migration spread through the countryside.

In sum, this experiment in popular justice added an additional layer of state courts on top of informal, indigenous forms of conflict management. It did not eliminate the informal courts, which continued to operate outside the Village Courts, sometimes but not always with the participation of current or former village court magistrates

(Gordon and Meggitt 1985). But the new system of courts was named after the village and was described as providing a form of settlement like that of indigenous systems of justice: adopting conciliatory procedures and enforcing customary rather than colonial law (Gordon and Meggitt 1985:214).

These examples suggest that popular justice has a critical temporal dimension. It often becomes absorbed into the formal legal system unless there is a sustained effort to recreate the revolutionary conditions that led to its development in the first place. Although each example has characteristics of different types, popular justice in China is predominantly socialist, in Sri Lanka reformist, and in Papua New Guinea communitarian. Each form gradually became incorporated into state law, yet each is also part of a local community and incorporates some of the discourse and organizational structure of that community. Popular justice is not simply an expansion of state law, but an arena in which state control struggles with local control.

American Community Justice

In the United States, all four traditions of popular justice were discussed in the 1970s, although attention focused on the first three (see further Harrington and Merry 1988; Silbey and Sarat 1989). Judicial, legal, and political elites developed reformist models for improving access to justice (Sander 1976). Socialist traditions from the Soviet Union, Cuba, and China were widely discussed in the legal and judicial literature (e.g., Lubman 1967; Cohen 1966, 1973; Garbus 1977; Li 1978; Crockett and Gleicher 1978; Berman 1969; Cantor 1974). Some legal elites and community activists urged a return to community moots modeled after prototypes in Ghana, Japan, Korea, and nineteenth-century America and inspired by a nostalgia for community (Danzig 1973; see further Abel 1982a:175). Some community organizers suggested recognizing and promoting indigenous dispute settlers who worked outside the legal system altogether (Wahrhaftig 1978, 1982:93–95).[12]

---

12. For example, Paul Wahrhaftig describes a mediation program initiated by a middle-aged black woman in Pittsburgh who already mediated problems in her own neighborhood. To start a program, she simply gathered together some other indigenous dispute resolvers and provided them a minimal amount of training. The program had no records and received no funding (1982:93–95).

The San Francisco Community Boards was a prominent and vocal proponent of communitarian traditions of popular justice in the late 1970s. It drew on that part of the communitarian tradition not grounded in religious or ethnic communities. The goal of SFCB was to use participation in local judicial forums to build neighborhoods, increase local self-governance, and empower local people. Neighborhood mediation panels were to be entirely separate from state law: they took no referrals from the criminal justice system, they imposed no penalties enforced by state law, and they received no financial support from the government.

SFCB located itself closer to indigenous ordering than to state law. Raymond Shonholtz describes the mission of the program as recreating the historical American communities in which community members took responsibility for their own conflicts (1987:46; see also 1984). Shonholtz says that the kind of popular justice he advocates requires building a community support base and developing the dispute-settlement system into a community institution. Although he places primary emphasis on the judicial capacities of communities, Shonholtz envisions the new justice system as working in symbiosis with (but not in a dependent relationship to) the formal system of police and courts by establishing limited links to state law (1987).

In some ways, the procedures of SFCB mediation replicate the forms of the court: the case, the neutral third parties, the table, the book of rules (in this case a loose-leaf notebook with a description of the Community Boards process), the claims to objectivity and the ability of those running the hearing to discern some kind of truth about the problems of the people facing them across the table. In other ways, the processes, the language of case handling, and the outcomes of mediation sessions are quite different from those of the court. The process emphasizes a discussion of feelings rather than facts and encourages, even forces, the parties to look at one another and talk to each other. Panel members and case developers are referred to as "community members." Mediators open hearings by describing themselves as neighbors of the parties. Those with problems are labeled first party and second party as a way of decriminalizing the process and emphasizing the mutuality of the problem. The sessions are public, so that other concerned neighbors can attend, although they rarely do. Symbolically, the session is defined as a neighborhood hearing, not a judicial process. Yet, the emphasis on its public nature is analogous to the judicial system and different from therapy.

Although SFCB endeavors to create and foster self-governing neighborhoods and to develop their indigenous systems of legal ordering, San Francisco urban neighborhoods do not seem well suited to these goals. They lack robust indigenous legal orders. My own work in similar neighborhoods in the northeast United States showed that systems of indigenous ordering were fragile in the urban neighborhoods of the region in the 1980s (Merry 1990). After prolonged periods of avoidance and putting up with problems, the first resort of most people is state law (Merry and Silbey 1984). Although there are many forms of private government in the urban United States, they do not seem to be rooted in neighborhoods but in institutions and organizations. Indeed, SFCB sought to *create* such neighborhood-based communities through popular-justice reforms, not to *build on* existing communities. Given the pervasiveness of legal ordering, the value on individualism, mobility, and legal entitlement in the average American urban neighborhood, constructing communities through this approach is difficult, as DuBow pointed out (DuBow, Goodman, and Hanawi 1985; see also Merry 1990). The weakness of indigenous legal ordering in the SFCB neighborhoods makes problematic the creation of a form of popular justice closely linked to that ordering.

On the other hand, SFCB appears to have created a specialized community of providers of mediation with their own language, culture, and forms of organization. It is the volunteers and the staff who constitute the new community discussed in the SFCB ideology, not the neighborhoods these centers serve, as Yngvesson describes in this volume. The program has in effect created an internal community of those who participate in the program as volunteers. They, not the people with problems, are called community members. SFCB volunteers participate in a wide range of activities, such as training in conflict-resolution skills, holding community educational meetings, training community residents to build a church-community support base, and working with local religious, police, school, and business associations to develop support for the community-justice system (Shonholtz 1987:49). They are drawn into an elaborate system of governance that puts into action the program's emphasis on self-government (DuBow and Thomson in this volume). Although dispute-resolution work is relatively infrequent, volunteers spend a great deal of time taking part in training sessions, governance meetings, social events, and retraining sessions (DuBow, Goodman, and Hanawi 1985). The program provides a language, a culture, a mission, and a social life that readily incorporates newcomers. Indeed, many of the volunteers are single people, new to the city, who lack extensive community ties (DuBow and McEwen in this volume). One could say that the community created by SFCB is that of the volunteers rather than that of the people who live in the neighborhoods.

Like other popular-justice tribunals, including other American community-mediation programs, panel members (mediators) are generally more educated and affluent than the parties who bring their problems to Community Boards (DuBow, Goodman, and Hanawi 1985). In my own research on a similar mediation program in Cambridge, Mass., a program inspired by San Francisco Community Boards and sharing its focus on community and social justice, I found a similar pattern of relatively young, highly educated, predominantly white mediators serving a predominantly poor, racially mixed population of litigants. Yet, the gap between SFCB mediators and clients in education, race, and social class is considerably less than is characteristic of more reformist-inspired American mediation programs (see DuBow and McEwen in this volume).

SFCB is not typical of the broader community mediation movement in the United States. Since the 1970s, the reformist tradition has always been dominant. The judicial and political elites who began the first neighborhood-justice centers expressed reformist rather than communitarian, socialist, or anarchic goals (Sander 1976). At the close of the 1980s, the reformist tradition remained predominant.[13] Remnants of the communitarian tradition continued to exist in the SFCB, other mediation programs it inspired, and in some religiously oriented programs (Beer 1986; Lederach and Kraybill in this volume),[14] but socialist and anarchic voices were distinctly silent. Most

---

13. As Christine Harrington and I have argued elsewhere, there were three distinct ideological projects in the community-mediation movement: one endeavoring to promote social transformation, one to improve the delivery of legal services, and one to promote personal growth (1988). The delivery of legal services project now seems to predominate in terms of funding, number of programs, and number of cases. Yet all three have contributed in important ways to constructing the social movement toward community justice.

14. This type encompasses both the personal growth and social transformation ideological projects, as discussed in Harrington and Merry 1988.

community-mediation programs were dedicated to improving the functioning of the formal legal system by providing a more accessible, speedy, and efficient service appropriate to the particular problems of each party (see Goldberg, Green, and Sander 1985). This version of popular justice, which Harrington and I labeled the service delivery project (1988), is dedicated to reforming and improving the legal system, not to transforming relations of power within the society. It does not criticize the principles of formal law nor the power relations that create and sustain it, but only the degree to which it has fulfilled its own commitment to providing equal access to due process.

Conclusions

This worldwide perspective on popular justice suggests some general conclusions. The space of popular justice, between state law and indigenous ordering, is a contested space. Based on my analytic framework, which locates popular justice at the juncture of state law and nonstate forms of ordering, it is possible to see the form of popular justice as derived from struggles between state law and local ordering. Moreover, understanding popular justice as pulled between two forms of ordering accounts for its temporality—its tendency to change shape and meaning over time. Although popular justice is often pulled under the control of state law, new forms of popular justice based on local, nonstate forms of ordering continually arise and challenge state law.

Popular justice has often been closely linked to state law and pervaded by the language, categories, procedures, and rituals of state law. Lawyers and judges often take over administration of these institutions, bringing with them the discourse of formal law and the codes of professionalism. Sometimes lay people who run popular justice forums also call upon formalism and the symbols of state authority to buttress their authority and to attract cases. Users may prefer more powerful institutions connected with the state, bypassing those that are community based and apparently less effective (Hayden 1984; Meschievitz and Galanter 1982). State law introduces new judicial forms clothed in the language and forms of indigenous law but governed by the authority of the formal legal system. Despite its cultural opposition to state law, popular justice often replicates and strengthens its language and cultural forms.

On the other hand, local people resist this legalization, reasserting demands for more informal procedures and local rules. Separatist or religious groups endeavor to block the intervention of state law, erecting barriers against its intrusion. Subordinate groups such as urban squatters create alternative forms of justice, uniting against a hostile state. Traditional chiefs in postcolonial societies, struggling to retain waning authority against the penetration of capitalist social relations and new forms of legal authority, adopt "customary" forms of conflict management. Community organizations such as the SFCB, working in advanced capitalist societies, attempt to establish a justice system opposed to state law and outside its jurisdiction and control.

Thus, the argument that informal justice is an expansion of state control by nonstate means is only one side of the story (Abel 1982a). On the other side are efforts by nonstate groups to capture this space for themselves, to counter the expansion of state law with forms of justice based on sources of authority outside the state. The contest waxes and wanes through processes of reform, counterreform, bureaucratization, decentralization, informalism, refusal to keep records, refusal to participate, and user preference for state law.

In each of the traditions described, the creation of popular justice is associated with a political agenda and the vision of some form of social transformation and is supported by particular class interests. Socialist traditions endeavor to restructure society to conform to the vision of a new elite, entrenching changes already accomplished through political change. Communitarian and anarchic traditions diminish central power and substitute more localized forms of power. Reformist popular justice seeks to increase the legitimacy of the system and contain discontent, while serving the interests of the dominant groups.

But, by and large, popular justice tends to reinforce and entrench relations of power rather than to transform them. The fact that SFCB did not create new forms of neighborhood ordering in San Francisco is not surprising. This reproduction of power relations occurs, I think, because popular justice rarely grows out of a base of power outside the state or the dominant classes. It is usually more closely tied to state law than to indigenous ordering. Anarchic popular justice is the most direct political challenge to existing power relations and is usually quickly quashed. Popular justice that grows out of indigenous ordering, the communitarian and anarchic traditions, has a greater possibility of challenging the hegemony of language and form exerted by state law. Paradoxically, because of the processes of colonization and domestication of more radical forms of popular justice, the potential for social transformation is greater for reformist popular justice operating within the hegemonic liberal legal order than anarchic popular justice pursuing more revolutionary objectives.

Most importantly, however, popular justice introduces a new ideology of conflict resolution based on nonviolence and opposition to the violence of law. Most forms of popular justice discussed here share a commitment to consensual, amicable resolution of conflicts. Whatever its impact on transforming power relations, popular justice is ideologically powerful in its capacity to imagine a nonviolent ideology of managing conflict.

REFERENCES

Abel, Richard L. 1982a. "The Contradictions of Informal Justice." In *The Politics of Informal Justice*, ed. Abel, 1:267–321. New York: Academic Press.

Abel, Richard L. 1982b. "Introduction." In *The Politics of Informal Justice*, ed. Abel, 1:1–16. New York: Academic Press.

Auerbach, Jerold S. 1983. *Justice without Law? Resolving Disputes without Lawyers*. New York: Oxford University Press.

Beer, Jennifer E. 1986. *Peacemaking in Your Neighborbood: Reflections on an Experiment in Community Mediation*. Philadelphia: New Society Publishers.

Bellah, Robert N., Richard Madsen, William M. Sullivan, Ann Swidler, and Steven Tipton. *Habits of the Heart: Individuals and Commitment in American Life*. New York: Harper and Row.

Berman, Jesse. 1969. "The Cuban Popular Tribunals." *Columbia Law Review* 69:1317–54.

Bossy, John, ed. 1983. *Disputes and Settlements: Law and Human Relations in the West*. Cambridge: Cambridge University Press.

Cain, Maureen. 1985. "Beyond Informal Justice." *Contemporary Crises* 9:335–73.

Cantor, R. 1974. "Law without Lawyers: Cuba's Popular Tribunals." *Juris Doctor* 4:24–27.

Chanock, Martin. 1985. *Law, Custom, and Social Order: The Colonial Experience in Malawi and Zambia*. Cambridge: Cambridge University Press.

Cohen, Jerome Alan. 1966. "Chinese Mediation on the Eve of Modernization." *California Law Review* 54:1201–26.

Cohen, Jerome Alan. 1973. "Chinese Law: At the Crossroads." *American Bar Association Journal* 59:42–44.

Cohen, Jerome Alan. 1977. "Criminal Law: Reflections on the Criminal Process in China." *Journal of Criminal Law and Criminology* 68:323–53.

Collier, Jane. 1977. "Popular Justice in Zinacantan." *Verfassung und Recht in Uebersee: Sonderdruck.* 3:431–40.

Cratsley, John C. 1978. "Community Courts: Offering Alternative Dispute Resolution within the Judicial System." *Vermont Law Review* 3:1–69.

Crockett, George W., and Morris Gleicher. 1978. "Teaching Criminals a Lesson: A Report on Justice in China." *Judicature* 61:278–88.

Danzig, Richard. 1973. "Toward the Creation of a Complementary, Decentralized System of Criminal Justice." *Stanford Law Review* 26:1–54.

DuBow, Fred, Oscar Goodman, and Nancy Hanawi. 1985. Preliminary Report of the Study of the San Francisco Community Boards Program.

Felstiner, William F. 1974. "Influences of Social Organization on Dispute Processing." *Law and Society Review* 9:63–94.

Fisher, E. 1975. "Community Courts: An Alternative to Conventional Criminal Adjudication." *American University Law Review* 24:1253–91.

Fitzpatrick, Peter. 1981. "The Political Economy of Dispute Settlement in Papua New Guinea." In *Crime, Justice, and Underdevelopment,* ed. Colin Sumner, 228–47. London: Heinemann.

Fitzpatrick, Peter. 1982. "The Political Economy of Law in the Post-Colonial Period." In *Law and Social Change in Papua New Guinea,* ed. David Weisbrot, Abdul Paliwala, and Akilagpa Sawyerr, 25–59. Sydney: Butterworths.

Fitzpatrick, Peter. 1989. "'The Desperate Vacuum': Imperialism and Law in the Experience of Enlightenment." *Droit et Société.*

Foucault, Michel. 1980. "On Popular Justice: A Discussion with Maoists." In *Power/Knowledge: Selected Interviews and Other Writings 1972–1977,* ed. Colin Gordon, trans. Colin Gordon, Leo Marshall, John Mepham, and Kate Soper. New York: Pantheon.

Garbus, Martin. 1977. "Justice without Courts: A Report on China Today." *Judicature* 60, 395–402.

Garlock, Jonathan. 1982. "The Knights of Labor Courts: A Case Study of Popular Justice." In *The Politics of Informal Justice,* ed. Richard L. Abel, 1:17–34. New York: Academic Press.

Gibbs, James L. 1963. "The Kpelle Moot." *Africa* 33:1–10.

Goldberg, Stephen B., Eric D. Green, and Frank E. A. Sander, eds. 1985. *Dispute Resolution.* Boston: Little Brown.

Gordon, Robert J., and Mervyn J. Meggitt. 1985. *Law and Order in the New Guinea Highlands: Encounters with Enga.* Hanover, N.H.: University Press of New England.

Halperin, Rhoda, and Sara Sturdevant. 1990. "A Cross-Cultural Treatment of the Informal Economy." In *Perspectives on the Informal Economy,* ed. M. Estellie Smith, 321–41. Lanham, Md.: University Press of America.

Harrington, Christine B. 1992. "Delegalization Reform Movements: A

Historical Analysis." In *The Politics of Informal Justice,* ed. Richard L. Abel, 1:35–74. New York: Academic Press.

Harrington, Christine B. 1985. *Shadow Justice: The Ideology and Institutionalization of Alternatives to Court.* Westport, Conn.: Greenwood Press.

Harrington, Christine B., and Sally Engle Merry. 1988. "Ideological Production: The Making of Community Mediation." *Law and Society Review* 22:709–37.

Hayden, Robert M. 1984. "Popular Use of Yugoslav Labor Courts and the Contradiction of Social Courts." *Law and Society Review* 20:229–51.

Henry, Stuart. 1983. *Private Justice.* Boston: Routledge and Kegan Paul.

Hsia, Tao-tai. 1978. "Legal Developments since the Purge of the Gang of Four." *Issues and Studies* 14:1–26.

Johnny, Nikontro. 1987. "The Relationship between Traditional and Institutionalized Dispute Resolution in the Federated States of Micronesia." Program on Conflict Resolution Occasional Paper no. 1987-3, University of Hawaii at Manoa.

Leng, Shao-Chuan. 1977. "The Role of Law in the People's Republic of China as Reflecting Mao Tse-Tung's Influence." *Journal of Criminal Law and Criminology* 68:356–73.

Li, Victor H. 1978. *Law without Lawyers: A Comparative View of Law in China and the United States.* Boulder, Colo.: Westview Press.

Lowy, Michael. 1978. "A Good Name Is Worth More than Money: Strategies of Court Use in Urban Ghana." In *The Disputing Process: Law in Ten Societies,* ed. Laura Nader and Harry Todd, 181–208. New York: Columbia University Press.

Lubman, Stanley. 1967. "Mao and Mediation: Politics and Dispute Resolution in Communist China." *California Law Review* 55:1284–1359.

Merry, Sally Engle. 1982. "The Social Organization of Mediation in Nonindustrial Societies: Implications for Informal Community Justice in America." In *The Politics of Informal Justice,* ed. Richard L. Abel, 2:17–45. New York: Academic Press.

Merry, Sally Engle. 1990. *Getting Justice and Getting Even: Legal Consciousness among Working-Class Americans.* Chicago: University of Chicago Press.

Merry, Sally Engle, and Ann Marie Rocheleau. 1985. *Mediation in Families: A Study of the Children's Hearings Project.* Cambridge, Mass.: Cambridge Children's and Family Services.

Merry, Sally Engle, and Susan S. Silbey. 1984. "What Do Plaintiffs Want? Reexamining the Concept of Dispute." *Justice System Journal* 9:151–78.

Meschievitz, Catherine S. 1987. "Panchayat Justice: A Brief History of State Sponsored Informal Courts in India." Typescript.

Meschievitz, Catherine S., and Marc Galanter. 1982. "In Search of Nyaya Panchayats: The Politics of a Moribund Institution." In *The Politics of*

Informal Justice, ed. Richard L. Abel, 2:47–81. New York: Academic Press.

Nader, Laura. 1969. "Styles of Court Procedure: To Make the Balance." In *Law in Culture and Society*, ed. Nader, 69–91. Chicago: Aldine.

Nader, Laura, ed. 1980. *No Access to Law: Alternatives to the American Judicial System*. New York: Academic Press.

Nader, Laura, and Linda Singer. 1976. "Dispute Resolution in the Future: What Are the Choices? *California State Bar Journal* 51:281–86.

Narokobi, Justice B. 1982. "History and Movement in Law Reform in Papua New Guinea." In *Law and Social Change in Papua New Guinea*, ed. David Weisbrot, Abdul Paliwala, and Akilagpa Sawyerr, 13–25. Sydney: Butterworths.

Ottley, Bruce L., and Jean G. Zorn. 1983. "Criminal Law in Papua New Guinea: Code, Custom, and the Courts in Conflict." *American Journal of Comparative Law* 31:251–300.

Paliwala, Abdul. 1982. "Law and Order in the Village: The Village Courts." In *Law and Social Change in Papua New Guinea*, ed. David Weisbrot, Abdul Paliwala, and Akilagpa Sawyerr, 191–219. Sydney: Butterworths.

Pe, Cecilio L., and Alfredo F. Tadiar. 1979. *Katarungang Pambarangay: Dynamics of Compulsory Conciliation*. Manila: UST Press.

Ranger, Terence. 1983. "The Invention of Tradition in Colonial Africa." In *The Invention of Tradition*, ed. Eric Hobsbawm and Terence Ranger, 211–63. Cambridge: Cambridge University Press.

Salas, Louis. 1983. "The Emergence and Decline of the Cuban Popular Tribunals." *Law and Society Review* 17:587–613.

Sander, Frank. 1976. "Varieties of Dispute Processing." *Federal Rules Decisions* 70:111–34.

Santos, Boaventura de Sousa 1977. "The Law of the Oppressed: The Construction and Reproduction of Legality in Pasagarda." *Law and Society Review* 12:5–126.

Santos, Boaventura de Sousa. 1979. "Popular Justice, Dual Power, and Socialist Strategy." In *Capitalism and the Rule of Law*, ed. Bob Fine, Richard Kinsey, John Lea, Sol Picciotto, and Jock Young. London: Hutchinson.

Santos, Boaventura de Sousa. 1982. "Law and Revolution in Portugal: The Experiences of Popular Justice after the 25th of April 1974." In *The Politics of Informal Justice*, ed. Richard L. Abel, 2:251–81. New York: Academic Press.

Scaglion, Richard. 1981. "Samukundi Abelam Conflict Management: Implications for Legal Planning in Papua New Guinea." *Oceania* 52:28–38.

Schwartz, Richard. 1954. "Social Factors in the Development of Legal Control: A Case Study of Two Israeli Settlements." *Yale Law Journal* 63:471–91.

Shonholtz, Raymond. 1984. "Neighborhood Justice Systems: Work, Structure, and Guiding Principles." *Mediation Quarterly* 5:3–30.

Shonholtz, Raymond. 1987. "The Citizen's Role in Justice: Building a Primary Justice and Prevention System at the Neighborhood Level." *Annals of the American Academy of Political and Social Science* 494:42–52.

Silbey, Susan S., and Austin Sarat. 1989. "Dispute Processing in Law and Legal Scholarship: From Institutional Critique to the Reconstitution of the Juridical Subject." *Denver University Law Review* 66:437–99.

Silbey, Susan S., and Sally E. Merry. 1986. "Mediator Settlement Strategies." *Law and Policy* 8:7–32.

Silliman, G. Sidney. 1981–82. "Dispute Processing by the Philippine Agrarian Court." *Law and Society Review* 16:98–115.

Silliman, G. Sidney. 1985. "A Political Analysis of the Philippines' Katarungang Pambarangay System of Informal Justice through Mediation." *Law and Society Review* 19:279–303.

Snyder, Francis G. 1981. "Colonialism and Legal Form: The Creation of 'Customary Law' in Senegal." *Journal of Legal Pluralism* 19:49–92.

Spence, Jack. 1978. "Institutionalizing Neighborhood Courts: Two Chilean Experiences." *Law and Society Review* 13:139–82.

Spitzer, Steven. 1982. "The Dialectics of Formal and Informal Control." In *The Politics of Informal Justice*, ed. Richard L. Abel, 1:167–207. New York: Academic Press.

Tan, Bayani K., and Ma. Gracia M. Pulido. 1981. "Katarungang Pambarangay Law: Its Goals, Processes, and Impact on the Right against Self-Incrimination." *Philippine Law Journal* 56:425–38.

Tiruchelvam, Neelan. 1984. *The Ideology of Popular Justice in Sri Lanka: A Socio-Legal Inquiry.* New Delhi: Vikas Publishing House.

Wahrhaftig, Paul, ed. 1978. *The Citizen Dispute Resolution Organizer's Handbook.* Pittsburgh: Grassroots Citizen Dispute Resolution Clearinghouse.

Wahrhaftig, Paul. 1982. "An Overview of Community-Oriented Citizen Dispute Resolution Programs in the United States." In *The Politics of Informal Justice*, ed. Richard L. Abel, 1:75–99. New York: Academic Press.

Weisbrot, David. 1982. "The Impact of the Papua New Guinea Constitution on the Recognition and Application of Customary Law." In *Pacific Constitutions: Proceedings of the Canberra Law Workshop VI*, ed. Peter Sack, 271–90. Canberra: Australian National University.

Westermark, George D. 1986. "Court is an Arrow: Legal Pluralism in Papua New Guinea." *Ethnology* 25:131–49.

Wolf, Eric. 1982. *Europe and the People without History.* Berkeley and Los Angeles: University of California Press.

Yaffe, James. 1972. *So Sue Me! The Story of a Community Court.* New York: Saturday Review Press.

The Future of Alternative
Dispute Resolution: Reflections
on ADR as a Social Movement

Peter S. Adler

The idea of using nonjudicial third parties to help settle big and small disputes has received considerable attention in the last decade. Enthusiasm for alternative dispute resolution (ADR) comes from a variety of sources. Some judges have endorsed it as a way of reducing court delays. Certain scholars have been attracted to ADR because it potentially expands access to justice. Business professionals like ADR because it avowedly reduces litigation costs. And community leaders—particularly those connected with the San Francisco Community Boards program and its kindred neighborhood justice centers—argue that ADR is an effective vehicle for mobilizing community talent, for preventing unnecessary violence, and for revitalizing the self-help capacities of ordinary citizens.

This chapter explores the range of places in which forms of alternative dispute resolution have been applied and describes its spread as a social movement. Despite the wide diversity of locations, there is an underlying similarity in structure and ideology of many forms of ADR. They share an interest in consensual, nonviolent modes of reaching agreements and an opposition to a formal, adversarial method of dealing with conflicts. Thus, this chapter suggests a wide variety of places in which some form of nonviolent, oppositional justice is possible.

Generally speaking, the phrase "alternative dispute resolution" describes various voluntary forms of mediation and arbitration. In the past decade, however, ADR has also come to include a panoply of other independent and sometimes unusual practices such as compulsory arbitration, administrative conciliation, minitrials, summary jury trials, confidential listening, and the use of special settlement masters. If these various dispute-resolution methods can be thought of as branches in an ADR tree of techniques, then mediation would be considered the trunk. Mediation in general—and, after a decade of experimentation, community mediation in particular—is the force that has invigorated this proliferation of methods.

Not unexpectedly, the adoption of mediation into various institutional settings such as courts and administrative agencies is now engendering complicated discussions about professionalization. When mediators from various settings gather together to discuss their work, conversations inevitably seem to turn to questions of evaluation, certification, the development of standards and codes of ethics, the need for qualifications, supervision, oversight, accountability, and the structuring of fee charging and service-provision schemes.

The success of mediation, however, invokes other issues as well. How, for example, do we explain the comparatively rapid development of mediation principles, practices, and rhetoric in seemingly divergent sectors and contexts? What are the wellsprings of this movement and what are its symbolic currencies? And what, moreover, of ADR's future, particularly the type of ADR that has been pioneered by the San Francisco Community Boards program? What does the larger transition from "innovation" to "trend" and from "reform" to "institutionalization" portend for proponents of community justice?

ADR: The Current Landscape

In the narrowest sense, ADR can be viewed as a toolbox of dispute-resolution methods that complements rather than acts as any real alternative to America's litigation and adjudication systems. ADR should, in fact, be defined, examined, and explained as a set of instruments toward various ends, most often but not always dispute settlement. Any contemporary inventory of ADR techniques certainly includes the core processes of arbitration (private judges), mediation (outsiders who assist with communications and negotiations), and fact-finding (third parties who act as investigators and dispute-resolution recommenders).

There are many variations and hybrids. In a recent survey the

Conference of State Court Administrators (COSCA) found 458 alternative dispute-resolution programs operating in forty-four states. The vast majority of these (306) were court-annexed or court-related mediation programs, although more than 25 jurisdictions reported the use of mandatory court-annexed arbitration systems. Similarly, a survey by the National Institute for Dispute Resolution (NIDR) (1983) found at least one community or neighborhood justice center in forty-three states and the District of Columbia. Programs ranged dramatically in size, staff, budgets, and problem foci. Both the COSCA and NIDR program counts are probably conservative.

The common denominator and supporting taproot for all of this activity is negotiation. As Marc Galanter notes, negotiation and bargaining are central to our experience of justice and to the larger arena of conflict resolution. "The master pattern of American disputing," he writes, "is one in which there is actual or threatened invocation of an authoritative decision-maker. This is countered by a threat of protracted resistance, leading to a negotiated or mediated settlement, often in the anteroom of the adjudicative institution" (1983:26–27).

For most ADR procedures, negotiation is an exceedingly prominent and central feature. Classic mediation strategy calls for bringing disputing parties together (or shuttling between them), helping each side clarify and articulate its interests, and assisting them in inventing or negotiating solutions. Variations on this theme—including the use of judicial settlement conferences, administrative conciliation panels, and special masters—often introduce other important factors in the form of deadlines, outside review of settlements, monitoring of the bargaining process, and the threat of penalties for bad-faith bargaining. The goals, however, remain the same: a negotiated end to the matters in dispute, a negotiated consensus on future relationships, or negotiated agreements that streamline the issues in contention.

All of this negotiating can simply be thought of, in Fisher and Ury's terms (1981), as the expansion of options and the solving of problems on a grand scale. From a slightly different angle, however, this same activity looks slightly sordid. Negotiation, in fact, has traditionally connoted compromising, dickering, bartering, haggling, niggling, trading, swapping, and back-room deal making. Recognition of negotiation as a serious and legitimate sociolegal activity thus seems to be something new.

Evidence for this appears bountiful. Only in the last decade, for example, has formal training in negotiation been introduced into law school curricula and continuing legal-education programs. Moreover, until the late 1970s, legal negotiation—what lawyers actually think about and do when they bargain with each other—remained virtually unstudied. Over the last decade, in fact, important scholarly works on negotiation have been contributed from a number of disciplines by writers like Bacharach and Lawler (1981), Druckman (1977), Pruitt (1981), Raiffa (1982), Rubin (1981), Williams (1983), Zartman (1978), Susskind, Bacow, and Wheeler (1983), Lax and Sebenaius (1986), and others. And in the popular press a steady flow of new writings continues to be published.

In one sense, then, it is possible to suggest that the ADR movement has been fueled, if not overtly driven, by the social legitimization of the bargaining process itself. What has been discovered, or perhaps rediscovered, is that many disputes that traditionally are conceptualized and treated as collisions of rights or as win-lose adversarial contests are indeed negotiable. In this sense the rise of the mediation movement is a concurrent extension of negotiation's newly acquired good name. The idea of a negotiated agreement has replaced the concept of imposed judgment as the guiding metaphor of dispute resolution. Indeed, if the master pattern of contemporary conflict management is negotiation, then mediation in all of its various mainstream and exotic forms and applications can best be viewed as a set of negotiation templates. All mediation strategies, however overtly or subtly, seek to utilize, build on, stimulate, enhance, or maximize opportunities for productive communication and problem solving.

Lawyers, Courts, and Neighborhood Justice Centers

In the United States, mediation is probably most stylized and institutionalized in the labor-relations field. Observers have long noted that collective bargaining models begin with the assumption of an inherently antagonistic relationship between labor and management, that is, a basic conflict of ends and goals. As opponents, however, labor and management are also interdependent. Each side has to insure the survival of the other to continue its existence. Labor mediators use the interplay that flows from these needs to conduct their work: the negotiated structuring of future relationships and the crafting and effectuation of agreements.

However much labor and management relations may be changing in the 1990s, it must be remembered that the use of mediation in this arena is a relatively recent phenomenon. The current administrative vehicle through which most of these transactions take place is the Federal Mediation and Conciliation Service (FMCS), an agency whose work is guided by the Wagner Act and National Labor Relations Board. Both of these legal frameworks developed early this century in the context of economic depression and class conflict. Only when unions had fought for and scored important economic and legal victories did collective bargaining become a reality. Once unions became legitimate bargaining units, the need for stable and predictable processes of conflict resolution arose and the practice of labor mediation came into being. And only, it should be added, against the backdrop of political and social empowerment.

The same can also be said of the Community Relations Service (CRS), a federal conciliation agency established in 1964. Born out of the human and civil rights movements, the CRS developed to help communities achieve amicable resolutions to racial and ethnic disputes. The idea of mediating such conflicts probably would not have come into place without the economic, social, and political confrontations of the 1960s and, more specifically, without the Civil Rights Act of 1964. The business of the CRS involved, in the broadest sense, helping communities, schools, prisons, and social agencies to negotiate implementations of the 1964 legislation (Salem 1985).

This pattern—of bargaining leverage being established, of legal relationships being defined, and of mediation then gaining credibility and favor as a dispute-resolution mechanism—can also be seen in other sectors such as conflicts over child custody and the processing of special education matters under Public Law 94-142, and in the National Environmental Policy Act.

If the landmark legislative actions of the 1960s and 1970s helped structure new social relations by redefining various rights and remedies, so too did it change the way the law itself was conceptualized and used. Analyzing the process of family breakup from a metalegal perspective, Robert Mnookin and Lewis Kornhauser noted the following: "We see the primary function of contemporary divorce law not as imposing order from above, but rather as providing a framework within which divorcing couples can themselves determine their postdissolution rights and responsibilities. This process by which parties to a marriage are empowered to create their own legally enforceable commitments is a form of 'private ordering'"(1979:950). The authors called this phenomenon "bargaining in the shadow of the law."

Mnookin and Kornhauser argued that, in very practical terms, laws and rules serve not so much as fixed principles for dispensing judgment but as public "bargaining endowments" that allocate and distribute private power. Since the laws that govern most classes of disputes are far from simple, the distribution of bargaining chips does not automatically simplify the resolution of disputes. Quite the opposite. It often creates substantive and procedural uncertainty that, in many circumstances, becomes an inducement to negotiate. If nobody knows how a judge or jury will decide and if the parties themselves are averse to risk, both sides may fare better through privately structured certainties.

One of the wellsprings of the mediation movement, therefore, is the development of rights and bargaining endowments in new sectors of society. Social movements, however, typically draw much of their vitality from what they stand against. (See for example Shonholtz 1982, and in this volume, DuBow and Thomson, Shook and Milner, Merry and Milner.)

The development of ADR, however, seems premised not so much on a critical and perhaps simplified view of the litigation process but on a tangle, perhaps even collision, of antilawyering and antijudging sentiments that have been invoked for larger ideological reasons. Various institutions in different social sectors, in fact, have adopted different ADR strategies for different reasons. In this regard, the genealogy of the neighborhood-justice centers (NJCs) concept provides an interesting vantage point from which to examine both the interplay of criticisms leveled against the legal extablishment as well as the evolution of a powerful discourse about the management of justice systems.

NJCs, many of which are currently led by lawyers, have their roots in conceptual models based on African moots, socialist people's courts, and on the American versions of psychotherapy and labor mediation. As originally proposed by Richard Danzig (1973), justice centers were to be independent community groups that fostered reconciliation rather than punishment through a complementary and decentralized system of criminal justice. In great part, Danzig's proposals aimed at deprofessionalization; that is, at controlling the work of lawyers, judges, jailers, and police and at reestablishing direct community involvement in the justice process.

His ideas were taken up and elaborated in somewhat different form by Sander (1976), McGillis and Mullen (1977), and by various legal scholars, social scientists, and court officials participating in the National Conference on the Causes of Popular Dissatisfaction with the Adminsitration of Justice (Pound Conference). Later still they were adopted by the U.S. Department of Justice under Attorney General Griffin Bell. At Bell's direction, a first round of organizational experiments were set up under the Law Enforcement Assistance Administration in 1978 in Atlanta, Los Angeles, and Kansas City and a second round in 1980 in Honolulu and Dallas.

Other states, counties, and cities followed suit with their own initiatives, and by 1981, even with the collapse of national funding, hundreds of community-mediation programs had been established. Although models and sponsorships differed dramatically from program to program, the idea of developing NJCs seemed attractive for many reasons. To judges and court administrators concerned with efficiency, nonjudicial forums looked like a way of reducing cases, costs, and court congestion. To those concerned with issues of access to justice, community-mediation centers appeared to be a mechanism for facilitating prompt hearings at convenient times and places with little or no involvement by the legal profession.

In the debates over court-centered versus community-centered ADR, the ideology of the community programs was most eloquently articulated by Raymond Shonholtz (see Thomson and DuBow, DuBow and McEwen in this volume). Regardless of their differences, both types of centers—the community models espoused by Shonholtz and the agency models launched by LEAA and the Department of Justice—have survived to share a common "theology" of ADR about the benefits of mediating and the drawbacks of litigating disputes.

The debate between agency and community models of mediation has also shrouded other ideological similarities between them (Adler, Lovaas, and Milner 1988). Paramount among these is avoidance of any real mention of rights and the function of rights in determining just and fair outcomes to disagreements. Nor is the role of the law as a source of rights critiqued either favorably or unfavorably. This lack of discourse is an interesting omission and understandable given the mediation movement's general goal of converting rights battles into an analysis and meshing of interests.

If the community-mediation movement's criticisms of lawyering rest primarily on the notion that litigation is an inherently poor social process, business leaders have taken a slightly different view. They criticize litigation as too costly and time-consuming, too disruptive of ongoing financial relationships, too uncertain in its outcomes, and too wasteful of talent and energy. Corporations have responded with a variety of ADR forms and with an ADR pledge. Trade and professional organizations, particularly in the insurance industry, focus their criticisms on the oversupply of lawyers, on the perennial search by attorneys for "deep pockets," on the tendency of liberal courts to act as social-welfare agencies, and on the surge of tort litigation in new areas of injury and product liability. More interesting still is the use of an ADR pledge that commits corporations like AT&T, Chrysler, Goodyear, J.C. Penny, Standard Oil, Motorola, Union Carbide, and Westinghouse that face business disputes at least in principle to try ADR techniques before full-scale litigation (Barnette 1984).

Just as criticisms of American litigation patterns have led to new initiatives in the community and corporate areas, so too have they brought about a wave of ADR experimentation and program development by court systems. Much of this activity aims at wrestling with congestion and delay on the trial track, problems noted by legal and judicial scholars like Roscoe Pound as early as 1906. As a critique that is more often implicit than explicit, judges and administrators now argue that lawyers are masters of delay and surprise and that, more often than not, it is the attorneys themselves who stall the process of justice. Thus, it is argued, courts that have traditionally been laissez faire in their attitudes can no longer afford not to exercise control over cases and the lawyers who plead them.

Generally speaking, court systems have attempted to address delay problems in four related ways: through administrative reforms, including the introduction of computerized information-management systems; by changes in the way cases are assigned to judges; by modernizing laws, statutes, and court rules; and through the adoption of ADR methods (Ebener 1981). One of the aims of these collective reforms is controlling the pace of litigation rather than leaving it in the hands of attorneys and their clients. A second aim is instilling in the litigants and counsel a greater sense of urgency and seriousness. In this sense, note Howard Bedlin and Paul Nejelski (1984), courts function as "a doomsday machine." The doomsday metaphor compels all of the parties in the dispute to assess their positions realistically in light of a potential loss at the end. The view that courts can and perhaps even should structure events and coerce litigants and their representatives into using them for negotiations is central to many of the emerging ADR techniques like court-ordered arbitration, court-related mediation, and the use of judge-run settlement conferences.

The question of general social litigiousness is particularly interesting for the ADR field because the increased use of mediation is often justified by a sense of increased disputatiousness coupled with a decline in the integrity and hold of traditional dispute-resolving institutions, despite evidence that Americans are no more or less contentious than they have always been.[1] Whatever its basis, along with the idea that there was once a "golden age of informalism" in the United States, excessive litigiousness is one of the mobilizing myths of the ADR movement.

Among the other foundational myths of the ADR movement are notions of voluntarism and empowerment. Mediation bases much of its appeal on the idea that the parties themselves can be and should be the architects of their own futures; that is, that the disputants, wherever possible, are to be the prime determinants of the processes by which their dispute will be heard and, even more ideally, the creators of actual outcomes. In mediation, these themes are central. Purists argue that in mediation (as opposed to adjudication) disputants are neither coerced to the bargaining table nor directed into specific agreements. The dispute, and any agreement to end the dispute, must come from the parties in conflict. Mediators may exert a great amount of control over the organization of the communication and negotiations processes, but ownership and responsibility for the outcome always rests with the parties. Empowerment and voluntarism, especially as they relate to the bargaining process, are fundamental to any discussion of what links and perhaps even unifies various ADR techniques. In this sense, they are the new myths offered by ADR to replace the perceived limitations of old myths, namely, legal advocacy and the adversarial process of assuring rights.

---

1. See Galanter 1983 for a persuasive argument questioning the view that Americans are very litigious.

Concurrent with these themes, however, are the larger social issues that extend from both the negotiation metaphor and the current organization of mediational activities by communities, courts, and corporations. These agendas, ranging from the rational-reformist contentions of corporate and legal adopters of ADR to the communitarian arguments of groups like the San Francisco Community Boards (see Merry in this volume), all hold constant the value of voluntary negotiations and settlement facilitated by skilled intervenors.

Cutting across and supporting these themes, however, is an even more implicit ideology of sociolegal informalism. This ideology, writes Christine Harrington (1985), has three elements to it. First, it is premised on the idea that there has been a general weakening of traditional notions of justice coupled with a search for new forms of legal legitimacy. Second, it assumes and promotes a pluralistic conception of politics dominated by the processes of accommodation and consensus. Third, it offers a replacement of the notion that the state's authority actually resolves disputes. In the new view, the state acts more as a facilitator of private accords than an arbiter of disagreements.

ADR as a Social Movement

Social movements, as described over the past quarter century by writers like Blumer (1951), Herbele (1951), and Turner and Killian (1961), are forms of collective behavior in which large and comparatively unorganized numbers of people seek to promote or resist particular types of changes. By definition, social movements arise in a more or less spontaneous fashion and serve diverse constituencies with both coherent statements of a perceived problem and articulated prescriptions for reform. The previously discussed thematic features distinguish ADR as both a movement within the American justice system and as a contributory current in a much larger stream of contemporary and political affairs.

The alternative dispute-resolution movement seems to echo if not directly parallel other movements in American society. Deane Neubauer has argued that ADR, as an emerging trend in the context of the law, is an analogue for what is taking place in the world of medicine (1985). The current crisis in American health care, he writes, derives from an interplay of events that includes recent technological and scientific progress, a broadening of opportunities for medical intervention, a consequent problem of overutilization, and a shifting class structure in which quality medical care is increasingly inaccessible because of costs. Just as the resolution of disputes has become institutionalized in courts and law offices, so too has health delivery come to be dominated by hospitals and doctors.

Like ADR, the alternative health-care movement gathers much of its organizing impetus from a negative critique of professionals and from the institutionalized rigidities that professionals support and represent. In the same way that the American health-care crisis has spawned a renewal of interest in traditional medical delivery processes (midwifery, community prevention, self-help, holistic health), so too has the legal crisis focused attention on the comparatively well-known techniques of mediation, arbitration, and fact-finding. In both cases the methods posed as alternatives are not truly innovations. They are old ideas dressed in new clothes and energized by changed economic and social conditions.

As reform efforts, however, ADR and the alternative health-care movement also exhibit similarly ambivalent if not outright contradictory tendencies towards professionalism and professionalization. Neubauer (1985) writes of the large number of people and professions that want to lay claim to health as a commodity and make a living out of delivering it. This, he notes, conflicts with the original ideology of prevention, which emphasizes the role of the parties themselves in dealing with their own illnesses, with the function of communities and of nonprofessionals, and with the separation of general health as a value and medicine as an expanding set of professional technologies.

Neal Milner (1985, 1986), in an analysis of movements advocating the rights of mental-health patients, shows even more dramatically how this pattern gets played out. Mental-health advocacy, he notes, has developed in two directions. The first, dominated largely by psychiatrists and psychologists bent on reforming perceived abuses within the medical establishment, emphasizes patients as medically dependent "bundles of needs." The second, urged largely by lawyers and other types of advocates, views patients as "bundles of rights" that need protecting. Both of these efforts come together to create a mythology of patient advocacy that invokes the ideas of care, concern, and change.

Building on the work of Murray Edelman, Milner shows how

both lawyers and doctors seek to protect their professional interests when larger political criticisms begin to threaten their legitimacy. "By seeing their work in terms of advocacy," writes Milner, "organizations that previously had held a rather paternalistic view of mental health patients could reassure themselves that they were now addressing themselves to the newly defined, serious problems in mental health" (1988:1–2). Thus "advocacy" becomes the code word for activities aimed at maintaining professional control.

Proponents of community and neighborhood mediation systems, perhaps not unlike those caught up in the currents and counter-currents of health care and patient rights, display great uncertainty about these issues and are at once infatuated and infuriated with the idea of professionalism. Those who seek to create various types of mediation certifications and associations argue their case in the name of consumer protection and the need for specialized, dispute-specific knowledge. Not everyone can or should be a mediator. Those who take various positions against professionalization maintain that mediation is more art form than science. What is essential are talents and competencies that lie beyond the ken of any one profession. Moreover, say those who oppose it, professionalization means an inevitable recapitulation of the innovation syndrome in which new ideas are colonized by aspiring or underemployed professionals, organized and monopolized into fee-for-service systems, and then subsidized through public dollars to keep them available to the poor.

In some mediation arenas, those that are more mature or that have garnered early support from traditional dispute-resolution insti-tutions, issues of professionalization take on a different complexion. Mediators of family disputes involving divorce and child custody, for example, typically come to their work in one of three ways: as lawyers specializing in family law; as social workers, counselors, or family therapists; and, to a lesser extent, as lay persons who have gained general mediation experience in neighborhood-justice centers. Much of the current debate in this area centers on discussions between lawyers and therapists over whose standards of practice should pre-vail, what qualifications and prerequisites family mediators should have, and which professional association can best represent the field. More or less excluded from these gatekeeping conversations are com-munity volunteers, who are rarely credentialed in either area.

While various emerging camps might disagree on who ought to

be the mediators of the future, almost everyone involved in alternative dispute resolution shares overlapping vocabularies about the work itself. Indeed, the mediator counterpart of "advocacy" in patients' rights conversations is "neutrality." Impartiality and neutrality—and the trust and confidence that theoretically stem from these qualities— are essential ingredients in most forms of alternative dispute resolution. Both concepts permeate the training, philosophy, and practice of mediation and arbitration and are articulated over and over again in program descriptions and organizational manuals.

Symbolically, this idea is most elevated (and professionalized) in the concept of the "super neutral" described by Colosi, Lebowich, Davis, Potter, and Sackman (1985). The super neutral, according to these writers, is an individual who has been trained in a variety of table processes and who can deftly apply his or her efforts to both public- and private-sector conflicts. Not unexpectedly, these writers advocate that such super neutrals be attached to and operate out of older and more established ADR organizations such as the American Arbitration Association (AAA) and the Society for Professionals in Dispute Resolution (SPIDR), which all of the authors are affiliated with.

The emergence of a professional discourse invoking central symbols and myths about the resolution of disputes is clearly on the minds of many practitioners and scholars interested in mediation. Regardless of one's position on the matter, the very fact that it is being debated can be interpreted in several ways. One can argue, for example, that the current interest in mediation circles on developing standards, certifications and collegial associations represents a co-optation of broader and more diffuse and spontaneous social objectives. One might also argue that the very emergence of such issues is an indicator that a social movement is alive and functioning as a force in contemporary society. From still a different perspective, it is possible to suggest that ADR is not in and of itself a coherent social movement but rather a modest professional reform effort and, at best, a side current in the changing stream of America's love-hate relationship with lawyers, judges, courts, and other forms of professional authority. Whatever the case, ADR issues resonate with other key reform issues in American society.

There have been many powerful criticisms directed against contemporary American ADR (Tomasic and Feeley 1982; Nader 1985 and this volume; Abel 1982; Fiss 1984; Cohen 1984; Lefcourt 1984; Neubauer 1985; Meeks 1985; Gnaizda 1982). While it is not the purpose of this chapter to attack or defend the propositions put forward by various practitioners and theorists, at least three general observations can be made about the collective concerns being raised about ADR. First, most of the arguments offered up against ADR have little to do with the technologies of mediation and arbitration themselves. Rather, they have to do with goals, ends, directions, and side effects.

Second, it is important to acknowledge the debate itself. In the comparatively short span of a decade, ADR has generated a not inconsiderable amount of discussion and argument for what still must be statistically considered relatively marginal methods of dispute resolution. Finally, every critic who takes alternative dispute resolution to task for one or more of its perceived failings either directly describes ADR as a "movement" or, in slightly more modest terms, as a set of trends. Whether ADR is a significant phenomenon or even a true social movement, it is clearly being treated as a conceptually serious change in the way Americans enact and handle disputes. ADR is generating both liberal and conservative reactions. Real or imagined, the tenor of these worries suggests something interesting is afoot in American society.

The Future of ADR

Contemporary social-movement theories suggest that movements can be understood in terms of how they succeed or fail in mobilizing human, financial, and social resources. John McCarthy and Mayer Zald believe that movements are just as often energized by people without a direct stake in the issues involved and by individuals who have no commitment to the values that underlie a movement (1977). If McCarthy and Zald were analyzing ADR, they would note the existence of a number of social-movement organizations that are attempting to represent and invoke the broad goals of the movement. Collectively, they might argue, these organizations—the National Conference on Peacemaking and Conflict Resolution (NCPCR), the National Conference for Dispute Resolution (NIDR), the Society for Professionals in Dispute Resolution (SPIDR), and the National Association for Community Justice (NACJ) to name but a few—form a loose-knit social-movement industry that is mobilizing people and money and struggling to manage both the internal and external conflicts of an emerging phenomenon. Some within this movement believe that the formal justice system must adopt mediation and other ADR methods. Others, particularly the San Francisco Community Boards and many of the neighborhood-justice centers organized on the community model, have argued against the annexation of ADR by courts and the growing use of voluntary or mandatory methods of administrative institutions.

Undoubtedly, many of the tensions and strains currently involved in the growth of mediation, particularly over issues of professionalization, can be understood in these terms. But does ADR offer a unified enough set of long-term agendas to truly be called a movement? After a decade of growth, it is also clear that practitioners of mediation have very different transformational agendas. Some of these are rational and reformist. Others are personal, interpersonal, or communitarian. At certain levels, the competition of agendas that McCarthy and Zald hold as a central facet of their movement theory is now appearing in ADR. Actors and players in all of these sectors are struggling to make their activities more permanent and arguing for technical and financial support from the few public and private sources willing to fund experiments and programs.

In the current competition of ideas over what its rightful goals should be, it is also useful to remember that ADR is still a new phenomenon in which the perceived need for services and the supply of able and willing providers seems to have outstripped actual demand. On the face of it, mediators and would-be mediators far outnumber the mediated upon, and surprisingly, perhaps, people do not easily volunteer their disputes for mediation. Quite legitimately both scholars and practitioners should be questioning why it is that the mediation movement's concepts and symbols are so powerful and attractive yet so very difficult to operationalize. Merry and Silbey (1984) suggest that mediation, with its instrumental emphasis on rational problem-solving, individualism, and free choice, probably does not take enough account of the emotional and normative characteristics that attend the disputing process. Hence voluntary mediation and perhaps other forms of ADR may never truly come into widespread use.

There may be other answers as well. Mediation might also be

viewed as nothing more than a modest innovation that has captured temporary attention because of its novelty but that carries no other intrinsic or extrinsic value. It may well be a set of techniques that can and will be adapted by different groups for different ends and that have—like athletic shoes and certain diets—achieved a certain degree of trendiness. Cultural currency of ideas, and particularly of economic, legal, and political ideas, does not automatically confer deeper and more important social significance. Thus those involved in ADR should stay open to the notion that the whole is less than the sum of its parts and that there is less to ADR than intially meets the eye.

Conversely, expanding interest in mediation may also be related to more profound and sweeping changes in American culture. The negotiation metaphor, by extension, implies such themes as better communication, improved exchange of information, self-help, collaborative problem solving, cooperative decision making, joint risk analysis and the shift from what John Naisbitt calls an "either/or" mentality to one built on the notion of "multiple options" (1982). All of these concepts may be part of larger cultural forces that are reshaping the way American society functions. While the use of mediation may not result from or even contribute to these trends, it at least mirrors some of them.

In a critique of Richard Abel's and Jerold Auerbach's books, Gabe Shawn Varges writes: "The informal justice or ADR movement is in the process of entering a third important stage of development. Whereas the first stage involved 'consciousness raising' about the need to try new methods of settling disputes, and the second stage saw the implementation of some of these new methods, the third stage is about assessing what the movement has accomplished, and in what direction it ought to go. In particular, it is about deciding the proper mix of law and informality that its mechanisms should have, and determining whose and which type of disputes are best resolved by judicial, quasi-judicial, or non-judicial methods" (1985:396).

While predictions are always risky, we should take note of some of the potential directions ADR might take in the future. Certainly the current interest in institutional acceptance suggests that ADR will be adopted as a short-term strategy by judicial and administrative agencies seeking relief from the old frustrations of long delays and high costs. Peter Edelman believes that the field of ADR is ripe for additional institutional development and argues for the development of second-stage models that include state-sponsored offices of mediation, multidoor courthouses, and increased visibility and funding for ADR applications (1984). This growing interest and attention will undoubtedly lead to mediation's becoming more and more a part of the traditional American occupational structure.

As that occurs, mediation will undoubtedly experience transformations that repeat what has happened in other professions. Social work, for example, was born in the slums of London and New York as unusual and high-minded volunteer work done by philanthropists and charitable reformers. As Roy Lubove demonstrates, the current field of social work, which is highly specialized and bureaucratized, derived from these early efforts but then rapidly moved through distinct stages of professional evolution involving (1) the development of diagnostic models; (2) the creation and acceptance of new theoretical structures; (3) the building of skill-based federations; and (4) the eventual incorporation of social work into the agendas of private and public agencies (1972).

In the context of greater adoption by institutions, programs with ambitious communitarian agendas would seem to face a problematic future. Programs like the San Francisco Community Boards will find it harder and harder to wall themselves off from the mediation and conciliation programs launched by courts, administrative agencies, and other dispute-managing institutions in the private sector. As the institutions of government and business adopt ADR, community-mediation programs will need to establish better working relations with those institutions and find creative ways to insure the incorporation, not just of the forms of ADR, but of the philosophic tenets that led to the start of community ADR programs in the first place.

In the long term, then, the future of ADR would seem to be tied most closely to the fate of activities in the justice world and to the future of the legal, judicial, and judicial-administration occupations. These professions may change dramatically in the next several decades. "The courts," writes Issac Asimov, "are in the uncivilized stage now" (1984). By this he means that the traditional legal and judicial ways of solving problems tend to be built on surprise, ambush, and delay, and not on communication, negotiations, and creative thinking. ADR may thus have its most profound impact, not on the small number of disputants actually being served or on communities in which such programs are embedded or on court caseloads, but on a generation of lawyers and judges newly schooled to the methods, art forms, and philosophic propostions involved in negotiated resolution of disputes.

But what if the profession of lawyering truly began to reform itself in the directions currently suggested by ADR advocates? Would ADR continue to be symbolically important if the American justice system cleared its delays and backlogs through better management of caseloads and the use of automation? What would the effect on the ADR movement be if highly sophisticated artificial-intelligence systems were developed that could accurately diagnose disputes and unfailingly match up appropriate cases to court-based mediators thoughtfully trained in the philosophies of empowerment and voluntarism? And if ADR systems were then fully incorporated into true multidoor courthouse systems, could programs like the San Francisco Community Boards survive apart? Probably not.

Conversely, however, we should also ask if mediation and, indeed, the whole metaphor of negotiated justice would continue to be credible if a new wave of rights-acquisition movements emerges. In fact, such a scenario seems quite plausible (McNally 1989). The 1990s are upon us. Scholars in diverse fields of endeavor—from Ravi Batra in economics (1985) to Arthur Schlesinger in history (1987)— have shown that significant economic, political, and social transformation seems to occur in American society in thirty-year cycles. In many ways, the coming decade is likely to echo much of the social turmoil of the 1960s.

It does not take a great deal of predictive imagination to see the reemergence of rights-oriented thinking by populist and grass-roots movements, to see a resurgence of shrill new demands for substantive justice and political participation, and to envision the development of a new radicalism focused on a deteriorating global environment, gross inequities in health care, and on the continuing suppression of human rights in many first-, second-, and third-world countries. In this context mediation may, like the once-honorable concept of community-based justices of the peace, be viewed as a quaint but archaic remnant of a bygone era. For the moment, however, programs like the San Francisco Community Boards are raising the critical issues, forcing the debate, and bringing about a much-needed challenge to America's traditional mythology of dispute resolution. For that alone they should be honored as a grand experiment in American social policy.

WORKS CITED

Abel, R. ed. 1982. *The politics of informal justice.* Vol. 2: *Comparitive studies.* New York: Academic Press.

Adler, P., Lovaas, K., and Milner, N. 1988. The ideologies of mediation: The movement's own story. *Law and Policy* 10:317–39.

Asimov, I. 1985. The next seventy years for law and lawyers. *American Bar Association Journal* 71:57–59.

Bacharach, S. and Lawler, E. 1981. *Bargaining: Power tactics and outcomes.* San Francisco: Jossey-Bass.

Barnette, C. 1984. The importance of alternative dispute resolution: Reducing litigation costs as a corporate objective. *Antitrust Law Journal* 53:277–318.

Batra, R. 1985. *Regular cycles of money, inflation, regulation, and depression.* Dallas. Venus Books.

Bedlin, H. and Nejelski, P. 1984. Unsettling issues about settling civil litigation: Examining 'doomsday machines,' 'quick looks,' and other modest proposals. *Judicature* 68, no. 1:9–29.

Blumer, H. 1951. Collective behavior. In *Principles of sociology,* ed. A. M. Lees. New York: Barnes and Noble.

Cohen, H. N. 1984. Mediation in divorce: Boon or bane? Paper presented at Conference of Women and Mediation, New York University School of Law, 21 Jan.

Colosi, T. et al. 1985. Conflict resolution and the superneutral. Society for Professionals in Dispute Resolution, Occasional Paper no. 85-1, 14–18.

Danzig, R. 1973. Toward the creation of a complementary, decentralized system of criminal justice. *Stanford Law Review,* 26:1–54.

Druckman, D. 1977. *Negotiations: Social-Psychological perspectives.* Beverly Hills, Calif.: Sage.

Ebener, P. 1981. *Court efforts to reduce pretrial delay: A national inventory.* Santa Monica, Calif.: Institue for Civil Justice.

Edelman, P. 1984. Institutionalizing dispute resolution alternatives. *The Justice System Journal* 9, no. 2:134–150.

Fisher, R. and Ury, W. 1981. *Getting to yes: Negotiating agreement without giving in.* Boston: Houghton Mifflin.

Fiss, O. 1984. Against settlement. *Yale Law Review* 93:1073–89.

Galanter, 1983. Reading the landscape of disputes: What we know and don't know (and think we know) about our allegedly contentious and litigious society. *UCLA Law Review* 31:4–72.

Gnaizda, R. 1982. Secret justice for the privileged few. *Judicature* 66, no. 1:6–13.

Harrington, C. 1985. Socio-legal concepts in mediation ideology. *Legal Studies Forum* 9, no. 1:33–38.

Herbele, R. 1951. *Social movements: An introduction to political sociology.* New York: Appleton-Century-Crofts.

Lax, D., and Sebenaius, J. K. 1986. *The manager as negotiator.* New York: Free Press.

Lefcourt, R. 1972. Women, mediation, and family law. *Clearinghouse Review.* July, 266–69.

Lubove, R. 1972. *The professional altruist: The emergence of social work as a career.* New York: Atheneum.

McCarthy, J., and Zald, M. 1977. Resource mobilization and social movements: A partial theory. *American Journal of Sociology* 82:1212–39.

McGillis, D., and Mullen, J. 1977. *Neighborhood justice centers: An analysis of potential models.* Washington: U.S. Government Printing Office.

McNally, P. C. 1989. Radicalism in the 1990s. *Justice Horizons* 1, no. 1:3–5.

Meeks, G. 1985. *Managing environmental and public policy conflict: A legislative guide.* Washington: National Conference of State Legislatures.

Merry, S., and Silbey, S. 1984. What do the plaintiffs want? Reexamining the concept of dispute. *The Justice System Journal* 9:151–178.

Milner, N. 1985. Viewing and assessing the mental patient rights movement. Paper presented at the Law and Society Association Meetings, San Diego.

Milner, N. 1986. The symbols and meanings of advocacy. *International Journal of Law and Psychiatry* 8:1–17.

Mnookin, R., and Kornhauser, L. 1979. Bargaining in the shadow of the law: The case of divorce. *Yale Law Review* 88:950–97.

Nader, L. 1985. Where is dispute resolution today? Where will it be in the year 2000? *Dispute Resolution Forum,* April 1985, 5.

Naisbitt, J. 1982. *Megatrends: Ten new directions transforming our lives.* New York: Warner Books.

National Institute for Dispute Resolution. 1983. *Dispute resolution directory.* Washington: National Institute for Dispute Resolution.

Neubauer, D. 1985. A fragment to chew on. Typescript. University of Hawaii Program on Conflict Resolution.

Pruitt, D. 1981. *Negotiation and behavior.* New York: Academic Press.

Raiffa, H. 1982. *The art and science of negotiation.* Cambridge: Harvard University Press.

Rubin, Jeffrey Z. 1981. *Dynamics of third party intervention: Kissinger in the Middle East.* New York: Praeger.

Salem, R. 1985. The alternative dispute resolution movement: An overview. *Arbitration Journal* 40, no. 3:3–11.

Sander, F. 1976. Varieties of dispute processing. *Federal Rules Decisions* 70:111–34.

Schlesinger, A. 1987. America's political cycle turns again. *Wall Street Journal,* 10 December, 140.

Shonholtz, R. 1981a. A justice system that isn't working and its impact on the community. Working paper, San Francisco Community Boards.

Shonholtz, R. 1981b. New justice theories and practice. Paper delivered at the Oslo Conference on Conflict Management.

Shonholtz, R. 1982. Neighborhood conflict resolution programs: Strategies for greater economic self-sufficiency and public policy viability. Working paper, San Francisco Community Boards.

Susskind, L., Bacow, L., and Wheeler, M., eds. 1983. *Resolving environmental regulatory disputes.* Cambridge, Mass.: Schenkman.

Tomasic, R., and Feeley, M., eds. 1982. *Neighborhood justice: Assessment of an emerging idea.* New York: Longman.

Turner, R., and Killian, L. 1961. *Collective behavior.* Englewood Cliffs, N.J.: Prentice-Hall.

Varges, G. S. 1985. Alternative dispute resolution: An international approach. *Negotiation Journal* 1:389–99.

Williams, G. 1983. *Legal negotiation and settlement.* St. Paul, Minn.: West.

Zartman, I., ed. 1978. *The Negotiation Process: Theories and applications.* Beverly Hills, Calif.: Sage.

Evaluation of Community-Justice Programs

Kem Lowry

There is a small and aging evaluative literature on community-justice programs. Some of it is published, but there are few recent published studies. Most evaluations remain in the "gray literature": unpublished, minimally circulated papers and reports assessing the success or effectiveness of particular programs in particular settings. These evaluation studies vary along predictable dimensions: the criteria by which success is judged, research methods, methodological rigor, and the audiences for which they are prepared.

Individually, these evaluations are important because of their impacts on decisions to fund (or refund) programs, on the morale of program staff, on the potential for conferring legitimacy on particular conflict-resolution techniques, and on decisions about whether to institutionalize particular programs. Collectively, these evaluations help establish the worth of community-justice and dispute-resolution forums. They shape agendas for research and training and priorities for funding. They direct attention to what is important in the mediation of community disputes.

What do these evaluations reveal about how success is defined in the community-justice movement? What criteria are used to evaluate programs? How consistently are these criteria used across evaluations? Are there additional or competing criteria that are used peripherally or not at all? Whose interests and needs are served by the choice of criteria? What research methods are used to generate and organize data for measuring success? How appropriate are these methods? How well are they used? To ask these questions is to engage in a type of metaevaluation (Scriven 1969; Cook and Gruder 1978).

There are several types of metaevaluation, the most common of which are empirical reanalyses of single or multiple data sets (Cook and Gruder 1978). However, in this analysis the emphasis is less on the results of analysis and more on the commonalities and divergences among evaluative questions that are raised (or ignored), the audiences served by attempts to answer those questions, and by the research methods used.

This review of the evaluative literature on community mediation is divided into four main sections. The first section is a brief description of the different types of community-justice programs. In the second section three broad types of evaluation applied to community-justice programs are identified: program research, program evaluation, and social criticism. The third section is a review of the evaluative literature on community-justice programs. The evaluative questions about community justice have been organized into three broad evaluative frames that reflect the different and sometimes divergent expectations of community justice. The *service-delivery frame* includes evaluative questions about the amount of mediation services offered and the efficiency and effectiveness of mediation services. The *informalism frame* includes evaluative questions about the degree to which community-mediation services offer more flexible rules, easier access, speedier resolution, and lower costs. The *community-building frame* addresses questions about the success of community-justice programs in promoting a greater sense of community. Throughout the discussion of evaluative findings there is particular emphasis on the findings from DuBow's study of the San Francisco Community Boards—the primary focus of the conference at which this paper was originally presented. In the final section some conclusions about the evaluation of community-justice programs are offered.

The Community Justice Enterprise

The community-justice enterprise includes a variety of programs offering nonjudicial methods and forums for dealing with a range of minor civil and criminal disputes. Community justice is partly a reform movement intended to address the delays, lack of access, and costs associated with traditional judicial processing of disputes. A second major theme in the movement is that judicial processing of disputes is alienating, that individuals can deal with disputes in ways that empower both individuals and communities.

The first community-justice programs were developed in the 1970s. There are now more than 180 programs (American Bar Association 1986). These programs vary widely in caseload and size of budget, sources of funding, sources of case referral, and size of geographic area served. Although they all use mediation, arbitration, or conciliation to deal with disputes, they vary with regard to goals, the number of mediators used in disputes, use of volunteers, and specific approaches to mediation and conciliation. Three basic types of programs have been identified: justice-based; community-based; and composite (McGillis 1986:20–21). Justice-based programs are sponsored by courts or other justice-system agencies. They rely heavily on the court system for referrals and frequently take minor criminal cases. The degree of coercion involved in getting disputants into the program is frequently high. Community-based programs are not affiliated with the justice system and frequently receive neither funding nor referrals from the justice system. Most such programs are explicit about their goal of using alternative dispute-resolution techniques as part of a larger program of developing community leadership, community building, and increased community autonomy. Composite programs tend to have some affiliation with the justice system, including some funding and referrals, but seek to maintain some independence. Some composite programs take minor criminal cases; others do not.

The Evaluative Enterprise

Community-justice programs have been the object of three basic types of evaluative analysis: program research, program evaluation, and social criticism. Program research is applied social research focusing on a particular social intervention or set of interventions. Program research aspires to develop "valid, generalizable knowledge about intervention, the social problems on which intervention is targeted and the social system within which intervention is implemented" (Cordray and Lipsey 1987:21).

In most program research efforts there is relatively little explicit evaluation. Impacts are identified and the reader is left to attach evaluative meaning to the findings. The dominant, although not exclusive, approach to doing program research is what Patton calls the

quantitative/experimental paradigm (1981) and House refers to as
quantitative methodology (1980).

There is some program research on mediation that is relevant to
community-justice programs. McEwen and Maiman, for example,
analyzed the degree to which mediation or adjudication was likely to
lead to payments of small debts (1984). Subsequent studies debated
whether it was the choice of forum (mediation vs. adjudication) or
case characteristics (whether the defendant admits partial liability) that
produces a greater degree of compliance (McEwan and Maiman 1984,
1986; Vidmar 1987). This research is remarkable primarily because
there is so little systematic research like it related to community justice.
There is very little research on why disputants choose (or ignore)
community justice as a dispute resolution forum (but see Merry and
Silbey 1984). Nothing has been reported about how, if at all, the race,
gender, or social class of mediators affects disputants' perceptions of
the fairness and justice of outcomes. Little is known about how the
cultural background of disputants or mediators operates as a variable.
We have little research on the effects of mediator styles or tactics on
outcomes. There is, in short, much that program research could
contribute to an understanding and evaluation of community-justice
efforts.

Program evaluation, in contrast to program research, is an immediate, responsive, service-oriented mode of inquiry, the aim of which
is to assess the merit of the program. Like program research, evaluation practice is dominated by the methods and norms of conventional
social science. However, there are significant alternative voices and
views about appropriate approaches to evaluation. Variations on eight
basic approaches can be identified (House 1980). These alternative
approaches are the result of more than two decades of evaluation.

All the major approaches to evaluation share the same basic logic
of evaluative analysis. This logic involves (1) establishing criteria of
merit; (2) gathering data relevant to these criteria; and (3) making
evaluative judgments. The first step is the choice of evaluative criteria.
In the early days of evaluation, evaluators tended to look at the
program's goals as the exclusive source of criteria for evaluating its
success. However, two decades of evaluation practice have made it
clear that goals are frequently a poor source of criteria. Goals are
often vague (Weiss 1977), latent, contradictory, or excessively modest
so as to insure achievement. They may also be overly optimistic in

order to insure political support and funding. Moreover, evaluators found that an exclusive emphasis on goals ignores other important impacts, whether positive or negative. The de-emphasis of goals as the source of evaluative criteria has made the process of developing criteria more complex. The evaluator can now develop criteria that emphasize the claims that clients or officials of the program make about its aims (Guba and Lincoln 1981), the information needs of key decision makers (Patton 1986), or other stakeholders (Bryk 1983), estimating the degree to which the needs of clients have been met (Scriven 1980), and other approaches. The dilemma is that when multiple interests are taken into account and no a priori reason exists for weighing some interests more than others, someone still has to establish priorities among potential criteria of evaluation.

The second step in evaluation is to gather data relevant to whatever criteria are chosen. In conventional evaluation of programs, key concepts are operationalized; empirical indicators are chosen as surrogates for satisfaction, fairness, or other concepts. Surveys, interview guides, and other data-gathering instruments are developed. Although most evaluations of community-justice programs have emphasized the quantitative measurement of outcomes such as client satisfaction, there is no necessary reason evaluations have to be so limited. Evaluating the effectiveness of a program frequently involves issues having to do with the program's context, nuance, or process. For these issues qualitative methods (Patton 1987), naturalistic inquiry (Guba and Lincoln 1981) or connoisseurship (Eisner 1979) may also be appropriate.

The third step in evaluation is to make evaluative judgments. What level of performance or impact constitutes success or effectiveness? Standards can be absolute or comparative. Absolute standards are appropriate in engineering and are used in educational evaluation (criterion-referenced tests), but absolute standards are arbitrary in most social programs—and certainly in community mediation. Performance standards are therefore comparative, but the practical issue is what sorts of comparisons are to be made. The social-science ideal is the "no-treatment control group" (Cook and Campbell 1979), but such control groups are difficult if not impossible for community-mediation programs. (Attempts to establish such control groups would raise substantial ethical issues as well.) There are at least three alternative comparisons. Outcomes from community-mediation programs (e.g., satisfaction of client, perceptions of fairness) can be compared with those of another similar program (the nonequivalent control group), with alternatives for handling disputers (e.g., the judicial system), or with individual feelings or perceptions prior to participation in a mediation program. While such comparisons raise questions of reliability and validity, explicit comparisons are usually preferable to evaluations that report performance without reference to any comparison group and leave it to the reader to attach significance to the level of performance.

The social critic offers a third perspective for assessing community-justice programs. Social criticism questions the givens in contemporary social and political order, treats the conventional wisdom as problematic, and examines the ideological basis of reforms such as alternative dispute resolution. Social critics are not concerned with determining the relative success of any particular community-justice program. Rather they focus on the premises and assumptions of community justice, on the historical and economic contexts within which community-justice programs are offered as an alternative forum for dispute resolution, and on explaining the evolution of alternative forms of dispute resolution (see, e.g., Abel 1982; Harrington 1985; and Hofrichter 1987. See also Fitzpatrick, Yngvesson, Harrington, Nader, and Merry in this volume).

A central theme in the critical literature on community-justice programs is the problematic treatment of informal procedures as a "reform." As Harrington notes:

> Informal procedures are idealized as non-adversarial, rehabilitative, and preventative methods for resolving conflict. The reform goal—informalism—is treated as non-problematic and invariably, analysis centers on barriers to implementing this goal. This approach leads to predictable and unilluminating evaluations of the politics of reform. (Harrington 1985:12)

Abel ofers one of the most explicit critiques of informalism:

> Informalism is a mechanism by which the state extends its control so as to manage capital accumulation and defuse the resistance this engenders. Its objects are not randomly distributed but rather are concentrated within the dominated categories of contempo-

rary capitalism: workers, the poor, ethnic minorities, and women. This is not accidental (or easily remedied). (Abel 1982 1:6)

Social critics regard conventional evaluation as irrelevant. As Hofrichter puts it:

> The liberal legal reformist perspective presents NDR (neighborhood dispute resolution) as a solution to problems of managing the courts and expanding access to the judicial system. It selects evidence for the success or failure of these programs in a way that justifies its ideology, such as caseload, processing time and disputant satisfaction. Within this framework no true evaluation of the programs can occur because the evaluation excludes a social context that sets boundaries or redefines the nature of the interaction between the parties in the mediation process. The evaluation of such programs depends on the interests that define the problems NDR addresses. (Hofrichter 1987:xxvi)

Or as Abel asserts:

> But informal institutions also foster disorganization much more directly, by instructing each party that he can, and must, resolve the controversy alone. The way in which the external environment of informal institutions measures their success imposes an incentive structure that reinforces these features: Evaluations are couched in terms of the number of cases handled and the satisfaction of individual parties, not in terms of the impacts on groups, the contribution to community, or the attainment of any other substantive goal. (Abel 1982 1:7)

One does not have to agree with the critics of community dispute resolution to be sensitized by the issues they raise and to be made aware of the need for a broader range of evaluative questions about community mediation, more skeptical treatment of the claims made in its behalf, and more attention to the limits and costs of reform.

Taken together, program research, program evaluation, and social criticism provide a rich array of evaluative questions to ask about community-mediation programs. In the sections that follow, some of these questions, the methods used to answer them, and findings are examined in more detail.

Evaluative Frames

A review of published and unpublished evaluations of community-justice programs reveals several evaluative frames: service delivery, informalism, and community transformation. Each frame represents an emphasis or set of expectations about community justice. This emphasis is manifest in the selection and prominence given particular criteria for assessing community-justice programs. These frames reveal the different and sometimes divergent expectations of community justice.

The Service-Delivery Frame

By far the most dominant evaluative emphasis to date has been to treat community justice as a service to be delivered as are other social services. This puts the evaluative emphasis on the amount of mediation services offered and the efficiency and effectiveness of service delivery. This evaluative frame is particularly characteristic of the agency model of community justice. Each of the basic service-delivery evaluative questions is discussed below.

What Are Program Caseloads? How Are They Changing over Time?

An emphasis on increasing caseloads as one measure of the success of community-justice programs is consistent with the image of community justice as an alternative forum for dispute resolution. Implicit in an emphasis on caseloads is the notion that there should be a reduction (or at least a slower rate of growth) in court cases involving the types of disputes handled in community-justice programs. There is also the notion that we should expect to see increasing mediation caseloads over time as the availability of mediation services becomes better known.

In practice, however, data on caseloads have to be interpreted with caution. First, caseloads are highly dependent on the types of cases handled by the program and the relationship of the program to referral sources. A survey of twenty-nine projects revealed that justice system–based programs had the largest caseloads, composite programs had the next highest, and community-based programs had the lowest level (McGillis 1986:48). However, the types of cases taken by each type of program also varies substantially. Minor criminal cases comprise a far larger proportion of the cases of the justice system–based programs; 90 to 100 percent of the programs McGillis surveyed (1986:114–15). In the community programs only one of the nine programs polled handled that proportion of criminal cases. Four other programs reported that about half their cases were criminal cases (McGillis 1986:118–19). Among the composite programs, only two of nine programs polled had caseloads that were comprised of 85 percent or more criminal cases (McGillis 1986:116–17).

A second critical factor affecting caseloads is the source of referral to mediation and the degree to which coercion is involved in getting disputants to mediate. The Neighborhood Justice Center evaluation reports that referrals from judges are most likely to result in mediation hearings, followed by police, prosecutors' offices, legal aid, and others in order of importance (Cook et al. 1980). The degree of coercion involved in such referrals ranges from very low in community-based programs to statutorily based compulsory nonjudicial processing at the other end of the continuum (McGillis 1986: 43–44). Not surprisingly, programs participating in mandatory mediation efforts report higher proportions of cases resulting in hearings.

For community-based programs and composite programs, getting voluntary cases remains a critical challenge. Caseloads for many programs are often substantially lower than justice-based programs. Whether because of a lack of public education about alternatives to adjudication, ambivalence about mediation on the part of the legal community, the availability of other conflict-resolution mechanisms, or avoidance, only a small proportion of disputants spontaneously take their disputes to community-based justice programs (Pearson 1982).

It is against this general background that we view the San Francisco Community Boards (SFCB) study. SFCB does not take referrals from the justice sytem if the justice system retains jurisdiction (DuBow 1987:5). Moreover, they are noncoercive in seeking to encourage people to settle disputes through the board system. SFCB has tried to get community agencies to refer conflicts, but "its principal efforts have been directed at appeals to the public and to countless community groups to recruit conflicts through community education" (DuBow 1987:6).

How well does this approach work? One of DuBow's surveys showed that more than 40 percent of the respondents were aware of its existence (1987:7). Dubow notes that this is a high recognition rate, but that caseloads are far lower: "Even though Visitacion Valley has a strong area office with more cases than any other office, the number of cases brought for mediation is quite modest, averaging about 175 in recent years of which 55 actually result in a hearing" (1987:7).

Drawing conclusions about the San Francisco Community Boards on the basis of data provided in the DuBow report illustrates the general problem of using caseloads in evaluations of community-mediation programs. DuBow described the caseloads as "modest," but modest compared to what? To previous performance? To expectations? To other community-based programs? In terms of impacts on caseloads? Without an explicit comparison, formal evaluative statements are arbitrary.

The DuBow report does break new ground by attempting to determine the need for mediation services. Dubow attempted to measure need in two ways. First, in a very short section, he reported efforts of the SFCB disputants to resolve their conflicts before coming to the boards. According to his data, only 23 percent had made no attempt to resolve their dispute before coming to the SFCB. At least 54 percent had made two or more attempts by contacting the other party, police, service agencies, or elected officials (1987:13). The second major effort to measure need for services is the study of police data. DuBow analyzed police log and incident reports for separate one-month periods. Each log and report was analyzed to determine whether it involved a conflict similar to those handled by the SFCB. In this analysis, 930 SFCB-like cases were identified (1987:17). DuBow then addressed the obstacles to meeting this need with SFCB-type services. The major obstacle he identified was the willingness of the police to make referrals and the acceptance of such suggestions by the parties (1987:37).

Measuring need for community-justice services is fraught with conceptual and methodological problems. For example, in the universe of community disputes, what proportion result in police calls?

However, comparing caseloads of particular programs to the community need for services provides a very useful perspective for making claims about the success of community-mediation programs.

How Quickly Are Mediation Cases Processed?

A second commonly used criterion for evaluating the delivery of services is the speed of handling cases. Case-processing time is generally calculated from the time intake occurs. The NJC study reported that centers organized mediation sessions an average of nine days after intake (Cook, Roehl, and Sheppard 1980:34). A Florida evaluation reported average time from referral to disposition was eleven days, and the median was eight days (Bridenback 1979). The speed of disposition is usually compared to courts. The NJC study reported an average time from filing to trial of ninety-eight days in Atlanta and sixty-three days in Kansas City for cases similar to justice center cases (Cook, Roehl, and Sheppard 1980:74). On the other hand, a more recent evaluation of New Jersey mediation programs indicated that the average number of days from court filing to a court date for a control group of mediation-like cases was thirty-nine days (Roehl and Hersch 1988).

How Efficient Are Community-Justice Services?

A third commonly used criterion is costs per case. The 1980 NJC study reported per case costs as low as $4.18 in one program and as high as $589 in another program with a small caseload (Cook, Roehl, and Sheppard 1980:101). Per-case costs vary as much as 50 percent depending on whether they are calculated on the basis of the number of referrals or the number of cases that actually go to mediation (Cook, Roehl, and Sheppard 1980:101).

It is difficult to compare costs per case. Calculating costs involves personnel (judges, prosecutors, clerical and other staff), buildings, utilities, and other costs for some average length of time it takes to process a mediationlike case to settlement or court decision. In one study, Felstiner and Williams calculated court-operating costs, based on

- the average amount of time consumed at different stages of the different forms of disposition;

• the court personnel present at all of those stages;
• the personnel whose activities support the work of those present at court stages;
• per minute costs of both types of personnel;
• personnel costs for each form of court disposition. (1982)

They conclude that the cost of the "pure" mediation approach used in Dorchester was greater than the savings in court costs by a ratio of 2.7:1 (1982:134). They note, however, that a "deep" mediation approach was used in Dorchester in which mediators "suppress fact finding and judgment formation in favor of disputant-initiated agreements about further conduct" (1982:140). They also note that the Dorchester approach requires far more time than the mediation-arbitration approach characteristic of some other programs.

Most recent unpublished studies of community-mediation programs have tended to de-emphasize costs per case as an indicator of efficiency. About 85 percent of the programs providing data to the American Bar Association report had budgets of less than $100,000 (1986). As noted above, caseloads also tend to be small. A Massachusetts evaluation of twenty-eight community-mediation programs reported that the median budget was $42,500 and that median number of referrals and mediations for these programs was 147 and 73 respectively (Davis 1986:x).

It is possible to construct indicators of efficiency that would better reflect on community-mediation programs than direct case costs do. For example, an evaluation could include at least some of the direct costs to disputants in mediation or the courts; costs such as legal representation and time off work. However, the design and implementation of such a study would be too expensive for most community-mediation programs.

What Is the Record in Case Dispositions?

All programs collect data on case disposition, but it is difficult to make interprogram comparisons or comparisons with court proceedings both because of problems with reliability of the data and because of the lack of common definitions. What, for example, does premediation "settlement" mean? Does it mean an explicit agreement was reached that addresses the issues in conflict? Is it simply that a complainant decided to suppress conflict rather than go through an unfamiliar process with uncertain outcomes?

The proportion of mediated cases in which agreements are reached is the standard indicator by which officials of programs gauge themselves and others. The ideology of mediation—with its emphasis on improved interpersonal communication through face-to-face discussion of issues with a neutral third party—justifies agreements as a measure of success. And, using this indicator, community-mediation programs are reasonably successful. The NJC analysis reported agreement in 65–78 percent of the civil mediations and 81–95 percent of the interpersonal mediations (Cook, Roehl, and Sheppard 1980). A New Jersey study of community-mediation programs indicated that 72 percent of mediated cases reached agreement (Roehl and Hersch 1988). A Massachusetts report of twenty-eight community-mediation programs indicated that rates of agreements were around 85 percent but noted that "available statistics on the number of agreements reached as a result of mediation were too diverse to merge into a concrete statistic" (Davis 1986:75).

One of the problems with using agreements as an indicator of success is that

> achievement of agreement at a hearing, while significant, can represent anything from a highly comprehensive and sensitive agreement reflecting an effort to solve the entire range of problems embedded in the dispute to the agreement by the parties regarding a marginal issue that may have some limited importance but leaves the vast bulk of the conflict unresolved. (McGillis 1986:57)

If proportion of mediated cases that reach agreement has been the primary emphasis in the data on case disposition, it is no longer the sole emphasis. There is increased emphasis on data that relates outcomes to referral sources, types of case, degree of coercion involved in getting the parties to mediate, and even the ethnicity and gender of the disputants (Roehl and Hersch 1988). In the San Francisco Community Boards study, DuBow reports standard data on case disposition for 1,576 cases between 1977 and 1982: number of hearings scheduled and outcomes of hearings; number resolved without hearings; number of parties who refused mediation services; number of cases deemed inappropriate; and number of cases in which one party could not be contacted. He also reports on the frequency with which issues were raised and the dispositions of cases by type (DuBow 1987:14). Generally such data on the dispositions of cases are more useful for monitoring than evaluation. They indicate trends and significant anomalies, such as particularly low rates of hearings for some types of cases. Making evaluative judgments from such data is more problematic. Comparative evaluation is possible, but, as noted above, without detailed information about what "agreement" means, evaluative comparisons are not meaningful.

The SFCB study illustrates another method of presenting and analyzing data on the dispositions of cases. In addition to the conventional quantitative summary, DuBow presented a series of mini–case studies on several types of disputes including domestic, juvenile, neighbor-neighbor, and noise. Each description of a specific case was followed by a brief analysis. These analyses were explicitly evaluative.

> In the domestic violence case the Panel displayed admirable skills on a number of occasions, particularly considering the fact that it was dealing with a highly complex, ongoing relationship between two people. There was also a level of unwillingness on the part of the disputants that was masked by overtly expressed interest in the SFCB process. The parties did not arrive at the appointed time and had to be fetched. They brought the children to the hearing, and these little ones created an amount of activity that bordered on chaos.
>
> By and large, however, the Panel was able to induce the parties to discuss their problems openly. It used personal examples of domestic experience to re-assure the couple that their troubles were not unique. It pinpointed each person's desire to be respected in the relationship. On particular occasions the Panel used effective devices in its intervention. For example, each party was asked to identify the three most important things they wanted in the relationship. And, as the session was drawing to a close, each was asked to tell something that each liked about the other person.
>
> The Panel did not seem to have the capacity to follow-up, to systematically bring together the bits and pieces of insight it had

revealed in order to construct an understanding between the parties that could help to solve their difficulties. The process that the Panel carried out did not seem to allow for such a capability. The practice of minimal intervention based on the principle that the disputants are responsible for resolving their own dispute, could not support them in a case where the parties did not know how to take the steps that would bring them together. As a proxy of the program the Panel was beyond its depth. It did the best it could in a two-hour period, carrying the hearing to Phase 2, and it ended the hearing session feeling good about its perform-ance. But the parties did not appear to the next appointed session a week later, nor did they appear when that session was re-scheduled for another time. (DuBow 1987:54)

Another analysis was more positive:

It was a very difficult situation that the Panel had to deal with, and through many chaotic moments it was able to extract sense and to find the means of building a resolution. It disengaged the disputants from the language of conflict and translated the asso-ciations that were flying around the room into the means of rational discourse. From careful listening it came to obvious but effective conclusions. For example: Both sides don't want to be insulted. It identified the older woman's fear of one neighbor's loud voice and got him to recognize it and tone it down, an important breakthrough in communication. The Panel directly suggested constructive ways of complaining as opposed to screaming, and it encouraged pragmatic solutions to the noise and other problems. When all else failed in its attempt to allay the fears of the older woman so that she could in the future communicate with her neighbors, it came from behind the table and did an extemporaneous role play in which it demonstrated how simple and unthreatening the communication could be.

The last, capping a bit of ingenuity worked, and a resolution was constructed that everyone subscribed to. They would get permission from the landlord to install rubber bumpers on the closet door; they agreed to a means of communication for future problems that might arise; and they all agreed to speak to each other with civility and respect. (DuBow 1987:63)

Some of the analysis is implicitly evaluative, such as this detail: "At most of the hearings our observers noted that panelists had their training manuals open and referred to them as they maneuvered their way through the 4-phase process" (1987:71). This detail conveys an image of insufficient training or experience and/or lack of "ownership" of the mediation process on the part of the mediators. Taken together these details provide context and a sense of process.

The context provided caused DuBow to reconsider the quantitative summary of the case dispositions:

> Eleven of the 14 cases ended with a resolution, about 80% of the total and similar to the success rate revealed in our archival study. But 4 of the 11 proved to be either incomplete or questionable resolutions in the light of further information. On the other hand, in the case involving the two juveniles, the panel perceived that the case had not been resolved, in large means, because one of the girls walked out, whereas the girls when questioned weeks later felt they have [sic] come to an agreement, and it was working. In any event, the more precise rate of success for our sample is 50% resolved, and 29% incomplete or questionable, and 21% definitely unresolved. While we cannot project from these percentages to adjust our archival data, we can see that the success rate for SFCB hearings is something less than the high figure in our case file analysis. Since follow-up is a weak point for virtually all conflict resolution programs, the same result would probably be true for other neighborhood justice programs as well. (DuBow 1987:47)

DuBow's analysis demonstrates that the conventional quantitative summaries of case dispositions have to be interpreted with great caution. They are useful for monitoring trends, but not necessarily for making evaluative judgments. His analysis also illustrates how mini-case descriptions can be used to convey a sense of how disputants are persuaded to participate, how mediators nudge the process along—sometimes brilliantly, sometimes haltingly—and how opportunities for resolving or mitigating disputes are created or missed.

How Satisfied Are Disputants with the Mediation Process?

Saisfaction with the mediation process is a popular criterion in the evaluation of community-mediation programs. Data on satisfaction are relatively easy to collect and can be easily interpreted by all the relevant audiences for community mediation. And the data on satisfaction with community mediation are impressive. The NJC study reports high levels of disputant satisfaction: An average of 88 percent across all centers (Cook, Roehl, and Sheppard 1980:47, 54).

Satisfaction is really a catchall criterion that includes disputants' general assessments of aspects of the mediation process, the fairness of mediators and the mediation, and the outcomes of the process. In addition to asking about general perceptions of satisfaction, a variety of empirical indicators have been used for each of the specific dimensions of satisfaction. One case study compared the degree to which defendants and complainants in mediated minor criminal cases felt they had an opportunity to explain their dispute as they saw it. Their responses were compared to a control group of defendants and complainants in a court process (Davis 1982). Another study examined satisfaction with the process by focusing on the degree to which participants in a small-claims mediation felt that the mediator completely or mostly understood what the complaint was about; whether they understood everything that was going on in the process and whether they were completely or mostly satisfied with their overall experience. These responses were compared to those of a control group whose claims were handled in court (McEwen and Maiman 1984). In all these studies, mediation participants were consistently more satisfied than court participants. The degree of difference varied depending on the specific questions and the type of case. Another study compared the satisfaction of complainants, respondents, and hearing officers (Conner and Surette 1980). Most unpublished evaluations of community-mediation programs report on the satisfaction of participants without a control group of court cases.

Satisfaction is sometimes assessed in terms of the perceived fairness of mediators and the mediation process. In the available comparisons to a court control group both groups are likely to view the mediator or judge as fair, but when the perceived fairness of the process or outcome is compared mediation is seen as fairer (Davis 1982; McEwen and Maiman 1981).

Satisfaction with outcomes have also been assessed in a few studies. The Brooklyn study found that those in mediation were more likely to be satisfied with the agreements than those in court proceedings (Davis 1982). In the San Francisco Community Boards study,

DuBow analyzed satisfaction with agreements; first- and second-party assessment of changes in their problem; satisfaction by type of outcome; and whether disputants would use the boards again. The collection of data from disputants by telephone calls from staff raises issues of reliability. There were complete data sets for only a portion of the cases, ranging from 81 cases for one question to 223 cases for another.

Satisfaction is likely to remain an important criterion for assessing community-mediation programs. It is relatively easy to collect, analyze, and understand. The general problem with disputant satisfaction as a criterion is that it is frequently not used precisely enough to allow for useful comparisons. Moreover, the variety of ways in which satisfaction questions are posed to disputants and the multiple scales and categories used to record responses make valid comparisons problematic. There are also problems of reliability associated with the collection of satisfaction from disputants by program staff. A more basic issue is the importance to attach to disputants' evaluations of the outcomes of mediation. Are disputants satisfied with their agreements (or other outcomes) because they think outcomes are "wise," "just," or "fair"? What is the correlation between satisfaction with an outcome and independent assessments of the wisdom and justice of these outcomes? The available literature is not very enlightening on this issue.

How Durable Are Agreements?

Stability or durability of agreements has been another primary criterion for evaluating community-justice programs. Stability has been measured in a variety of ways. In the NJC study a sample of complainants and respondents were interviewed six months after reaching mediated agreements to assess whether the other party had kept all the terms of the agreement. More than two-thirds of both complainants and respondents indicated that the other party had kept all the terms of the agreement (Cook, Roehl, and Sheppard 1980). The Brooklyn study, which dealt with mediation and court adjudication of criminal cases, used several indicators of durability: complainant problems with defendants' behavior; frequency of intervention by the criminal-justice system with the disputants during the follow-up period; the degree to which complainants feared revenge from defendants; and the degree of anger experienced by complainants against defendants (Davis 1982). Significantly, the number of problems experienced and the frequency of police intervention was similar for both mediated and court cases. However, about twice as many court complainants feared revenge or experienced anger as did mediation complainants (Davis 1982). The Maine small-claims mediation study examined the frequency and amount of claims paid and the degree to which defendants in mediated and adjudicated cases felt an obligation to pay. They found that not only did nearly 71 percent of defendants in mediated cases pay in full (as compared to 34 percent in adjudicated cases), more than two-thirds of defendants in mediation reported some or a strong legal (and moral) obligation to pay (as compared to one-third in adjudicated cases) (McEwen and Maiman 1981). The authors concluded that agreements fashioned by the parties led to this greater sense of responsibility. Conner and Surette found that complainants' satisfaction increased after three weeks, although 41.5 percent of the complainants and 35.6 percent of the respondents reported that the problem remained unsolved (1980). In the SFCB study, DuBow compared first- and second-party assessments of whether agreements were working, assessments at follow-up for different case outcomes, and parties' assessments of changes in their problems since going to the San Francisco Community Boards. In the small sample of cases ($n = 143$) in which follow-up data are available for both parties, 75 percent of the first parties reported improvements in their situation, while 84 percent of the second parties felt their situations had improved (DuBow 1987:77).

Although the available data suggests that mediated agreements are more durable than court decisions, there is much that we do not know about this stability. Two questions are paramount: how does stability vary by type of dispute and how does it vary by the characteristics of the mediation program? We might expect stability to be high—as it frequently is—when an agreement involves a single act, such as repayment of a debt. However, we know less about stability in cases that involve an ongoing web of interactions such as a custody agreement or neighbor-neighbor disputes over noise or shared space. Moreover, we know least about the types of mediation structures and processes that foster stability.

How Do Characteristics of Mediators, Mediation Styles,
Program Structure, and Other Variables Affect
Program Outcomes?

If one thinks of community mediation as a dispute-resolution service analogous to other community social services, one of the major
gaps in the literature has to do with how interprogram variations in
service delivery affect program outcomes. Education, mental-health,
substance-abuse, and other community services are frequently treated
as service technologies or modalities that can be compared in an
effort to determine which approaches are most effective in different
circumstances. While there are a few comparisons of community-
mediation outcomes with court outcomes (as noted previously), there
is surprisingly little published research on the impacts of variations
in the number of mediators, the degree of coercion in getting parties
into mediation, the different techniques of mediation in different programs, the use of volunteers versus paid staff, the recruitment of
mediators, training and retention practices, average length of hearings, and a host of other potentially important variables.

Much of the available research on mediation processes is neither
explicitly evaluative nor focused on community-justice programs.
Tactics of mediators in a variety of settings for mediation is one
aspect of process that has received some attention. Pruitt and his
colleagues tested two models of mediator behavior. The first was a
three-stage model developed by Kressel (1972). This model, based on
interviews with labor mediators, suggests that mediators employ three
distinct types of tactics in sequence: reflexive tactics designed to establish rapport with the disputants and orient the mediator; nondirective
tactics designed to aid the disputants to develop a solution; and
directive tactics designed to promote particular solutions. The second
model suggests that sets of tactics are related to five distinct stages
in the mediation process: information gathering; posing issues; generation and evaluation of alternatives; urging decision making; and
facilitating planning for implementation (Pruitt et al. 1989). They
found that "mediators follow a logical series of steps, starting with
clarification of ground rules, moving to efforts to gain information
and keep order, then to efforts to pose and solve issues, and finally
to implementation" (Pruitt et al. 1989:389). (They note, however, that
there was little consistency between what tactics mediators used [as

noted by observers] and what mediators said they did in completing mediator checklists after completing the mediation [1989:384]). Other research indicates that mediators are adaptive in their choice of mediation tactics; they use different tactics in different situations to achieve success (Carnevale, Lim, and McLaughlin 1989). This same research suggests that some tactics are contingently effective in the sense of being more likely to be associated with success under some conditions than under others. Process-related research has been done on the competence of mediators in communicating (Donohue 1989), on the effects of caucusing (Pruitt et al. 1989; Markowitz and Engram 1983; Silbey and Merry 1986), and on the effects of three different mediation/ arbitration conditions on disputant behavior (Pruitt et al. 1989).

The ideology of program mediation emphasizes a process leading to tailored, individualized dispute resolutions. Evaluations of such processes require methods that allow detailed attention to program nuances, settings, complexities, idiosyncrasies, and context. The methods of qualitative evaluation—in particular observation and in-depth interviewing—make it possible for the evaluator to "focus on capturing program processes, documenting variations, and exploring important individual differences between various participants' experiences and outcomes" (Patton 1987:14). As Patton notes, "The qualitative-naturalistic approach to evaluation conceives of programs as dynamic and developing, with 'treatments' changing in subtle but important ways as staff learn, as clients move in and out, and as conditions of delivery are altered" (Patton 1987:18).

Detailed observation and in-depth interviewing would seem to be ideal methods for exploring the relationship between program processes and outcomes. They are not widely used for two reasons. The first is that qualitative methods are expensive and time-consuming. They require well-trained researchers over a period of weeks or months. Staffs of small programs with limited budgets regard such evalutions as simply too expensive. In addition, the methods of qualitative research (observation in particular) are regarded as too intrusive.

A second constraint is that the methods of qualitative evaluation are too unfamiliar to the sort of audiences for which community-mediation evaluations are prepared. The limited number of interviews that can be conducted and observations that can be made sometimes raise questions about the validity of the conclusions, even when purposeful sampling strategies are carefully developed and implemented. Hence, detailed evaluation of process remains one of the underdeveloped research areas of community mediation.

The Informalism Frame

Informalism describes a set of benefits ascribed to alternative dispute-resolution programs, of which community mediation is a part: flexible rules, easier access, speedier resolution, lower costs, and the like. Most evaluative efforts have focused on the degree to which these benefits have been delivered. However, a few critics have raised important questions about the premises of informalism and about the impacts of informalism on the rights of disputants. Some of these questions are reexamined in this section.

To What Extent Has Community Mediation Increased Access to Justice?

In the most literal sense, community-justice programs have the potential for increasing access to dispute resolution services by 1) charging no or minimal fees for service; 2) not requiring lawyers; 3) holding hearings at times convenient to all parties to the dispute; 4) providing readily understandable rules and procedures; and 5) providing multilingual staff to serve non-English-speaking disputants (McGillis 1986:87).

Those who see community mediation as increasing access recognize that the flexible hours and reduced costs of mediation are necessary conditions for increased access. However, they have a more profound meaning of access in mind. They assume that there is an unmet demand for disputing services, that there are categories of disputes and disputants that are dealt with inadequately in the court system. Identifying and measuring the degree to which community-mediation programs deal with this unmet demand is viewed as one more way of evaluating these programs.

At present, inferences about unmet demand for disputing services are typically based on three types of data: 1) mediation caseloads; 2) comparisons of demographic characteristics of disputants in medi-

ation with those in the judicial system; and 3) determining the degree
to which cases in mediation do not duplicate court cases.

As noted previously, data on caseloads is the most commonly
collected information about community-justice programs. These data
are useful as an overview of program activity and of changes in
program activity. While data on caseloads is important in determining
the types of cases handled by community-mediation programs, it is
not, by itself, a valid indicator of changes in access to services. That
is to say, even if caseloads are increasing, it does not necessarily
follow that access in increasing.

The demographic characteristics of disputants are also used as
an indirect indicator of unmet demand. The assumption is that legal
costs, formality, and the inconvenient hours of the court are an
impediment to access by the poor, the uneducated, and ethnic minorities. Thus if the poor and ethnic minorities are increasing users of
mediation services, it must be that these services are more "accessible."
There are data to support the claim that users of community mediation are more likely to be poor and ethnic minorities. The NJC
evaluation indicated that complainants in Kansas City and Atlanta
were much more likely to be black and female (Cook, Roehl, and
Sheppard 1980:152–57). The Brooklyn study also showed that the
majority of users were young, poor, black or Hispanic, and uneducated (Davis 1982:32–33). One might infer from these and other
similar studies that the community-justice programs do increase
access, if these disputants are in mediation as a matter of choice.
However, some proportion were in mediation because their cases were
referred by the courts. In addition, Merry (and others) have noted
that the poor are already users of the court system (Merry 1979).
Hence, we do not know from the conventional way in which demographic data are reported to what degree community mediation
represents the dispute-resolution forum of choice for the poor, the
uneducated, and ethnic minorities.

A third way of assessing unmet demand is to focus on disputes
that are not dealt with by courts or other dispute-resolution forums.
For example, McGillis cites a Florida study that concludes that approximately 78 percent of the programs' caseloads hold the potential for
formal judicial processing. He notes: "If 78 percent of the cases handled by the five programs studied have the potential for formal judicial
processing, then the remaining 22 percent of cases may represent

disputes receiving a clear increase in access to justice" (McGillis 1986:94). In short, access is viewed as increased if these community programs are dealing with unmet demand for dispute-resolution services.

Using indirect indicators for making inferences about the degree to which community-mediation programs increase access to justice is problematic, at best. There are obvious conceptual problems with the concept of "unmet demand" and validity problems with the standard indicators of demand for mediation services. It may be possible to demonstrate that there are classes of disputants who, in the absence of community-mediation programs, would suppress their conflicts or engage in avoidance. For them, communmity mediation could represent an increase in access to justice provided that the other party or parties participate as well.[1] It is difficult to determine from the available data the degree to which such participation is occurring.

What Is the Quality of Justice Provided by Community-Mediation Programs?

The alternative dispute-resolution movement of which community justice is a part is partly a response to 1) the perceived lack of procedural and substantive justice to minor offenders and 2) claims that courts cannot effectively address social demands expressed in complex disputes (Harrington 1985:34). Community justice, it is argued, provides a dispute-resolution forum that is more flexible than courts in its processes, not limited to purely "legal" issues, conducive to addressing the complexity of neighborhood disputes, and built on the sanctions and incentives of ongoing relationships to encourage compliance and agreements.

Evaluators have not addressed the issue of quality of justice directly. Rather they have treated quality of justice as synonymous

---

1. Harrington argues that second-party participation in mediation is a key issue. She notes that evaluative studies overstate the satisfaction of disputants because they focus only on those who participate. She notes: "One conclusion of this study is that mediation programs, such as the Neighborhood Justice Center, do not increase critical party participation. Thus even if we assume that there is a correlation between increased participation in dispute processing and more effective order maintenance, the Neighborhood Justice Center does not significantly contribute to enhancing it" (Harrington 1985:162).

with "quality of dispute-resolution services." They have focused on the flexibility of the process, the opportunities for disputants to explain their situation, the satisfaction of the disputants with mediators or with the mediation process, proportion of hearings ending in agreements, compliance with agreements, subsequent problems with other parties, and similar measures of general and specific satisfaction discussed previously.[2]

Hofrichter offers a more critical evaluative perspective on the quality of justice offered by community-mediation programs:

> Few would dispute the value of flexibility, informality, and responsiveness in dispute processing. Yet the instrumental and apolitical approach of the reforming liberal denies the objective interests that generate social conflict by obscuring those struggles that express class interests. Reformist analysis stresses the benefits of mediation to individuals and measures the success of these institutions according to the number of disputants who reached agreements and were satisfied. This interpersonal view of disputes ignores the ways in which individuals may benefit qua individuals but lose as members of a larger social class whose interests cannot be fully satisfied through law or private case-by-case resolution of personal grievances because the issues involve questions of political power that extend beyond legality. (Hofrichter 1987:xxvi)

"The major objective of conflict resolution," he argues, "is not primarily justice but order maintenance and problem-solving" (Hofrichter 1987:xxv).

Harrington also focuses on the order-maintenance function of community mediation, although she uses the term less pejoratively than Hofrichter: "Order maintenance is a term that refers to a style of intervention by officials or a type of 'control system.' Conflict is handled informally on a case-by-case basis rather than by the enforcement of legal standards" (Harrington 1985:44). Harrington's primary

---

2. McGillis, quoting Thibaut and Walker, notes that the major elements of the quality of justice include precision in bringing relevant facts to the surface, consistency of outcomes for similar cases, disputant satisfaction, and compliance by disputants with judgments or settlements (1986). McGillis notes that precision and consistency are difficult to measure. His subsequent review of the literature focuses exclusively on indicators of satisfaction and compliance.

thesis has to do with the degree to which community mediation promotes participation and the relationship between participation and the maintenance of order. However, she concludes with some comments on the quality of justice. She argues that

> substantive demands for social justice have been overshadowed by experimentation with techniques of alternative dispute resolution. This focus on dispute techniques has separated the politics of problem solving from the politics of taking rights seriously.
>
> We need to turn our attention to the substantive rights and claims for justices that are expressed in the dispute-processing context. Once we understand that the exercise of rights, making claims of rights, is an expression of social problems (e.g., social and economic inequality), then we can move forward with the view that rights are one context or framework in which social problem solving takes place. (Harrington 1985:173)

The degree to which ADR protects (and promotes) rights of disputants is likely to be a major theme in the next generation of evaluative studies. Taking rights seriously in an evaluative sense is likely to involve supplementary indicators of dispute satisfaction with third-party judgments about the degree to which rights are protected.

Community Mediation and Community Building

One of the six major goals of the original NJC program was to "contribute to the reduction of tension and conflict in the community" (Cook, Roehl, and Sheppard 1980:17). Community-based mediation programs have a more ambitious agenda than mere conflict resolution. Adherents of community-based programs see these programs as playing a central role in community building. Merry has provided a succinct description of the community-based mediation agenda:

> Community mediation could provide a means to counteract a state of anomie, isolation, alienation, and fear in a community by facilitating communication between people who would otherwise remain distant acquaintances, even locked into relationships of hostility and conflict.
>
> Mediation could provide a valuable means to counteract this

social isolation by providing a mechanism for people to communicate with each other, breaking down hostilities founded on
misunderstanding. Even if the actual number of disputes resolved
is small, the improvement in the quality of neighborhood life
could be great. (Merry 1982:187)

Community-based programs share many of the goals of justice-
system models of mediation, including increased access to justice.
The primary difference is their emphasis on the need to develop
increased community self-awareness, greater capacity for managing
the community, and the development of indigenous community
leadership (McGillis 1986:25).

How Successful Have Community-Based Programs Been
in Fostering a Greater Sense of Community?

Assuming that it is possible to achieve some consensus about what
community means (spatially bounded; socially bounded?), it might
be possible to develop surrogate indicators of "sense of community"
or "empowerment"; changing patterns in individual feelings of alienation and anomie could be surveyed. Perceptions of identification
with and attachment to the community could be documented. Measures of autonomy and efficacy in the community could be developed
(e.g., the degree to which citywide land-use regulatory authorities
follow community recommendations).

To date, only the SFCB study addresses the issue of community
empowerment. The study emphasizes the impact of training and
participation on the volunteer mediators. This emphasis is justified
if we assume that the development of community leadership skilled
in the techniques of mediation is a necessary condition for empowerment of the community. To analyze empowerment DuBow compared the interview and survey responses of forty-two trained
volunteers with eleven nontrainees. According to DuBow, San Francisco Community Boards members see themselves as part of a social
movement:

Community Boards in its training and day-to-day operations
functions on a premise that its practices are more than just
efficient or effective techniques to deliver a dispute settlement

service. They are conceived of as aspects of a correct and valued view of conflicts in society. Community Boards' participants view the way they do things as informed by a set of political and social values that other conflict resolution programs may not share. For example, they believe that the settlement of a conflict is less important than getting people to express their differences and to improve their communications. Getting disputants to see their own responsibility in the conflict and to become actively involved in finding a resolution are tenets about the sort of approach individuals in society should take to the conflicts they encounter in their lives. They also have come to see dealing with disputes in an autonomous neighborhood context as qualitatively different and superior to other geographic and institutional settings for the settlement of most interpersonal conflicts. (1987:32)

Perhaps because of this sense of participating in a social movement, volunteers report that the single most satisfying aspect of SFCB work was the sense of community they felt (DuBow 1987:41). Volunteers report that participation is a "significant experience in their lives." They believe that the SCFB is an important organization and their efforts are contributing to its success (1987:44).

DuBow then investigated the degree to which participation had a measurable effect on the volunteers' "connectedness" to the neighborhood. He focused on comparisons of volunteers and trainees' perceptions of neighborhood, knowledge of neighborhood, behavioral ties to neighborhood, and attitudes toward the justice system. The overall responses indicated that both groups were "more integrated" into the community, but the differences between trainees and nontrainees were generally not statistically significant, suggesting that the experience may not account for these increased feelings of integration (DuBow 1987:45).

Trainees also rated themselves at two points in time on a number of communication and organizational skills such as ability to speak to a group, help run an organization, do publicity work, lead groups discussions, communicate with people, help people solve problems, and be a good listener. The trainees did not report an increase in skills, perhaps, as DuBow notes, because the SFCB experience "made the volunteers aware of the difficulty and complexity of these tasks and how much still is involved in performing these tasks well" (1987:51).

It is perhaps not too surprising that the SFCB study focuses more narrowly on empowerment of the mediator than on empowerment of the community. Building or empowerment of the community is difficult to document, and, in any case, development of leadership is viewed as a necessary condition for such empowerment. What is more surprising, given the early rhetoric of the community-mediation movement, is that not only have there been no studies of empowerment, there is almost no current mention of it. In a recent issue of *Dispute Resolution Forum* six directors of community-mediation centers commented on various aspects of the community-justice movement (National Institute of Dispute Resolution 1988). When asked about successes and problems, not one director mentioned community building as either a success or an area for improvement. It is not clear whether the current lack of emphasis on building the community represents an abandonment of the objective of empowerment.

Conclusions

Most of the published and unpublished evaluations of community-justice programs treat those programs as social services. The evaluative emphasis is on simple measure of delivery efficiency (e.g., costs per case), effort (e.g., caseloads; caseloads per mediator), and outcome (e.g., percentage of agreements and satisfaction of disputants). What is remarkable about this emphasis is that it has changed so little in the last decade. Current unpublished evaluations and individual data reporting forms use the same concepts and the same indicators.[3]

This emphasis on delivery of services occurs for several reasons. The first and most obvious is that the criteria and indicators seem to relate most directly to the original expectations of community-justice programs; increasing access, decreasing costs, and decreasing court

---

3. I base this comment on a review of a sample of these forms. In the summer of 1988 I wrote to about sixty community-justice programs asking for evaluations and data-gathering forms. Of the twenty-three programs that responded, most reported that they had not recently been evaluated. Several programs sent unpublished evaluations and/or data-gathering forms.

caseloads. However, if the interviews with the six directors reported in NIDR's *Forum* are any guide, the present agenda of community-justice programs has less to do with reducing the public costs of disputing and court caseloads than with increasing access to justice and the quality of justice (NIDR 1988). (Community-justice programs, it should be recalled, are not having a demonstrable impact on court caseloads. Per case direct costs are also frequently high.)

A second impetus to the service-delivery emphasis is that much of the data are relatively easy to collect. Caseload data, costs per case, referral sources, types of cases, and the like are all indicators that any new program minimally concerned about public account-ability is likely to collect. Even data on satisfaction and compliance of disputants can be collected by program staff (although doing so raises serious problems in the reliability of the data).

Third, evaluations using these data are relatively cheaper to con-duct, and cost is a major factor in the conduct of evaluation. Most community-justice programs have small staffs—1.4 paid staff mem-bers was the median for twenty-eight programs in Massachusetts—and budgets of less than fifty thousand dollars.

Finally, the principal audiences for these evaluations—funding agencies, in particular—do not seem to ask for anything more pro-found. Indeed, the service-delivery evaluation data is generally ger-mane to decisions about whether to continue funding. In sum, the existing organization of evaluative studies provides predictable infor-mation to the already-persuaded.

The service-delivery frame of evaluation is likely to continue to dominate evaluations of community-justice programs, at least as long as accountability and funding decisions remain the dominant concern of program managers and funding agencies.

There are, however, other questions and audiences that need to be addressed with supplementary evaluative studies. One such ques-tion has to do with regard to what mediation approaches are most effective in different circumstances. There is a tendency to treat medi-ation as a single technology. Each program has its own training procedures and manual, sometimes carefully adapted over a period of years. These procedures impart a particular technology of medi-ation, having to do with the number of mediators, a sequence of mediation steps, ground rules, settings, and the like. Although medi-ators may have great faith in their own technology, there is relatively little critical analysis of other approaches in other programs. Given the "movement" characteristics in the development of community justice nationally, this is not surprising. It is, nevertheless, somewhat disturbing: if one of the principal values of mediation is to help disputants create custom-made agreements, we need to know much more about processes of mediation. How do particular types of processes affect outcomes? Are there processes that work better for some types of disputes? How, if at all, do gender, class, ethnicity, education, and other characteristics of disputants and mediators affect outcomes? How are disputants educated about mediation? How does this education affect expectations, outcomes, satisfaction, and stability? What types of hearings are more conducive to promoting communication among the parties?

A second primary audience for evaluation is the bar and officials of public agencies. Among other things, they need to know how informal community-justice procedures affect the rights of disputants. What types of cases can be referred from the justice system without eroding individual rights? What are the impacts of mandatory referral programs on satisfaction of disputants, compliance, and stability? What are the impacts of mandatory referral on processes of mediation? What are the impacts of referring minor neighborhood disputes over zoning variances, height limits, building code violations, and similar disputes to community-justice programs?

Third, where does community justice fit in the larger mosaic of official and unofficial efforts to promote community participation? What are the impacts of community-justice programs on particular geographically or socially defined communities? How, if at all, do they contribute to an increased sense of community, to community autonomy?

All these questions necessarily involve comparisons; comparisons of program processes and outcomes over time; comparisons with other programs, and comparisons with court processes. Comparative analysis is expensive, even limited comparisons of the sort published in the original NJC study. Large-scale evaluation requires a financial commitment on the part of public agencies and foundations. Evaluation has not been a priority among funding agencies, perhaps because it has been so narrowly conceived.[4] Finally, the existing

4. One recent RFP explicitly excluded program evaluations from the list of projects it would fund.

organization of community-justice evaluations treats programs in isolation from their total context. How do the political, social, and administrative contexts of programs interact with their processes and outcomes?

Community-justice programs have developed multiple habitats in the ecology of community dispute resolution. Some thrive nearer the shadow of the courthouse; a few are taking root on the hard ground of the community away from official agencies and referrals. Each type is evolving an ecological niche. Those nearest the courthouse feed off the court system. Those further away scramble for cases. Patterns of ecological succession for these different types of programs are likely to be very different. We need to think about how evaluations can be tailored to be more sensitive to these different contexts and processes.

REFERENCES

Abel, Richard L., ed. 1982. *The Politics of Informal Justice:* Vol. 1: *The American Experience.* Vol. 2: *Comparative Perspectives.* New York: Academic Press.

American Bar Association. 1986. *Dispute Resolution Program Directory.* Washington, D.C.: ABA Special Committee on Minor Dispute Resolution.

Bridenback, Michael L. 1979. *The Citizen Dispute Resolution Process in Florida: A Study of Five Programs.* Tallahassee: Florida Supreme Court, Office of State Courts Administrator.

Bryk, Anthony S. (1983) *Stakeholder-Based Evaluation.* San Francisco: Jossey-Bass.

Carnevale, Peter J. D., Rodney Lim, and Mary E. McLaughlin. 1989. "Contingent Mediator Behavior and Its Effectiveness." In *Mediation Research,* ed. Kenneth Kressel, Dean G. Pruitt, et al. San Francisco: Jossey-Bass.

Conner, Ross F., and Ray Surette. 1980. "Processing Citizens' Disputes outside the Courts: A Quasi-Experimental Evaluation." *Evaluation Review* 46: 739–68.

Cook, Royer F., Janice A. Roehl, and David I. Sheppard. 1980. *Neighborhood Justice Centers Field Test: Final Evaluation Report.* Washington, D.C.: U.S. Department of Justice.

Cook, Thomas D., and Charles Gruder. 1978. "Metaevaluation Research." *Evaluation Quarterly* 2, no. 1:5–51.

Cook, Thomas D., and Donald T. Campbell. 1979. *Quasi-Experimentation.* Chicago: Rand-McNally.

Cordray, David S., and Mark W. Lipsey. 1987. "Evaluation Studies for 1986." *Evaluation Studies Review Annual,* vol. 11, (ed. Cordray and Lipsey). Beverly Hills, Calif.: Sage.

Davis, Albie M. 1986. *Community Mediation in Massachusetts*. Salem: Administrative Office of the District Court.

Davis, Robert C. 1982. "Mediation: The Brooklyn Experiment." In *Neighborhood Justice: Assessment of an Emerging Idea*, ed. Roman Tomasic and Malcolm M. Feeley. New York: Longman.

Donohue, William A. 1989. "Communicative Competence in Mediators." In *Mediation Research*. ed. Kenneth Kressel, Dean G. Pruitt, et al. San Francisco: Jossey-Bass.

DuBow, Fredric L. 1987. *Conflicts and Community: A Study of the San Francisco Community Boards*. Draft. Chicago: Center for Research in Law and Justice, University of Illinois at Chicago.

Eisner, Elliot W. 1979. *The Educational Imagination*. New York: Macmillan.

Felstiner, William F., and Lynne Williams. 1982. "Community Mediation in Dorchester, Massachusetts." In *Neighborhood Justice: Assessment of an Emerging Idea*, ed. Roman Tomasic and Malcolm M. Feeley. New York: Longman.

Guba, Egon G., and Yvonna S. Lincoln. 1981. *Effective Evaluation: Improving the Usefulness of Evaluation Results through Responsive and Naturalistic Approaches*. San Francisco: Jossey-Bass.

Harrington, Christine B. 1985. *Shadow Justice: The Ideology and Institutionalization of Alternatives to Court*. Westport, Conn.: Greenwood Press.

Hofrichter, Richard. 1987. *Neighborhood Justice in Capitalist Society: The Expansion of the Informal State*. New York: Greenwood Press.

House, Ernest. 1980. *Evaluating with Validity*. Beverly Hills, Calif.: Sage.

Kressel, Kenneth. 1972. *Labor Mediation: An Exploratory Survey*. Albany, N.Y.: Association of Labor Mediation Agencies.

McEwen, Craig, and Richard J. Maiman. 1981. "Small Claims Mediation in Maine: An Empirical Assessment." *Maine Law Review* 33:237–68.

McEwen, Craig, and Richard J. Maiman. 1984. "Mediation in Small Claims Court: Achieving Compliance through Consent." *Law and Society Review* 18:11–49.

McEwen, Craig, and Richard J. Maiman. 1986. "The Relative Significance of Disputing Forum and Dispute Characteristics for Outcome and Compliance." *Law and Society Review* 20:439–47.

McGillis, Daniel. 1986. *Community Dispute Resolution Programs and Public Policy*. Washington, D.C.: National Institute of Justice, U.S. Department of Justice.

Markowitz, J. R., and P. S. Engram. 1983. "Mediation in Labor Disputes and Divorces: A Comparative Analysis." *Mediation Quarterly* 3:21–40.

Merry, Sally Engle. 1979. "A Plea for Thinking How Dispute Resolution Works." *Mooter* 2, no. 4:37–40.

Merry, Sally Engle. 1982. "Defining 'Success' in the Neighborhood Justice Movement." In *Neighborhood Justice: Assessment of an Emerging Idea*, ed. Roman Tomasic and Malcolm M. Feeley. New York: Longman.

Merry, Sally Engle, and Susan S. Silbey. 1984. "What Do Plaintiffs Want? Reexamining the Concept of Dispute." *Justice System Journal* 9:151–78.

National Institute of Dispute Resolution Forum. 1988. "How Community Justice Centers Are Faring." *Dispute Resolution Forum*, December, 7–14.

Patton, Michael Q. 1981. "Making Methods Choices." *Evaluation and Program Planning* 3:219–28.

Patton, Michael Q. 1986. *Utilization-Focused Evaluation*. Beverly Hills, Calif.: Sage.

Patton, Michael Q. 1987. *How to Use Qualitative Methods*. Beverly Hills, Calif.: Sage.

Pearson, Jessica. 1982. "An Evaluation of Alternatives to Court Adjudication." *Justice System Journal* 7:420–48.

Pruitt, Dean G., Neil B. McGillicuddy, Gary L. Welton, and William R. Fry. 1989. "Process of Mediation in Dispute Settlement Centers." In *Mediation Research*, ed., Kenneth Kressel, Dean G. Pruitt, et al. San Francisco: Jossey-Bass.

Roehl, Janice A., and Rebekah Hersch. 1988. *Evaluation of New Jersey Complementary Dispute Resolutions Programs*. Institute for Social Analysis.

Scriven, Michael. 1969. "An Introduction to Meta-evaluation." *Educational Product Report* 2:36–38.

Scriven, Michael. 1980. *The Logic of Evaluation*. Inverness, Calif.: Edgepress.

Silbey, Susan S., and Sally E. Merry. 1986. "Mediator Settlement Strategies." *Law and Policy* 8:7–32.

Vidmar, Neil. 1987. "Assessing the Effects of Case Characteristics and Settlement Forum on Dispute Outcomes and Compliance." *Law and Society Review* 21:155–65.

Weiss, Carol. 1977. "Research for Policy's Sake: The Enlightenment Function of Social Research." *Policy Analysis* 3:531–45.

Part 2

San Francisco Community Boards and the Meaning of Community Mediation

Community Boards:
An Analytic Profile

Frederic L. DuBow and Craig McEwen

This chapter uses the data collected through the evaluation project to describe and analyze the conflict-resolution activity of San Francisco Community Boards (SFCB) during the period between 1977 and 1984. SFCB changed considerably both during and subsequent to the study reported here. The portrait and analysis presented here should thus be understood as time bound. The analytic limits of this chapter should also be understood; the second author has drawn from the data reported in draft manuscripts and documents from the evaluation project, many of them by Frederic DuBow, for this over-view and summary of findings.

The early prominence of San Francisco Community Boards in the field of community-conflict resolution, its longevity, and some of its special features as a program make even a limited description and analysis of its early years potentially significant. This historical examination of SFCB can serve to raise larger questions about the special issues and challenges of carrying on dispute resolution in urban neighborhoods and more generally about the nature and meaning of popular justice.

Five general questions guide the summary of both SFCB and the massive set of data collected to evaluate it: 1) What was the program's ideology, and what implications did that ideology have for program organization? 2) What kinds of conflicts and people did SFCB draw into its dispute-resolution network? 3) How did SFCB handle its

We acknowledge the helpful comments of Kem Lowry, Vicki Shook, Sally Merry, Neal Milner, Ray Shonholtz, Judy Rothschild, and Barbara Schwartz.

caseload and with what consequences? 4) Who were the volunteers and what impact did the SFCB experience have on them? 5) What impact, if any, did SFCB have on the neighborhoods it worked in?

An Overview of San Francisco Community Boards

Program Ideology

San Francisco Community Boards was incorporated in 1976 as a nonprofit corporation whose primary goal was the resolution of conflict at the neighborhood level. The philosophy of the program was summarized by its president and founder, Raymond Shonholtz, in *Prospectus*, the SFCB newsletter. "Conflict and violence often occur between people who know each other; neighbors, family members, roommates, business partners, lovers" (*Prospectus* 1985:2). Yet, the formal justice system "views conflicts apart from the community or setting in which they occur, and often returns these disputes, unresolved, to the neighborhood, school or family from which they came." In contrast, "community conflict resolution mechanisms are among the few effective tools for early intervention and the reduction of anger and hostilities between people who know each other."

As a consequence, Shonholtz argued, "we should look to community-based conciliation programs as our 'courts of first resort . . .'" while recognizing that "community conflict resolution work is not a program. It is a long-term social investment in the health and stability of individuals and communities. This approach will need to be in place for 10–15 years, with the support of schools, communities and cities, to change the way Americans manage conflict" (*Prospectus* 1985:2).

San Francisco Community Boards was the brainchild of Raymond Shonholtz, an attorney and former clinical associate of law and co-director of the Legal Clinic at the University of San Francisco Law School. His entrepreneurship and persuasive capacity were instrumental in building the organization, articulating the philosophy, and securing the funds from many foundations to make the program operational.

Although unique in several respects, many aspects of the organization of Shonholtz's "community-based conciliation program" paralleled that of neighborhood- or community-mediation programs across the United States. It was built around a core of paid staff who coordinated the work of hundreds of volunteers in advertising the program ("outreach"), intake, meeting individually ("case development") with complainants ("first parties") and respondents ("second parties"), and hearing the disputes in face-to-face sessions ("panels") with three to five mediators. SFCB has preferred the term *conciliation* rather than mediation for the process it employs, but most observers would be hard-pressed to distinguish it from face-to-face mediation. Clearly, one of the distinguishing features of this program was its language for describing dispute-resolution work, a language that was at the core of a "program culture" that helped build and sustain identity and solidarity—an "internal community"—among the large pool of volunteers.

As we shall see, the far-reaching ideology of SFCB shaped the way that it approached voluntarism, linked its work to particular San Francisco neighborhoods, and utilized its resources.

The Use of Volunteers

Unlike most other community dispute-resolution programs, SFCB since its inception has viewed the recruitment, organization, and training of its volunteers as being at least as important as the actual delivery of conflict-resolution services. The program gave primacy to volunteers in its self-description: "Community Boards is a neighborhood-based conflict resolution program which trains community members in conciliation, case development, outreach and related skills" (*Prospectus* 1985:4). This emphasis on a large volunteer base grows from the premise that one can promote order in urban neighborhoods by encouraging and training residents to take on local issues and problems. Within the limits of its resources, the San Francisco Community Boards program thus sought to maximize the number of neighborhood residents it trained. As a consequence, there were virtually no selection criteria for volunteers (*Dispute Resolution Forum* 1988:11).

The program has thus faced the continuing challenge of maintaining a sense of engagement on the part of the large pool of volunteers, especially since their numbers have typically approximated the program's annual caseload of roughly 365 cases. Rather than developing a small cadre of highly skilled mediators as do many other programs (Harrington and Merry 1989), SFCB engaged as many volunteers as possible in the dispute-resolution process from intake to the mediation panels that hear cases. The program estimated that 80 percent of its work in outreach, case development, and hearing panels was done by these volunteers, half of whom might be active in providing service at any one time. In addition, volunteers served on area committees that helped to organize and deliver these services, reflecting SFCB's commitment to "democratic organization building" as well as to dispute resolution. Estimates of time spent on service delivery as compared to other SFCB activities suggest that roughly 25 percent of volunteer time goes to work on disputes and 75 percent to organizational work and training. Clearly, the time and energy of paid staff were consumed in large part by the demands of recruiting, coordinating, and training the volunteers.

Areas Served by San Francisco Community Boards

The early development of San Francisco Community Boards was closely linked to "neighborhoods"—geographical areas whose residents had some sense of shared identity. These were the areas, after all, whose capacity to handle conflict was supposed to be developed through the work of SFCB. This focus on area or neighborhood contrasted sharply with the practice of the Neighborhood Justice Centers piloted by the United States Department of Justice about the same time (Cook, Roehl, and Sheppard 1980). In each of these centers, a single program served whole cities with ties to courts rather than to local areas and institutions.

San Francisco Community Boards was launched in 1976 with the opening of a store-front field office in Visitacion Valley, and, shortly thereafter, a second office in Bernal Heights, both located in the southeastern part of San Francisco. In subsequent years the program expanded geographically both by enlarging the service areas of established field offices and by adding new offices. By 1982 it had opened four new field offices in the areas known as Mission, Noe Valley, Western Addition, and Haight-Ashbury/Fillmore. By 1984 each field office was staffed by an area coordinator and a full-time volunteer organizer and operated at an average annual cost of roughly $47,000. In addition, clerical, support, and central administrative staff worked in a central office. By its own estimates SFCB served an area of roughly one-third the city of San Francisco with a total population of 210,000. Largely as a cost-saving measure, the program reduced its field offices first to three and then to one in 1984–85 but maintained service to the same areas.

The areas of San Francisco served by SFCB ranged considerably in size and social characteristics. The data presented in table 1 give a sense of this variation, although the five neighborhood areas described there only roughly approximate the service areas of SFCB offices.[1] Nonetheless, the statistical data provide a useful orientation to the varied social and economic contexts in which the work of SFCB was carried out.

Two of these areas were predominately black, one predominately Hispanic, one predominately white, and one of mixed ethnicity with Asians constituting 22 percent, Hispanics 27 percent, blacks 11 percent, and whites 40 percent of the populaton. The educational and socioeconomic characteristics of the areas also varied enormously, with 42 percent of one area's residents having college educations compared to 15 percent in another. Average household incomes varied from approximately $13,000 to $21,000. In two areas just over half of the residents were single, while in two others only 30 percent were. Thus, the areas where SFCB opened its offices provided substantial diversity in the populations served.

This demographic profile can be fleshed out with more detailed descriptions of two of the neighborhoods drawn from a Reactions to Crime study (Lewis and Salem 1986) completed just prior to the birth of SFCB.[2]

Visitacion Valley was a small (population 9,000) working-class area of single-family homes—largely owner occupied—set out on quiet, well-kept streets. A modest commercial area consisted largely of shops. A lock company was the only large employer in the area, though few Valley residents worked there. Two large and poorly cared-for multiple-family housing developments stood in sharp contrast to the rest of the Valley: a public housing project and a low-income high rise. Crime problems seemed to emanate from these

---

1. These data were collected by the San Francisco United Way and summarized in Rothschild 1986:62–66.

2. The descriptions of Visitacion Valley and Mission that follow are paraphrased from the work of Dan Lewis and Greta Salem with their permission (Lewis and Salem 1986:29–41).

TABLE 1. Selected Socioeconomic Characteristics of San Francisco Community Boards Neighborhood Areas and San Francisco, 1980

	Neighborhood Areas					City
	Bernal Heights/V.V.	Mission	Ingleside (V. V. Office)	Western Addition	Haight/Noe Valley	Total Pop.
Population Characteristics						
Total Population	105,592	40,312	17,717	35,743	74,977	677,704
% White	40	28	18	30	66	58
% Black	11	6	62	54	6	13
% Spanish	27	50	10	6	12	12
% Asian	22	13	10	6	9	21
% Under 18 yrs.	33	30	34	31	32	34
% Single (never married)	32	41	31	50	51	39
% Not completed high school	36	46	31	31	15	26
% With 4+ yrs. of college	18	15	16	23	42	28
% aged 16+ yrs. employed	59	56	60	54	70	60
% Blue collar civilians	48	54	47	38	26	33
% Exec/prof/tech	20	16	22	26	41	32
Household Characteristics						
Total Households	25,264	15,495	6,204	17,154	37,912	299,867
% Female head of household	21	30	25	48	21	21
Mean household income ($)	20,732	13,596	21,072	12,811	20,775	20,554
% Household income over $25,000	34	14	34	13	28	28
% Households with public assistance	12	21	14	21	7	11
% in overcrowded units	23	37	17	16	8	16
Mean value of housing unit ($)	86,441	87,795	73,815	143,198	141,895	117,940
% Moved in last 5 yrs.	42	60	41	63	63	52

units. An adjacent townhouse project for young professionals failed
to hold the intended clientele, and the "bars and safety devices on
these townhouses serve[d] as a visible symbol of the fact that virtually
all the residents have had at least one experience as a burglary victim"
(Lewis and Salem 1986:37). People complained too about the public
parks and playgrounds, which were all thought to be unsafe. A local
golf course was strewn with litter, and fairways had become drag
strips for young people in the area. Overall, the reported crime rate
in the Valley was substantially above the San Francisco average, and
fear of crime was very high.

Less ethnically heterogenous than many other areas in San Francisco, the Valley's population nonetheless was 27 percent black and
11 percent Hispanic. It was a changing area, but still could boast
that 69 percent of its residents had been there over five years and 25
percent over twenty years. This relative stability may be related to
the tradition of civic participation in the Valley. For example, an
Alinsky-style (see Harrington in this volume) All People's Coalition
(APC) complemented the work of two older neighborhood organizations, and all seemed to draw substantial participation. APC, for
example, successfully orchestrated a mass demonstration at the San
Francisco Board of Supervisors (city council) that achieved its goal
of including the area in a pilot crime-prevention project.

In contrast, the Mission was one of San Francisco's most ethnically diverse and transient areas, as well as the sunniest in its
microclimate. With a population of over 50,000, it was also five times
the size of Visitacion Valley. The majority Hispanic population
included people from over twenty-six countries, living alongside
whites, blacks, Filipinos, Samoans, and Native Americans. Over 80
percent of Mission's residents rented quarters in the multi-family
dwellings that constituted most of the area's housing stock, and well
over a third of the housing units were overcrowded. Not surprisingly,
over 60 percent of residents had moved within the last five years.
Two public housing projects with reputations for danger added to
the housing stock. By the late 1970s several large employers—including furniture companies and breweries—had departed the area, contributing further to the relatively high rates of unemployment (14.5
percent), poverty (34 percent with incomes under $10,000 in 1980),
and public welfare (21 percent).

Once known as "miracle mile," Mission's shopping area remained the second largest in San Francisco, despite the growth of suburban shopping centers and the inroads made by pawn shops, adult bookstores, pornographic theaters, and transient hotels. With these came some shabby streets with homeless people in doorways. Residents in some areas still thronged the streets, however, patronizing the small restaurants and grocery stores where they met and talked with friends and neighbors. Despite the friendly personal interchanges on the streets, community organizations did not prosper in the Mission. Many of the residents felt relatively powerless and ill served by local government.

Funding, Budget, and Costs

The funding of San Francisco Community Boards was secured almost exclusively from private foundations, which between 1976 and 1984 contributed to a total of $3.1 million. Over the years more than thirty foundations funded SFCB, including the Public Welfare, Ford, Charles Stewart Mott, Hewlett, and Aetna Life and Casualty Foundations. In its initial stage the program also received public subsidy through the utilization of CETA-funded workers. During the mid-1980s SFCB unsuccessfully sought public funding from the city of San Francisco and the state of California.

From expenditures of $127,000 in its first full year of operation (1977), the program's total budget grew to $407,000 in 1981 and $523,000 by 1984. In 1984, for example, the operation of the six field offices cost $283,000. This translates into a rough cost of $750 per case referred. In addition, the work of the central program administration, including training and public education, cost about $241,000. Compared to community programs relying on court referrals, these very rough "per case" costs appear high. For example, the Dorchester Community Mediation Program cost roughly $330 per referral (Felstiner and Williams 1980:35), and the Dade County Citizen Dispute Settlement Program only $36 per "matter handled" (Moriarity, Norris, and Salas 1977:53).

Such comparisons are potentially quite misleading, however. SFCB invested considerable time in each case. For example, time logs kept by volunteers for twenty-two cases showed a range of seven to thirty-three hours spent per case that went to hearing, an average of roughly twenty-one hours. For cases not going to hearing the time devoted ranged from fifteen minutes to almost eleven hours, and averaged just over three hours per nonhearing case. Comparable data are not available from other programs, but descriptions of their work suggest far less time devoted to each case.

Moreover, these data on costs illustrate vividly the multiple goals of SFCB and the consequences of its refusal to rely on court referrals. Programs relying on court referrals hide some of their overhead in uncounted justice-system costs. Most important, the SFCB commitment to and heavy investment in continuing volunteer development substantially affected its costs of operation.

In 1981 SFCB developed the Center for Policy and Training, a separate organizational unit that operated alongside Community Boards of San Francisco, the service delivery arm of the program. The center was responsible for disseminating the dispute-resolution program model outside of San Francisco, largely through provision of training institutes and technical assistance for other programs. The center also began a "school initiatives" project that introduced conflict resolution into selected elementary, junior, and senior high schools within San Francisco. Originally conceived to be a "profit center" that would subsidize the rest of the program, the center failed to fulfill that expectation, despite the fact it became nationally prominent for its dispute-resolution training and generated 20–25 percent of SFCB's income.

Conclusion

The San Francisco Community Boards vision is not simply or mainly of a service that processes individual cases. Instead, it focuses on developing neighborhoods and the capacity of their residents to be engaged with each other in resolving conflicts before they reach the formal justice system. Because SFCB works both on conflict resolution and on skill building among its volunteers, a full description of the program requires attention to both. In the rest of this chapter, therefore, we first examine in some detail the kinds of cases coming to SFCB and the way they were handled by the program. Second, we look at the experience of volunteers and the impact of the program on them. Finally, we try to understand the cumulative effect of this program on the neighborhoods where it has been in operation for the longest time.

San Francisco Community Boards Cases
and Disputants

Where San Francisco Community Boards Cases
Come From

Because SFCB was committed to establishing "an alternative justice system," it generally resisted referrals from courts and police, relying instead on cases brought to it voluntarily by individuals or groups. Unlike any other programs that began with that hope but soon abandoned it to build caseloads from police and court referrals, SFCB persisted, drawing almost 90 percent of its caseload from people who had heard of the program from media, leaflets, friends, personal experience, or social agencies (see table 2). This pattern contrasts sharply with that reported for the Dorchester mediation program, where 89 percent of the cases came through referrals from the courts and another 4 percent from the police (Felstiner and Williams 1980:15).

According to data from intake sheets collected by SFCB from complainants, 81 percent of its cases are brought by people who heard about the program and decided on their own to initiate contact. In 35 percent of the cases, the initiators reported that they had seen or heard some form of the publicity that SFCB distributed—the direct payoff for SFCB's extensive public relations efforts in the neighborhoods: flyers, posters, public presentations, and knocking on doors. Another 8 percent learned about SFCB through the fairly extensive coverage SFCB attracted in the metropolitan and neighborhood newspapers and on local radio and television shows. Thus, SFCB achieved its goal of drawing most of its cases from walk-ins who decided to try the program without having pressures to do so placed upon them by criminal-justice agencies.

Direct acquaintance with SFCB through work as volunteer or staff or previous experience as a disputant also generated a substantial proportion of "walk/call-ins" (15 percent) and of referrals from individuals familiar with SFCB (8 percent). It is particularly striking that repeat disputants are present in 10 percent of all cases. These latter cases can be viewed both as a sign of satisfaction with previous SFCB experience and an acceptance by a few residents of mediation as a primary dispute-resolution mode.

Only 11 percent of SFCB's cases came from the police or prosecutor or a juvenile justice agency. None were from the courts. SFCB apparently took some cases at the suggestion of justice officials but kept its commitment not to hear complaints where litigation or criminal charges were pending.

Because they were exceptional, it is useful to take a closer look at the cases referred to SFCB from the formal justice system. Clearly, there was an element of legal pressure or threat in these cases that was not evident in others. As a consequence, such cases appeared particularly likely to go to a mediation hearing, a pattern similar to that found in studies of the Kansas City Neighborhood Justice Center (Harrington 1985) and the Community Mediation in Dorchester, Massachusetts (Felstiner and Williams 1980:18). Illustrations of cases referred by the justice system come from the brief case summaries of all cases coming to SFCB from 1977 through 1982. These were compiled by the evaluation team from program files. For example:

TABLE 2. Self-Reported Sources of San Francisco Community Boards Cases 1977-82

Percentage of Cases (N=1,450)			
Justice System Referrals			11%
Police	6%		
District Attorney's Office	2%		
Youth Guidance Council	3%		
Non-Criminal Justice Referral/Information			
Source			81%
SFCB materials/presentation		35%	
Media	8%		
Direct program contact		15%	
Former disputant	10%		
SFCB volunteer	4%		
SFCB staff member	1%		
Interpersonal referral		11%	
by a former disputant		1%	
by a SFCB volunteer		5%	
by a staff member		2%	
by others		3%	
Referral by other organizations and			
agencies		12%	
Community organizations		1%	
Social Service		2%	
School		1%	
Legal services		4%	
Lawyer		1%	
Mayor's office/City Council		3%	
Source unknown			9%

Note: Totals sum to 101% due to rounding error.

791216 The police refer a merchant who wants to recover the cost of stolen beer from a youth. At the hearing the youth agrees to pay for the stolen goods and to avoid trouble in the future. The merchant agrees to settle the account and to restrain himself in the event of future problems.

771020 There is a referral from the police involving a feud between two girls which resulted in physical violence. The girls meet with a school counselor and other school officials but no formal resolution is reached. At the Board hearing the two parties agree to stop fighting and promise to meet again should there be any future problems.

771026 The Youth Guidance Council refers two boys accused of breaking into a nursery school, stealing items and causing some damage. At the hearing the boys agree to work, monetary restitution and apologies to the school officials.

781072 School counselors report chronic truancy to a student and their concern that the parents do not support the child in school attendance. The mother feels it is the school's responsibility to place the child in special classes. At the hearing the school representatives agree to place the child in a special class. The student agrees to regular attendance as well as summer camp attendance. The mother agrees to regular contact with school officials and a referral to family counseling. All parties agree to a follow-up meeting which never occurs.

Despite their official source, these exceptional referrals appear subtly different from those that predominate in programs relying heavily on court referrals. The involvement of third parties such as school officials, the early referral before criminal charges were pending, and the emphasis on restitution help distinguish these cases in the aggregate from those consisting largely of criminal assault charges against individuals.

At the same time that it was successful in drawing a high proportion of its cases from walk-ins, SFCB was not so successful in continuing to expand the number of cases coming to it as its reputation and service areas grew. Table 3 indicates that by 1979 SFCB had reached its peak intake of cases. Subsequent expansion to new areas of San Francisco and the cumulative experience and reputation of SFCB produced no net growth in caseload. During its first six years of operation, the program managed to take in for initial processing an average of roughly 365 cases per year. This yielded roughly 100 mediation hearings per year for the entire program, although, as noted below, SFCB frequently intervened extensively in cases that did not go to hearing.

The caseload growth over six years does not fully test Shonholtz's claim that in ten to fifteen years the American approaches to conflict could be altered by communitywide efforts at conflict resolution. SFCB was well established in some but not in other neighborhoods during this period, and there is little evidence that schools and other local institutions had helped to make the effort "communitywide." Nonetheless, the fact that the caseload reached a plateau so quickly and that subsequent expansion did not lead to steady increases raises challenging questions. Are there fewer conflicts of the sort that do make their way to SFCB than we might think? Are the barriers to revealing conflict to public third parties (see Merry 1990; Merry and Silbey 1984) even more difficult to alter than hoped? These unanswered questions go to the heart of the long-term community dispute-resolution enterprise as envisioned by SFCB.

In the face of these unanswered questions, there are some hints that organizational and strategic choices may have played at least a partial role in limiting the growth of the caseload. Obviously, the decision to minimize criminal-justice referrals was paramount. Another less obvious choice might be inferred from the fact that only 1 percent of case referrals came from organizations such as churches or other voluntary associations. This fact may reflect the lack of commitment

TABLE 3. Total Cases Referred to San Francisco Community Boards by Area, 1977–82

	Visitacion Valley	Bernal Heights	Mission	Noe Valley	Western Addition	Haight	Total
1977	31						31
1978	100						100
1979	117	270					387
1980	135	209					344
1981	101	95	117	37			350
1982	153	62	85	51	10	13	374

in these organizations to conflict resolution, but if that is the case, it is a lack of commitment that SFCB did little to change. The decision not to do so follows from the program's ideology, which envisioned urban life in terms of the estranged and individuated "mass public" rather than in terms of preexisting formal and informal social networks. Urban life was disorganized rather than organized. As a result, heavy emphasis was placed on using the media and leafleting to inform individual residents about the program. Substantial energy was also devoted to speaking at Sunday masses or inserting notices in church bulletins, and thus using other preexisting audiences or networks to get out the message. But the appeal was still to individuals *through* organizations rather than to the organizations themselves. It appears that little was done to establish alliances with church organizations, neighborhood-improvement associations, fraternal groups, and others in order to mobilize their organizational resources (as opposed to their individual members) on behalf of conflict resolution.

From what we know about the characteristics of volunteers, the recruitment strategy was successful because it drew in a large number of people seeking attachment in the face of urban isolation (see discussion of volunteers below). However, this same strategy may have been less appropriate for building caseloads. Research about the adoption of innovations (see, for example, Coleman, Katz, and Menzel 1966) makes clear that preexisting social networks structure a large proportion of the diffusion of new ideas or products. The word of mouth advertising that one would expect to lead to steady growth in cases over the years works best when it occurs through the community organizations already in place, reinforced by the persuasion and pressures from group leaders.

The Nature of San Francisco Community Boards Cases

The conflicts that came to SFCB concerned a wide range of issues generated in the course of daily life. In the examination of the program's case file, the 1,481 cases referred to SFCB between 1977 and 1982 were characterized in terms of a primary issue. In over two-thirds of the cases a secondary issue was identified as well.[3] The

---

3. Since the number of issue characterizations is over 2,500 and there are only 1,481 cases, the percentage of cases with a particular issue adds to more than 100 percent.

existence of multiple issues in conflicts suggests that one should talk, for example, not about "assault cases," but about "cases with assault issues." Table 4 lists the frequency of dispute issues. These focus predominantly on the petty aggravations of neighborly life—noise, litter, pets, parking, property care, insults, and varied forms of community disorder.

This distribution of complaints differs from that found in many other community-mediation programs that rely heavily on court and police referrals and from the entire nature of complaints brought to the police (see DuBow and Currie in this volume). Rather than representing episodes of violence between people in continuing relationships, SFCB cases drew far more heavily on neighborhood problems. For example, in the Dorchester Urban Court mediation program, 47 percent of the cases were assault cases (Felstiner and Williams 1980:21) compared to 11 percent in SFCB. Many of the assault cases in Dorchester were domestics, involving spouses, family members, or lovers, but such incidents made up only 2.5 percent of SFCB cases. Many have questioned the value or appropriateness of mediation in assault cases, which frequently involved psychological or alcohol problems (Felstiner and Williams 1980:46). In contrast, neighborhood conflicts often appear better suited to resolution through mediation and clearly are of great importance to the people who bring them. Ironically, although one of Shonholtz's major goals in advocating a "primary justice system alternative" to the formal criminal courts was to reduce violence within the community, SFCB's caseload contained only a minority of conflicts that appeared likely to lead to serious violence if unresolved. Eleven percent of the cases involved an assault or violence and another 18 percent included issues of verbal harassment or personal insults.

Who Uses San Francisco Community Boards:
The Disputants

The common image of community mediation is of two individual disputants who meet with a mediator to try to resolve their conflicts. This image is shaped in part by the fact that courts and police often define conflict in this fashion, and many community-mediation programs draw cases already defined in part by legal officials. However, while a single disputant was involved in most SFCB conflicts, many

TABLE 4. Frequency of Dispute Issues (N = 1,481)

Rank Order	Issues	No. of Cases	% of Cases
1	Noise	268	17.9
2	Inappropriate Behavior	261	17.5
3	Insults/Harassment	234	15.7
4	Communication Breakdown	198	13.2
5	Violence/Assaults	166	11.1
6	Pet Behavior	153	10.2
7	Vandalism	125	8.4
8	Parking/Access	116	7.8
9	Property Care	100	6.7
10	Litter	96	6.4
11	Child Behavior/Rearing	93	6.2
12	Health Hazards	64	4.3
13	Eviction	57	3.7
14	Theft of Personal Property	56	3.5
15	Poor Goods	53	3.5
16	Poor Service-Public Agency	45	3.0
17	Nonpayment of Bills	44	2.9
18	Territoriality	41	2.7
19	Domestic	38	2.5
20	Tenants Complaint	33	2.2
21	Long-standing Feud	31	2.1
22	Breakdown of Personal Relationship	25	1.7
23	Breaking and Entering	21	1.4
24	Character Defamation	20	1.3
25	Nonpayment of Rent	17	1.1
26	Complex Neighborhood Problem	17	1.1
27	Fire Hazard	16	1.1
28	False Accusations	16	1.1
29	Drug Possession or Use	16	1.1
30	Illegal or Unlicensed Business	16	1.1
31	Mental Health Problems	13	0.9
32	Tenant Misbehavior	13	0.9
33	Loitering	13	0.9
34	Nonreturn of Security Deposit	12	0.8
35	Group Communication Breakdown	10	0.7
36	Truancy	10	0.7
37	Group—Multiple Problems	9	0.6
38	Shoplifting	8	0.6
39	Nonpayment of Loan	6	0.4
40	Nonpayment of Salary	3	0.2
41	Abandoned Building	2	0.1
42	Educational Practices in School	1	0.1

cases have more than one individual involved on one or both sides (see table 5). Two-thirds of all cases involved a single initiating individual; 14 percent involved a family or a couple, and in 5 percent of the cases the initiating party was a group or organization. Respondents were almost as likely to be several individuals—a couple, family, or organization—as they were to be a single individual. As a consequence, more than half of all disputes had more than one individual on at least one side of the dispute, and almost one-quarter of all disputes had more than one individual on both sides of the dispute. This pattern contrasts sharply with the characteristics of disputants in the Dorchester program, which relied almost exclusively on court referrals. There only 13 percent of the cases involved more than two disputants (Felstiner and Williams 1980:20). San Francisco Community Boards thus appears to have been unusual in the extent to which it has drawn in multiperson disputes. Further, it acknowledges in its hearings the multiperson character of many neighborhood disputes. In particularly complex, large-group cases, the program composed mediation panels of people trained in the additional complexities and problems of intervening in multiparty conflict.

A clearer sense of the character of these multiparty cases comes from the brief case summaries:

> 792233 Neighbors complain about the behavior of the students of Balboa High School in their area. SFCB arranges large group hearings (three of them with 59, 28, and 44 people attending respectively). These include students, the school's principal and staff members, and neighbors. The neighbors, who have previously called the police, are very pleased with how the issues are being resolved.

TABLE 5. Organizational Characteristics of First and Second Parties in San Francisco Community Boards Cases ($N=1,576$)

	1st Parties	2d Parties
An individual	67%	47%
More than one unrelated individual	10	9
Couples/families	15	22
Groups/organizations	5	11
Unknown	3	11
	100%	100%

792229 Two 14 year old girls have a fight and one accuses the other of getting a group of older friends to assault her. The families get involved. The issues are resolved to everyone's satisfaction in a hearing that is conducted in Spanish.

802005 and 792214 A case started with an incident of a gay being "trashed" by neighborhood youths. The merchant brought in other merchants who had been having problems with the youths, to act as complainants in the first hearing. A second hearing was held, with only the bar owner acting as complainant, to work out the issues involving only that business. At that hearing, however, the youths claimed harassment by police, resulting in a third hearing with police as the second party.

821069 A group of Latino students at a high school bring a case against a group of Filipino students, regarding fighting, badmouthing, harassment. Although the school administration was perceived by each side as showing favoritism to the other side, this was only one of many issues and the administration did not become involved in the series of three hearings.

One of the striking features of SFCB is the range of the disputants' socioeconomic backgrounds. Most community programs for which some data are available draw heavily on low-income populations with relatively low levels of formal education (see, for example, Merry 1990; Harrington 1985; Cook, Roehl, and Sheppard 1980). Those programs that rely heavily on court referrals reflect the socioeconomic mix of defendants in the lower criminal courts.

Because it attracted cases from different sources, however, SFCB worked with disputants who represented a much wider range within the community. Although data on social class and ethnicity of the parties are unavailable for the entire set of cases referred to SFCB, they exist for about two-thirds of the Intensive Care Study sample (Rothschild 1986:110–11). This study followed forty representative cases from their inception through completion (see Rothschild 1986 for a full description of the methodology). Fully 57 percent of the sixty-three parties for whom data are available had at least some college education and 30 percent had at least some graduate training. This distribution suggests a population of users somewhat similar to, but even more diverse than that reported by Jennifer Beer in the suburban Philadelphia program she studied (1986). Incomes of SFCB disputants, however, appeared to be somewhat lower than their educational attainment would suggest, but still above San Francisco's median. Fifty percent of the disputants had incomes over $20,000.

Even the minimal picture of disputants provided by these data distinguishes SFCB from most other community dispute-resolution programs. Issues of community order among neighbors (the issues that predominate in SFCB) appear to come more often from a middle- or working-class population, whereas cases of assault among family members or lovers (frequently referred to programs by the police) "are more often brought by the poor and the unemployed" (Merry 1990:186). Thus, it appears that SFCB provided a forum for a wide range of residents to air grievances and seek resolution to problems for which other forums may not have been available. It did not serve primarily to divert cases from the courts. The higher social status of the parties may reflect the typical characteristics of people who seek help with neighborhood problems.

The ethnicity of disputants also suggests a diverse clientele, one that represented the wide range of ethnic groups within San Francisco, but did not mirror precisely their distribution in the city. Rothschild reports that in the Intensive Case Study sample, 60 percent of the disputants were white, 20 percent Hispanic, 14 percent black, and 8 percent Asian (Rothschild 1986:108). Although it underrepresents Asians, this distribution comes quite near to that in San Francisco in 1980: 58 percent white; 13 percent Hispanic; 12 percent black; and 15 percent Asian.

With respect to gender, SFCB disputants reflected patterns found in many other dispute resolution programs: the complainants were disproportionally individual females (56 percent), whereas individual males constituted only 34 percent of the complainants (the other 10 percent involved multiple complainants). Just the reverse was true of respondents, 50 percent of whom were individual males in the intensive case study and 23 percent individual females. Women were less overrepresented in these cases than in other community-mediation programs, however (see Merry 1990). For example, the Dorchester mediation program drew 66 percent of its cases from individual female complainants (Felstiner and Williams 1980:20). Presumably, these other programs drew more heavily on court referrals and received in return a high quota of domestic-violence cases involving spouses, lovers, or former lovers.

Conclusion

In sum, the characteristics of both cases and disputants distinguish SFCB from most other neighborhood dispute-resolution programs. As Sally Merry (1990) has pointed out, class and community structure shape the nature of the conflicts that surface for processing by courts or other institutions. Drawing cases as it did from a variety of relatively stable, working- and middle-class neighborhoods of San Francisco, SFCB's caseload reflected a concern with community stability and order, especially in the face of change. Other programs whose cases often come from the courts tend to draw heavily from lower-class populations from less stable areas. With fewer resources and less control over lives beyond their own apartments or houses, the issues of order relate to interpersonal ties rather than to the quality of neighborliness. San Francisco Community Boards has thus tapped a dimension of conflict in the United States that has rarely been recognized in community dispute resolution.

The Dispute Resolution Process of San Francisco Community Boards

An Overview

San Francisco Community Boards described its dispute-resolution process as follows:

1. Volunteer outreach workers educate the neighborhood about the program and how to use it.
2. When a case is called into a neighborhood office, a volunteer case developer visits the first party, then the second, encouraging each to conciliate the dispute.
3. If the parties agree, a panel (conciliation) hearing is scheduled at a time and place convenient to all. Sometimes referrals are made instead or the problem is resolved prior to the hearing.
4. At the hearing a panel of trained community residents helps the parties reach their own, voluntary agreement.
5. The specifics of the agreement are written down, and the parties and panel chairperson sign it.
6. Follow up is provided, often by volunteer follow up workers. (*Prospectus* 1983:2)

Complaints and Case Development

Typically a case was initiated when one of the parties to the conflict contacted SFCB by calling an area office. A staff person did a brief intake by phone, soliciting and giving minimal information. In about 7 percent of the complaints, this led to a decision that the case was inappropriate for SFCB, often concluding with a referral to another agency:

> 771013 A townhouse tenant complains of a junk car parked in the parking lot and claims the lights in the parking lot are out. The complainant is referred to the townhouse owner who has the lights repaired. The complainant is referred to an appropriate agency for action on removing the junk car.

> 813017 A group of employees claim they are being sued for defamation of character by a former employee. The case is not pursued because of pending legal action.

> 781057 A woman claims she has been subpoenaed for putting her daughter up for adoption. The case is referred to San Francisco Neighborhood Legal Assistance Foundation.

If the case appeared appropriate and the complainant willing, however, a staff person then typically assigned a volunteer to be the "case developer." This person would make a personal visit to the complaining party in the hope of clarifying the nature of the conflict and convincing the party to use the SFCB hearing process. The role played by the case developer is highly unusual in community mediation and is one more example of the labor-intensive nature of SFCB's conflict-resolution work.

In 14 percent of the cases at this stage, the complaining party withdrew the complaint because of the sense that SFCB was not an appropriate forum for resolution, because of fears about proceeding against the other party, or for other reasons:

> 821132 A resident claims a neighbor's sons have burglarized his two other neighbors' homes. As contact with the case developer proceeds, the complainant becomes reluctant and withdraws, feeling that the matter is too serious to be resolved with the SFCB process.

781076 A public housing tenant complains of insults and character defamation from another tenant. The complainant declines further action because of fear of retaliation.

If the first party was willing to attend a hearing, the case developer then visited the second party to obtain his/her cooperation in scheduling a hearing. Presumably, having a person knock at one's door and announce that they were "neighbors" working with SFCB to deal with neighborhood conflicts would have a compelling quality that could not be achieved by a letter or even a phone call. In this role the case developer also served an important but unintended go-between role in communicating disputes—often for the first time. In only 25 percent of the roughly fifteen hundred cases in SFCB files had the complainant made direct contact with the respondent in order to try to resolve the problem before coming to SFCB. In a substantial but unknown proportion of cases, the respondent simply did not know there was a problem before the arrival of the case developer. In contrast, programs relying on court referrals often do much of their intake in the courts, where both parties may be present. If the complainant is not there, the respondent is at least on notice that there is a problem.

In some cases the contact by the case developer with the second party proved sufficient to yield what the parties viewed as a resolution (4 percent) or what would have been one if followed through on (5 percent).

771022 A consumer complains that the TV set he recently bought does not work and that the seller refuses to replace or repair the set. After contact with the case developer, the seller agrees to resolve the issue without a hearing.

792150 Ten neighbors complain about a dog barking at night. A SFCB case developer talks to the owner who agrees to take the dog in at night.

781043 A tenant claims that the landlord is illegally holding his possessions. The landlord claims the tenant's name is not on the lease and therefore his occupancy is illegal. With the involvement of the case-developer and the legal aid agency, the tenant is allowed to remain in the apartment until new housing is found by the Housing Authority.

791195 A resident complains that a neighbor's high weeds are a fire hazard and haven for rats. The second party declines a hearing but promises to immediately resolve the issue by cleaning up the yard.

In fact, however, case developers were not supposed to resolve conflicts themselves. Their role was to encourage all parties to come to a mediation panel for a hearing.

There were other ways that the case could have been concluded at the case-development stage. A substantial proportion of the cases had already been resolved by the parties themselves (9 percent) or the problem had ended, as when for example the complainant moved away (5 percent).

780150 A woman complains that she and her son are being threatened by neighbors because her son has hit their son. Before a hearing takes place, the complainant reports that the situation has improved and she withdraws.

813113 An elderly resident complains of noise from a neighbor's pet. The complainant then gets her landlord to write a letter to the second party. The case is dropped.

813036 A tenant complains about the noise from his combative neighbors. The second parties move away and the problem ends.

In another 6 percent of the cases, the respondent could not be located, and the case ended, perhaps with a referral:

781066 A consumer complains of false advertisement from a car dealer. The second party is unreachable. The complainant is referred to legal avenues.

801059 A tenant complains about noise from an upstairs neighbor. The second party cannot be reached.

Even when contact was established, the respondent could, and in 19 percent of the cases did, refuse to respond to the complaint or proceed with the case. Under these circumstances SFCB was powerless to proceed and in essence closed the cases:

> 791204 A tenant complains about regular semi-annual rent increases, and claims that the landlord is gouging him. The landlord denies the problem and refuses a hearing.

> 821124 A resident complains of a neighbor's tree which is ruining her driveway and entrance. The respondent refuses a hearing.

> 792231 A resident accuses his neighbor of littering, of abuse about parking conflicts, and of causing water damage. They have different lifestyles and do not communicate. The neighbor refuses a hearing.

By the conclusion of case development, thus, roughly 70 percent of the cases initially brought to SFCB had been concluded in one fashion or another.

Scheduling Hearings and the Problem of No-Shows

If both parties agreed, a mediation hearing was scheduled to be held at a location in the area such as the Community Boards field office, a church, a school, or a community center. Twenty-nine percent of cases initially brought to SFCB reached the point where a hearing was scheduled. Of course, not all of these hearings took place because of no-shows in 2 percent of the cases (7 percent of scheduled hearings).[4] For example:

> 812025 A public housing tenant complains that her upstairs neighbor is noisy and causes parking problems. The second party denies the noise problem and claims that the complainant harasses her. A hearing is scheduled, but the complainant cannot attend because of health problems.

---

4. These rates of no-shows in Community Boards fall within the range of those in court-connected programs such as the Neighborhood Justice Centers, where they ranged from 3 percent in Venice-Mar Vista to 15 percent in Atlanta (Cook, Roehl, and Sheppard 1980:34–39).

782050 A man claims his car was rear-ended, and the second party, who does not want to report the accident to his insurance company, will not pay him to get his car repaired. The complainant does not show up to the first scheduled hearing, and neither party shows at the second.

813108 A group of neighbors feel that a man in the neighborhood is a threat. The second party claims he is being harassed. At the scheduled hearing the second party does not show but the complainants agree to have a spokesperson talk directly with the second party about their concerns and have men present when the women talk to the second party about his behavior toward them. They also agree to refer the second party to a veteran's counselor in the area.

In this latter case, the mediation process produced a creative outcome despite the no-show, but that was rarely the case.

The Hearing Process

The hearing is the focus of most SFCB training and the activity most celebrated by the program in its internal and external publicity. The mediation process at the hearing was distinctive in several respects (see also Rothschild 1987:75–79). First, rather than single or paired mediators, SFCB used three to five volunteers who acted as panelists to mediate the conflict. Second, SFCB was committed to and, in observed cases, generally successful in making the panels reflective of the social characteristics of disputants. The panels in size and composition were also an effort to represent "the community" and its concerns in the conflict-resolution process. Third, rather than being closed and elaborately confidential sessions as in most community-mediation programs, the hearings were semipublic: that is, they were generally open to the public but not advertised, so that few or no observers were typically present.

Fourth, private caucuses between panelists and parties were prohibited; all of the mediation was done face-to-face. Fifth, according to Terry Amsler, the current executive director of San Francisco Community Boards, "[A] substantial phase of dispute resolution process emphasizes communication and appropriate relationship building between the parties as opposed to being primarily agreement oriented"

(*Dispute Resolution Forum* 1988:12). This means that in some sessions the mediators were preoccupied with having the parties express their feelings while the parties themselves were concerned with reaching a solution (see the coffeehouse case described in detail below). The SFCB analysis of conflict placed heavy emphasis on problems of communication and saw the major goal of a panel hearing as establishing that communication, especially about the feelings of participants (see Rothschild in this volume). For mediators, success was not supposed to be measured by agreements but rather by the degree to which communication was established and feelings were expressed. Nonetheless, mediators tended to be acutely disappointed in the rare cases (9 percent) where no agreement was reached in mediation.

Several of the unique features of SFCB mediation are suggested by a description of the four-step process that guided training and practice in the program.

These four phases were sandwiched between an opening in which, according to program materials, the panel "welcomes people formally and explains the nature of the hearing and the ground rules," and a closing in which the "panel finalizes the agreement between the people and the community." The four-phase process was so central to training and to practice that many panelists kept a summary of the phases in front of them during a hearing. In other programs that make heavy use of a few experienced mediators working alone, such reliance on "the process" might appear slavish. In SFCB, however, reliance on the four-phase model served important support and coordination functions in a program where panelists were often inexperienced and had rarely worked together as copanelists.

By having each party talk in turn about their perceptions and feelings, the first phase was supposed "to help the parties define the problem and express how they feel about it," according to program materials. The panelists then asked questions for clarification and summarized the main concerns of each party before proceeding to phase two. In phase one each party interacted with the panelists.

The goal of the second phase was to help the parties understand "how the other experiences the problem." Panelists were directed in this phase to "select one issue or concern and encourage the people to talk about it." During this process the panelists encouraged the parties and noted points of understanding expressed by them. In this phase the parties were supposed to be interacting with each other and expressing their feelings about one another and the problem at hand. That fact was symbolized by the request that they turn their chairs toward one another.

In phase three, the panelists were directed to help "the parties understand that to solve the problem, each must be willing to acknowledge what new understanding they have about the dispute." Direct questions about the new understandings and about how the parties would handle the situation if it arose again were supposed to facilitate the growth of mutual understanding. If both parties agreed at this point that they were willing to move forward to develop a solution, phase four began.

The panelists tried in phase four to help the parties reach agreement by asking each in turn what they thought would be a fair solution, and by using questioning and listening techniques to help the parties find a specific agreement. When parties reached an agreement (in about 91 percent of cases going to hearing), it was then summarized, written up, and signed. Agreements contained both concrete actions and behavioral changes as clauses.

The Hearings in Practice

Hearings generally lasted about three hours. Panelists were briefed before the hearing about the case by the case developer and were debriefed afterwards by a trainer. In the debriefing the trainer used the time to provide supportive—but almost never critical—feedback to panelists.

Examples of the cases going to hearing include the following:

791215 There is an ongoing feud between elderly neighbors in which the first party claims he has been sprayed with water in an altercation. The second party claims provocation by the complainant. At the hearing both parties air their feelings and then shake hands and apologize. They both agree to be more civil in the future and to avoid calling the police.

791200 An ongoing feud between families erupts into a large fight. At the hearing both parties agree to have one of the landlords erect a fence between the two properties. Both parties agree to communicate with each other about problems, and to maintain respect in their communications. Both parties agree to otherwise avoid contact with each other and to contact the District Attorney in the event of future problems.

821051 An elderly resident complains that he cannot use his garden because a neighbor's dirt clogs his drain. The neighbor agrees to complete a steel retaining wall to stop the problem. The complainant also agrees to take steps to help avoid a drainage problem. Both parties agree to contact each other directly in the future.

Extended Examples of Hearings

Somewhat more detailed descriptions of hearings come from the observations done as part of the Intensive Case Studies and help illustrate more clearly the mediation process. Take, for example, a dispute between a coffeehouse owner and an employee, both women, over twelve hundred dollars in cash and six hundred dollars in checks that had disappeared through carelessness (see Rothschild 1986 for a more detailed account). In this case the panel concentrated heavily on the four-step process, particularly the feelings of the parties, even though the disputants appeared to the observer to be far more concerned about issues of money and responsibility. In fact, each of the women at an advanced point in the hearing began to respond with some sarcasm to the repeated probes asking "How do you feel about that?" or "Will you tell her how you felt when you heard her say that?" One disputant asked in frustration, "Are we going to keep telling each other how we feel?" The panel persisted, however, in moving through the stages and resisted "premature" efforts at resolution.

The situation was in fact an emotional one. During the hearing, the employee broke down in tears and continued to testify in that state for at least fifteen minutes. But her emotion seemed to relate to her acknowledgment of her own carelessness in the loss of the money and her fear of possible demands of repayment, demands that she could not afford to fulfill. Subsequently, when the disputants were moving toward a resolution, the mediators ignored or missed suggestions by the owner regarding restitution through charitable service. Finally, this idea was recognized and became the basis for an agreement that was viewed by both parties as reasonably satisfactory.

In another case the salience of the process to the mediators was emphasized by their creative and successful divergence from it (see Rothschild in this volume for a more detailed description). In this case the disputants included Salvadorans and other Hispanics, and the hearing was conducted in Spanish. The central complaint by a single, older woman was directed at the noise made by a neighboring family who happened to be relatives by marriage. In particular, she complained about the banging of a closet door at all hours of day and night. However, before the hearing was over, there were also accusations and counteraccusations of threats, cockroaches, refusals to communicate, and disrespect. A lurking issue was the fact that the walls were thin, but no one would complain to the landlord because the rents were cheap, and they were fearful of eviction.

The panelists were unusually active and spontaneous during the tense and stormy hearing. The older woman knew that her neighbors thought that she was crazy. She was fearful of answering her door when a neighbor came to talk with her about their conflicts because she was alone, and she was not tall enough to see the face of the person through the peephole. As a consequence, she could not attain what she seemed to want—human contact and the respect of her neighbors. During the hearing the mediators tried to solve the practical problems of establishing communication even by telephone, but the older woman rejected them all. Her only suggestion for solving the problem was "Don't slam the closets."

Faced with this difficult and somewhat chaotic situation, the panel worked to translate the language of conflict into a discourse that might lead to resolution. The panel concluded, for example, that neither party wanted to be insulted and that the older woman was particularly afraid of one neighbor's loud voice, a fact that he was encouraged to accept and promised to respond to. The panelists made numerous concrete suggestions about ways to complain without screaming and methods of controlling the noise problem. When their suggestions seemed to have failed to allay the fears of the older woman, the panelists came from behind their table and did an extemporaneous role play to demonstrate how simple and unthreatening communication could be. This last strategy worked, and a resolution was constructed that pleased everyone. It included a request for the landlord's permission to install rubber bumpers on the closet door, an agreement to speak with civility and respect in the future, and a method of communication in the face of future problems.

Ironically, the panel, which had operated so effectively, revealed considerable uncertainty in the debriefing about their departures from the SFCB process. They were concerned about the fact that they were repeatedly confused about which of the four phases the hearing was in. The trainer reassured them that the departures from the process in this instance were acceptable and complimented them on their good work. As it turned out, however, this hard-won resolution became irrelevant when soon afterward the landlord sold the building and evicted all the tenants.

As this case and some others suggest, SFCB, like other community dispute-resolution programs and courts, was necessarily limited in its capacity to deal with some disputes. In those instances where larger economic and social forces overrode the choices of disputants or where underlying social or personal problems produced the problems, mediated or adjudicated outcomes often have little tangible effect (Felstiner and Williams 1980). Thus, in other instances, too, the agreements reached could not be implemented:

821024 A woman has concerns about the conditions in an absentee landlord's adjacent property. She wants the fence and retaining wall to be rebuilt. She also has complaints about the neighboring tenants. The second party, however, feels that the complainant is harassing her and also has problems with the realtor who has allegedly mishandled affairs at her property. Since the complainant is Filipino, a Tagalog speaker acts as an interpreter at the two hearings that are held. Although the hearings clarify issues, both women are too poor to do anything material about the situation, and it remains basically the same.

813057 A SFCB staff member refers a case between a teenager and his parents. The teenager has behavioral problems and is disrespectful. The boy claims his father abuses him. At the hearing the son agrees to a schedule of work, to changing his behavior, and to attend weekly family meetings. The father agrees to stop abusing his son and to seek counseling help for alcoholism. The agreement soon breaks down on both sides.

Resolution and Compliance

Ninety-one percent of the cases that went to mediation ended with a resolution. These rates of "successful" mediation compare favorably with those achieved in programs drawing their cases through referrals from courts and other criminal-justice agencies with consequent pressures to settle. Felstiner and Williams, for example, report 89 percent of the cases in mediation in Dorchester reached agreement (1980:22). However, 9 percent of SFCB cases ended without a settlement, such as the following cases:

> 821013 This case is almost an identical re-hearing of a case that is a year old. Neighbors are concerned about an illegal car repair business, boozing, noise, parking problems and property damage. The man accused and his buddies agree to a hearing, claiming that they are being harassed. The man shows up at the hearing drunk, however. Not much is accomplished.

> 821086 A resident claims work done to repair damage to his house is an eyesore and wants the work redone properly. The workman claims the materials used were the only ones available. At the hearing the negotiations break down, and the respondent walks out.

The evidence is sketchy about the implementation of agreements reached in SFCB hearings. Follow-up evaluations were done inconsistently by SFCB staff. Data from the 150 cases where both parties had completed evaluations were examined in the evaluation research. In these cases both complainant and respondent had answered follow-up questions. Seventy-nine percent of complainants and 58 percent of respondents reported the agreement was still working in full or in part, while 14 percent of complainants and 30 percent of respondents said it was not working. Agreements reached without a hearing appeared slightly more durable than those reached through a hearing (90 percent vs. 81 percent working at least in part). In over 90 percent of the cases one or both of the parties reported improvement in their problems since contacting SFCB. Over 90 percent of the disputants reported satisfaction with the SFCB experience overall.

San Francisco Community Boards' Impact on Volunteers

The Study of Volunteers

While some conflict-resolution programs may view the recruitment and training of volunteers primarily as a means to provide capable but inexpensive mediators, SFCB saw the development of volunteers as an important end in itself. Volunteers were also neighbors and community members. To train them in conflict resolution was not simply to staff a program but to upgrade the capacity of neighborhoods to deal with conflict peacefully.

As a result, the Hewlett-funded research focused in part on these volunteers and the program's impact on them. To obtain longitudinal data on the volunteers' experience questionnaires were administered to several groups of prospective volunteers at orientation sessions leading up to SFCB training in the spring of 1983. These people were then reinterviewed one year later. By administering questionnaires at orientation sessions, data were obtained on individuals before they had a significant amount of contact with the program. Among the eighty-two persons who filled out the questionnaires in March of 1983, fifty-seven went through the training and became volunteers while twenty-five did not. In the spring of 1984, eleven of the twenty-five nontrainees (44 percent) and forty-two of the fifty-seven trainees (74 percent) were questioned again. Additional data were gathered through interviews and questionnaires of random samples of volunteers who had been with the program for one to two years (twenty-two recent actives); over two years (eighteen veteran actives); and volunteers who had ceased work with SFCB (nine former actives). These data provide the basis for a portrait of Community Boards volunteers.[5]

Characteristics of Volunteers

San Francisco Community Boards recruited widely and almost continuously in order to create and maintain as large and diverse a pool

---

5. This analysis also draws insights about the work of volunteers from observations of a wide variety of Community Boards meetings in which volunteers participated.

of volunteers as possible. Recruitment through the media, pamphlets and brochures, and word of mouth produced a volunteer population that represented reasonably well the diversity, if not the distribution, of San Francisco's population.

A little over two-thirds of the surveyed volunteers who completed training were white, 18 percent black, and the remainder Hispanic (8 percent) and Asian (4 percent). This distribution overrepresents whites and blacks compared to the San Francisco population, which in 1980 was 58 percent white and 13 percent black. It underrepresents substantially the Asian and Hispanic populations, which together accounted for 29 percent of San Francisco's population. Nonetheless, SFCB was generally able when called upon to put together mediation panels that reflected the ethnic and language mix of disputants.

In addition, the volunteer population included a similar percentage of renters and a larger percentage of low-income people as compared to San Francisco as a whole. Volunteers were substantially more likely (90 percent) to have had some college than the general San Francisco population (49 percent). Although these volunteers were "overeducated," they had less formal education than the volunteers in some other community dispute-resolution programs. For example, Jennifer Beer (1986) reports that of the thirty-seven volunteers in the Friends Suburban Project near Philadelphia thirty had graduate degrees and all had college degrees.

Like those in other mediation programs (see Pipkin and Rifkin 1984), the San Francisco volunteers were predominantly female—60 percent. The vast majority were also under forty-five years of age (83 percent). Finally, the volunteers were substantially more likely to be unmarried (82 percent) than the city population as a whole—48 percent.

In general, the characteristics that separated the volunteers from other city dwellers would appear to be less demographic and more political or social. Comparing a small (200) citywide sample of interviewees with the volunteers makes clear that the volunteers were generally more gregarious, engaged in their neighborhoods, and concerned about the future of those areas. This engagement and sense of civic responsibility is indicated by the following: 61 percent of the volunteers had visited neighbors in the past two weeks compared to 43 percent in the citywide sample; 59 percent of the volunteers compared to 30 percent of the citywide sample had talked recently with others about neighborhood problems. Volunteers were almost twice as likely as the citywide sample to identify particular problems as existent in their own areas—problems ranging from drug use to graffiti, to family disputes, to litter, to abandoned buildings. At the same time, the volunteers' concern about the neighborhood reflected a decided optimism; 60 percent of the volunteers felt their neighborhood had improved in the last few years compared to only 18 percent in the citywide sample.

When asked about their goals in joining SFCB, the volunteers' major emphasis was on personal development through learning mediation and communication skills. Secondary goals related to getting to know neighbors better and helping to improve the neighborhoods. The picture that emerges from these data is thus of volunteers who were relatively unattached, young, and well educated but not economically comfortable, and who were deeply concerned about the areas in which they lived. They were drawn into the SFCB program as a way to express their own sense of responsibility for the fate of their neighborhoods and also to develop their own skills and to meet new people.

These characteristics of volunteers contrast sharply with those reported in many other studies of voluntary associations and to some degree with the experience of other community dispute-resolution programs. Social attachment and engagement in social networks typically characterize volunteers in other settings (Smith 1975). Many other dispute resolution programs (though not all, by any means— see *Dispute Resolution Forum* 1988) rely heavily on well-educated and economically comfortable individuals to sustain their efforts (see also Harrington and Merry 1989).

Training of Volunteers

Volunteer training was a prerequisite for joining SFCB, but the formal training program served as the only significant screening device. That is, any interested person who devoted twenty-six hours to training over two successive Saturdays and five weeknights in a two-week period could become a "community member." Although substantial, this training was somewhat shorter than the thirty to forty hours common in other community programs. The length and scheduling of the training were designed to be convenient and accessible to the diverse volunteers drawn to SFCB. The program generally offered two or three introductory training sessions per year with between fifty and a hundred volunteers participating. By 1984 the program reported that it had trained over one thousand San Franciscans in conflict resolution (Rothschild 1986:71).

Many trainers were volunteers themselves, a few of whom had little or no experience in actual mediation sessions. They worked together with staff members in a training program guided by the training manual and built around the four-phase model of a hearing that is unique to SFCB. These training sessions emphasized the "right way" to do things and applied these lessons in role plays focused on two-party disputes. This focus on the four-phase model was viewed as essential in order to provide a shared framework of expectations that could coordinate the work of three to five panelists who typically had never worked together previously. Further, the structure was viewed as important to support the involvement of volunteers of diverse backgrounds.

The training sessions also stressed the primary importance of "getting the feelings out" as compared to dealing with the substance of the conflict. Trainees were taught to elicit feelings using such techniques as role reversal and requesting one party to tell the other about how they feel about the conflict. Success in these sessions was viewed primarily in terms of establishing communication about feelings and differences especially—and only secondarily in terms of resolution of the issues of the dispute (see also Rothschild; Milner and Shook in this volume).

In addition to training for the mediator role, SFCB early on devoted segments of the formal training to case development and outreach and later developed separate tracks for those wishing to learn these roles. Thus, outreach volunteers learned public speaking and how to answer questions in workshops. Those who wanted to become trainers took specialized workshops at a later date. So, for example, the first issue of *Prospectus*, the SFCB newsletter, announced a Trainers Institute to "provide understanding, skills and models necessary to train community members in the three essential roles of a neighborhood-based conflict resolution program: outreach worker, case developer and panelist (conciliator)" (1983:1). Other workshops were intended to build skills for hearings and for participation in SFCB governance, touching on topics such as meeting facilitation, homophobia, racism, and family disputes.

Unlike many other training programs, SFCB had no requirement of apprenticeship in real hearings or as case developers as part of the training process. Nonetheless, efforts were made to pair paid staff or experienced volunteers with neophytes in each of the varied roles in order to do on-the-job training. The fact that hearing panels were composed of three to five members cushioned the impact of inexperienced members on the conduct of these hearings. In addition, after each hearing a trainer (either a staff person or volunteer) would conduct a debriefing. On occasion, he or she would also present a pre-hearing review of the four-phase process. Given the expectation that training would continue on the job, it is not surprising that only 21 percent of trainees felt prepared to do case development and 53 percent to do hearings at the conclusion of their formal training. Thus, unlike most other community dispute-resolution programs, which make their training investment before starting practice, training was an integral and substantial part of the continuing SFCB experience.

Volunteer Roles and Participation

From the outset SFCB made clear to new recruits the expectation of substantial time commitment. Trainees indicated that they expected to spend a median of seven hours per month in their work for SFCB, precisely the average estimate of time devoted to the program by the volunteers one year into their work. This time was devoted primarily to attending meetings, participation in hearing panels, case development, social events with other "community members" and outreach to the neighborhood on behalf of SFCB.

Of these activities, the most highly valued was work on the hearing panels. The hearing process was central to training of new volunteers and in some sense to the public image of the organization. The program newsletter regularly carried stories of successful panel hearings, although they constituted a small proportion of the time commitment to the program for volunteers. Case development, which staff increasingly shared with volunteers during the early years of the program, came to make up a substantial portion of direct service work. Nonetheless, it received relatively little notice in publicity. Given the importance of development of skills to volunteers, meetings devoted to further training were presumably rewarding in their own right, as were the social opportunities so central to the life of the program.

Not only did SFCB depend more than other programs on volunteers for a variety of roles, but it also appears to have distributed work widely and quite evenly among its volunteers. This observation is particularly striking because many such organizations seem to rely heavily on a small core of workers (Harrington and Merry 1989). In SFCB, however, roughly two-thirds of the active volunteers surveyed had been involved in case development and had participated on hearing panels. About one-third had done one of these within the past month. Fifty percent of the volunteers had done two or more hearings of cases. These findings are especially striking since at any one time the program claimed about 350 to 400 people on its list of volunteers.

Volunteer Commitment and Internal Community

Volunteers felt considerable enthusiasm for SFCB. Of the 1981 training cohort roughly 56 percent remained active one year after training, 36 percent two years after, and 25 percent three years after. Later cohorts seemed to experience lower attrition rates. The reasons for dropping out, however, appeared quite consistent—lack of time or moving from the area.

Just as new recruits were drawn to SFCB by the opportunities for self-development as well as by the chance to do "civic work," so veterans were sustained by these twin interests. If anything, the veterans were even more deeply committed to personal development through acquisition and application of new skills in communication and conflict resolution. Over half of the veteran volunteers indicated a desire to work in a job where mediation skills were important, for example.

At the same time, participation in SFCB seems to have reinforced the longing on the part of volunteers to be part of communities with a high degree of social interaction and an abundance of mutually supportive relationships. The program was organized to foster these values by building an internal community that filled and sustained some of those needs. One symbolic indication of this emphasis was reflected in a decision in 1980 to excise the term *volunteer* from the SFCB literature and replace it with *community member.* In practice, the informal ties among volunteers were substantial, with more than half the veterans indicating that they socialized on occasion with as many as six other volunteers. Thus, the single most satisfying aspect of SFCB work reported by the volunteers was the sense of community that they felt.

The sense of internal community was not surprising given that most of the salient aspects of the work of the organization were collective in nature: training sessions, meetings, and social activities. Even the hearings were done by a small group, and it was not uncommon that the disputants were sent off by themselves after the hearing while volunteers focused attention on one another in a debriefing. This pattern contrasts sharply with that reported by Barbara Schwartz in the New York State Dispute Resolution Centers, where volunteers function autonomously after initial training (1989).

Considerable organizational time and resources were devoted to building and sustaining relationships among volunteers and between staff and volunteers. The cohesiveness was built also on the sense of the uniqueness of and personal commitment to the SFCB mission. The organizational culture emphasized, on the one hand, the negative features of the formal justice system and, on the other, the uniqueness of SFCB in providing an alternative forum for justice. Rather than trying to integrate volunteers into the larger dispute-resolution movement, the organization stressed its own special qualities.

In many respects, SFCB itself resembled a social-movement organization. Members were linked by a sense of shared mission, summarized in the training manual as five values:

1. Viewing conflicts as a normal part of life from which learning and change can take place;
2. Peaceful (verbal) expression of conflict is desireable because it provides an opportunity to identify "deeper" community issues and lays the groundwork for resolution and safer neighborhoods;
3. Individuals and neighborhoods must take responsibility for expressing and seeking solutions to conflicts;
4. Participation in the dispute process and in making agreements must be voluntary;
5. Respect for cultural diversity and other differences must exist. (*Training Manual* 15–17)

The positive mission to implement these values was complemented by the negative views of the formal justice system and the professionals who work in it.

Although the conflict-resolution practices at SFCB did not differ dramatically from those of other programs, there was a substantial difference in the understanding and perception of these activities. The ideological framework of the program emphasized a larger mission than resolving individual conflicts. It viewed civic work as a means to influence neighborhood life and to provide citizens with important personal experiences that would make them more responsible members of their neighborhoods.

Self-development and Change among Volunteers

Volunteers valued not just that sense of community and collective mission, however, but also the sense of competence and expertise in specific skills that the training and experience provided for them. Most volunteers reported that their ability to handle conflict in their own lives had improved since joining SFCB. Seventy percent reported improvement in their ability "to help people solve problems"; 56 percent in their interpersonal communication skills; 31 percent in discussion leading; and 33 percent in public-speaking skills. At the same time, comparisons of self-ratings in a variety of skills before training and after a year of experience showed no pattern of increase in self-rated skill level. This finding is inconsistent with the volunteer's perceptions of personal growth and may have resulted from greater sophistication about skills and higher standards for self-assessment after training and experience. It may also have resulted from lack of confidence arising from the infrequency with which volunteers were able to apply their skills in actual mediation sessions.

The general conviction not only that their skills had grown but that these were important life skills prompted 60 percent of the volunteers to teach some of these techniques to family members or roommates; roughly 67 percent to teach them to friends; and just under half to teach them to coworkers. Further, over two-thirds of the volunteers reported frequent use of these skills in their own lives. Forty percent of the volunteers said that they had used the four-phase process for conflict resolution in disputes outside of the SFCB context. This pattern of widespread utilization and dissemination of dispute-resolution skills sets SFCB apart from many other dispute-resolution programs, where the application of skills remains confined to the program context (Schwartz 1989).

Before and after measures of the attitudes of trainees compared to nontrainees suggest few changes that can be attributed to the SFCB experience after a year with the program. Only self-assessed knowledge of the neighborhood and distrust of the formal justice system showed statistically significant increases for volunteers. Other perceptions of the neighborhood (such as valuing cultural diversity or feeling a part of the neighborhood) and behavioral ties to it (such as number of visits with neighbors or belonging to a neighborhood organization) were relatively unchanged. Although these measures did not show it, it is clear from interviews that a substantial proportion of SFCB volunteers believed that their participation had had a profound effect on their lives.

They felt, for example, a greater sense of efficacy and privilege derived from their work as mediators. By virtue of their twenty-six hours of training, they gained access to intimate aspects of disputants' lives. Unlike professionals such as doctors, psychologists, and social workers who gained such access only after years of training, SFCB volunteers had to invest relatively little to be part of emotionally charged encounters and significant human dramas. This engagement, unlike the superficiality of much day-to-day social interaction, was experienced as rich, meaningful, and consequential.

For several of the volunteers, participation in SFCB was viewed as the turning point in their lives. For example, one volunteer claimed that SFCB had "saved her life." She had been depressed, sickly, and on welfare when she first heard about SFCB. Through her work first as a panelist and later in various training, outreach, and governance roles, she remade her life into one that was worthwhile and satisfying. Such stories were not common, but this one was certainly not unique. They illustrate much about the potential of SFCB to assist its volunteers as much as or perhaps more than the disputants who seek assistance in conflict resolution. It also exemplifies the ideology of personal growth that is at the heart of SFCB's strategy for improving neighborhood capacity for resolving conflict.

Conflict Resolution and the Transformation of Neighborhoods

Through engagement with SFCB, volunteers appear to have reinforced their already high sense of civic responsibility and developed conflict-resolution skills that they applied in their work and personal lives. To what degree did the program's impact extend beyond its individual volunteers into the sections of San Francisco where it was strongest? It would be remarkable to find any evidence of transformation in general public attitudes and behavior attributable to the continuing presence of SFCB in the loosely organized, large, and heterogeneous urban areas where the program operated. No matter how visible and effective in conflict resolution and public education SFCB was, it remained, if anything, only a tiny part of the urban experience for most residents. Nonetheless, building neighborhood capacity for civic work and conflict resolution and thus more generally for neighborhood change was part of SFCB's public presentation of itself.

An opportunity to test the possibility of impact of SFCB on neighborhood residents at large emerged by chance from the completion in 1977 of a telephone survey about fear of crime and views of the neighborhood from a sample in Visitacion Valley as well as from samples in another section of San Francisco (Sunset) and the city at large. This research was carried out as part of the Fear of Crime Project (Lewis and Salem 1986), but its timing just as SFCB was initiating its office in Visitacion Valley provided the opportunity for later replication. In 1983 the telephone survey was repeated to see whether patterns of change were evident in the attitudes and perceptions of Visitacion Valley residents that could be attributed to the active presence of SFCB there during five years.[6]

The survey provided striking confirmation of the extent of that presence; 2 percent of the respondents were SFCB volunteers and 40 percent were aware of the program. A large percentage of people knew of the organization and its work. This evidence, together with the ability of SFCB to draw cases without active sponsorship and case referral by the criminal justice system, supports the conclusion that San Francisco Community Boards had succeeded in establishing a local capacity to hear and resolve conflicts.

That enhanced capacity, which was SFCB's primary goal, had not altered, however, the average residents' views of their neighborhoods. Visitacion Valley residents were no more or less likely than those of Sunset (another neighborhood) or San Francisco as a

6. Rather than using random digit dialing as in the first study, the second survey used a sample of phone numbers from the published city directory. Both survey samples totaled six hundred in their coverage of Visitacion Valley, Sunset, and San Francisco at large.

whole to show an increase or decrease in sense of attachment to the neighborhood, confidence in neighborhood improvement, involvement in civic work with neighbors, or to be fearful of crime. None of these measures, of course, directly taps approaches to perceptions of conflict-resolution capacity—the core of San Francisco Community Boards activity. The data suggest, however, no evidence of peripheral effects of the program in creating stronger community ties and diminishing fear of crime among residents at large. Given the indirectness of their relationship to SFCB activity, such findings should not surprise us.

When these data are tied to the fact that caseloads peaked very quickly rather than growing steadily as neighborhood recognition, reliance, and capacity developed together, they should introduce a note of skepticism regarding the most inflated claims for the broad, transformative effect of community dispute resolution on whole communities (see Shonholtz in this volume). As Shonholtz noted himself, dramatic change in communities can ultimately come only when all their institutions—schools, churches, voluntary organizations, public agencies—are working together on the same mission. SFCB began its work as a lonely crusader, developed a substantial following of individuals, spread widely its message and skills, and drew to it—as few other programs have—neighborhood conflicts for resolution. Yet, by the early 1980s SFCB had not seen the emergence of the coalition for institutional change that might have further transformed the San Francisco neighborhoods where it worked.

Conclusion

SFCB has been unusual among dispute-resolution programs in its vision of the central importance of building neighborhood capacity to resolve conflict. It has also been unusually successful in following through on its vision by drawing in a wide array of neighborhood conflicts involving people of varied socioeconomic status and ethnicity who come to SFCB on their own rather than through court referral. Its experience contrasts sharply with that of court-connected programs, whose cases largely involve assaults among intimates. In that sense SFCB has served to open up an "alternative justice system."

At the same time, SFCB has found only a limited market for its services. This ceiling is either the result of cultural limits on the willingness of people to pursue complaints outside the formal justice system or the result of strategic choices in developing referral networks for cases. The relatively low volume of cases has meant an extremely high cost per case. These costs, however, may be somewhat misleading because this program has devoted many of its resources to building and maintaining a large volunteer network as an end in itself. For SFCB, service to the community has meant training large numbers of people in conflict-resolution skills as well as providing mechanisms for conflicts to be heard.

Unlike many other community dispute-resolution programs, SFCB has utilized face-to-face mediation by panels of mediators in sessions open to the public. Thus, despite its extensive private funding and independence from the courts, SFCB has made itself accountable to the people it serves. The SFCB program is also unusual in that it resisted the tendency to individualize conflict that is so common in the United States. It permitted and even encouraged couples, groups of neighbors, groups of teenagers, and others to come together to face and try to resolve problems. Not only did it accept the fact that parties to conflicts might consist of more than one person, but that there could well be more than two parties. In this sense, SFCB acknowledged the complexity of neighborhood conflicts and was responsive to the ways in which parties understood and defined the issues. At the same time, the program chose not to become an advocate by itself, encouraging linkages between complainants. Thus, when a single tenant complained about a landlord, SFCB did not pursue other tenants to learn if they had similar problems. But, then, by permitting cases to move forward with multiple actors or with two actors, SFCB resisted the transformation of disputes. At the same time, however, it sometimes imposed its own ideology of emotional expression on those who entered mediation panels (see Rothschild in this volume). These varied dimensions of assessment and comparison cannot, of course, wholly encompass the complex social phenomenon that was and is SFCB. They tell us as much perhaps about the hopes and perceptions and critiques of those outside the program as about the program itself. Whatever they suggest about SFCB's successes and failures, however, they provide an important basis for thinking further about community justice and its relationship to popular justice.

BIBLIOGRAPHY

Beer, Jennifer E. 1986. *Peacemaking in Your Neighborhood: Reflections on an Experiment in Community Mediation.* Philadelphia: New Society Publishers.

Coleman, James E., Elihu Katz, and Herbert Menzel. 1966. *Medical Innovation: A Diffusion Study.* Indianapolis: Bobbs-Merrill.

Cook, Royer F., Janice A. Roehl, and David I. Sheppard. 1980. *Neighborhood Justice Centers Field Test: Final Evaluation Report.* Washington, D.C.: U.S. Department of Justice.

Dispute Resolution Forum. 1988. December.

Felstiner, William, and Lynne Williams. 1980. *Community Mediation in Dorchester, Massachusetts.* Washington, D.C.: U.S. Department of Justice.

Harrington, Christine. 1985. *Shadow Justice: The Ideology and Institutionalization of Alternatives To Court.* Westport, Conn.: Greenwood Press.

Harrington, Christine, and Sally E. Merry. 1989. Ideological Production: The Making of Community Mediation. *Law and Society Review,* 22:709–35.

Lewis, Dan A., and Greta Salem. 1986. *Fear of Crime: Incivility and the Production of a Social Problem.* New Brunswick, N.J.: Transaction Books.

Merry, Sally Engle. 1990. *The Paradox of Legal Entitlement: Law, Power, and Resistance among Working-Class Americans.* Chicago: University of Chicago Press.

Merry, Sally Engle, and Susan S. Silbey. 1984. "What Do Plaintiffs Want? Reexamining the Concept of Dispute." *Justice System Journal* 9:151–79.

Moriarty, William F., Jr., Thomas L. Norris, and Luis Salas. 1977. *Evaluation: Dade County Citizen Dispute Settlement Program.* A report for Dade County Citizen Dispute Settlement Program, Dade County, Florida.

Pipkin, Ronald, and Janet Rifkin. 1984. "The Social Organization in Alternative Dispute Resolution: Implications for Professionalization of Mediation." *Justice System Journal* 9:204–27.

Prospectus. 1983. Fall/Winter.

Prospectus. 1985. Spring/Summer.

Rothschild, Judy H. 1986. "Mediation as Social Control: A Study of Neighborhood Justice." Ph.D. diss., University of California, Berkeley.

Schwartz, Barbara. 1989. "The Construction of Neutrality in American Community Mediation Practice." Paper presented at the annual meeting of the American Anthropological Association, Washington, D.C. November.

Smith, David Horton. 1975. "Voluntary Groups and Voluntary Action." *Annual Review of Sociology* 1:247–70.

Organizing for Community Mediation: The Legacy of Community Boards of San Francisco as a Social-Movement Organization

Douglas R. Thomson and Frederic L. DuBow

> Popular justice and collective justice operate from very
> different premises.
>
> —Hofrichter 1987:100

The history of the San Francisco Community Boards program has been dynamic and full of changes, controversies, contention, and acclaim. In examining this history, we can identify several stages of development: initiation and identity formation (1976–79), expansion and experimentation (1980–83), contraction and accountability (1984–86), and consolidation and adaptation (1987–89). As the following analysis will make clear, a strategy, or motive idea, was associated with each of these descriptive stages of development. Thus

This chapter results from a major evaluation of SFCB begun in 1983 by the second author and continued until his death in April 1987. The first author, who was not involved in the original fieldwork, joined the project in October 1986. He has drawn on data and materials gathered, field notes, and interim reports prepared by Fred DuBow and various evaluation associates, notably Oscar Goodman and Nancy Hanawi (e.g., Dubow, Goodman, and Hanawi 1987). Hence the chapter focuses on SFCB from its inception in 1976 to 1985, when the collection of evaluation data ended. We place special emphasis on the 1983–85 period, when the greatest evaluation activity took place. In one respect that emphasis is fortunate, because the first stage emphasized cooperation, the second empowerment, the third governance, and the fourth "the work," that is, the institution-alization of conflict-resolution services. We will see that this sequence of strategies and organizational development contributed to SFCB's prominence and reputation and to its success in attracting funding while sharply constraining its achievements toward popular justice.

Throughout much of this history, organizational battles centered on an ironic situation: SFCB was committed to democratic empow-erment of citizens, neighborhoods, and communities, and its internal governance sought widespread participation by volunteer members of the program and encouraged mutual accountability between staff and volunteers. Meanwhile, however, authority remained hierarchi-cal, the making of policy decisions was essentially centralized, and SFCB's image was identified strongly with the persona, opinions, and commitments of its founder. This tension dissipated as the organi-zation moved to consolidation and adaptation, acquiring a new direc-tor, establishing new programs and funding sources, and developing a structure and a climate that seem more than ever like those of a conventional social-service organization.

Consider how two knowledgeable observers summarize SFCB's origins and midcareer status:

---

those years roughly marked an era of great experimentation and turmoil in the program.

    The first author also visited San Francisco for a few days in February 1989 to interview SFCB's founder, Raymond Shonholtz, and several other veteran participants. I call these individuals by the pseudonyms Elliot, Gale, Jessie, Morgan, and Val. Four of these persons had been employed by SFCB for several years; the fifth, who is quoted only once, is a veteran volunteer. Sometimes I have edited quotes or have provided transliterations to aid communication. Because this is neither a linguistic nor primarily a semiotic analysis, this procedure seems acceptable. I also treat the interviews as accounts (Scott and Lyman 1968) reflecting the respondents' stated opinions and perceptions, although sometimes they also represent consensuses regard-ing events and their patterns.

    In addition to the aforementioned materials, we rely heavily on the report of an organization analysis of SFCB made by Oscar Goodman and Nancy Hanawi in 1985. Their report was a preliminary draft of the major evaluation mentioned earlier. Because Goodman and Hanawi did much of the fieldwork during the evaluation, and indeed worked for or with SFCB in some capacity until 1985, their account gives our analysis the benefit of first-hand witnesses, although it is treated here as secondary data. In view of the controversy associated with their report, we occasionally present alternatives to their interpretations and recast the tone of the original. For the most part, however, we conclude that our analysis leads to conclusions (albeit tentative) compatible with those reached by Goodman and Hanawi.

CBP started out as [a] crime prevention program that intended to divert great numbers of cases from the justice system. It used an accepted mediation process that was implemented by volunteer panelists on five-person community boards. The additional intent of developing resident empowerment and neighborhood accountability evolved into substantial activities to effect community governance and neighborhood socialization and cohesion. One of the moves in that direction was to expand the roles of community volunteers in the performance of dispute resolution services. The program has also, to a limited extent, attempted to educate the community at large and the volunteers about the methodology of the program and its effect on disputes. CBP also sees its training functions as part of a process of affecting the lives of people living in close proximity to one another. Volunteers are trained in communication skills, in the implementation of the dispute hearing, in the role of panelists, in case development for the hearings, and, to a lesser extent, in outreach and follow-up. Some are also trained to function as trainers of other volunteers and others to participate in governance and planning. The perception still remains, however, that the central volunteer activity is participation as a panelist to hear cases. (Goodman and Hanawi 1985:11–12)

This description reveals an identity centered on mediation in itself rather than on either crime prevention or democratic empowerment.

This passage also highlights other important issues. What happened to SFCB's broader aims? Why did "resident empowerment" not become collectivized? Why did it remain largely a matter of individual and interpersonal development instead of a more highly organized, more politically engaged phenomenon? Why is there so little evidence that "community governance" was enhanced in Visitacion Valley, Bernal Heights, Mission, Noe Valley, Western Addition, and Haight-Ashbury/Fillmore? Why was "community governance" effectively translated as concerning how SFCB itself was organized and operated instead of as greater democratic participation and power in the neighborhoods and in the city?

An understanding of these questions and conflicts is central to an assessment of SFCB's legacy. We will examine these themes in the remaining sections of the chapter, but first we will review how SFCB presented itself, and how it used and was constrained by its resources in developing its identity.

The Local Context: San Francisco as Scene and as Power Politics

San Francisco seemed in the 1970s and 1980s to provide a remarkably supportive social, cultural, and political environment for the planting and cultivation of SFCB. The city offered a history of tolerance of diversity, sophistication in political behavior, and willingness to try social inventions. A large proportion of its residents had experiences and capabilities compatible with SFCB's goals and technologies.

Thus, on the basis of popular perceptions, one is tempted to think of San Francisco during this era as a locale especially receptive to the ideology of conflict as beneficial (see Becker 1971). Yet San Francisco's historical "culture of civility" (Becker and Horowitz 1971) and its "mystique" (Davis 1971), including its nurturing of bohemian and hippie cultures in the 1950s and 1960s (Smith, Luce, and Dernburg 1971; Wirt 1971), contrasts with the city's interest group struggles of the 1970s (Wirt 1974; Zisk 1973). These struggles echo the bossism prevalent in San Francisco in the latter nineteenth and early twentieth centuries. They reflect a generally muted history of racial tensions (Hippler 1971) and the dominance of financial interests, which seem to have avoided much scrutiny, perhaps partially in contrast to more dramatic radical movements (Lyman 1971). These movements include sometimes momentous student protests in Berkeley, as well as the more engaging attempts at populist reform (Carlin 1971).

A prosaic local political movement set the stage for SFCB and its early rhetoric:

> The community empowerment issue in Community Boards was also related to a broader local control issue which in San Francisco was marked by the successful referendum in 1976 to bring district representation to the Board of Supervisors. The slogans were "self-sufficiency" and "community participation." (Goodman and Hanawi 1985:30)

Thus SFCB emerged in a section of San Francisco called Visitacion

Valley. This emergence reveals its original hopes and plans as well as its responsiveness to specific events.[1]

Visitacion Valley in the late 1970s was a little-known neighborhood that matched a favored profile for community organizers: it was an "underserved" area that was not "overorganized" but offered promising informal ties and associations. Visitacion Valley was a place where "there was some room to move and come in and work" (Jessie). It also was "noted for its ethnic and racial diversity" (Podolefsky 1983:207). Two prominent centers of power there, frequently at loggerheads, were the All People's Coalition (APC) and those allied with Henry Shindell, the "mayor of Visitacion Valley" (Baker 1976; Podolefsky 1983:207–33). In 1969, Shindell, along with the Schlage Lock Company (the only large, institutional source of jobs in Visitacion Valley) and key members of the merchants' association successfully lobbied the mayor's office to place a beat cop on Leland Avenue. This action reflected fear of crime and perceptions of a substantial crime problem in the area (Podolefsky 1983; Reactions to Crime project [hereafter RTC] 1977:330608–11, 331048–55). It also revealed the influence that elements of the local business community could wield.

In 1976 (the year of SFCB's founding) an APC ally, the Citizen Safety Project (CSP), persuaded the Cala Mart to employ a private security guard in response to complaints from many residents about purse snatching. The "old power structure," which included the Visitacion Valley Coordinating Council, the Visitacion Valley Improvement Association, and the Visitacion Valley Community Center, in addition to the business interests mentioned above, had been "steadily eroding" since the 1971 founding of the APC, "an Alinsky based community organization" working on recreation, land use, and jobs issues (Baker 1976; Podolefsky 1983). Shindell said that the CSP would not work because the APC "wants all the glory" (RTC 1977).

SFCB tended to align itself initially with APC. There was evidence of collaboration between CSP and SFCB regarding organizing possibilities shortly after SFCB received some funding.

SFCB emerged in an era of concern about crime and interest in

---

1. This analysis benefits from the systematic and well-documented analyses contained in Northwestern University's archives of the Reactions to Crime project, and also draws on published materials of Podolefsky and DuBow (1981) and Podolefsky (1983).

the possibilities of community crime prevention; it was involved with and even had some personnel in common with efforts such as the Reactions to Crime project. This profile made Visitacion Valley an especially attractive site for initiating the community-mediation effort.[2]

This background also should have enabled SFCB to build on the extant and latent capacities for collective action, to generate some degree of political empowerment with democratic participation. The strength and the record of the APC, together with its early cooperative attitude toward SFCB, were also promising. In addition, SFCB's primary organizer and strategist at this time, Bruce Thomas, was a prominent veteran of National Welfare Rights Organization campaigns.

In addition to these forces, another feature of SFCB's early history in Visitacion Valley should have facilitated a collective approach. From its inception SFCB built coalitions across racial groups and across other diverse groups as well. SFCB organizing was based more on group dynamics, however, than on political action (Shonholtz 1989). But in view of their potent working relationship, why didn't SFCB develop its alliance with APC, especially given SFCB's strength in Visitacion Valley after that time? Wasn't that the ready link to collective action and broader concerns about popular justice that have been missing in SFCB? Other comments by Shonholtz, from the same account, suggest some possible explanations:

> We had gone in and done some straight organizing, a lot of experiments in organizing, a lot of mistakes . . . strategies that didn't work, period. It was really a credit to Bruce Thomas, who was a black organizer who did a lot of work . . . with welfare rights organizing, who . . . figured out that what we were organizing was a service. We weren't really organizing advocacy.

---

2. A large-scale survey conducted in 1977 (Podolefsky 1983:18–21) showed that Visitacion Valley residents ranked crimes such as burglary and robbery as more significant problems than did residents in nine other community areas in San Francisco (Mission and Sunset), Philadelphia, and Chicago. Because crime was a major concern in Visitacion Valley, the residents generally showed greater involvement in community crime-prevention activities (Podolefsky 1983:217–28). In comparison to the mean for the other community areas, for example, Visitacion Valley residents reported much more involvement in "collective anti-crime activities" such as holding meetings, pressuring police, and organizing the neighborhood (Podolefsky and DuBow 1981:238–52).

This account suggests that this early strategic choice for service organizing rather than advocacy organizing shaped SFCB's future and may have directed it away from continued, effectual alliance with APC.

In fact, SFCB training turned toward group dynamics rather than organizing and political action. Group-dynamics training could have been a prelude to political training, but instead the training turned to mediation skills. This quieter side of the popular-justice movement prevailed from the start. This was the root of SFCB's ultimate movement to community social service rather than community empowerment.

Resource Constraints and Opportunities

Organizational Self-Presentation

A picture that appears often in the organization's publications captures SFCB's image most accurately. "Conflict Managers at Paul Revere School" (Community Board Program 1983b) neatly depicts SFCB's rhetorical strategy. Several grade-school youths, multiracial and multiethnic, wear "Conflict Managers" T-shirts. They look informal, and they constitute a group. Even the name of the school suggests the charge of spreading the word. Throughout SFCB's transformations, this element seems to have been a constant of SFCB: it got out the message.

SFCB consistently articulated its public self in a flow of newsletters, annual reports, proposals, press releases, and other documents. This material seems to have reinforced the staff and volunteers in the internal communications network; it was also a key component of SFCB's successful public relations and funding efforts and communicated its willingness to "act as a neutral in the resolution of disputes" (Goodman and Hanawi 1985:12).

The newsletter alone reached approximately twenty-two thousand persons (Wahrhaftig 1982:92). To serve an educative function, early issues of the newsletter provided detailed analyses of hearings. By late 1981, these had given way to brief summaries. By 1985 the newsletter presented "a picture of a program that is no longer experimenting, assessing, and developing" (Goodman and Hanawi 1985:20–21).

The very earliest reports of the program were measured in tone and relatively free of high-sounding rhetoric. The 1978 mid-year report contains solid content and does not inflate the actual accomplishments of the program. By the end of that year, however, the tone has changed and all later reports are filled with hyperbole. An image of serious experimentation, vigorous trial and honest effort is replaced by one that projects the interests and talents of effectively marketing a program. (Goodman and Hanawi 1985:21)

Early in its history, SFCB attempted to obtain cases from agencies but failed, reportedly because of the "newness of the idea" (Jessie). Consequently it turned its attention to neighborhood referrals. According to one veteran, "[T]hat was a mistake because lack of sustained attention to city government and agencies meant a lot of work had to be done later to establish a track record when SFCB shifted focus" (Jessie). Indeed, SFCB's small caseload has been something of a legend, generally running about four hundred cases and one hundred hearings a year during the middle years (DuBow and McEwen in this volume). Nevertheless, police referrals accounted for about 30 percent of the cases even during those years when the emphasis was not on agency referrals.

The SFCB literature's emphasis on decentralization contrasted with the actual centralization of the organization. Evidence of centralization included the central office as a constant and as a symbol of continuing dominance of decision making by the executive director; continuity in key staff personnel as well in several community members; and the Visitacion Valley office, which opened in 1977.

Funding and Referrals

By the beginning of the period of contraction and emphasis on accountability (roughly 1984–86), the organization was still small, with only about fifteen staff, but involved about 350 active community members in the six areas encompassing neighborhoods with a total of over two hundred thousand persons in them. Its annual budget was estimated to be somewhere between $375,000 and $525,000 for a program conducting about one hundred hearings a year, processing four hundred cases, and training 175 volunteers (Goodman and Hanawi 1985:14).

SFCB originally sought, and in the beginning received, some government monies (mostly CETA), but very early announced its aversion to such arrangements due to: 1) the founder's success in private fundraising, 2) a desire to avoid government regulations, and 3) an aversion to justice-system entanglements (Goodman and Hanawi 1985). This approach was also consistent with the prevailing ideological sentiment of the time (circa 1977), with the Carter administration stressing deregulation and the planned elimination of the Law Enforcement Assistance Administration, a primary assignment of Attorney General Griffin Bell. Interestingly, for a dozen years SFCB refused opportunities for LEAA funds "because of the politics and the community's feelings" (Jessie).

But SFCB did not need government funding, as it established its now well-known funding record (Goodman and Hanawi 1985:8). There were about thirty "substantial funders" for SFCB from 1976–84, granting more than $4 million.[3] While this approach brings advantages, it also poses the danger "that the program will become market driven" (Goodman and Hanawi 1985:8, 11, 60–61).

After this remarkable record of attracting private funding over a period of several years, SFCB began to experience difficulties in attracting such monies in sufficient amounts to maintain all six area offices. This prompted the closing of three of them in 1984, and the demise of having area forums in every neighborhood in the city (Community Board Program 1983b:15). Critics saw SFCB giving a "double message" on public funding in 1984, as it tried to satisfy two audiences, public policy (and funding) and private funders, and the "expansionist goal became detached from the ideology" (Goodman and Hanawi 1985:61–62).

Constriction of private funding spurred the application for city funding (1984), a major turning point. SFCB made a profound shift to increased reliance, even dependence, on government funding (Shonholtz 1987). With this, SFCB increased its involvement with

---

3. Funders during the first year or two included the Robert F. Kennedy Memorial, the Gerbode Foundation, Haas, Rosenberg, Hancock, Sachem, Veatch, and New World foundations, the Police Foundation, Law Enforcement Assistance Administration (U.S. Department of Justice), Comprehensive Employment and Training Act (CETA/U.S. Department of Labor).

established agencies, formalizing referral mechanisms and articulating working relationships. Hence, SFCB has reinstitutionalized in a form that may be more stable and familiar.

By 1985, SFCB was "making concerted efforts to get public funding," turning to the state and the city to provide funding for expanded community-based dispute-resolution programs (Goodman and Hanawi 1985:6). By 1989, about half of the budget came from private foundations and corporate giving, with the other half coming from the state and special projects. SFCB received increased city and county support through the California Dispute Resolution Act and generated revenues through its own marketing to clients. It had recently received a grant from the state Department of Mental Health for a research and writing project, was exploring peace education to go with its schools' work, and was discussing with the Delinquency Prevention Commission a California Youth Authority grant to survey "systemwide approaches to dealing with delinquency" (Jessie). The transition to governmental affiliations is a major development.

It has even produced an arrangement in which SFCB is now obliged to report back to referring police officers the outcomes of cases (Community Board Program 1988:3). As one veteran put it:

> SFCB has learned to deal with change, it has adapted. It's hard to get direct referrals, it's hard to reeducate people, so it made sense to hook up with the police department. (Jessie)

To further boost referrals from the police, SFCB was planning to pitch the program in visits to all police roll calls in the city (Jessie).

There appears to be some embarrassment within SFCB over the vocalness and tone of its earlier eschewing of entanglements with established agencies. But this takes place in the context of recognition and acceptance of what the organization has been and accomplished, even as witnesses modestly demur from some of the expansive expectations that years of visitors to SFCB activities have harbored for SFCB.

Why did this transformation occur? Does it represent a displacement of the organization's goals? Is it a case of goal succession—turning from its commitment to empowering communities and transforming social structures? Or does it suggest that SFCB has transcended a fixation with tactical engagements, that it has achieved all that it could, that it is time for other social forms to more appropriately pursue the empowerment agenda while SFCB attends to mediating community disputes, to personal development, and to keeping the organization fit for such business?

Such questions suggest the tensions that persisted throughout SFCB's history between the goal of empowerment and the development of the community-mediation program and organization.

Organizational Issues: The Competing Promises and Demands of Empowerment, Governance, and Program Development

This section examines these tensions by looking first at SFCB's mission of empowerment and then its mission of democratic governance. It then turns to what has emerged as SFCB's dominant focus: "the work," or conflict-resolution service in itself.

The Empowerment Mission

Like any new organization operating in uncharted waters, SFCB needed to establish an identity and then to use that identity to grow. Empowerment became an important, albeit ambiguous, part of that identity. SFCB's initial ambitions encompassed nothing less than a "neighborhood building" endeavor, bringing people together to establish communication networks to identify "community needs" and "to work together on a constructive project," with the ends of forging a collective identity and "reduc[ing] anxiety, fear, and stress in the community," while improving neighborhoods (Center for Social Redesign 1980:9, 10).

In SFCB's middle years, the centrality of democratic empowerment and its link to the core service work of the program were captured in its own statement of purpose:

> The purpose of Community Board is to maintain an organization of democratic neighborhood forums to enable neighborhoods and their residents to express and resolve a broad range of individual and community conflicts. (Community Board Program 1983a:1)

Thus we find that even as late as 1983, during the period of retrenchment and contraction, SFCB's rhethoic continued to highlight, ves-
tigially perhaps, the mission of community empowerment.[4]

This ethos valued citizens taking ownership of their conflicts
(Christie 1977). Hence, it is the ideology of "the work" that SFCB
leaders viewed and advocated as empowering. Some of the key terms
of SFCB ideology appear: a new "primary justice system," a pre-
emption of (rather than an alternative to) the formal, now secondary,
justice system; "civic work" as the purpose of the rippling efforts at
conflict resolution; "self-governance" as process and product. Yet
SFCB would soon find that mediation was structurally problematic
for fostering empowerment in the face of disparities in power between
the parties, with landlord-tenant relationships as an example (Gale).

The Early Days of Empowerment

We find some uncertainty and disagreement about what SFCB was
in the beginning, before the period of empowerment. Wahrhaftig
(1982) says that SFCB developed apart from and other than formal
justice agencies. Goodman and Hanawi (1985) mention institutional
sources of support for SFCB and cite early plans for collaboration
with justice agencies. One CB veteran had never thought of SFCB
as "a community organizing thing," but observed acerbically that it
"depends on who you talk to" because one cannot know "what someone said at some meeting in 1976" (Jessie).

From 1976 to 1979, SFCB groped for its identity. Notions of
community problem solving, self-governance, and empowerment

---

4. Consider the larger frame into which SFCB placed its purpose, one that harks
back to the early sense of empowerment:
   The effect of this success has been to establish Community Board forums as a
   new neighborhood justice system. This neighborhood justice work compels
   broader conceptual consideration of democratic ideology and neighborhood self-
   governance. As a primary justice system of "first call" in the neighborhoods,
   Community Boards not only stands apart from the traditional justice agency
   system, but also represents a new model of civic work and activity within the
   urban community. Community Boards provides a service that is derived from
   the direct participation of community members who are seeking to ameliorate
   conflicts within their neighborhoods. This is a self-governance activity of the
   neighborhoods and it is work that promotes the democratic role of citizens in
   voluntarily performing civic responsibilities. (Community Board Program
   1983a:2)

accompanied notions of civic responsibility and primary justice. Certain strategies were rejected or highlighted. Yet with the presence of seasoned community organizers Bruce Thomas and Dan Carroll (Shonholtz 1989; Jessie), and despite some early discussions of prospects for direct action, SFCB soon rejected confrontation and collective action as possibilities. Empowerment appeared on the agenda. As Goodman and Hanawi observed:

> the program began with the concept of working within or complementing the traditional justice process. Its stated purpose was to handle, from a community base, the large volume of police cases that are dismissed from or plea-bargained out of the misdemeanor courts. The expectation was that referrals would come from law enforcement and social service agencies, and directly from the community. (1985:7)

But despite this effort to look toward the justice system for cases, SFCB attempted to set itself apart from the system:

> An additional goal was to develop resident empowerment and neighborhood accountability in minor dispute resolution, essentially a way of recognizing community ownership and control. The latter was to become the dominant theme as the program's mission developed. (Goodman and Hanawi 1985:7)

In fact, an early SFCB proposal ("Proposal for the Implementation of Community 'No Fault' Boards Within the Criminal Justice Process" [Shonholtz 1979]),[5] consistent with the program's initial amenability to some government funding, saw the new community-mediation program working closely with justice agencies.

---

5. Note how this proposal appropriates a concept and term ("no fault") current at the time and used regarding other issues (divorce, insurance, automobile accidents) and applies it to the founder's area of interest. This appears to have been a common working strategy of his, and indeed I presume of many other successful program entrepreneurs. This development also highlights the civil-law origins of the SFCB community-mediation effort, origins that may have complicated its picking up on criminal and quasi-criminal cases and interfered with efforts to foster community empowerment.

Goodman and Hanawi capture SFCB's organizational culture at its origins in these terms:

> At this initial stage the organizational stance was democratic and cooperative from a staff as well as a community point of view. The staff thought of themselves as community organizers setting out on a joint venture with the community to effectuate vital social change. There was evidently a sense of adventure and risk in the enterprise as meetings were held in a number of neighborhoods to tell people about the idea of no-fault boards, and to learn from them what the community needed and how the model of conflict resolution might be implemented in the neighborhoods. (1985:7–8)

SFCB developed in a rather opportunistic and cautiously experimental fashion. It eschewed confrontation and more explicit forms of community organization associated with both mass and neighborhood forms of popular justice. This was fateful for SFCB's possible alliances and for its own achievements of popular justice. Apparently, early on some argued for the alternative:

> There were debates about whether to use the "conflict model" or the "network model" of community organizing. Should CB use local issues to build community consciousness, or should it network and use the power, status and legitimacy of existing organizations to build the program? There were cautionary concerns about politicizing the program countered by desires to take all the risks necessary to deal with the deeper causes of community unrest. Eventually it was the careful attitude toward survival of the process and of the organization that won over the ideological political and social issues. (Goodman and Hanawi 1985:32)

Empowerment through Policy and Training?

Of SFCB's various organizational forms, the Center for Policy and Training (CPT), created in 1981, is a particularly significant illustration of the changes in SFCB's objectives, procedures, and activities. Originally a vehicle for disseminating the SFCB message, it internationally represented its identity as a social movement and encapsulated the meaning of training in SFCB. The founders of CPT wanted it to articulate policy as well as to provide training, but after the emergence of the new governance forms of 1983 and 1984, the decline of the area forums, and the eventual closing of five of the six area offices, it subtly shifted to being a vehicle generating resources for the organization. Eventually, it lost its quasi-autonomous identity and was folded back into the general operations of SFCB.

CPT demonstrated that SFCB was not strictly a direct-service agency. It showed that training was central to SFCB's mission. Its striving for multiple identities epitomized SFCB's expansive and path-breaking sense of its domains. In addition, CPT was perhaps the most explicit social-movement component of SFCB, both in its focus on policy and in its search for constituencies beyond San Francisco. SFCB's changing identity is revealed in the very fact that CPT no longer exists as a separate entity.

CPT represented "a significant stage of development" that produced much of SFCB's "national work." It increased opportunities to work with staff members, to provide training, and to lecture (Gale). Paradoxically, CPT, with its national focus, took SFCB beyond local concerns.

Training, however, was an essential component of SFCB before CPT. In the early days, when cases and hearings were few and far between, training was a tactical necessity. SFCB's mass training sessions created the base of skills and personnel and generated an awareness of the program's existence, which subsequently made it more visible as a provider of a useful service. SFCB also used the mass training to establish "model communities" (Gale), presumably in service of the empowerment mission.

SFCB sought ways "to use training as an organizing tool, trying as much as possible to build the community through training and service" (Gale). By 1984, SFCB stated that it had trained one thousand San Franciscans in conflict resolution (DuBow and McEwen in this volume); this figure is consistent with Goodman and Hanawi's estimate that it was training about 175 volunteers a year (1985:14). Thus, to date, SFCB presumably has trained thousands of persons, including several hundred of its own volunteers (community members).

Despite CPT's prominence during the era of empowerment, SFCB abolished it in 1988. It died in part because it had outlived its usefulness

and in part because of a change of regime that called for streamlining
operations and for simplifying SFCB's jargon (Jessie).

The Mission of Democratic Governance

SFCB began by emphasizing democratic governance for the community but shifted to internal democratic governance as a way of
modeling community and building capacity. When that effort failed,
SFCB shifted again to empowerment. Now, however, it emphasized
microempowerment, which dovetailed with conflict-resolution services and thus brought SFCB full circle.

Governance as Transition from Empowerment to Service

Although it had a short life (1984–86), the San Francisco Governing
Board captured an important phase in the organization's history. It
represented the culmination of the experiments with representational
forms of governance while paving the way for more conventional
mechanisms of coordination and accountability. Shonholtz recounts
the process:

> [T]he San Francisco Governing Board . . . had a function of hav-
> ing elected representatives who had credibility in the community.
> Having gone through a series of processes and experiments to
> find that element of representation and finally finding some way
> of finding a group of volunteers who could speak for the mem-
> bership, we experimented with Area Committees, and we exper-
> imented with Chairs of Area Committees meeting, and in an age
> when I think everyone felt that they couldn't make a decision
> without checking with everybody they could possibly check
> with. . . . Only with the creation of an elected leadership that was
> authentically elected out of the area membership could we get
> a board that could make some decisions. (1989)

Hence the transition in emphasis from empowerment to governance
emerges as a natural process of finding organizational vehicles to
channel popular energy. Shonholtz (in this volume) also alludes to
the difficulties that plagued the decision-making process.

SFCB's initial approach to governance was quite conventional.

It established a Board of Directors, which still existed in 1989 and which appeared to be the primary locus of policy decisions. Much had happened in the intervening years, however.

As SFCB grew in its early years, expanded into more community areas, and grappled with the realities of its claims to empowerment, it began to experiment with alternative forms. Perhaps the first of these, which appeared in 1977 (Gale), was the Forums, a vehicle for decentralized administration including recruitment and training of volunteers (community members). *Forum* denoted where the hearings took place, "a forum for resolving conflicts," but it also referred to all neighborhoods served by a particular area and to the people living within its boundaries. The Forums no longer exist in the early form. Now SFCB has divided the city into twenty-four neighborhoods; maps and alphabetical lists show who lives in each neighborhood (Val).

SFCB continued to struggle for governance mechanisms that would involve members in decision making while maintaining the technology and ideology established by the founders of SFCB. To supplement the area forums and area offices (Jessie), volunteer committees emerged in 1979 and grew over the next two years. A new governance form, the Advisory Council, succeeded the committee of area chairs in 1982. One consequence was "the elimination of area representation on the Board of Directors," because SFCB now viewed itself as a national endeavor (Goodman and Hanawi 1985:42–44).

Originally the only conceivable role for volunteers was panel member or, more generally, conciliator (Jessie). Fairly early, however, SFCB began to stress other roles: case developer, trainer, evaluator, lecturer. In fact, the expansion of volunteer roles was part of the reason for the mass training sessions mentioned earlier (Jessie): SFCB sought to "find out what they liked and what they considered garbage work, and then to train them to be trainers" (Gale).

Role expansion accompanied geographic expansion to Noe Valley and the Mission (1981). Casework, outreach, and follow-up were added as volunteer functions, along with panel work and training new panelists. The two forms of expansion complemented one another, allowing spreading of staff (Goodman and Hanawi 1985:38), but it also brought anxiety for the staff members who waited in vain for clarification of their new roles.

In particular, volunteers found that the informal networks that had developed among them were now diffused by program expansion.

Even the addition of new roles for volunteers, a clear and forthright message of empowerment, did not assuage volunteers, because panelist continued to be the most prized role (Goodman and Hanawi 1985:39).

Disgruntlement united staff and volunteers against SFCB administration, which responded in part by creating the Planning and Evaluation Groups (PEGs) in 1982 to accommodate demands for increased participation in organization governance. This was not enough, however; Goodman and Hanawi offer a view that contrasts sharply with that of a SFCB veteran we quoted earlier:

> Many of the more vocal and active volunteers felt that the PEGs simply made busy work for them since all of the policy and budget decisions were already made by the Executive Director before their participation commenced. (1985:40)

In 1982 and 1983, the "major focus was on thinking through governance" (Gale). Eventually this process of experimentation revealed tensions between empowerment and governance and between area participation and central control:

> Within the whole concept of empowerment as the central office of CB responded to it was the notion of the "charter." It appears repeatedly with the various community governing bodies that have been developed, including the Area Committees. It is a curious legal concept to have inserted into the context of community empowerment and local control. Since the act of chartering is the confering [sic] of power from some authority, the unfortunate assumption is suggested that Community Boards, rather than the community, has the power to grant. In any event, to argue that a community governance mechanism did not have a clear charter was regarded as sufficient to eliminate it and develop another. (Goodman and Hanawi 1985:42)

In 1984 SFCB leadership created the Governing Board, which CB veterans now view as a "transitional stage, frustrating and crazy" (Val). They suggest that problems in democratic governance resulted from the lack of benchmarks and of plans for monitoring, and eventually from a governance structure that put staff in the predicament of circular accountability (Gale).

Eventually both the Board of Directors and the Governing Board decided to dissolve and to reconstitute a new Board of Directors. One veteran reported that the current board communicates better internally than did the Governing Board, and that current SFCB administration involves the board more fully in policy making than did the previous administration (Morgan). Another veteran suggests a long-term organizational benefit from "the governance struggle": it left a core group of resilient volunteers who play visible and key governance roles on the present board (Jessie).

Community Members and the Energy of Governance

Volunteers were known as "community members" (CMs). By this self-consciously employed term, SFCB attempted to convey that its volunteers were much more than the free labor force and dues payers they might be in other, more conventional membership organizations. This term suggested that they were members of an organic entity. SFCB was saying to its community members, "This isn't a piece of it; you are it" (Jessie). In this sense, they were conceived of as empowered within this purposive polity.

Thus even in the early days, CMs exhibited substantial authority in interviewing and hiring new staff members (Jessie); this responsibility is not typically associated with the role of volunteer. Later, SFCB called on the CMs to take on roles beyond that of panelist, even the role of training the trainers. Still later, during the period of struggles over governance preceding the creation of the Governing Board, staff members were held formally accountable to CMs (Gale).

Beyond its implications for organizational governance, the term *community members* suggested that CMs also were emissaries to their neighborhoods. They would bring back their skills and insights to reshape life in their home communities. At the same time, however, SFCB saw the community members' commitment as reinforcing the value of the SFCB's overall work within the community (Jessie).

Thus, as various participants testify, governance required a huge commitment of time by everyone, including "hundreds of hours by volunteers" (Jessie). Even so, SFCB heard numerous complaints about "not enough democracy and too much hierarchy." Let us examine more closely what happened to SFCB's intentions of democratic governance, and why.

Transformation of the Hearings

Hearings were central for volunteers, who experienced the most gratification in this area. They showcased SFCB's work, made tangible what it was about, and gave SFCB a community presence. Yet the hearings, too, changed, both in context and in their meaning.

Consider what hearings were like in 1985:

> Hearings are held in a CBP area office, a local church, school, or other available space in the neighborhood. A hearing is usually open, but it is not widely advertised so that the audience usually consists of a very few directly interested parties or observers (such as evaluators or site visitors). (Goodman and Hanawi 1985:12)

By 1989 the hearings had become less accessible by virtue of location as well as ideology (Val). This change reflected the program's newer, more traditional focus on providing a helping service, on mediation as an end in itself rather than as a means to accomplish something broader, such as community empowerment. Disputants may have desired less accessible hearings, which would protect their privacy from inquisitive observers.

SFCB's four-phase conciliation process, with its emphasis on getting feelings out, on the conflict's belonging to the parties, and on the passive, facilitative role of panelists (Goodman and Hanawi 1985:13), structured SFCB's efforts away from collectivist empowerment while providing little as a model of governance for volunteers. The volunteer panelists could (and sometimes did) steer disputing in directions they considered desirable (see Rothschild in this volume); evidence from the hearings and the interviews suggests that volunteers were much more comfortable with the SFCB mediation process as ideology than were the disputants. Yet both of these senses of the volunteers' power undercut the formal, public goals of the program, toward collective empowerment internally and externally. At the same time, the presence of trainers at every panel may have impeded the CMs' sense of controlling even the hearing, at least when that role was filled by staff members (Elliot). Eventually, however, the volunteers came to be in charge of the panels (Elliot). Compared to the experiences of conventional alternative dispute resolution (ADR) programs (Hofrichter 1987), this was no small achievement in itself in terms of empowerment and democratic governance.

When SFCB consolidated from six offices, each one with a well-defined service area, to one office, the veterans found it "heartbreaking." Earlier, there had been a vision of expanding to eight, ten or eleven area offices (Val).

Even so, the consequences for the hearings are less dire than one might expect. SFCB staffs all cases out of the Visitacion Valley office, but it holds the hearings in forty sites scattered throughout they city; in this way it provides "a continued neighborhood presence" (Jessie). Thus although it lacks a permanent physical facilities in these locations, SFCB continues to work by means of decentralized hearings. Three Forums remain, but they are organized for large sections of the city (north, central, and south) rather than by smaller community areas (Val).

Some thought that contraction actually offered organizational benefits:

> I think there was a time there when in SFCB the direction got a little looser. And you simply couldn't maintain the funding level to allow six field offices. . . . (I)t's only in the last couple of years that CB's really begun to think, hey, we can serve the city. . . . So while it was perceived as a setback organizationally when you had to close offices, I thought it was a real plus. It is the work which is central and which has carried the neighborhood involvement, even though it is more difficult now in terms of volunteers being able to get together. (Jessie)

Throughout the changes, the conciliation panel seems to have remained a constant. This organizational form is significant, especially in the mission of empowerment. It represents a residual recognition of empowerment because the panel symbolized SFCB's resolve to broaden the ownership of conflicts and to bind local residents together in the process. Persistence in using the panel partially counters the stronger trend in SFCB toward institutionalization and smoother functioning.

As the numbers of volunteers grew, SFCB faced increased difficulties in honoring both democracy and responsible management
(Jessie). This situation, combined with some middle-management
problems in the early 1980s that created delays in hiring, led SFCB
to develop "different ways of dealing with volunteers" (Jessie). SFCB
began to treat the CM role in more routine fashion, more like that
of other volunteer organizations.

External forces accelerated this process as critics noted that
SFCB's focus on "internal community building" impeded efficiency.
From 1980 to 1983, for example, the numbers of CMs increased 332
percent while caseloads increased only 9 percent. These figures suggest a substantial commitment to governance, but also threatened to
create high turnover among volunteers who lacked work. According
to SFCB ideology, volunteers were central to governance by way of
committee work and peer training.

Communication and Control

SFCB's system of communication also contributed to what SFCB
became and to what it did not achieve. Goodman and Hanawi
observed that staff communication occurred through role identification, supervisory conferences, periodic staff meetings, memoranda
and reports, and informal contacts (1985:16). Although this system
included participative and informal approaches, it emphasized structured, top-down communication. More significantly, the isolation of
the field offices and CMs contributed to the maintenance of hierarchical control because they were denied effective access to decision
making. Large-scale, face-to-face comunication among volunteers in
the areas seems to have declined along with the decline in focus on
SFCB democratic governance in the mid-1980s.

Thus, ironically, that transformed emphasis on top-down communication seems to have undercut the power of extant intermediate
forums, limited as they were, and to have reduced the opportunities
for empowerment of volunteers latent in larger, more democratic
meetings. Instead, communication among volunteers occurred mostly
through contacts regarding work, developing identities as community
members, training workshops, SFCB's newsletter, and informal contacts such as celebrations (Goodman and Hanawi 1985:16). These
means of communication were either controlled by the central office

or were task-oriented, sporadic, or substantially social. Thus SFCB's
system of communication prevented volunteers from different areas
from having direct contact with one another, enticed a small number
of volunteers to be involved more deeply in representative deliber-
ations, enhanced and formalized central control while promising
expanded participation, and diverted volunteers' interactions from
modes likely to influence governance.

In the long run, as Goodman and Hanawi stated aptly, SFCB
"has been caught in the ambiguity of a stated democratic grassroots
ideology that is coupled with tight organizational control" (1985:47).
They note the complexity of SFCB's governance system, given the
small size of the organization, and observe that in fact there were two
governance systems in 1985. The system for the staff was hierarchical;
that for the volunteers was "structured democratically." Even so,

> [s]ince the CM system is not self-governing, its democratic forums
> are limited to its internal workings; policy decisions are made
> in the program organization, and those decisions govern the CM
> system. The staff hierarchical organization tends toward a per-
> vasive central control. (Goodman and Hanawi 1985:5)

Goodman and Hanawi conclude, harshly perhaps, that SFCB
had overextended itself and had become a victim of its own extrav-
agant claims and expectations, of a vigorous but ill-conceived attempt
to realize them, and of a dynamic, powerful, and intractable leadership (1985:45–46). The aspirations and direction of the CMs themselves have changed. Today's CMs tend to be young, ambitious, and
career oriented, much like mediators in conventional ADR programs
(Hofrichter 1987). A common path to SFCB is first to learn about
ADR and then to discover that "the granddaddy of all" is in San
Francisco. The newer CMs tend not to understand how SFCB began
or to grasp its original meanings and aspirations.

Although some of the contemporary CMs are effective, others
show little interest in improving neighborhoods, "whereas the earliest
people, through 1983, most[ly] came in wanting to help other people."
The original CMs "wanted to make the world a better place," but
their contemporaries frequently are "very self-interested people."
Although "they aren't bad people," indeed are "attractive" and
"easier," their presence "changes the atmosphere for those who aren't

as educated and young, and [aren't] white" and eventually discourages some of the neighborhood CMs from participating. To a degree, then, the CM corps is becoming somewhat less multiracial and multiethnic (Val).

SFCB's standard of "not wanting to say no to anyone," of letting everyone in, helped produce such gentrification. In 1989, SFCB was planning to implement its own affirmative action program in recruiting CMs to counter this "curse of being successful" (Val).

> People are moving in and out very quickly so that we aren't developing the experience and depth that the older people have. These new people take it with them like a commodity. It's all "skills, skills, skills." You observe them doing all the right things self-consciously; the old-timers did cringeable things, but it worked. (Val)

Thus in addition to the pernicious effects of gentrification and institutionalization, CB now must deal with the possibility that technique will dominate and subvert value (Ellul 1964).

The Pronouncement of Community and the Redefinition of Empowerment

In general, the mission of empowerment was superseded by the mission of democratic governance, whose frenetic activity produced burnout. The result was a leaner, more conventional organization focusing on "the work," which came more and more to be defined as the conflict-resolution process itself (see Rothschild in this volume). Empowerment came to be understood increasingly as a matter of interpersonal relationships with personal development. Meanwhile, the understanding of "community" shifted subtly from the neighborhood to SFCB itself (see Yngvesson in this volume). We must remember that volunteers, and perhaps most staff members, never embraced collective empowerment as a key mission of SFCB. Hence SFCB's commitment to democratic governance contributed to the subversion of the mission of community empowerment and yet proved too shallow to sustain itself.

"The Work:" The Mission of Conflict Resolution Revisited

By 1983 the demise of SFCB's empowerment mission was clear and official, as the following statement by the founder makes clear.

> I believe that potentially one of our valuable contributions to building community justice programs lies in "discovering" the right mixture of direct and representational processes that will make an effective democratic organization.
>
> Two important warnings: Service, not governance, is the program's primary function.
>
> The primary task of this neighborhood justice system is conflict reduction. (Community Board Program 1983b: 13, 19, 21)

Such statements contrast strikingly with the image of a social-movement organization committed to neighborhood empowerment.

Empowerment had vanished completely from the picture, and governance was subordinated to service. The emergence of the Governing Board in the following year made the shift official. After a half-dozen years of existence, SFCB had effectively ended its flirtation with ambitions for popular justice. Significantly, the major evaluation began at this point, after much of the excitement and promise had passed. In this way the stage was set for the difficulties that would plague the evaluation: it sought to study something that essentially was no longer there.

SFCB retains traces of what it originally announced as its missions, and many of the participants, both staff members and volunteers, are veterans of the experiments in democratic governance. Yet however much of that distinctive ethos remains, few people would deny that it plays a more modest, more institutionalized role today.

Why were empowerment and then governance displaced by service as SFCB's primary goal? At an abstract level, of course, such displacement is part of a conventional process of institutionalization experienced by virtually all organizations that survive for any length of time (Selznick 1957). More concretely, perhaps the answer is simple: it may be that SFCB's staff and volunteers fell in love with the mediation work. We suggest unglamorously that SFCB displaced its overarching goals of empowerment and democratic governance with "the work" and its management.

At the organizational level of analysis, we find that the transformation of goals responded in part to shifts in resources and in conceptions of legitimacy. In short, SFCB found both money and acceptance for the intrinsic value of mediation (Jessie). This shift also suggests that SFCB became more appropriately modest about its claims and returned to its very early emphasis on cooperation (Gale).

Along with these external shifts, SFCB seems to have altered its approach to management. In getting "down to fighting weight," it has reduced staff, has focused more sharply on the size of its caseload (Val), and has begun "recruiting in a more sophisticated way" as it has begun to receive public funds and has expanded its sources of referrals to feature public agencies (Jessie; Gale). In short, SFCB now emphasizes efficiency in its internal operations as it becomes more isomorphic with its environment (Aldrich 1979).

The emphasis on efficiency reflects the reality that SFCB now confronts "much more work" with the smallest staff it has had in years. Thus SFCB's services are not all that they were in the past. For several years, SFCB generally has not gone to the homes of first-party disputants to develop cases. Exceptions are cases concerning juveniles, the presence of language problems, or the possibility of a misunderstanding about the voluntary nature of the program. Under the new regime, more case development is handled by staff, partly in response to the complexity of cases now being received from the Department of Social Services, for example, and its demand for speedy processing (Val).

Finally, SFCB has made the important shift not only to receiving referrals from public agencies, but also to providing feedback to these social-control organizations.

> To get cases to SFCB, police give cards to the kids. There are no sanctions for not showing up, but there are grey areas in terms of awareness of subtle coercion, e.g., Youth Guidance, Social Services, and Juvenile Court. (Jessie)

This description represents a SFCB radically different from that which captured the attention of the ADR field as a *community* mediation alternative. Now SFCB stresses informing the police when referred disputants use SFCB's services.

Any meaning left for empowerment in SFCB exists at the personal level (Val). The skills-and-spread form of empowerment has always been part of SFCB ideology; now it stands alone as the only conceivable form.

> People have used mediation back home or at work, meaning that personal empowerment is a natural by-product of the work. It's skills, not institution building. It's like breathing and eating; if you start breathing and eating, you'll do it someplace else. Most of this stuff works, it's not fancy and it's no big deal. It's the simplest stuff in the world. (Jessie)

The Political Meanings of SFCB

Although SFCB has enjoyed widespread praise, it also has faced criticisms throughout its history. Some of the most telling critiques focused on issues of empowerment and leadership within the organization. Wahrhaftig predicted that after its funding ended, SFCB probably would continue to survive because of the successes of case development and volunteer recruitment and training, but that it had not positioned itself to "leave a more valuable legacy of dispute processing institutions" (1982:92, 93). He attributed the latter of SFCB's failure to build on existing organizational capabilities in the neighborhoods it covered and contrasted it with the experience of the Community Association for Mediation in Pittsburgh.

Both of Wahrhaftig's predictions have been realized. SFCB has survived its funding difficulties and appears to have done so with vitality. It has a mix of community members and community elite members on its board, which is actively involved in policy making. New but experienced leadership, appropriate to current circumstances, has emerged. Yet SFCB's legacy differed from the original vision. Even SFCB veterans sometimes acknowledge their suspicion that SFCB's early funding successes may have damaged its development (Jessie).

Even without government funding, however, organizational processes seemed to be diverting SFCB from its mission of community empowerment. Possibly not the least of these processes was the symbolic usefulness of this mission as a generating and energizing force for the organization. To develop, SFCB needed such "grandiose plans" (Jessie). They were of mythic proportions, and as such they promised more than they could deliver. By definition, then, SFCB could not succeed or be sustained for long. This point is worth keeping in mind, although such a gap between plans and possibilities is not sufficient to explain the politics of the process and to identify its organizational and institutional consequences (Harrington 1985:38, 39). Unfortunately, we lack the data to examine whether something more modest than transformation resulted.

A Legacy of Ambiguous Claims

SFCB has not located its mediation offerings within an analytic framework that challenges hegemony. It has not linked mediation as a personal and interpersonal resource with a political strategy for collective action to address structural inequities that underlie recurring patterns of disputes. In fact, SFCB may have perpetuated a personalized view of disputing that constricts political discourse (Marcuse 1968) to the possibility of popular justice via community mediation. Its recent history, as outlined above, suggests that SFCB has begun to work with social-control agencies in ways that go beyond the personalization issue to raise again the specter of complicity in coercion.

If we must assess what SFCB was and has meant, the conclusion lacks splendor. SFCB was a symbol of hope, an innocuous effort in itself, expensive but promising and inspiring. Yet it did not transform San Francisco or even any of its neighborhoods, and it did not achieve the successes in political empowerment enjoyed by its contemporaries in the new populism. But neither did it do any great harm. SFCB suffers from guilt by association, and some of that misplaced. It also shares its legacy with the community-mediation movement that it propelled and reflected—a modest effort in contemporary urban republicanism, one strand of the ADR movement that required its own analysis and evaluation. Ultimately, then, SFCB was neither colonization nor empowerment; it was a deprofessionalized and quasi-indigenous initiative in "civic work" that became institutionalized as a more conventional social-service agency, difficult to classify and difficult to assess.

Perhaps the absence of a realistic, well-articulated plan for achieving empowerment and democracy, and (more fundamentally) the existence and the convincing communication of such grandiose claims, contributed to the disappointed criticism that SFCB has received along with the praise. This interpretation suggests analogies to analyses of Progressive Era social inventions such as probation and parole (Rothman 1980) and of more recent court reforms (Feeley 1983), which explain how inadequate understanding of perceived problems and exaggerated expectations of proposed reforms produce the disappointments that arise from their failure. As Scull (1982) states, however, such explanations do not take us quite far enough. They suggest merely a failure of implementation. Scull's analysis of the history of community corrections proposes instead that it may be foolish to expect political empowerment to flow from an effort as dependent on establishment funding, premises, and legitimation as was SFCB.

Beyond this observation, some thoughtful commentators have voiced troubling concerns that SFCB was part of a counterempowerment movement, either in the sense of being used rhetorically, symbolically, and with funding by those who sought to limit popular access to the courts, or at least in the diversionary sense of absorbing human energy, funds, and other resources that might have gone otherwise to other new populist endeavors more oriented toward collective action. Indeed, SFCB directed its efforts more toward individual fairness than toward collective justice.

Perhaps the main regret felt by us, the friendly critics, who are blessed with acute hindsight and who support the goals of popular justice of the people's community-mediation movement but are concerned about the possibilities of co-optation, is that SFCB did not align itself actively with new populist organizations such as Citizen Action and ACORN. Such coalitions could have benefited from the combination of macrolevel analysis of issues and strategies of collective and direct action with the mobilizing ideology, the empowering technology, and the overall respectability of community mediation. Whether such opportunities for cooperative coalition existed and were viable and, if so, why they were not realized are central issues that lie beyond the purview of this chapter.

REFERENCES

Abel, Richard L., ed. 1982. *The Politics of Informal Justice*. Vol. 1: *The American Experience*. New York: Academic.

Aldrich, Howard. 1979. *Organizations and Environments.* Englewood Cliffs, N.J.: Prenctice-Hall.

Baker, Kim. 1976. Reactions to Crime Project Field Notes, Northwestern University Archives, Evanston, Ill.

Becker, Howard S., ed. 1971. *Culture and Civility in San Francisco.* New Brunswick, N.J.: Transaction Books.

Becker, Howard S., and Irving Louis Horowitz. 1971. "The Culture of Civility." In *Culture and Civility in San Francisco,* 4–19. See Becker 1971.

Carlin, Jerome E. 1971. "Store Front Lawyers in San Francisco." In *Culture and Civility in San Francisco,* 125–50. See Becker 1971.

Center for Social Redesign. 1980. *Dispute Resolution and Neighborhood Governance: The Evolution of the Community Boards Program.* San Francisco: Center for Social Redesign.

Christie, Nils. 1977. "Conflicts as Property." *British Journal of Criminology* 17:1.

Community Board Program. 1983a. A Funding Proposal to Support Neighborhood Conflict Resolution Forums: An Experiment in Democracy and Self-Governance.

———. 1983b. *Community Board Newsletter* 4, no. 3, June–July.

———. 1988. *Community Boards Newsletter,* Fall.

Davis, Fred. 1971. "The San Francisco Mystique." In *Culture and Civility in San Francisco,* 151–61. See Becker 1971.

Delgado, Gary. 1986. *Organizing the Movement: The Roots and Growth of ACORN.* Philadelphia: Temple University Press.

DuBow, Fredric L., Oscar Goodman, and Nancy Hanawi. 1987. "Conflicts and Community: A Study of the San Francisco Community Boards." Photocopy.

Ellul, Jacques. 1964. *The Technological Society.* New York: Basic Books.

Feeley, Malcolm M. 1983. *Court Reform on Trial.* New York: Basic Books.

Fischer, Frank, and Carmen Sirianni, eds. 1984. *Critical Studies in Organization and Bureaucracy.* Philadelphia: Temple University Press.

Goodman, Oscar, and Nancy Hanawi. 1985. "Visions of Neighborhood Justice." Photocopy.

Harrington, Christine B. 1985. *Shadow Justice: The Ideology and Institutionalization of Alternatives to Court.* Westport, Conn.: Greenwood.

Hippler, Arthur E. 1971. "The Game of Black and White at Hunters Point." In *Culture and Civility in San Francisco,* 53–75. See Becker 1971.

Hofrichter, Richard. 1987. *Neighborhood Justice in Capitalist Society: The Expansion of the Informal State.* New York: Greenwood.

Lyman, Sanford M. 1971. "Red Guard on Grant Avenue." In *Culture and Civility in San Francisco,* 20–52. See Becker 1971.

Marcuse, Herbert. 1968. *One-Dimensional Man.* Boston: Beacon.

Podolefsky, Aaron. 1983. *Case Studies in Community Crime Prevention.* Springfield, Ill.: Charles Thomas.

Podolefsky, Aaron, and Frederic L. DuBow. 1981. *Strategies for Community*

Crime Prevention: Collective Responses to Crime in Urban America. Springfield, Ill.: Charles Thomas.

Reactions to Crime Project. 1977. Field notes, Northwestern University Archives, Evanston, Ill.

Rothman, David. 1980. *Conscience and Convenience: Asylums and Their Alternatives in Progressive America.* Boston: Little, Brown.

Scott, Marvin B., and Sanford M. Lyman. 1968. "Accounts." *American Sociological Review* 33:46–62.

Scull, Andrew. 1982. "Community Corrections: Panacea, Progress, or Pretense?" In *The Politics of Informal Justice,* 99–119. See Abel 1982.

Selznick, Phillip. 1957. *Leadership in Administration: A Sociological Interpretation.* Evanston, Ill.: Row, Peterson.

Shonholtz, Raymond. 1987. "The Citizen's Role in Justice: Building a Primary Justice and Prevention System at the Neighborhood Level." *Annals of the American Academy of Political and Social Science* 494:42–52.

———. 1989. Interview with Douglas R. Thomson, 9 February.

Smith, David E., John Luce, and Ernest A. Dernburg. 1971. "The Health of Haight-Ashbury." In *Culture and Civility in San Francisco,* 77–100. See Becker 1971.

Wahrhaftig, Paul. 1982. "An Overview of Community-Oriented Citizen Dispute Resolution Programs in the United States." In *The Politics of Informal Justice,* 75–99. See Abel 1982.

Wirt, Frederick M. 1971. "The Politics of Hyperpluralism." In *Culture and Civility in San Francisco,* 101–24. See Becker 1971.

———. 1974. *Power in the City: Decision Making in San Francisco.* Berkeley and Los Angeles: University of California Press.

Zisk, Betty H. 1973. *Local Interest Politics: A One-Way Street.* Indianapolis: Bobbs-Merrill.

Justice from Another Perspective: The Ideology and Developmental History of the Community Boards Program

Raymond Shonholtz

The origins and development of the San Francisco Community Boards (SFCB) ideology and program are a phenomenon more than a specific, descriptive event. Some of the chapters in this book look at SFCB from different analytical perspectives. Beyond the requirements of different disciplines, perhaps this is the only recourse that other writers can take, not having experienced the early birth or growth of the SFCB program or its development in the years they are writing about. Analysis is a form of intellectual mining, where things are broken apart for study and for the purpose of learning patterns and making comparative critique. In contrast, synthesis is a way of bringing everything together. It is the intent of this chapter to bring together as much of the phenomenon of the SFCB's ideology and work as possible.

For the reader's appreciation of the enterprise of the SFCB program, its vision and accomplishments, this chapter seeks to create a comprehensive working picture. The motivational quality of the founding participants, the organizational shifts, the geographic expansion, and the ideological terrain are presented as an integrated pattern. In creating a structure such as the SFCB to carry forth a new concept, many elements that others may analyze in isolation are in reality intertwined. For example, volunteer recruitment, community outreach, case development, staff development, training models, approaches to dispute resolution, funding strategies, board development, external political and neighborhood forums, and development of internal organization capacity were contemporaneous activities in the early years of the SFCB program.

Beginning in 1977, San Francisco Community Boards was a movement of energy and creativity in the city of San Francisco. Espousing a citizen's approach to conflict, crime, civil dissonance, and disorder, the organization engaged the imagination and commitment of hundreds of residents, volunteers, disputants, and agency and school personnel in some of the city's most difficult neighborhoods. The excitement and commitment to SFCB came from the direct work and involvement of neighborhood people creating from a simple concept a new reality for themselves and their communities.

SFCB set out to demonstrate several points: that urban residents would step forward and, through training, learn a new skill that directly related to assisting their neighbors in the early resolution of conflicts; that neighbors in conflict would accept a forum created by their neighbors to express and resolve their differences; and that a dispute-settlement process could be developed that would apply to most neighborhood conflicts. The success and power of this demonstration is detailed in this volume.

SFCB offered a new approach to handling recurring conflict and interpersonal differences that had a potential for violence in urban neighborhoods. The program emerged out of an understanding that the vast majority of homicides and felonious assaults are between people in long-standing, ongoing relationships. With this knowledge, SFCB understood the importance of a community-justice system that is able to address conflicts early and, ideally, intervene to prevent or thwart any pending violence (Shonholtz 1976a).

In developing a rationale for its endeavor, SFCB presented a critique of the formal justice system that is as valid today as it was fifteen years ago, one that community people could relate to and acknowledge. SFCB argued that the system was formal, procedural, after-the-fact, and did not address the ongoing conflictual relationships of youth, families, neighbors, teachers, or merchants.

The critique set forth in 1976 in "A System of Justice That Isn't Working and Its Impact on the Community" highlighted several points (included in Shonholtz 1984). First, the justice system forces communities and individuals to tolerate conflict until some law is broken, a person is injured, or property has been damaged. Second, a justice system based on an after-the-fact response to alleged violation of rights without any mechanism for prevention or early intervention leaves individuals at risk and communities unsafe. Third, the legal system does not address the underlying personal needs or interests that generate interpersonal conflict and often aggravates tensions between disputing parties. Fourth, the legal system suppresses and evades conflict by its language, boundaries, codes, and procedural requirements. Even within a court, emotional content is given little, if any, validation or recognition, though it might express the real needs of one or all of the parties. A party's search for recognition, acknowledgment, or an apology is difficult, if not impossible, within the adversarial process.

Fifth, the legal system makes adults dependent upon processes that often strip them of their sense of responsibility and integrity. Sixth, the value of the conflict is "stolen" from disputants by transforming what is significant in the conflict to the disputants into what is relevant to be considered by the legal process (Christie 1977). Seventh, the legal system has limited, if any, prevention or early intervention capacity and is in reality a crisis management system, even for potentially explosive conflicts that are known to friends and relatives.

Eighth, since the law treats everyone as "equal," there is no tolerance for cultural, linguistic, ethnic, racial, or value diversity. Although considered irrelevant within the legal context, factors of diversity often infused conflict, and the failure to address them leaves many people, especially minorities, feeling that the legal system is insensitive and unresponsive to their needs.

A final critique relates to the delivery of services. Public services are generally delivered to individuals who come through "deviancy channels": police; probation; social services; and welfare. In each instance, the person's need must be first documented before any service can be provided. Thus, like the formal justice system, the condition must exist and be deemed sufficient or serious enough before public services are provided. Consequently, many service agencies are themselves after-the-fact oriented and represent a static, crisis-response model.

Further, preventive service delivery is difficult for agencies. Documentation is always required because services are generally delivered based on some legal or provider justification. Not functioning at the neighborhood level, most agencies are unaware of the escalating dynamics of a potential case and are unable to receive the case early or in a preventive condition. The staffs of most agencies are oriented toward a crisis; most agencies are understaffed for prevention and lack strategies for early intervention.

This critique, experienced on a daily basis, encouraged the development of a system of justice and service that dealt with problems before the traditional, often times dysfunctional, justice system was needed. The SFCB program turned to the neighborhoods because this was where the problems were and where the people who knew about them lived. The program's intent was to create a link between those in need with those who could offer assistance. In this sense, SFCB represents a modern cultural analog to the communal interactions of an earlier American period that Auerbach discusses in *Justice without Law?* (1983).

Beyond being one of the earliest community-justice programs, SFCB offered the community-justice movement an ideological framework, organizing strategy, and organizational structure. Beginning in one community in 1976, SFCB by 1986 covered all the neighborhoods of San Francisco. Its development, successes, and longevity sparked a sustained debate in the legal community about the role of citizens in the delivery of justice services.

The Ideology of Community Justice

The SFCB program gives expression to a modern vision of a workable community-based justice service located in diverse urban neighborhoods. The vision of a community able to address its conflicts galvanized the energies of volunteers and staff and gave momentum to similar justice efforts in hundreds of communities throughout North America.

Buoyed by its ideological position and organizing strategy, SFCB did not experience the uncertainty or pessimism evident in some other programs (Beer 1986). Likewise, the organization considered its work to be a direct expansion and refutation of the narrow communal limits placed on the concept and work of community justice as described by Jerold Auerbach's *Justice without Law?* (1983). In a review of Auerbach's book (Shonholtz 1984), concern was expressed that he failed to look at contemporary examples of a working community-justice system that closely approximated what Auerbach described as existing in early American life. In many respects, SFCB can be seen as a cultural analog to the social cohesion, historical continuity, and shared interpersonal values more prevalent at an earlier point in American history. The analog shows up in the fact that even without many of the elements of community cohesion (as experienced in New England communities of the 1600s and 1700s), a new system of neighborhood justice could be achieved.

A modern community-justice system sustained through the values and labor of volunteers and the self-interests of disputants can be developed in highly diverse neighborhoods, enlisting hundreds of people in its training and service programs, and providing a first-resort conflict-settlement service for local residents outside the perimeters of the formal legal system.

One of the great advancements in the field of dispute resolution, having significant social, political, and psychological implications, has been the successful experiment in enabling citizens to directly resolve their own conflicts. This avenue, long part of the early American tradition (Auerbach 1983), has been so systematically reduced that it is now necessary to organize community-justice services anew in nearly every American urban community. Such efforts remind citizens of the powers they already possess and of their right in society to effectuate them. One of the great promises of community justice has long been its potential to reawaken citizens to their power as disputants and dispute resolvers. Without the community base for the peaceful expression and early settlement of conflict, how are communities to deal effectively with individual conflict, community disputes, or cultural, religious, or ethnic differences?

The ideology of community or informal justice is at one end of a spectrum, with the formal, legal system at the other end. With the former, individual citizens resolve their own conflicts or assist others in the nonlegal resolution of differences. From the perspective of "keeping disputants powerful," this spectrum is schematically set forth in figure 1. At the latter end, disputants have allocated to judges and third parties the responsibility and right to make decisions for them.

The demise of the historical infrastructure associated with early forms of community justice, so well articulated by Auerbach, is no accident. It is a conscious process of diminution of community power in favor of more centralized and formalized structures. SFCB created

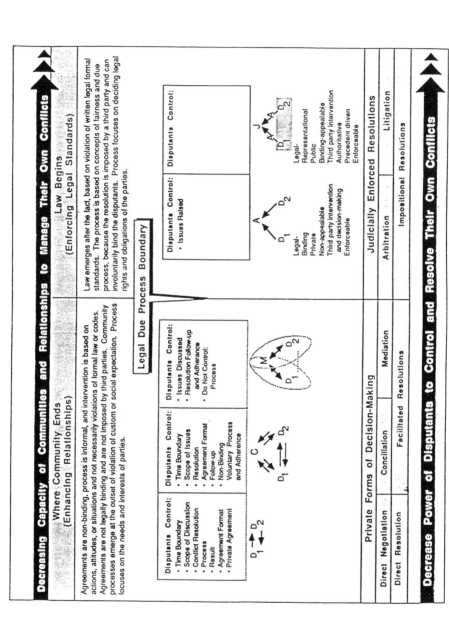

Fig. 1. Disputant power in conflict resolution models. (*Source:* Prepared by Raymond Shonholtz for the San Francisco Community Board, 1983.)

a community base for a justice experiment that went beyond building cohesive ethnic, religious, or social groups. It provided an opportunity for diverse citizens in a multiethnic and multiracial society to exercise their power to reduce local tensions and hostilities by encouraging citizens to establish and use a new, neighborhood conciliating structure.

SFCB was designed with a strong belief in citizen power and as a radical departure from the formal justice model. The SFCB concept devolves to the most essential unit of democratic society, the citizen, the full power and ability to effectuate a range of rights and responsibilities without any governmental or intermediary structure. The organizing activity of SFCB was designed to reach citizens and to place them in a context of democratic work within their neighborhoods. Through community organizing and organizational development, the program sought to build new capacity in urban neighborhoods to resolve daily conflict. Community organizing was based on the rationale that in a democratic society only citizen-based conflict-settlement mechanisms could reach disputes early and provide some reasonable process for their peaceful expression and resolution. Legal institutions constrained by statutory boundaries could not prevent or diminish a conflict without first establishing some basis for intervention. Citizens, working within a local mediating structure, have no such limits (see fig. 1).

Accordingly, the number of cases a neighborhood dispute-resolution service receives or hears, its impact on the courts, its relationship with agency personnel and police, the scope of the dispute-resolution service, and its costs compared to other social systems are all important, yet are secondary concerns to the central ideological themes inherent in community justice: the renewed, reclaimed, and restated role and function of the citizen as the primary intervener in the early settlement of conflict.

The Politics of Community Justice

Understanding the ideology of SFCB will give the reader a more critical perspective when reading other chapters in this book. While each author presents a different analysis, no chapter challenges the community-justice movement's central theme of citizen power and the important role of citizens in dispute settlement.

The concept of the citizen as a genuine actor in democratic society (beyond the vote) has always been unnerving to those in control of institutional life. SFCB was early on described as an antijustice program by those within the legal community. The concept was attacked for not seeking to reduce courts' caseloads, being too expensive, not having professionals hearing cases, requiring too much community-organizing time, or being too inward and intraorganizationally oriented. Legal theorists attacked it for being a new form of informal social control that enabled the state to intrude into the lives of citizens through new state-supported or state-connected mechanisms. Some of these critiques are found in different chapters of this book. Mostly, the chapters reflect the vitality of some of the early issues associated with SFCB, when the Law Enforcement Assistance Administration (LEAA) saw it as an "anti-justice project" in the Evaluation of the Neighborhood Justice Centers; as presented to the National Evaluation Advisory Committee; and when Professor Rick Abel viewed it as a possible social-control initiative (1982). Dr. Dan McGillis considered it as a new model for neighborhoods (1978). And scholars like Nils Christie (1977) and Jacek Kurczewski and Kaximierz Frieske (1978) articulated it as an evolution of people's own sense of power and democratic action. The latest attack against community justice can be found in the disclaimers of "harmony theory" and its community expression, the SFCB program.

Nonetheless, many of the chapter critiques further our understanding and appreciation of how to improve community-justice systems and amplify their central premise of citizen initiative. This book is a microcosm of an ongoing debate.

Community Boards: The Historical Perspective

To achieve a realistic understanding and, perhaps, appraisal of the SFCB program, its philosophy and endeavor, it is important to understand why it was organized, how it was formed, the goals it articulated, and the achievements it realized.

At the Beginning

The seminal idea for the SFCB program emerged while I served as the task-force leader of a penal code reform project on criminal justice for the California Assembly in 1974. The task force was responsible for redrafting the state penal code. Two staff members of the task force examined programs that kept first-offender youth from penetrating too far into the juvenile justice system. Citizen panels attached to juvenile courts in King County, Washington, and Edinburgh, Scotland, were specifically examined. These two jurisdictions were diverting pre- and postfiled cases out of the juvenile system and forwarding them to panels composed of community leaders and residents. Although there was no intent of passing legislation, a bill was prepared for the Assembly committee's consideration that proposed the creation of citizen panels based on high school districts throughout the state of California.

The task force completed its work in 1975, and I took a position as a Criminal Law Associate and co-director of the Criminal Law Clinic at University of San Francisco's School of Law. Throughout the year, I continued to think about the concept of citizen panels and wrote a concept paper on the creation of "Community 'No-Fault' Boards" (1976a).

This paper presented the case for a community-based approach to civil and criminal justice and the rationale for the SFCB program. Working from this paper, I presented the concept of a new form of neighborhood justice and process to over fifty community and legal groups in San Francisco. Although there was some skepticism, there was little or no opposition to the concept of building an early-intervention- and prevention-oriented, neighborhood-based system of conflict resolution. The most responsive groups included minority churches, especially black, and the local neighborhood organizations. In addition, the San Francisco Bar Association, legal-assistance offices, and police department indicated either support or no opposition to the community-justice experiment. The city of San Francisco at this time was run by the Moscone-Burton liberal wing of the Democratic party. Mayor Moscone had strong credentials in the city's neighborhoods and in Delancy Street, the city's premier residential facility for felons. Delancy Street asserts an influential role in city politics and neighborhood affairs. The SFCB program soon developed a close working relationship with Delancy Street, and Mimi Silbert, its codirector, served for several years as the chair of SFCB's Board of Directors.

In 1976, I took a leave from the USF Law School, became a Fellow of the Robert F. Kennedy Memorial, and began the process of developing an organization, staff, office, board of directors, funding strategy, and a host of other like activities relevant to launching the SFCB program. The concept received considerable attention when Professor Dan McGillis included it in *Neighborhood Justice Centers*, his U.S. Department of Justice study of four promising conflict-resolution models (1978). McGillis's inclusion of the SFCB model legitimated the experiment, made it more visible, assisted the fund-raising effort, and articulated the program's ideological and organizational model. About the same time, Professor Fredric DuBow was managing a seven-city program for the Law Enforcement Assistance Administration's Reactions to Crime project. One of the neighborhoods in San Francisco selected by DuBow's team was Visitacion Valley, an area the SFCB program independently selected and developed as its first neighborhood conflict-resolution forum.

The major experimental work took place in the first two of the organization's many neighborhood forums: Visitacion Valley and Bernal Heights. Visitacion Valley is a low-income, primarily working-class community with considerable white/black racial tension. During one of the SFCB's planning meetings, the leading community organization in Visitacion Valley divided along racial lines over continued white resident involvement in the Reactions to Crime project.

After several unsuccessful organizing efforts in the black housing projects, a successful organizing strategy was designed by Bruce Thomas, a highly skilled organizer, who had worked for George Wiley's Welfare Rights Organization. Thomas had a unique sense for what SFCB was not: namely, an advocacy organization. After assessing the limitations of earlier organizing attempts, Thomas articulated a service-delivery model of organizing that brought volunteers together to do something for themselves, as opposed to mobilizing them to put pressure on "Downtown" or the mayor. Thomas's organizing brought the first group of volunteers into the program.

The Dispute-Resolution Panel

Two initial dispute-resolution trainings for volunteers were conducted first by the Community Relations Service of the U.S. Justice Department and then by the American Arbitration Association. Both trainings, involving approximately twenty-five community residents, proved to be too formal and rigid for the case and hearing needs of the program. Volunteers in 1977 were asked to go through a third training. This was conducted by Philip Zeigler, a therapist and trainer. Zeigler developed a model that related to the emotional and expressive needs associated with those in conflict. The training model was linked to the conflict-resolution process model that David Straus from Interaction Associates and I developed. Zeigler subsequently trained Kenneth Hawkins, then a staff case developer, to be the organization's lead community trainer.

The explicit assumptions underlining the dispute-resolution panel process included: a panel of three to five trained dispute resolvers; panelists living in the same community as the disputing parties; the panelists meeting with all the disputants together and none of them privately; the disputants inviting whomever they pleased to the hearing; the panel having no contractual, legal, or formal power or authority over the disputants or the dispute; and the panel fairly representing the composition of the community it served.

An innovation of SFCB that heightened citizen involvement and became a hallmark for community-justice programs was the panel and the hearing process. The panel was conceived as a counterbalance to the authoritarian structure of the judicial system and as a multi-faceted expression of the community's interest in conflict resolution.

The panel represented the third entity in the victim-offender paradigm: the community. Violence and conflict take place within a community. The community was conceived as a stakeholder in any dispute. The presence of the community through the panelists served to reduce the propensity for violence or bad behavior between disputing neighbors during the hearing process and, hopefully, afterwards.

This concept of a visible community presence in the panel serves as an analog to the early American community dispute-settlement practices presented by Auerbach (1983). The panel can fairly approximate the demographic characteristics of the community and assist disputants in feeling comfortable in the voluntary dispute-settlement process. It can demonstrate teamwork and the forms of cooperation that it sought from the disputing parties themselves. The panel is an expression of resident skills in action and the ability of local people to administer a justice process on behalf of their peers. It serves as an expression of the civic commitment of residents to provide to their peers a forum for the early expression and resolution of conflicts.

The panel process and interactions preclude any panelist from dominating or taking sides. The panel provides on-the-job training for new panelists and a monitoring process for the transmission of knowledge and skills.

The panel presents in microcosm various aspects of the community-justice model. Disputants retain the full power to resolve their own matters while they are provided a balanced ethnic and racial group of trained citizens to assist them. Through the panel, the neighborhood provides a visible and cooperative process for residents to use to ameliorate differences and to reduce tensions regardless of the legal definition of the situation. The panel expresses the civic quality of community life and the relevant work of citizens. Furthermore, it defines an authentic realm for citizen participation in justice at the community level. But most significantly, it presents a model for the exercise of democratic power and responsibility by the disputants themselves. Not extracting power from them nor "stealing" their conflict, "as is common within the legal process" (Christie 1991), the panel models how disputants in democratic society can remain powerful in the peaceful expression and resolution of their own conflict.

SFCB Terminology

In the development of SFCB, a conscious effort was made to delete the term *volunteer* from the organization's lexicon. To many people, especially in low-income and minority communities, the term volunteer has a negative or perjorative connotation and often refers to the donated time of women. Since the program was building a service of justice in the neighborhoods, there was a need to strengthen the community's regard for the status of the volunteer worker. To achieve this end, the term *community* was linked to the term *member.* Externally, *community member* referred to one who lived in the neighborhood he or she served. Within the organization, community member refers to one who has completed the program's training in one or more roles and is competent to offer a service to his or her neighborhood. The distinction between these external and internal definitions has not been fully understood by some of the writers in this volume.

After several neighborhoods were organized they were grouped into a forum, which had a local field office, staff, and community members able to provide services to the neighborhoods within the forum's district. One of the forum's services was the panel hearing, a process through which trained volunteers assist disputants in the expression and resolution of their conflict. Community members trained to communicate with disputants and encourage their use of the neighborhood-forum process are called *case developers*. Persons who are trained to inform the community about the service and training programs are referred to as *outreach workers*.

The process developed for the hearing panels was termed *conciliation*, derived from the Latin *conciliare* or "one who brings people together." In conciliation, the goal is to reunite the parties physically and psychologically. The conciliation process encourages disputants to express to one another their feeling about the conflict before they get into the back-and-forth of negotiations. Generally, the entire conciliation process is done in the open without the use of separate meetings with disputants. Thus each disputant becomes intimately aware of the real issues and emotional concerns of the other party. Since most disputants are in some continued relationship, using the conflict as a vehicle toward better emotional understanding can be extremely important and, at times, perhaps more valuable than a mechanistic resolution. This would be the case where roommates need to continue to live together, teachers need to continue to teach in the classroom where a student is acting out, or business partners need to continue their working relationship with greater understanding if their labors are to succeed.

Some writers in this volume highlight disproportionately the "feeling" aspect of SFCB's dispute-resolution process over the contextual and negotiating components (see Rothschild in this volume). Clearly all three parts are necessary. Nonetheless, it is clear from hundreds of conciliations that have reached written resolution that for the agreements to hold up it is necessary for disputants to fully express the emotive content in their conflict, to come to mutual understanding as to what is important about the dispute from the other disputant's perspective, and to make some reasonable accommodations based on this new understanding. To achieve an agreement in a limited period of time where the parties might be initially distrustful, suspicious, hostile, or uncertain of one another requires grounding the dispute-settlement process in the emotional needs of the disputants. If this can be addressed and reasonably satisfied, the nonlegal agreement will hold up without force of law or formal authority behind it. This has been one of the great learning experiences of the community-justice movement that warrants greater study, development, and application.

The organization's terminology has been used by SFCB from nearly its inception and adopted by hundreds of community and school programs in the United States and abroad.

The Motivation to Serve

From the beginning, SFCB generated strong involvement and commitment by community members and staff. The motivational energy comes from the positive nature of the work, the skills and new abilities people learn, and the visible impact of the process on conflicts. SFCB sought to create within the community a new dimension of civic work exclusively under the control of neighborhood residents. SFCB created new civic work space for neighborhood people and made it exclusively theirs.

The ownership of the work and the recognition that community people are building something new in their neighborhoods has sustained a very high élan throughout the program's history. While many community members initially came to the Community Boards out of negative experiences with the legal system, this alone would not account for an average of 120 hours of donated time per community member per year (DuBow 1987; see DuBow and McEwen in this volume). Nor would it account for the nearly 25 percent who became community members after first being disputants (DuBow 1987). Specific attributes of the organization's mission to create a community-justice system deepened the bond of participants to the organization. These included the nature of the work; the relations it generated between community members and neighborhood residents; the friendships created between community members; the satisfaction with making a contribution to one's community; and the incorporation of negotiation and communication as important personal social skills.

SFCB began to manifest the elements of a movement by 1979. The organization, through its community members and staff, espoused vision, commitment, community involvement, energy, and control of one's life and important aspects of the neighborhood. While many personal examples of commitment abound, like the woman who left money to SFCB in her will or the people who found through the work personal value that overcame a need for antidepression medicine, the best account can be seen in something as simple as potluck dinners. By 1978, it was well known in the southern part of San Francisco that you ate really well at SFCB work potlucks. People, many of whom had little in their own lives, brought ample quantities of excellent food. For many, the program was providing something very important, both personal and communitarian. The preparation of food is a statement of caring and nourishment, both of which were in abundance in the organization's developmental period.

It became common for one family member to go through the training only to be followed by another at the next training session. Families were incorporating the communication and conciliation skills within their own home, work, and community domains. It was this understanding of what the skills and service could mean for the neighborhoods that sustained hard-working community members and their willingness to attend organizational meetings, training sesssions, and community-outreach functions. Some authors of chapters in this volume have misunderstood this development and classified it as an organizational goal. This interpretation is an inversion of the objective context: it was the shared participation in civic work that created the context for relationship building, rather than relationship building being an organizational goal in order to perform or deliver a social service.

Scope and Limits of SFCB's Organizing

SFCB sought to build a new capacity or resuscitate an earlier capacity of communities to reduce tensions and hostilities between people in conflict. It developed this capacity by recruiting and training neighborhood residents to perform a service to their community. Through the service, the neighborhoods would be stronger for the relationships that had been built, the new skills that were developed and shared, and the disputes that were expressed and resolved. As envisioned, SFCB serves to enhance the quality of community life. Yet this was not the organization's primary task. SFCB staff and volunteers were not primarily about the business of building community. The organization has been about the business of building capacity in neighborhoods to better manage individual and community issues and conflicts.

SFCB never took as its mission the direct restructuring of political power, economic relationships, or issues of social conditions (poverty, bad housing, racism, illiteracy, etc.). Nor has SFCB sought to build an internal community through voluntarism and the empowerment of individuals, as Professor Barbara Yngvesson suggests in this volume.

In the early days, SFCB staff, community members, and members of the board of directors struggled over the question of whether SFCB was an organizing project using conflict resolution as a vehicle, or a conflict-resolution program needing a community base. The answer to this question was taken very seriously, as it would shape the allocation of resources, the type of staff brought in, the external relationships of the program, and the organization's work. After nearly two years of examination and struggle over this question, from 1977–79, SFCB developed a mission statement that placed emphasis on its conflict-resolution dimension over organizing as a priority area of attention and focus:

> The purpose of the SFCB Program is to enable neighborhoods and their residents to express and resolve a broad range of individual and community conflicts through neighborhood forums.

The purpose of the organization was not to build community per se, but to build a capacity within the community to enable a range of conflicts to be heard by the community itself. SFCB, after 1979, explicitly moved away from any form of traditional community organizing and adhered to a service-organizing model that promoted the community's capacity to hear and resolve its own disputes. In this endeavor, SFCB has been extremely successful. These distinctions in organizing and the mission of SFCB formed the subsequent development of the program.

By being advocates for a service system of conflict management in the neighborhood, SFCB removed itself as a traditional community-advocacy organization. It therefore did not compete with local advocacy groups nor espouse their issues. This was one of the major reasons SFCB enjoyed the local support of neighborhood advocacy organizations. Moreover, by not taking an advocacy stance on larger social or structural issues, it enabled disputants to raise and address these questions in a SFCB forum where all could participate.

A Vehicle for Large-Group Disputes

The model that SFCB developed relates primarily to issues that can generate violence and hostility between people. As such, the program's primary focus is on disputes between people who have ongoing or prior relationships. SFCBs did not hear its first large-group dispute until 1980.

To address complex and large-group issues, SFCB developed a large-group hearing format, which was initially designed by several active community members/panelists under the leadership of staff member Georgia Quinones. This format allows for the expression and negotiation of social and economic issues between disputants.

This was illustrated in SFCB's first large-group hearing, concerned with the location of a halfway home for mentally ill seniors in the community of Bernal Heights. Over 125 residents attended the hearing. The function of the five-member SFCB panel was to facilitate a dialogue between the promoters of the halfway home, the immediate residents who opposed (mostly out of fear), and the surrounding neighborhood residents, who had a series of concerns regarding the planning for the needs of the seniors (e.g., availability of recreation, food, and transportation). While SFCB brought all the parties together and informed the neighborhood of the meeting, it did not seek to organize the neighborhood around "structural issues," promote a political agenda, or frame the dialogue for the parties. Nonetheless, in four hours of community discussions, issues were clarified, major concessions made by the promoters, fear was reduced, and the Dan Carrol House (named after a SFCB staff member who died in a car accident) became a residential reality for mentally ill seniors in Bernal Heights.

SFCB's dispute-settlement process focused on disputants articulating their concerns and achieving resolutions relevant to their needs, while using their time together as an opportunity to improve communication and understanding and reduce tensions and potential hostilites. Many matters that bring people to violence have larger social dimensions (e.g., racism, poverty, poor housing, tense work lives), yet SFCB organized itself to let these issues arise and be worked on by local, Saul Alinsky–styled advocacy organizations. In communities with diverse community organizations this approach generated respect for the San Francisco Commuity Boards' unique role and function and enabled social advocates to bring countless large-group disputes to the panels. By developing a service versus advocacy strategy that excluded no one or issue, SFCB's dispute-settlement dimension grew steadily over time.

Training as a Change Agent

The program learned by 1980 that training crossed race, ethnicity, and gender lines in the city's diverse neighborhoods. Training as an outreach strategy significantly contributed to SFCB's being one of the most multiethnic and multiracial volunteer organizations in the city. Moreover, training residents in conflict-management skills proved to be a powerful organizing tool.

Armed with this knowledge, the organization decided to embark on a major training effort that would introduce third-party conflict-resolution skills to as many neighborhood residents as possible. Thus, well beyond the organization's need for conciliators or community members, an initiative was undertaken in the latter part of 1980 to enhance the internal organization's capacity to train at least a hundred residents at a time. SFCB's mass training gave it broader recognition in the neighborhoods and city, while introducing people to one another from the many different communities. The interactions from these training sessions were extraordinarily positive. By the late 1980s, SFCB had over 2,200 residents trained in third-party dispute-settlement skills.

Through training, SFCB saw itself as advancing a new process and skill in the city. Moreover, the more the organization came to appreciate the important role of early intervention and prevention in the management of conflicts, the more it sought to make these skills available to residents in the home, at work, and with peers. During the 1980s, training became as important as of the panel, case development, or outreach functions, and a critical part of the base-building effort.

SFCBs as a First Resort Service

By 1983, SFCB began conducting more panel hearings than the city court held jury trials. Prior to this date, the program worked in selected areas of San Francisco. With city-wide expansion came more calls for service. SFCB learned early on that not all calls for service are conflicts and those that are may be inappropriate for a neighborhood forum (e.g., welfare recipient's dispute with the welfare department over the amount of the welfare check). Operationally, the program accepts any conflict as long as the parties voluntarily want to discuss it. There are no conceptual, practical, or organizational limitations to the types of issues a neighborhood forum can hear.

By creating a neighborhood-justice system of first resort and educating residents and agency personnel about its mode of operation, many cases can come directly to a neighborhood forum. For example, in assessing the police log data collected during the evaluation, 16.8 percent of cases reported to the police involved ongoing relationships and were suitable to SFCB's process. Indeed, as many as 60 percent of the 541 incidents in the police logs could be categorized this way. Moreover, a significant percent of cases handled by SFCB had a history of violence or fear of violence, with nearly 47 percent having prior police contacts. In short, SFCB could handle a significant percent of current police cases, including those having some associated violence (DuBow 1987; see DuBow and Currie in this volume).

A first-resort neighborhood system of justice has implications for the reduction of hostilities and violence in urban communities, especially in cases where disputants are intimate or have close working relationships. Moreover, community-justice systems can generate new insights that can be translated into public policy. For example, the evaluation's police study revealed that nearly one-third of the disputants had tried unsuccessfully to use some agency service before using SFCB (see DuBow and Currie in this volume). A policy that more directly encouraged disputing parties to use a SFCB forum would be highly appropriate in these cases.

Such a policy would reflect a strong educational program informing citizens when and how to use an early intervention, conflict-prevention system operating in their neighborhoods. The policy would also integrate police call responses with neighborhood dispute-resolution services and improve, thereby, the discretionary capacity of the police to elect the best response among a range of options while affording citizens a state-encouraged process of settlement.

The Program's Growth and Operational Themes

During the formative years, from 1978 through 1984, the program had four major operational themes. These included growth and development, building the capacity of forums, organizational stability, and governance and democratic ideology.

Growth and Development

From 1977 to 1982, SFCB embarked upon a major period of organizational growth. During this period, the program expanded into nearly a dozen neighborhoods of San Francisco and opened five community offices; recruited and trained several hundred volunteers to serve as community members; developed as roles for community members all the various functions associated with delivering the conflict-resolution service (case developer, outreach worker, panelist, and trainer); developed community-member leadership and area committees to supervise and coordinate forum activities; developed a program to train community members as trainers of new members, which enabled the organization to train nearly 125 members at a time; established planning and evaluation groups attached to local forums composed of trained community members; and built a trained staff able to coordinate the work of the community members, recruit new members, and participate in a diverse range of forum training and activities.

Building Forum Capacity

During this same period, the program embarked upon one of its most successful thematic operations: building the organization's capacity to deliver service. At the beginning of the 1980s, attention was devoted to building the capacity of the neighborhood forums. "Capacity building" came to mean the ability of a local forum to perform all the service work with limited involvement by staff.

By the end of 1981, SFCB was engaged in capacity building. "The intent behind the capacity effort focused on reducing neighborhood dependency on a large paid staff [and] making more of the work of a conflict resolution forum the activity and responsibility of community members and neighborhoods" (Community Boards Program 1981). The leadership for this level of highly intensive staff and community-member work came from several people within the organization. Paul Rupert, Program Manager, was a key figure in the early success of the program. He brought a unique blend of organizational know-how, commitment, drive, and loyalty that linked staff and community members' mutual aspirations for the program.

By the end of 1982, with the inclusion of the Western Addition and Haight/Fillmore areas, SFCBs covered nineteen neighborhoods of the city amalgamated into six forums, each having a local field office, and serving a total constituency of approximately 250,000 people.

The forums developed in Visitacion Valley and Bernal Heights, the first two SFCB areas, became the organization's models for the new areas. The initial two staff leaders, Georgia Quinones and Rita Adrian, the former later to serve as the first Director of SFCB of San Francisco and the latter to serve later as coordinator of the SFCB service citywide, promoted leadership, skills, and commitment for the new area-forum staffs and community members.

The most critical success factor during these early years related to the equality of the community members. These volunteers were the creative and inspirational energy for the program. The list of early community-member leaders in the program is too long to set forth without inadvertently failing to give recognition. Nonetheless, the leadership of Betty Parshall, Luisa Esquierrro, and Martin Harrington from the early neighborhoods of Visitacion Valley, Mission, and Bernal Heights would be commonly validated.

By the end of 1984, each forum had a cadre of trainers able to train new community members in the case, hearing, and outreach roles; a pool of case developers who could meet with disputants and, if appropriate, bring a case to hearing; a diverse body of panelists able to conduct individual, large group, or bilingual hearings (in over six languages) in single or multiple sessions; trainers who could observe the hearing and discuss techniques with the panelists in post-hearing sessions; outreach workers who could inform the community through knocking on doors and making presentations at school, church, or community-organization meetings about the scope of SFCB's conflict-resolution service and training program, and recruit for cases and new community members; and an elected member managing the daily service, governance, and planning and evaluation needs of his or her local forum. By 1985 an increasing number of hearings were "staffed" only by panelists who were community members, case developers, and trainers with no paid staff person in attendance.

An additional dimension of the capacity-building initiative concerned the development of a community base for each forum. Community members were trained by Judith Lynch, SFCB's director of communications, in presentation and outreach skills. Each forum's outreach workers developed annual plans to enhance and strengthen the forum's connections with community groups, schools, churches, housing projects, and business organizations. This educational and service approach contributed to local forums receiving awards from neighborhood organizations for exemplary community service.

The capacity-building program is one of SFCB's great successes and served to deepen the organization as a communitarian service program in the neighborhoods. Some authors in this volume critique this endeavor as creating a "community of volunteers or community members" instead of creating community generally. Some of the critics have not understood the rationale for the capacity-building initiative and have only observed one aspect of its success: the bonding of community members and their commitment to the organization. While such association is understandable given the amount of training and service time each volunteer generally commits (nearly 120 hours per year per community member), this was not the goal or intent of the capacity-building initiative. The primary purpose of the capacity initiative was to make each forum more self-reliant.

Through enhanced capacity, each forum became more independent and capable of planning and organizing special trainings, outreach programs, and case-development strategies appropriate for their different neighborhoods without requiring additional staff. Over time the staff in each area forum was reduced from four to two as community members took on more of the service and governance roles. The capacity-building program transformed SFCB from an organization with discrete activities performed by trained volunteers to a comprehensive, volunteer, service-delivery system, decentralized at the neighborhood level, operating throughout the city of approximately 720,000 citizens.

Organizational Stability

In 1983 through 1984, SFCB's focus shifted to a greater emphasis on stabilizing the entire multioffice enterprise. Improvement in service delivery, recruitment of new community members, revised training formats, and training and educating more residents in conflict-resolution skills became part of each forum's work. Likewise, learning how to better coordinate 45–120 volunteers associated with each forum became increasingly important, and various experiments in coordinating staff and community members were undertaken. Similarly, the central office took on more responsibility in programwide coordination, planning, and budget work, and became more closely affiliated with the Governing Board, a body elected from the forums and responsible for the daily management of the neighborhood conflict-resolution service throughout the city.

The overall stabilization of the program required refinement in central management to coordinate the diverse aspects of the program, including the expansion of community members' roles and functions; the expansion of the community service to include both conflict resolution and training; geographic expansion of the program through the city's neighborhoods; and development of the democratically elected Governing Board.

The central and field staff received more organizational training and a Tavistock organizational consultant assisted in improving the quality of intrastaff communications and the overall continuity of operational performance. These were demanding years, necessitating a committed staff willing to work in excess of sixty hours a week and community members willing to attend countless meetings.

Governance

Concomitant with its expansion of services through volunteers, SFCB in the early 1980s gave increased attention to democratic structural forms, decision-making processes, and organizational governance at the level of the forum and citywide.

Expanding the democratic aspects of the SFCB proved a new challenge. By 1981, the organization was quite diverse, representing different neighborhoods and engaging many different organizations and racial and ethnic constituencies. The democratic thrust devolved to community members the overall responsibility for program and budget within the forums and for the operations of SFCB of San Francisco. This devolution of responsibility and authority away from the central office was reflected in the program's mission statement in 1982:

> The purpose of SFCB is to maintain an organization of democratic neighborhood forums to enable neighborhoods and their residents to express and resolve a broad range of individual and community conflicts.

Prior to 1982, the mission statement did not refer to either "an organization" or "democratic neighborhood forums." At this historical juncture, attention focused on the formation of area committees to manage the neighborhood forums. Each of the six area committees had elected representatives from the local community membership, who were responsible for a broad range of forum activities.

On top of the area-committee structure was the Governing Board, composed of two elected representatives from each of the six area forums and two members of the Board of Directors. Elected representatives on the Governing Board also sat on the local area committee. The Governing Board received a formal written charter from the Corporate Board of Directors that enabled it to hire a director for Community Boards of San Francisco, plan forumwide activities within the six areas, and dispense an annual budget ranging over the years from approximately $160,000 to $300,000. The Board of Directors held responsibility for oversight of the organization's national center (see below).

The Governing Board served to internalize the democratic ideology of the program. It also enhanced the authority and responsibility of the community members while reducing the strong staff line personified in my role as president and founder. The Governing Board promoted greater working relationships among the diverse neighborhood forums. By 1987, the success of the Governing Board and the anticipated passage of the state legislation on dispute resolution (see below), warranted amalgamation of the corporate board into the Governing Board structure.

From its inception, SFCB through its president espoused strong democratic and civic themes. At graduation ceremonies it was common to read sections from the Ninth and Tenth Amendments to the U.S. Constitution that affirm the rights reserved to citizens and to link the civic actions of SFCB as a demonstration of the rights and responsibilities intended by the reservation clauses of these amendments.

SFCB's funding proposals, annual reports, newsletters, and special publications all stressed the importance of civic democracy at the community level as a right and responsibility of citizens.

The interrelationship between the constitutional guarantees of civic power and service are well summarized by the following: "The neighborhood justice work compels broader conceptual consideration of democratic ideology and neighborhood self-governance. SFCB provides a service that is derived from the direct participation of the community members who are seeking to ameliorate conflicts within their neighborhoods. This is a self-governance activity of the neighborhood and is work that promotes the democratic role of citizens in voluntarily performing civic responsibilities" (Shonholtz 1987).

Neighborhood governance became an overarching theme for the organization's work, and included the importance of civic work and the civic roles and functions of citizens; conflict prevention and reduction as a neighborhood responsibility; the importance and positive value of conflict; diversity as a community strength; and service as a right of citizenship founded in the Constitution (Shonholtz 1983, 1985).

The Impacts of a System of Community Justice

The success of the SFCB experiment can be seen in the graph originally prepared by the Center for Social Redesign (CSR) for the San Francisco Foundation in 1982 (see fig. 2). After extensive interviews and observations of hearings, cases, and the work of community members, the CSR evaluation sketched out an impressive range of possible impacts associated with a community conflict-

Primary effects	Secondary effects	Tertiary effects and beyond	
Provides a forum for the clarification of norms and values	Builds common understandings about appropriate behavior	Develops informal social control, reduces public deviance	Reduces fear of crime
Provides a justice forum that teaches individual and collective responsibility	Promotes sense of responsibility in other situations	Gives community a sense of control	Increases local autonomy
Builds skills, gives individuals feelings of accomplishments	Develops local leadership, participation, and problem solving		
	Gives sense of accomplishment		
Provides an opportunity for a diverse set of people to work together on concrete problems	Decreases fear of groups unlike oneself		
Facilitates communication, especially when hostile relationships occur because of different life-styles	Builds understanding of and respect for different life-styles	Builds sense of relatedness to others in the community	Counteracts alienation and isolation
Provides a forum for the transformation of individual grievances into collective problems	Allows important local issues and local resources to be identified	Gives impetus to action for social reforms	
Provides a new vehicle for solving disputes that appears fair and just to participants	Provides solutions for cases that defy resolution	Promotes acceptance of a more formal, less faultfinding justice system	Reduces alienation toward others and toward social institutions
	Heightens understanding of the role, pervasiveness, and potential benefits of conflict		

Fig. 2. Possible effects on the community of a community-based conflict resolution system. (*Source:* Evaluation Profile of Community Boards by Center for Social Redesign, 1981.)

resolution program. A close examination of the "primary effect" category provides a constructive insight into the importance of developing an early intervention and prevention system at the community level to reduce the potential for aggravated conflict. In many respects, the chart summarizes what many staff and community members experienced in developing and maintaining the neighborhood-justice service. Moreover, the chart serves as a good social index for the relationship between a community-justice program and issues common in urban neighborhoods: fear, conflict, neighborhood diversity, intolerance, and alienation.

Much of the summary items listed in the chart were subject to further documentation in the DuBow evaluation, especially in the studies of the cases and intensive cases, community members, and neighborhood recognition. The chart provides another window into the complex potential of community-justice programs. There are many indications of the chart's primary and secondary effects in both the CRS study and the DuBow evaluation. Many of the chapters in this volume highlight this information, especially Professor Craig McEwen and Fred DuBow's. Some of the most challenging impacts are those listed under "tertiary effects and beyond." Here we begin to see the larger social implications of a citizen-based initiative and the sociopolitical character of the results.

The secondary and tertiary conclusions set forth in figure 2 were subject to further documentation in the DuBow evaluation, especially in the studies of cases, intensive cases, community members, and neighborhood recognition. The chart provides another window into the complex potential of community-justice programs. While the primary and secondary effects noted in the chart are underscored in the DuBow data samples and studies (e.g., DuBow and McEwen in this volume; Merry in this volume), it is the tertiary effects noted in the chart that highlight the challenging position of community-justice systems and ideology. Here the larger implications of a volunteer justice service are presented, which respond to the deeper need of modern urban residents.

Given the increasing ethnic and racial diversity of urban communities, and the growing tensions within them, it is significant that the neighborhood-justice mode offers "less fault finding," "reduces alienation," "builds a sense of relatedness to others in the community," "counteracts isolation," "reduces fear of crime," and "gives impetus to action for social reforms."

As citizen participation in civic affairs and decision-making become the accepted pattern of urban governance, the ability of social justice programs, like San Francisco Community Boards, to "increase local autonomy" and foster "a sense of community control" warrant the urgent support of policymakers.

Broadening and Sustaining Community Justice through a National Center

Beginning in 1983 and continuing through 1987, SFCB moved into a period of institution building while simultaneously developing a strategy to reduce its dependence on the support of private foundations. To achieve these ends, the program embarked on four interrelated initiatives: developing links with local agencies; developing a national center to spread ideas and to generate income; drafting and implementing legislation that would promote community-justice programs and provide new sources of income; and promoting a national organization of community-justice programs that would further the ideology, innovative funding schemes, and legislative activities of community justice.

As early as 1981, the organization received a grant from the William and Flora Hewlett Foundation to explore the development of a national center. The Community Board Center for Policy and Training was created soon afterwards, and it became the vehicle for implementing the above initiatives.

Linkages, Dissemination of Ideas, and New Forms of Income

The Center for Policy and Training served as the laboratory for many new conflict-resolution projects and institutes, including the School Conflict Managers Program, Community Justice Planning and Development Institutes, Native American Conflict Resolution Institutes, conflict resolution in housing projects, youth employment and training programs, conflict-resolution programs for incarcerated youth, and conflict-resolution models for corporations and transportation industries. The development of the University of California Community Justice Board for faculty, student, and administrator disputes emerged through the center's work with UCLA's ombudsman, Donald Hartsock, who led the movement for university-based conciliation programs. By the end of 1987 the center, under the able leadership of Terry Amsler (who began with SFCB as a neighborhood case developer in 1978), generated approximately 20–25 percent of the total organization's revenue. Several of the center's projects, most notably the School Conflict Managers Program, have been replicated in thousands of schools in the United States and abroad, and provide a sustained source of revenue to the organization over the past several years.

The School Conflict Managers Program was one of the nation's earliest primary and secondary student conflict resolution training initiatives. Now in dozens of San Francisco's public and parochial schools (grades K–12), the Conflict Managers Program brought the entire organization closer to the city's schools and to many youth-serving organizations. Under the leadership of Gail Sadalla, the two initial school experiments expanded to several dozen through an innovative teachers' training-for-trainers program. School district resource personnel were trained as trainers with the mission to train teachers how to establish conflict-manager programs and train the youth as conflict managers. This approach became the format for the Conflict Manager Institutes conducted throughout the United States and Canada that effectively placed the Conflict Managers Program in the hands of thousands of students in North America.

The success of the Conflict Managers Program encouraged the Johnson Foundation to give a grant for the development of communication and conflict resolution curriculum, grades K–12. Meg Holmberg and Manti Henriquez, in collaboration with Gail Sadalla, developed a primary and secondary curriculum that is one of SFCB's bestsellers.

Consistent with its goal to create linkages for the neighborhood-justice service, the center by 1985 had developed third-party dispute-resolution procedures in youth employment and training organizations, juvenile probation and residential facilities, and special child-abuse cases referred from juvenile court. It is significant to note that the latter program attracted more black and Hispanic community members for special training and service than any other SFCB project.

Further, the center developed conflict-management training programs in police and fire departments, and community groups working with youth gangs. Many of these new trainings were developed by Kenneth Hawkins, the organization's gifted director of training, who began his conflict-resolution work in the early days of SFCB.

While the strategy of linkages expanded case referrals, agency relationships, and funding opportunities, it reflected a change in the organization's original service design. Through the formalization of agency relationships, the neighborhood organization shifted away from being totally separate from the formal justice system, a strategy of SFCB in the developmental years. With community acceptance and understanding, with nearly 75 percent of the cases coming out of the neighborhoods, and with a committed community membership, the organization could forge institutional links without jeopardizing the community's control over its own neighborhood service system. Moreover, the organization was building linkages and promoting statewide legislation that would institutionalize community-justice services in California.

Legislation

The Center for Policy and Training was involved in several legislative efforts in California and developed the prototype legislation that ultimately passed as Senate Bill 2064, the state's Dispute Resolution Bill. Susan King, the center's policy expert, supervised a significant part of the center's legislative work. She organized the community dispute-resolution programs in the state into a body able to make constructive input into the draft statute and subsequent regulations. From the present legislation, which enables counties to increase their civil filing fees up to $3 per filing, the SFCB program was able to secure close to $125,000 for its 1988 neighborhood conflict-resolution service.

Legislation has always been a two-edged sword for community justice. The desire for funding makes the passage of legislation important. However, the impact of legislation on creativity and independence and the increased pressures to reduce costs per case have been considered negative aspects of uniform state legislation.

Between 1986 to 1987, the California Bar Association moved from modest interest in the mediation legislation to active dominance and control. The bar's intransigence generated the formation of a statewide network of community conflict-resolution programs. Senate

Bill 2064 fulfilled the fears of many community programs by incorporating the language of neighborhood mediation in the preamble and the regulatory scheme of an agency. The bar's management of the bill resulted in legislation that failed to appreciate the impact of uniform agency and funding requirements on county community-justice services. Many of the original fears about legislation circumscribing community control and innovation in managing a distinctive form of justice were realized in the final passage of SB 2064 and its regulatory scheme that brought neighborhood justice within the orbit of the formal legal system.

Legislation has now become the major approach that the American Bar Association and state bars are using to corral mediation within the orbit of formal justice. By designating the scope of work for mediators, requirements to be a mediator, and how mediators are to receive cases, the legal system has made conflict resolution an extension of the legal processes. Instead of placing conflict resolution processes prior to the legal system, a model has been created that makes most mediations available only after a case is filed in court—at the back of the legal system. The most extreme example of legal control over the management of disputes is the Florida legislation that essentially makes attorneys (with minor exceptions in family disputes) the only qualified persons to receive a case referred by courts for mediation or arbitration. Community-justice programs cannot ignore the serious impact that legislation can have on their survival and funding.

National Strategy

Since 1981 the Center for Policy and Training has been conducting special institutes to train people from different cities in how to develop community-based conflict-resolution systems. In a few years, several dozen cities were initiating SFCB experiments. By 1984, developing an association of community-based programs became a serious consideration. An association that centered around the SFCB program was considered, but rejected. Rather, a larger association was envisioned, which became the National Association for Community Justice, which incorporated the leadership of both the community-justice and religious-tolerance groups in the United States and Canada. Susan King served as director of the organization during the formative years.

The primary purpose of NACJ was to raise the issue of community justice beyond the confines of any one program or geographic area. NAJC gave voice to the social need for communities to undertake civic action in the area of conflict management. NACJ organized an impressive and needed agenda for the further development of community-justice ideology, legislation, and programs in the United States.

The national program, however, was severely limited by available funds, which resulted in significant reprioritization of goals and operational objectives. The organization's geographic diversity, multiple interests, limited dollars, and issues of consistent leadership made NACJ a less effective national voice for urban and community issues than had been originally anticipated.

Nonetheless, throughout the 1980s, NACJ served as an important clearinghouse for hundreds of individuals and organizations seeking ways to build community and school conflict-resolution programs. Moreover, NACJ had an impressive legislative agenda and series of working sessions on legislation, underscoring the importance of legislation in the mid-1980s for community-based programs. By the end of the 1980s, NACJ decided to transform itself into a network organization communicating relevant issues and concerns through a newsletter published by Paul Wahrhaftig's Conflict Resolution Center International.

The Promise of Community Justice

SFCB has demonstrated both the value and ability of establishing in diverse ethnic and racial urban neighborhoods a first-resort justice system based on the services of trained volunteers. Arguing for a dynamic role for citizens and communities in resolving conflict and engaging conflict in socially constructive ways, SFCB pioneered a new form and rationale for informal dispute-settlement processes prior to the use of formal, agency-based justice mechanisms. Standing apart from the formal system, SFCBs shaped a unique model of conflict settlement that empowered both disputants and neighborhoods.

While several factors contributed to the organization's uniqueness, probably none proved more significant and relevant to its community support, recognition, and vitality than the organizing component, the quintessential dimension of all community-justice services. SFCB understood from the very beginning that staff and volunteer organizing time and resources had to be committed to building the program's neighborhood base. This is the stage so often skipped by would-be neighborhood justice programs and undervalued in the California dispute-resolution legislation, to the forfeiture of the neighborhood program as a first-resort system and its ultimate dependency on agencies for cases and support.

As documented by Rick Abel and Bonaventura de Sousa Santos at Dean Nils Christie's Oslo symposium on community justice in 1980, the integrity of community justice lies in the complex relationship between the informal quality of the justice service and the community its serves. The more the community understands the functions of the service, the more it will use it. Thus it is significant that the early DuBow data from the community awareness surveys reported that three out of every four households in the program's oldest neighborhoods were aware of the program and one out of four understood the service it provided. These are extremely high awareness and recognition figures for a community service initiative.

Moreover, SFCB and the like neighborhood-justice services hold a promise to middle- and working-class communities facing potentially explosive issues of community change and stability, as noted in Fred DuBow and Craig McEwen's article in this volume.

The potential for a first-resort, informal system of justice at the community level can be a reality. SFCB has proven this. Now it is a question if it can be a genuine reflection of a public policy that does not suffocate, co-opt, or destroy it. A first-resort system of justice holds out a promise of community stability to middle- and low-income communities facing potentially explosive interpersonal issues and needs.

In their chapter, Craig McEwen and Fredric DuBow highlight an important aspect of community justice's promise:

> Even the minimal picture of disputants provided by these data distinguishes SFCB from most other community dispute-resolution programs. Issues of community order among neighbors (the issues that predominate in SFCB) appear to come more often from a middle- or working-class population, whereas cases of assault among family members or lovers (frequently referred to programs by the police) "are more often brought by the poor and the unemployed" (Merry 1990:186). . . . As Sally Merry (1990) has

pointed out, class and community structure shape the nature of the conflicts that surface for processing by courts or other institutions. Drawing cases as it [does] from a variety of relatively stable, working- and middle-class neighborhoods of San Francisco, SFCB's caseload reflect[s] a concern with community stability and order, especially in the face of change. Other programs whose cases often come from the courts tend to draw heavily on lower-class populations from less stable areas. With fewer resources and less control over lives beyond their own apartments or houses, the issues of order relate to interpersonal ties rather than to the quality of neighborliness. San Francisco Community Boards has thus tapped a dimension of conflict in the United States that has rarely been recognized in community dispute resolution. (DuBow and McEwen in this volume, pp. 144–45)

Informal justice services simultaneously strengthen a neighborhood's capacity to meet the local needs of citizens and build a more cohesive, interactive community. A first-resort justice service outside the perimeters of the institutional system can be perceived as a threat to formal justice agencies. Certainly it creates an alternative for the engagement and settlement of conflict, which disenfranchises the formal system's monopoly on dispute settlement. This does not mean there are not useful points of intersection, as noted earlier.

Nevertheless, formal justice has systematically sought to limit the capacity of informal community-justice processes and to restrict and screen their caseloads. The most effective mechanism for circumscribing the work of community justice has been the incorporation of the community system into the agency and court systems and the latter's subsequent distribution of approved cases to informal processes. Thus instead of living up to its potential as a first-resort system, the community process is linked to the legal institutions as an after-the-fact referral service for cases it really does not want to pursue but seeks to control. This co-optation compromises the integrity and legitimate purpose of community-justice mechanisms with the concomitant effect that most programs integrated in this fashion suffer a dramatic decrease in the participation of ethnic and minority volunteers, a significant drop in awareness of the program in the local community, and serious diminution of cases referred from the community. From a cynical perspective, it could be postulated that such results are precisely what formal justice integrationists hope to achieve.

Such cynicism is given added credibility when it is understood that agency and court mediation cases "tend to draw heavily from lower-class populations from less stable areas [where] the issues of order relate to interpersonal ties rather than to the quality of neighborliness" (DuBow and McEwen in this volume, p. 144), a sensitive area of continuous justice interest and control. Perhaps one of the most profound studies undertaken by DuBow concerned the number of calls for police service that were clearly appropriate for SFCB, and in which police could exercise discretionary referral prior to citing for criminal violations, which nonetheless were logged into the formal criminal-justice system. (See DuBow and Currie in this volume.)

Where issues of community stability are concerned, it is important to examine how community-justice forums fit into the constructive mosaic of community order and stability. A National Institute of Justice study underscores the significance of neighborhood involvement and police support in achieving stable urban communities (Kelling and Stewart 1989). Community stability can be enhanced through neighborhood-justice services.

In summary, the issue before policymakers seriously concerned with issues of civic work, volunteer service systems, neighborhood cohesion, and the relevant issues associated with community justice (as detailed in fig. 2) is how to design a public policy that fosters such initiatives and protects them from the co-optation and integration efforts of formal justice.

In a very real sense, the success of community justice and the need for new public policies to advance it present a challenge for change not unlike the call for "perestroika" in other societies. For America, an urban perestroika would renew civic participation, promote community service, build community cohesion through civic work, and place democracy as the empowering vehicle for civic initiative throughout society.

Citizens are the appropriate agents of civic work and their efforts strengthen and stabilize communities. While some may critique dimensions of SFCB or community justice, as some academics in this volume do, the boards demonstrate that in democratic society citizens can exercise a primary responsibility to preserve the social order, stabilize their communities, and secure their neighborhoods through their own efforts. Moreover, citizens have been motivated to achieve these ends not through the instruments of state authority, but through community-designed and -implemented informal intervention and prevention mechanisms.

Given that most criminal conduct is between persons who know one another and who have consistent negative interactions based on their ongoing or prior relationships, it is not surprising that the DuBow police studies demonstrate the potential for preventing crime or harm through neighborhood-justice systems. In democratic society, where crime triggers a formal justice intervention, only informal, nonstate mechanisms can intervene in conflicts before a criminal statute has been violated. In short, community justice and citizen intervention are the prerequisites to successful crime prevention.

The promise of community justice is to transform the dormant power and responsibility of citizens and communities into a dynamic form of service and prevention. Solidifying this transformation into a public policy strengthens civil society. The SFCB program, as an experiment testing the vitality and viability of a functional informal justice system in urban neighborhoods, is a success. The next test, which cannot be an experiment, is to fashion this first-resort, volunteer service-delivery system of informal justice into an integral part of urban American society.

As peoples around the world are experiencing new forms of democracy and the exhilaration of civic initiatives, a perestroika for urban America can be envisioned: a renewal of civic participation and community service through the efforts and resources of Americans in their own community. Why not make the community the foundation of public policy for justice? Why not bring the desperate sectors of neighborhood life and the alienated individuals in our communities and bond them in civic work that directly relates to their own safety, quality of life, and community stability? Who, better than the citizens themselves, can do this work? And, why should we have anyone else do it, if they are competent and most able? Anyone can critique the concept of community justice, but can it really be said that in a democratic society citizens do not have a primary responsibility to preserve the social order, stabilize their communities, and secure their neighborhoods through their own civic labors? And isn't the best way to accomplish these important tasks through informal processes and early intervention/prevention mechanisms, rather than through forms of state directives and control? Who but citizens can prevent crime or harm before it happens? Who but communities can actually realize and promote the early peaceful settlement of conflict? Where else but in democratic society do citizens have such power and responsibility?

The promise of community justice is to transform the dormant power and responsibility of citizens and communities into a dynamic form of service and justice. Solidifying this transformation into public policy will sustain this civic activity. The form and practice of citizens learning how to assist citizens can be modeled for our children, promoted in our religious and civic organizations, and made part of our public education. The experiment to test the vitality and viability of an informal system of neighborhood dispute resolution has been very successful. The work ahead is to create policies that make the achievements and service of community justice an integral part of our daily lives.

WORKS CITED

Abel, Richard L. 1982. "The Contradictions of Informal Justice." In The Politics of Informal Justice, ed. Abel. Vol. 1: The American Experience. New York: Academic Press.

Auerbach, Jerold S. 1983. Justice without Law? Resolving Disputes without Lawyers. New York: Oxford University Press.

Beer, Jennifer E. 1986. Peacemaking in Your Neighborhood: Reflections on an Experiment in Community Mediation. Philadelphia: New Society Publishers.

Christie, Nils. 1977. "Conflict as Property." British Journal of Criminology 17:1–15.

———. 1991. Unpublished paper. Community Board Program. 1981. Annual Report. Mimeo.

DuBow, Fredric L. 1987. Conflict and Community: A Study of the San Francisco Community Boards. Draft. Chicago: Center for Research in Law and Justice, University of Illinois at Chicago.

Kelling, George L., and James K. Stewart. 1989. Neighborhoods and Police: The Maintenance of Civil Authority. Washington D.C: National Institute of Justice, U.S. Department of Justice.

Kurczewski, Jacek, and Kaximierz Frieske. 1978. "The Social Conciliatory Commissions in Poland: A Case Study of Non-Authoritative and Conciliatory Dispute Resolution as an Approach to Access in Justice." In Access to Justice, ed. M. Cappelletti and J. Weisner. Vol 2: Promising Institutions. Milan: Guiffre; Alphen aan de Rijn: sijthoff en Noordhoff.

McGillis, Daniel. 1978. *Neighborhood Justice Centers: Four Models.* Washington D.C.: Law Enforcement Assistance Administration, U.S. Department of Justice.

Shonholtz, Raymond. 1976a. "Community 'No-Fault' Boards." Typescript.

———. 1982. "Civic Institution Building." Community Boards Publication.

———. 1984. "Neighborhood Justice Systems: Work, Structure, and Guiding Principles." *Mediation Quarterly* 5:3–30.

———. 1984. Review of *Justice without Law? Resolving Disputes without Lawyers,* by Jerold S. Auerbach. *Arbitration Journal of the American Arbitration Association.*

———. 1985. "Developing Community Volunteer Service: Delivery Systems as a Public Policy." San Francisco Community Boards. Typescript.

———. 1987. "The Citizens' Role in Justice: Building a Primary Justice and Prevention System at the Neighborhood Level."*Annals of the American Academy of Political and Social Science* 494:42–52.

What Mediation Training Says—or Doesn't Say—about the Ideology and Culture of North American Community-Justice Programs

Vicki Shook and Neal Milner

An advocate of community-justice programs had this to say about the values of mediation and the role that training plays in achieving these values.

> We view teaching and practice of mediation as a social good of the hightest order, even a revolutionary act of empowering the people. . . . It is through this outreach, this wide dissemination of mediation skills, that a fundamental change in society will occur. The more programs reach out to teach mediation to the public, the sooner we will be a nation of peace makers.(Bean 1989:5–6)

Training takes on a broad political and ideological dimension here. It is not simply a transfer of technology. Teaching people to mediate is the key in this social-transformation theory, which links visions of informal justic to broader visions of social change (a "nation of peace makers"). Training is the foundation for the strategies necessary to achieve these visions. People must be taught these skills in order to be empowered ("The more these programs reach out to teach mediation to the public"). Here training is presented as a given, as is its connection to social change.

Like any ideological statement, this view of mediation makes assumptions about what is problematic and what is not. In this view, training is so integral that the assumptions about what it's worth require no examination.

In fact, there is a good deal to examine. First, is training necessary? Second, is training necessarily a prerequisite for social transformation? Even when the culture expects explicit socialization, this training may not be tied to social transformation. Third, what are the hidden cultural assumptions embedded within training programs? Much of our own culture, particularly those aspects conveyed in communication behaviors, is hidden from us (Hall 1973, 1976). Training relies heavily on communication and carries hidden cultural messages. Indeed, one of the hidden messages is the strong value placed on formal education itself. "Everyone knows" that skills are best imparted through formal training. It is hard to stand outside of one's own culture, whether as an analyst writing about informal justice or as an advocate of a mediation program. But to answer the three questions, one must stand outside and look at what other cultures believe and do about mediation.

In this essay, we try to discover some of these hiding places by using comparative analysis and cultural juxtaposition. By first describing and then comparing San Francisco Community Boards (SFCB) training programs with others, particularly the Mennonite Conciliation Service (MCS), and the Honolulu Neighborhood Justice Center (HNJC), we are able to bring to light some of the variations and implicit ideological dimensions of mediation training. What is considered a given in one program may be highly problematic in another. However, the comparative analysis described above is too limited because each of these three programs is a part of a contemporary informal justice movement in North America. All three share some commonsense notions about dispute resolution, so certain cultural assumptions can remain hidden (especially if the analysts, like ourselves, are part of that same milieu), unless there are also more disorienting sorts of comparisons made on the basis of cultural milieus that are quite different from the three modern North American mediation programs that are our focus here (Marcus and Fischer 1986:111–86). In this paper we use *ho'oponopono*, a traditional form of Hawaiian dispute resolution, as an additional source of comparison.

We explore three issues in this paper. First, we consider the relationship between training and ideology by describing three U.S. community-justice programs and the traditional Hawaiian practice of *ho'oponopono*. Next, we elucidate five basic premises of community-justice mediation training and point out how these are linked to particular cultural and ideological frames. We argue that North American community-justice training programs arise from assumptions about expertise, knowledge, communication, and emotion that are not shared across cultures. Finally, the paper considers the problematic link between training and social transformation. We contend that this training-transformation link is far less direct and far less certain than it is described by the advocate of community justice quoted above. Formal training is only one way to impart mediation skills. Indeed, such training may limit the possibilities of social transformation.

The Ideological Frames of Training: A Look at Three Contemporary Programs

San Francisco Community Boards Ideology and Training

Three crucial aspects of SFCB[1] ideology have a direct impact on its training: (1) the delineation of the destruction of community and its potential reformulation; (2) the emphasis on education as a means of revitalizing community; and (3) the link between communication and citizenship skills.

The community, which to SFCB means the geographic neighborhood, is at the hub of SFCB ideology. Communities/neighborhoods are seen as the core of political and social life, that have lost their ability to maintain their own standards, handle their own problems, and resolve their own conflicts. The formal legal process fosters these losses by professionalizing the resolution of conflicts. Activities formerly carried out between neighbors are now seen as the province of law enforcement and judicial processes. This shift away from the

---

1. Primary sources in SFCB include the *San Francisco Community Boards Conflict Resolution Training Manual;* Hawkins's handbook for trainers (1986); Lash's workbook (1985); policy papers and articles by Shonholtz (undated, 1984, 1987); secondary sources include DuBow's research (1987); and a paper by Adler, Lovaas, and Milner (1988).

grass roots form of social control has left communities feeling more vulnerable and less safe. While the formal legal system will step in to deal with overt violence, police officers, judges, or lawyers can do little about alleviating the disputes that are not legally constituted as violations of the law.

The way to get the power and influence back, according to SFCB, is by restoring the central role of informal processing of neighborhood disputes. This potential can be tapped through the creation of a nonprofessional organization that reminds people of the value of handling disputes at the neighborhood level and teaches them the skills to do so. Many of these roles and skills in dispute resolution have been lost, so organizations and training are essential at the community level (Shonholtz 1987:47).

San Francisco Community Boards ideology has broad communitarian visions that see training for mediation as a training for democratic citizenship. The characteristics necessary for dispute resolution— self-confidence, empathy, fairness, compromise, assertiveness—are precisely those seen as lacking in American political life. The right combination of these traits fosters cooperation, which, in the words of a SFCB member, is "a pivotal theme of democratic life" (Adler, Lovaas, and Milner 1988:320). By learning how to handle neighborhood disputes, individuals develop the skills and confidence necessary to make politics less alien and more controllable. Politics is transformed—SFCB ideology would say retransformed—to the grass roots, where democracy has the best chance of flourishing.

Teaching these lost or diminshed skills is the basis of this link between transforming disputes and transforming politics, but they take on a psychological dimension since they are defined as self-expression (Shonholtz: n.d.2).

Most of these skills involve communication. According to SFCB ideology, people must learn to express themselves clearly and must learn to delve into and appreciate the feelings of others. The lack of such skills is a reflection of the destruction of community. Communications skills create the sense of self-efficacy and empathy for others that is necessary for successful public citizenship and civic work.

San Francisco Community Boards looks for volunteers from diverse backgrounds to participate in the training. In order to become a volunteer a person must reside in the community, (i.e, geographic neighborhood) and be at least fourteen years old. There is also an attempt to have the pool of volunteers match such neighborhood demographics as ethnicity, sexual preferences, renter/homeowner, youth/elderly, and so forth (DuBow 1987:127).

The basic conciliation training is a twenty-six hour program that spans two weekends and is designed to develop skills such as active listening, public speaking, facilitation, counseling, writing of agreements, mediation, training, and publicity (Shonholtz and Bosley 1984:19). In addition to preparing individuals to do the work of San Francisco Community Boards, the training is seen as having broader applications that "empower" community members. Trainees become better able to address disputes more skillfully in their family, workplace, and general community.

> The letter that is sent inviting people to become trainees states, "The skills you will acquire will help you in your family, social, and work life and will prepare you to join [other] community members in . . . doing the work of peacemakers." (DuBow 1986: 186).

Training stresses conflict-resolution techniques, particularly communication skills, but there are also broader socialization objectives.

> After a brief consideration of general communication skills, the manual and the training concentrate on the San Francisco Community Boards process in its ideal form . . . The training sessions emphasize doing things in a prescribed manner. This appears to reflect a strategy of laying a foundation of common understandings and practices. It gives the group a shared set of experiences and a language in which to describe what it is doing. (DuBow 1986:179)

Completion of the training enables members to do the work of San Francisco Community Boards, including outreach, conciliation hearings, public education, and perhaps later, training—all on a volunteer basis. Individuals also have conferred upon them a new identity— "community member."[2]

---

2. San Francisco Community Boards makes it a point to refer to the men and women as "community members" rather than "volunteers." There is a distinction

The training process continues after this first basic two-week session. Each hearing is seen as a further training opportunity. The three panelists who conduct the hearings are overseen by a trainer. He or she conducts a "debriefing" after each hearing. Trainers rarely give specific criticism to the panelists but are apt to compliment and offer general suggestions.

> The debriefings appear to serve more to affirm the group's work and to correct deviations from Community Board's policies than they are to provide individual skills improvement. (DuBow 1986:182)

After some time serving on panels, the trainees may be recruited to become volunteer trainers, although they may not see themselves as very experienced. This is another opportunity to learn more about the San Francisco Community Boards orientation and process (like the adage "teach what you need to learn") and is a way of strengthening commitment to the organization.

There are some additional educational and training opportunities. SFCB offers advanced training on some specialized subjects like intercultural relations and conflict in organizations. The newsletter and other SFCB publications offer additional information. However, the primary exposure to SFCB remains the general training program. So it is the training process, embedded in SFCB's ideological context, that initiates the volunteers into their roles as community members. SFCB's vision is that collectively the community members constitute a new grass-roots leadership who spread skills in dispute resolution and thereby strenghten the community.

Mennonite Conciliation Service Ideology and Training

Peacemaking is part of a three-hundred-year-old tradition in the Mennonite church. The most obvious example of this is the Mennonites' refusal to serve in the military, but the roots of pacifism go much deeper than this political stance and rest on values about the centrality of inner peace and reconciliation in a person's spiritual life. Inner

---

between these community members and other community members who have not been through SFCB training.

peace and reconciliation are interdependent. Without a concern for reconciliation, inner peace is trivial, merely a relaxation technique (Kraybill 1980:7). There must be a linkage between being at peace with oneself and working to establish peace among others, so that the most effective and authentic peacemaking has a profound effect on the peacemaker and becomes a way of life. This authenticity can happen only as a result of reconciliation.[3]

Although Mennonites are conscientious objectors and will not take oaths of office, Mennonite teaching encourages participation in secular activities. Mennonites envisage the duty of peacemakers to work for social justice by bringing these standards of inner peace and reconciliation to bear on the larger world. One must work for both peace and social justice. Their beliefs do not advocate doing this in a way that overtly promotes their view of Christianity. As one of MCS's founders put it, the challenge for handling conflict is to maintain a presence "without imposing a Christian agenda" (Kraybill 1980:18).

Mennonites see a wide range of disputes as falling within their arena as peacemakers. There are conflicts over religious issues within Mennonite congregations, nonreligious conflicts between members of those churches, and finally, disputes of a more secular nature, often involving people who have no link to any Mennonite congregation. Since MCS is grounded in a theology that closely links the need to achieve both individual peace and social responsibility, it places a greater emphasis on group conflict and on tactics that are more manifestly political than those used by most community-meditation programs.

MCS activities and training reflect this encompassing peacemaking ideology. The organization began in 1979 as a response to conflicts within Mennonite congregations. There was a particular concern that this church, so strongly based on peacemaking, was doing little to keep its own house in order, or more appropriately, in reconciliation. But as MCS has grown and developed, it has become involved with an extraordinarily broad range of conflicts, including work in developing nations. It is not tied to any single neighborhood or jurisdiction. Its focus is in dispute resolution and training others to do so.

---

3. Primary sources on the Mennonite Conciliation Service (MCS) are writings by Kraybill (1980); Lederach (1986, 1989); Lederach and Kraybill (in this volume); MCS training materials and articles in *Conciliation Quarterly*; a secondary source is Adler, Lovaas, and Milner (1988).

MCS training programs reflect these broad concerns. The training manual is a diverse compendium of essays and instructions on conflict resolution, including a bit on Mennonite teachings, a few examples of church disputes, and a heavy dose of standard mediation and facilitation techniques (Mennonite Conciliation Service 1988). Training materials make no clear distinction between religious and nonreligious disputes. The training manual does not explicitly prescribe which techiniques are most applicable to which settings or types of disputes. Although other Mennonite writing talks of advocacy and community organization as part of dispute resolution (e.g, Kraybill 1980), the training manual emphasizes peacemaking skills to mediate disputes.

This mix reflects the Mennonite belief that a concern for peacemaking transcends one's own religion. The training programs are offered to people with the understanding that the skills, however important to Mennonites, can and should be used in all sorts of settings by non-Mennonites as well. MCS advertises its training programs nationally through its newsletter, *Conciliation Quarterly,* and in other alternative dispute-resolution publications and attracts a diverse group of participants to its training sessions. MCS is also asked by other groups to assist them in resolving conflicts. MCS may respond by offering a program that instructs people how to do conflict resolution, or by utilizing consultation or group facilitation led by its own staff. The manual acts as a basis for instruction for both types of interventions.

Recently, MCS has begun to rethink its approach to training, particularly in regard to the applicability of this training to settings outside of the United States. The new orientation stems from the realization that many things about North American mediation are peculiar to that place and culture. Consequently, there is a recognition that a standardized form of MCS training conducted outside of North America may actually be a form of cultural imposition (Lederach 1986). For example, MCS trainers see a difference between the rule-oriented, highly structured North American mediation model and the less structured traditional forms of dispute resolution in which neutrality and expertise in technique are less important than prior relationships. Reflecting MCS's experiences in Central America, Lederach (1989) describes a more traditional approach as one based on *confianza,* or relationship ties (see Lederach and Kraybill in this volume).

The critique of a standardized training program has emerged because training may be based on an irrelevant set of assumptions, but also because the usual method disempowers people by implying that outside experts can decide what is best for them. By using new approaches in place of a preconceived training program for people outside of North America, MCS trainers empower communities by helping them see and develop the existing resources in their own culture that are available to resolve the dispute. Frequently these resources have become hidden, trivialized, or ignored. This approach is not reflected in the basic training manual, but some attempts have been made to apply it in North American settings also.

Honolulu Neighborhood Justice Center Ideology and Training

Like San Francisco Community Boards, HNJC[4] is a nonprofit, volunteer-based organization that was formed, grass roots–style, in the late 1970s to enlist and train volunteers to mediate a variety of disputes in the surrounding community.[5] In the HNJC view, conflict is seen as a "vehicle for personal, social and political change." Mediation is seen as a conflict activity that has great potential for facilitating this kind of change.

A number of fundamental ethical premises guide mediator training at HNJC: (1) mediator neutrality (operationally understood as a guarantee that the mediator has no prior relationship with the parties), (2) impartiality (lack of favoritism), (3) confidentiality (mediation is a private forum), (4) no advice-giving (mediators are not acting as therapists or attorneys and can only "encourage and assist" participants), and (5) a striving for a power balance between parties (negotiations should be balanced, not manipulative or intimidating). These ethical premises imply a degree of formal distance between the

---

4. Sources for information on HNJC include the mediator's training binder (from 1985 with updates through 1988); and the personal experience of the authors, who have both been through HNJC training.

5. Presently it has four distinct program areas: (1) neighborhood mediation (e.g., landlord-tenant, consumer-merchant, neighbor, and other community-type disputes, including cases mediated at the small claims court), (2) family and divorce mediation, (3) juvenile restitution, and (4) conflict management (for complex, multiparty disputes, such as land use or environmental issues). Over fifteen hundred cases are mediated annually.

disputing individuals and the mediators. Mediators are taught that by using these ethical guides with the mediation model, the disputing participants will be empowered to handle the conflict in their best interests. However, mediators are not seen as representing the community values in any substantive way. In that sense they are not seen as representatives of the community, except that through the mediation procedures they are providing a safe forum for the expression of community values and norms.

Interested adults who wish to be HNJC mediators go through an application and interview process. The training consists of fifty-plushours of work over a few weeks, followed by an additional twenty or more hours at later dates for mediators who would like more specialization. Participants learn to mediate alone and with a co-mediator. Like SFCB, the HNJC staff trainers are joined by many volunteer mediator trainers.

The content of the training includes an overview of the HNJC philosophy, policies, and model of mediation. Most of the emphasis is placed on learning and practicing specific communication strategies. In the past few years the communication-skills training has become more elaborate. Trainees are taught to utilize variations of specific interventions called "listening, asking, and moving" at different stages of the mediation in order to move the process along. The meaning of listening and asking is fairly self-evident. The "moving" interventions are those designed to help the disputants see and understand the issues in a new, broader context, thus enabling them to move through the disputing process. This strategy is similar to "reframing" responses in therapy.

Providing Cross-cultural Contrast: Ho'oponopono

The traditional Hawaiian process for addressing conflicts in the family is called *ho'oponopono*.[6] This process comes out of a system of fundamental beliefs about a triadic relationship among the forces of the cosmos: gods, nature, and human beings. All things are seen as related within this sacred web of life.[7] Conflict impedes, blocks, "jams

---

6. Sources on *ho'oponopono* are Shook (1985) and Shook and Kwan (1987).

7. It was important for people to understand how to relate to the varieties of life force—whether of rocks, animals, fellow human beings, or the gods, since wrongful or disrespectful actions could have negative reverberations throughout the web. Spiritual forces operate in many ways within the Hawaiian cosmology. In this par-

up" the relationships. It disrupts the harmonious balance and, if unresolved, can bring about illness or misfortune. *Ho'oponopono* is used as a way to restore harmonious relationships in the family, and by extension, with the spiritual and natural forces. Literally meaning "setting to right," *ho'oponopono* is guided by a person, the *haku*, who is not usually involved in the conflict but is intimately known to the parties. Often the *haku* is a respected elder family member. The family conference is opened and closed with prayer. The leader guides the discussion to uncover the multiple layers of the problem.[8] Each problem has negative entanglements between family members, known as *hihia*. When these have been examined it is possible to perceive the initial transgression, or *hala*. When an aspect of the problem has been fully aired, then each person apologizes and receives forgiveness for their part. This mutual forgiveness opens the way for harmonious family relationships to be restored. After one or more sessions the process draws to an end when the family members agree that their relationships are "free and clear" once again. A prayer of affirmation and thanksgiving is followed by a snack or shared meal. The family then resumes regular patterns of interaction and activity.

Traditionally, since *ho'oponopono* was a regular part of family life, individuals learned how to lead the sessions through repeated participation. There was no special instruction or apprenticeship. Respected status, often by virtue of age, and intimate knowledge of the family members were important attributes of leaders. Today, few Hawaiian families have grown up with the formal process and those who wish to use *ho'oponopono* need to be reintroduced. Renewed interest in traditional Hawaiian practices and concepts grew during the 1960s and 1970s and led to a revival of *ho'oponopono* practice. Initially the revival was tested out by a few individuals in consultation with Hawaiian elders and Western mental-health professionals. Later materials, including videotapes, manuals, and other documents were developed to support training efforts. However, very few formal trainings have been conducted. The few conducted have been provided

---

ticular triadic network, the "self" is a relational construct. Individual behaviors are tied to others—direct kin as well as ancestors and ancestral gods. These relationships are conduits or channels for positive and negative consequences.

8. The problems are discussed in an atmosphere of humility, truthfulness, sincerity, and self-scrutiny. The talk will often be concerned with individual perceptions and about emotions, but the tone should remain cool to avoid creating further entanglements.

to workers in social-service agencies who had a modern-day, sanctioned context in which to use the practice.[9]

The Premises of Training

With three community-justice programs outlined we turn our focus to an examination of the phenomenon of dispute-resolution training, and to the key role it plays in the ideology and operation of community-justice organizations. The following five premises represent some of the key assumptions we believe are made by the organizations. Examples from *ho'oponopono* are also used to highlight differences and similarities in assumptions.

> Premise One: People Lack the Skills Necessary to
> Resolve Their Own Conflicts

In forms of dispute resolution used by SFCB and HNJC, mediation is a cultural "add on." It is not a process that is generally learned in the family, school, or church.

> People [in SFCB neighborhoods] don't think of mediation as an alternative for dealing with conflicts. When they are informed about a mediation alternative, they have little basis in direct or vicarious experience upon which to formulate a sense of what types of conflict it can handle. (DuBow 1986:127)

This contrasts with the traditional Hawaii example, where a specific conciliatory practice has been a part of the ongoing community life. Even when families do not use formal *ho'oponopono*, they often have a general understanding of its meaning and implication. The presence of conflict-resolution training programs in American communities is indicative of the lack of indigenous, structured conciliation strategies. To some extent, MCS differs from SFCB and HNJC because peace-making is a tradition in the Mennonite churches, but MCS has, until recently, made the add-on assumption about those outside the church seeking MCS assistance.

---

9. See Shook (1985:100–101) for possible culturally based explanations for the reluctance of individuals to begin using the practice in their families of communities.

Premise Two: Training Mediators Is the Way to
Overcome the Community's Deficit of Informal
Dispute Resolvers

For SFCB, training is a passport to mediation. The techniques
imparted through training, rather than through experience or social
connections, are the ones necessary to resolve disputes. Mediators
are drawn from the community, but their selection is not related to
finding linkages between the disputing parties and the mediators.
Indeed, such linkages are not trusted because they might very well
violate the "neutrality" of the process. For SFCB, neutrality means
distance from the parties, and those with close ties to the values of
a particular neighborhood are not considered to be good mediators
(Harrington and Merry 1988). Although SFCB ideology speaks frequently and positively about the rebuilding of communities, its theory
of community rebirth gives little attention to the power of those who,
without training, are acting as natural peacemakers in the communities. Instead, SFCB seeks to rebuild such communities by imparting
the skills.

Similarly, HNJC distrusts preexisting relationships between the
parties and the mediators, and, not surprisingly, HNJC training programs increasingly place a heavy reliance on techniques of mediation
and on selecting trainees for their ability to master these techniques.
This is consistent with HNJC's ideology. HNJC no longer builds its
programs on the basis of neighborhoods or any similar collectivity,
and it does not see its goal as rebuilding or maintaining traditional
or already existing linkages.

MCS training is more ambivalent toward the need for close links
between the parties and the mediators. The recent revisions of MCS
training indicate that the organization has become more interested in
adopting dispute-resolution models of cultures where linkage is more
important than technique. MCS has recently attempted to empower
trainees by emphasizing that the ability to resolve conflict already
lies in their own culture or group. That shift in MCS training reflects
a renewed belief in the importance of local knowledge and social
linkages that already exist. Church conflicts also offer opportunities
for preexisting networks to act as a mediating force. The best mediator
might be the pastor of the church that the parties attend or someone
who attends the same church as the disputants. Even when the church

dispute is so rancorous that someone from MCS is called in, the MCS mediator, as part of the same religious tradition, shares some history with the parties. On the other hand, many of the examples in the MCS manual and much of the training material is geared toward developing the same skills and basis of neutrality as those found in SFCB or HNJC.

Again the contrast with Hawaii is instructive. A person becomes a *ho'oponopono* leader, or *haku*, not by virtue of training, but by being a *kanaka makua*, or respected, mature adult. Qualities like ascribed wisdom, status, or age might be considered more important than any particular skill. Leaders learn their role and responsibilities through many years of participating in community and family life, including straightening out misunderstandings. Also, the traditional Hawaiian style of learning is based on observation and participation, rather than explicit instruction,[10] whereas in U.S. programs there is an assumption that effective dispute resolvers must go through some formal training process. San Francisco Community Boards promotes the idea that most citizens can be trained in the desired skills, which may even have an impact on changing attitudes (Hawkins 1986:75). MCS has referred to some attributes like "cooperation" and "presence" as the fundamental skills for a mediator to learn (MCS Training Manual, sec. C). HNJC also believes that certain attitudes and personality attributes are important indicators of success as a mediator, and the organization screens training applicants according to their attributes.

Premise Three: Knowledge and Expertise in
Communication Skills Are Paramount for Mediators

The San Francisco Community Boards training program emphasizes skills that they believe assist parties to hear each other and speak clearly about their concerns and allow the conciliators to intervene in ways that further dispute resolution. Listening skills, particularly what is called active listening (involving paraphrasing and reflecting both the substantive content and emotional quality of the message), is the primary skill. Active listening is conveyed verbally and non-

---

10. See Gallimore, Boggs, and Jordon *Culture, Behavior and Education: A Study of Hawaiian-Americans* (1974) for more on differences in style of learning. As we previously mentioned, training has become a more important way of learning *ho'oponopono* as it has been reintroduced to new culture settings.

verbally and is done in a nonjudgmental manner. Questioning skills are used to clarify the issues in a dispute. Another skill that relates more directly to the experience of being a trainee is "constructive criticism." Trainees are taught to give and receive feedback that is "helpful," i.e., avoids blame, is specific, and describes a person's behavior rather than personal attributes. ("I think that you might have spent a little more time explaining the panel process to Mr. Smith" as opposed to "You didn't do the opening statement right.")

HNJC and MCS use the same basic stock of communication skills in their trainings. As mentioned earlier, HNJC has articulated a somewhat complex schema of communication skills in their listening, asking, and moving framework that is used by mediators to move the process along. SFCB and MCS also spend time during their basic training on other communication skills, such as public speaking and persuasion (SFCB) and group facilitation (MCS). Since SFCB trains case developers and public educators as well as conciliators, they include sections on persuasive public-speaking techniques (Hawkins 1986:79–84). MCS covers group facilitation skills to be used in intra- and intergroup conflicts.

The training manuals of all three programs reveal a similar repertoire of training methods. For example, SFCB's manual for trainers lists the following: lectures, demonstrations, experiential learning ("role plays and practice exercises"), discussion, reading, and modeling (Hawkins 1986:15–16). Recently, MCS has begun to question the universal application of some pedagogical techniques based on their experience doing training outside of North America. During a conference for contributors to this volume, Lederach told a story that illustrated the cultural limitations of role-playing, even when the script of the role play has been adapted to fit the culture. During the exercise one Central American observer noted that the role players looked and sounded like gringos. In other words, role-playing wasn't a culturally familiar way to learn, even if the dialogue was culture-specific.

Premise Four: There Are Core Communication
Patterns That Can Be Applied Universally to
Disputing Activities

The earlier premises suggest that training itself, with its communication skills orientation to dispute resolution, is basic to the operation of the three mediation programs. The communication perspective also influences the way that conflict and its resolution are perceived, expressed, and resolved.

The teaching of a multistage dispute-resolving process, as done in all three programs, underscores a particular ordering of disputing activities. SFCB's process is delineated in four stages: defining the problem, discussing the issues, understanding the other disputant's concerns, and making an agreement. This ordering assumes that a conflict can be examined in a logical fashion outside of the disorderly vicissitudes of everyday life. By training volunteers to name and delineate the stages of the dispute-resolution process the trainees' sense of belonging to the SFCB community is reinforced, and some of the ambiguities and the complexities of the dispute are reduced. Trainees report having confidence in the process. HNJC mediators are likewise encouraged to trust in and follow the process, and many echo their faith in it.

While the benefits of this structured model are an increase in cohesion and common understanding within the community of mediators, such models assume certain kinds of conflicts. Day-to-day disputes may not lend themselves to this format, and complex disputes may require alternative approaches. Again, MCS's experiences in Latin America are instructive. The ordering of dispute resolution into discrete stages, where people speak one at a time while others listen, is a North American speech structure reflecting our culture's value of formalism (Lederach 1986). A predilection for formalism influences a number of other factors: the setting where the mediation takes place—indoors and usually in a public facility; the importance of specifically articulating the rules and procedures of mediation; and the timing and sequencing of speaking itself—for example, the rule that people speak one at a time and are not to be interrupted (Lederach 1986).

Lederach's description of more typical dispute-resolution behavior in Latin America violated all of these rules (1986). Disputes were often discussed out-of-doors; they did not have a discernable beginning, middle, and end; more than one person spoke at a time; and multiple topics were included. Similarly, ho'oponopono may look similar to mediation in terms of its formal structuring, which perhaps explains why many Westerners find it appealing. However, the aspects that don't conform to American values or speech rules are the very ones that are most frequently dropped or changed (Shook 1985:98–

99). For example, traditionally all speaking was directed to the *haku*, rather than between the offending family members. This rule, which is understood by Hawaiians as a way to keep the lid on emotional outbursts, is seen by some non-Hawaiians as unnecessary because of a belief that it's good to allow people to express themselves directly—"to get things off their chest," a view closer to HNJC and SFCB.

Premise Five: The Expression of Emotions Assists the Resolution of Disputes

Although each of the contemporary programs address the emotional dimensions of conflict resolution in slightly different ways, all believe the expression of emotions is appropriate in mediation. In HNJC the expression of feelings is understood as a necessary prelude to the main objective—negotiating agreements. Whereas some expression of emotions is expected and encouraged, exploration of this dimension is seen as inappropriate for mediation and is labeled as "a counseling issue" (Shook and Kwan 1988:44). The MCS training manual is not very explicit about the role of emotion in the mediation process, but in a recent issue of their newsletter devoted to "reconciliation," emotional expression was related to forgiveness, emotional healing, and restoring relationships. The following excerpt gives a sense that while Mennonites value the emotional dimensions, they also recognize that mediators may feel that they are on slippery ground when moving beyond issue-oriented negotiations.

> Whatever the terminology, we all know in our personal lives that moving through brokenness to renewed relationship is what we most yearn for in the face of conflict. But in our professional lives, as teachers and practitioners of conflict resolution, many of us shy away from such matters. Some of us are simply uncomfortable with the expression of strong emotions—both our own and those of others. Others would willingly take on the emotional level of conflict, but feel lacking in practical skills. Yet another group may believe that emotional healing is better left to psychological and spiritual counselors; mediators should stick close to the "issues" and leave the "feelings" to others. (Price 1988:1)

For SFCB, the *expression* of the personal experience of the conflict may be more important than the actual settling of the dispute (DuBow 1986:180). In a way this places SFCB more in line with the Hawaiian view, because in *ho'oponopono* most of the discussion is spent expressing one's *mana'o*, or thoughts from one's "gut." These heartfelt exchanges are thought to promote deeper understanding, which pave the way for forgiveness and restoration of family harmony. In contrast to SFCB, however, in *ho'oponopono* little attention is paid to articulating agreements about future behavior. Where there is understanding and forgiveness, the future will take care of itself.

There is another difference between *ho'oponopono* and SFCB regarding the context in which emotions are placed. Although SFCB stresses the importance of the emotional dimension, the value is articulated mostly in terms of benefits to the individual, or to an interpersonal relationship. The cultural worldview that supports *ho'oponopono* locates the significance of emotional expression beyond the individual. Conflict creates emotional entanglements that extend to the family and have repercussions throughout the community— social, physical, and spiritual. In some cases the reflection of this condition, coupled with self-correction and seeking at least spiritual forgiveness, may be sufficient to ameliorate the problem.

The Limits to Training as a Key to Social Transformation

Dealing with Diversity: How Training May Diminish Rather Than Empower People and Cultures

In some ways, community-justice programs underestimate their role in discouraging the voice of other cultures. Training has a mixed effect on promoting cultural diversity. Both HNJC and SFCB talk about the need for cultural diversity, and both attempt to recruit an ethnically diverse group of mediators. Nonetheless, the approach to training is still essentially monocultural. There is a standard training program accompanied by an assumption that the techniques and values learned in these training sessions set people off on the right path toward protecting cultural diversity. MCS's recent changes in training indicate an awareness of the culturally homogenizing effects of training. These changes emerge as a result of MCS's concern that training in its standard contemporary North American form is a cultural imposition. MCS sees both the process and the content of training as an act of power, while the other two North American programs are silent on this possibility.

MCS's recent changes suggest another SFCB limitation regarding the empowerment of minority cultures. SFCB and HNJC training approaches are based on a deficit model. Without training, people lack the resources to resolve their own disputes and maintain their own communities. The deficit model can create a self-fulfilling prophecy, where in the interest of returning informal justice to the community, the already existing cultural resources are ignored. It is not clear that is what has happened to SFCB, but it is clear that this possibility has received little attention.

Promoting diversity itself may be an uncertain basis for strengthening contemporary communities. Diversity is not a goal or outcome of dispute resolution in some, particularly more traditional, homogenous cultures. In *ho'oponopono*, for example, the concern is not so much to legitimate diverse individual interests as it is to relate these interests to a larger shared and spiritually based network.

HNJC, SFCB, and MCS in their secular work face the complexity of working with parties who do not necessarily share an assumptive system of beliefs, values, and practices. SFCB literature suggests that there are recognizable neighborhood standards, albeit possibly latent, and that SFCB plays a key role in making these standards more explicit, communicating them to others, and encouraging their use. Let us assume, as SFCB does, that there are, in the contemporary urban neighborhood, values that are shared, discoverable, and supportive of community cohesion (Shonholtz and Bosley 1984:13; compare Cohen 1985). SFCB training offers little guidance about how to discover these values, or how to help create them.

There are some important silences in the training programs' attempts to link informal justice with broader social transformational issues. San Francisco Community Boards training illustrates a view that in some ways criticizes individualism, in other ways celebrates it, and in still other ways is not explicit about the relationship between the individual and the community. SFCB tries to reinvigorate and strengthen the neighborhood and promote group solidarity, but faces difficulties since the organization emerges from an American culture that has never shown much concern or sympathy for this kind of solidarity. Reflecting this culture, SFCB training pays little attention to some key issues concerning the relationship between individuals and larger collectives. Mediators are not taught pragmatic ways to link the individual to social transformation. The disjuncture and disparity reflects the individualistic culture of which SFCB is a part.

SFCB claims that although modern urban communities are inexorably diverse, community and diversity do not have to be incompatible. Community mediation can teach people to cope with this diversity and to build upon it (Shonholtz n.d.:16). Ideally, SFCB training is designed to legitimize diversity in three ways. First, participants learn what the community values are. Second, they develop a tolerance for diversity, particularly through working together with ethnically different mediators and disputants. Third, they develop the skills necessary to resolve disputes emanating from the range of conflicts that are a part of the modern neighborhood. Thus, through the experience of being trained and working on panels, the mediator/community organizer develops a body of knowledge about two aspects of community life: (1) the values that are shared throughout the community and (2) the multiple, particularistic values that emerge from diverse communities.

MCS, especially in regard to secular disputes, promotes some of the same kind of delicate balance between individuality and the larger collective as SFCB does. Church conflicts, however, present a different community context. Although Mennonites celebrate individual conscience and dissent, religious conflicts among Mennonite community members take place within a context of some shared history and assumptions. These arise not only from close ties between the individual parties and the larger community, but also from a three-hundred-year-old history in which terms like *peace* and *reconciliation* have some shared meaning.

Both SFCB and HNJC, to a lesser extent, assume that social transformation will emerge as the number of trained mediators increases. MCS training indicated less willingness to assume the link between individual and social change. Still, what is interesting about MCS is how *similar* its training has been to SFCB and HNJC. If someone taking the MCS training did not know of the religious tradition, he or she would not likely discover it in the mediation training. The broad range of tactics mentioned in general Mennonite literature about peace and justice receive little attention in the MCS training manual.

SFCB training, reflective of SFCB general ideology, is silent about other important approaches to the relationship between the individual and social change.

One alternative makes a collectivist orientation an integral part of a formal training or socialization process. There is a tradition of this approach in European democratic socialist parties (Stephens 1979). Community in this example does not necessarily refer to geographically based relationships. Instead the emphasis is more on the community of shared interests. What most differentiates this approach from the SFCB approach, and for that matter fom most politics in the United States, is the emphasis the collective approach places on the need to have a variety of socializing institutions that generally present the same ideology. There is in a sense some very explicit training, but the training is less task oriented and more doctrinal. So, for example, political parties and labor unions are closely allied, and both these organizations teach lessons about the relationship between individuals and the larger political world.

U.S cultural traditions discourage this kind of linkage between individuals and politics. Labor unions have never had success with this apporach, and even when they made some inroads during the early twentieth century, American socialism was not so organized (Aronowitz 1973). U.S. political parties traditionally pay little attention to developing these transformational connections. The concern with collective solidarity has not resonated and does not resonate with the predominant American values, which are oriented toward individual rights. The experience of the worker-controlled companies in the United States, which on the surface appear to encourage collective solidarity, are indicative of the difference between this value and those of the predominant culture, and of the consequences of this difference. Workers in these companies do not take these notions of equality and cooperation with them when they leave the plant. Instead, outside of their work, they too accept individualistic ideologies. The workers are just as individualistic and privatized in their personal politics as those who work in less communal and egalitarian settings (Greenberg 1987).

When there are collective responses in American neighborhood politics, they are often based on perceived threats to individual values. One powerful example in contemporary politics are "NIMBYs" (standing for "not in my backyard"). In these conflicts neighbors unite to oppose the placement of a structure, program, or activity (for example, a half-way house for disabled adults) in their neighborhood. The backyard metaphor connotes the strength of individual property rights. Another example where community response has been strong, active, and unified is opposition to school desegregation. In each of these situations, people see outsiders, often the government, as encroaching upon their individual freedoms "to live the way I want," or "to decide what is best for my family." The response may be collective, but at the base are individual values. "Leave me alone" is the basis for the collective response. Furthermore, the response is typically contingent upon a single issue rather than a pattern of concerns. When the issue is resolved, the collective response dissolves.

In this volume, Nader and Rothschild show how SFCB de-emphasizes the link between the individual and the larger political world. They demonstrate this by contrasting SFCB to a San Francisco consumer organization that aims to get individuals to see the relationship between their own hassles as consumers and the larger economic context. In the consumer-action case, the goal is to get consumers to broaden the conflict by banding together. Rothschild's essay shows how SFCB's behavior maintains an approach to politics that individualizes disputes. Issues are seen as conflicts between individual parties. As DuBow's assessment of SFCB pointed out, SFCB was not comfortable when it tried to concern itself with cases that were broad in scope (1986).

Another approach to political organization and social transformation is more spontaneous and depends less on explicit training than on political participation. The recent political developments in central European countries have often emanated from social movements that were not self-consciously developed. In such political movements training programs do not dominate. There were no self-conscious attempts to make distinctions between individual and collective action. Collective action emerges on the job, so to speak, as does the focus on transformational politics. People learn by doing in response to a specific crisis. This model is clearly more situational and organic than the SFCB or HNJB approach, but it is an approach to conflict resolution nonetheless. Strategies emerged from the particulars of a dispute, rather than from an already formed dispute-resolution format. From this perspective, the American programs, with their emphasis on preexisting dispute structures, careful training, and individual change, might appear to stifle rather than encourage community empowerment.

This spontaneity also runs against the grain of the broader political culture in the United States. Such activities are typically less organized and law-abiding than our culture generally accepts. People in the alternative dispute-resolution movement are more interested in structuring conflict rather than letting it evolve and work itself out in these less predictable ways. The more organic approaches leave little room for imparting expertise through formal training.

These alternatives remind us that SFCB is consistent with dominant political ideologies in the United States. Like these dominant ideologies, SFCB is silent about some important ways of doing politics. What appears in one culture to be very flexible, liberating, or relevant can in other settings be quite the opposite. From the standpoint of the spontaneity approach, SFCB ideologies and activities appear very procedural, orderly, and civil. From the standpoint of the collective approach, SFCB appears not to build community, but rather to emphasize and strengthen individualism within a geographical area.

Conclusion

It appears that in many ways SFCB ideology not only critiques, but also shares, much of the dominant U.S. political ideology. The silences suggest that SFCB takes a typical U.S. approach to community building, and, like those approaches, SFCB is likely to move away from the broader and more transformative political strategies. Since traditionally there has been in the United States a discomfort or ambivalence about the idea of community because of its perceived threat to individualism, it is doubtful that SFCB will emerge as a community builder in the transformational sense. Shonholtz's essay in this volume suggests that SFCB is indeed moving away from this community-building approach and more toward the view that SFCB should be a social-service agency within a particular geographically defined community. There are signs that social transformation is disappearing from the community agenda in U.S. community-justice programs. A publication of the National Institute of Dispute Resolution (NIDR) indicates this movement in an article by McGillis (1988), and in interviews of the directors of the most influential programs, including the present executive director of SFCB (*Dispute Resolution Forum* 1988:7). The question addressed in this issue is "how are community justice centers faring?" Links between mediation and community building were not a part of the criteria used to answer this question. Funding, caseload, program survival, and disputing parties' perceptions of success totally dominated the responses. Only the SFCB director hinted at the broader concerns, but his focus, too, was elsewhere. Rather than being problematical, SFCB's training programs may in fact be consistent with their emerging set of concerns. Training may not be the transformational linchpin after all.

SFCB sees its training and ideology as adaptable across cultures. In one sense that is certainly the case. A rainbow coalition of people use it in San Francisco, and programs in very different cultural settings, like the Tribal Council Program in the state of Washington, have adopted the SFCB approach (Adler, Lovaas, and Milner, 1988). In another sense, however, the problems of cultural diversity are not so easily overcome, because SFCB, like the other examples of dispute programs we have discussed, is culturally bounded. The more spontaneous and collective responses that SFCB ignores have been successful in other cultures, even for, perhaps particularly for, people without much political power. As MCS's reassessment suggests, the standard, contemporary North American approaches to mediation, which train people to follow a set of procedures, may actually take away power from other cultures or subcultures within the United States, by slighting idigenous expertise and resources or by stopping more spontaneous, collective, possibly less orderly responses to a problem. North American mediation programs, regardless of their claims about community orientation, may not have much to teach other cultures about the way to balance individual and collective wants or about the way to respond to serious and threatening political problems that suddenly arise.

The silences about the individual-collective link leave all sorts of unanswered questions about the nature and desirability of community (see Yngvesson in this volume). SFCB attempts to develop community in a broader American political culture that is strongly individualistic and anticollective. SFCB training produces a program that promotes individual growth and skill development. If there is a social transformation, it is limited to individual actions by some volunteers who attempt to make a personal-political link, rather than through collective community action.

How does SFCB define and understand the nature of community? Can these trained, caring, feeling, listening people be expected also to be neutral and distant from the parties in dispute—their neighbors? Are these individuals, who are trained to be committed to procedural fairness and neutrality, different from those in their community who are more committed to particular values, who are more willing to fight passionately in behalf of these values, or who wish to exclude others who do not agree? What kind of communities do we perceive as having failed, and what kinds do we envision in the modern U.S. city? The homogenous, experienced-based, historically formed enclaves like the Mennonite communities? The racially exclusive ethnic village? The Amish of the film *Witness*, or the whites of South Boston? To regret the loss of community is to regret the end of the racially stratified small town of the rural South as much as the friendly, potluck church supper. Is there a way to salvage community in order to get cohesiveness based on something other than homogeneity? Can we build such cohesiveness in a society that esteems individualism so highly? These remain questions that are unanswered and ignored by community-justice movements.

REFERENCES

Adler, Peter, Karen Lovaas, and Neal Milner. 1988. "The Ideology of Mediation." *Law and Policy* 10: 317–39.
Aronowitz, Stanley. 1973. *False Promises.* New York: McGraw-Hill.
Bean, Ralph, 1989. "The Importance of Community Justice." Paper presented at National Conference on Peacemaking and Conflict Resolution, Montreal, 6 March.
Cohen, Stan. 1985. *Visions of Social Control.* London: Polity Press.
DuBow, Frederic L. 1987. "Conflicts and Community: A Study of the San Francisco Community Boards." Photocopy.
Gallimore, Ronald, Joan Boggs, and Cathie Jordon. 1974. *Culture, Behavior, and Education: A Study of Hawaiian-Americans.* Beverly Hills, Calif.: Sage Publications.
Greenberg, Edward S. 1987. *Workplace Democracy.* Ithaca, N.Y.: Cornell University Press.
Hall, Edward T. 1973. *The Silent Language.* New York: Anchor Books.

————. 1976. *Beyond Culture.* New York: Anchor Books.

Harrington, Christine, and Sally Engle Merry. 1988. "Ideological Production: The Making of Community Mediation." *Law and Society Review* 22:709–37.

Hawkins, Kenneth. 1986. *Handbook for Conciliation Trainers.* San Francisco Community Boards.

"How Community Justice Centers are Faring." 1988. *Dispute Resolution Forum,* 7 December.

Kraybill, Ronald S. 1980. *Repairing the Breach.* Scottsdale, Penn.: Herald Press.

Lash, Rozlyn. 1985. *Conflict Resolution Workbook.* San Francisco Friends of San Francisco Community Boards.

Lederach, John P. 1986. "Mediation in North America: An Examination of the Profession's Cultural Premises." Comprehensive examination paper, Department of Sociology, University of Colorado.

McGillis, Daniel. 1988. "What's Gone Right—and Wrong—for Community Justice Centers." *Dispute Resolution Forum,* 5 December 5, 7.

Marcus, George E., and Michael M. J. Fisher. 1986. *Anthropology as Cultural Critique: Experimental Moments in the Human Sciences.* Chicago: University of Chicago Press.

Mennonite Conciliation Service Mediation Training Manual. 1988.

Price, Alice. 1988. "Beyond Negotiation: Restoring Relationship. *Conciliation Quarterly.* Fall, 1.

San Francisco Community Board Conflict Resolution Training Manual. No author or date specified.

Shonholtz, Raymond. 1987. "The Citizen's Role in Justice: Building a Primary Justice and Prevention System at the Neighborhood Level." *Annals of the American Academy of Political and Social Science* November 494:42–52.

————. Undated. *Community Board Policy Papers.*

Shonholtz, Raymond, and Bruce Bosley. 1984. "Public Policy Paper for Community Conflict Resolution Services." Photocopy.

Shook, E. Victoria. 1985. *Ho'oponopono.* Honolulu: University of Hawaii Press.

Shook, E. Victoria, and Leonard Ke'Ala Kwan. 1988. "Straightening Relationships and Settling Disputes in Hawaii: Ho'oponopono and Mediation." Program on Conflict Resolution Working Paper no. 1987-10, University of Hawaii.

Stephen, John D. 1979. *The Transition From Capitalism to Socialism.* London: Macmillan.

Dispute Tranformation, the Influence of a Communication Paradigm of Disputing, and the San Francisco Community Boards Program

Judy H. Rothschild

A transformational perspective on disputing starts with an awareness of disputes as socially constructed phenomena (Mather and Ygnvesson 1980–81). Disputes are considered "fluid" (Merry and Silbey 1982), "subjective, unstable, reactive, complicated and incomplete" (Felstiner, Abel, and Satrat 1980–81). Language, participants, and audience are key features in shaping disputes (Mather and Ygnvesson 1980–81). The "naming" of issues serves to define their meaning (Felstiner, Abel, and Sarat 1980–81), and power differences between participants in the disputing process influence *how* the definitional process occurs and *who* assumes the dominant role (Nader and Todd 1978; Mather and Ygnvesson 1980–81). Mather and Ygnvesson argue that

> [t]ransformations occur because participants in the disputing process have different interests in and perspectives on the dispute; participants assert these interests and perspectives in the very process of defining and shaping the object of the dispute. (1980–81:776)

This chapter examines the process of rephrasing disputes by describing the way disputes are transformed through the interactions of

265

disputants and the representatives of a neighborhood-based conflict-resolution program, the San Francisco Community Boards (SFCB). Discussed are different stages of dispute transformation that occur in the course of SFCB's response to disputes; how the interests of disputants and program representatives affect the rephrasing of disputes; and the consequence of SFCB's intervention with regard to dispute transformation.

The primary purpose of this chapter is to show how the SFCB approach to conflict resolution involves a highly interactive process that rests on what I refer to as a communication paradigm of disputing, whereby conflicts and disagreements, including fights over interests, are rephrased as interpersonal problems of communication (Rothschild 1986a). This orientation towards disputing is based on assumptions about the interpersonal value of conflict. Conflicts which come to the attention of the program are seen as arising from misunderstandings or miscommunications (Rothschild 1986a; Merry and Silbey 1982). I argue that a communication paradigm of disputing leads program staff and volunteers to direct attention (theirs and disputants') to the relational and emotional aspects of conflicts. Consequently, social, legal, and economic dimensions of disputes, while often perceived by the SFCB staff and volunteers, are rarely if ever addressed during case intake or mediation sessions.

A second and related purpose of this chapter is to highlight the critical relationship between the intake and hearing phases of dispute processing. This topic has received little attention in the study of American alternative dispute-resolution programs, despite evidence suggesting that only about 30 percent of disputes progress from intake to mediation in voluntary mediation programs such as SFCB, or in court-affiliated programs where mediation is voluntary (Harrington 1985; Beer 1986; DuBow and McEwen in this volume).

Concluding comments address the tension between SFCB's vision of "community empowerment through conflict resolution" and the observable effects of the SFCB approach to disputing.

The Data

This chapter draws from the data and findings of the Intensive Case Study component of the San Francisco Community Boards Evaluation Project, one of the data sets discussed by McEwen and DuBow (in this volume). A deep appreciation of the transformational nature of disputing informed this component of the research, as well as the overall research concerns and multistudy design of the San Francisco Community Boards evaluation. I discuss the findings of the Intensive Case Study from the vantage point of one of the primary researchers involved with this study.

The aim of the Intensive Case Study was to acquire an in-depth understanding of how conflicts came to the attention of the SFCB, and the program's role in the transformational process whereby *conflicts* came to be defined as *disputes* and SFCB *cases*. Forty disputes were monitored from the point of case intake to two months after the program closed the case. Research methodologies included ethnographic fieldwork, nonparticipant observation of case intake (case development) and hearing sessions, and intereviews with disputants, program staff, and program volunteers.[1]

A third of the cases (n = 13) included in the Intensive Case Study progressed beyond the intake phase to include a SFCB hearing. As

---

1. The Intensive Case Study was a panel study of forty disputes that came to the attention of SFCB in 1984. Sampling was inclusive rather than exclusive. Any inquiry for assistance that met the program's criteria for acceptance as a case was considered eligible for the study. The sample was drawn from three of the program's field offices, specifically the three oldest, most established, and fully staffed offices. As the sample grew, screening criteria were employed to ensure that the sample reflected the array of disputes commonly processed by the program. In addition, cases were sought that would fill theoretical gaps. In the tradition of grounded theory (Glaser and Strauss 1970; Glaser 1978) and ethnographic research, various techniques of in-process analysis were used to keep abreast of meaningful categories of analysis as they emerged during the data collection process.

The research design involved monitoring each dispute from the point of intake to two months after SFCB "closed the case." All forty cases came to the attention of the program during a five-month period. Data collection continued for approximately a year, given the longitudinal design that required follow-up interviews with disputants two months after the program officially closed their case.

Data collection techniques included ethnographic fieldwork, nonparticipant observation, and survey methods. Data collection began with program staff interviews, when a request for program assistance was received. In more than half of the disputes, a member of the research team observed SFCB staff and volunteers during in-home intake meetings with disputants. Structured interviews were conducted with intake workers both prior to and following their intake meetings with disputants.

Structured interviews with disputants occurred at up to three points in time. Attempts were made to interview all parties to a dispute after the intake meeting with SFCB representatives. Interviews occurred at the time disputants decided whether or not to use the program's services. For those disputants who chose to use mediation (i.e., the SFCB hearing process), a second interview occurred in the week following noted above, this rate is consistent with findings from other studies. Follow-up interviews with disputants revealed that in 70 percent of the mediated disputes (n=9), the hearing and/or other subsequent events had led to an end to the conflict. In two other mediated disputes, the disputants described the conflict as partially resolved, and in an equal number the disputes had continued. A descriptive overview of dispute and disputant characteristics and data about case dispositions of the cases comprising the Intensive Case Study are provided below, and in the appendix to this chapter (See also DuBow and McEwen in this volume).

To illustrate the analysis presented in this chapter, discussion focuses on a single case from the Intensive Case Study, "The Promised Land" dispute. "The Promised Land" dispute moved smoothly from intake to mediation but stalled at the hearing session when the mediators were unable to facilitate a resolution or settlement because the disputants refused to sustain a definition of the dispute as a problem of communication. "The Promised Land" example *is not intended* to be indicative of the SFCB's general rate of success or failure at conflict resolution.

I selected this case for a number of reasons. In the sociological tradition of looking toward "deviant" cases to expose normative expectations, this case serves as an example of an occasion where reality did not conform to normative expectations. As such, it provides valuable insights about the expectations of mediators and disputants and the underlying assumptions that inform the SFCB approach to disputing. Second, although the SFCB hearing in this case did not lead to a resolution of the dispute, program staff and volunteers' orientations and responses to the conflict and the processing of the dispute were consistent with the overall findings of the Intensive Case Study. Third, contributing to the qualitative analysis presented in this chapter, this case provides an ethnographic description of how the SFCB's intake phase plays a central role in the transformation of disputes. I hope this account helps remedy a void

the "hearing. Attempts were made to interview all disputants again two months after the program officially declared the case closed.

Hearing sessions (including the prehearing briefing and posthearing review) were observed by a member of the research team. A member of the mediation panel was interviewed shortly after the hearing.

Members of the research team also attended SFCB training sessions and local area-office meetings.

in the literature about this critical stage of dispute processing. Fourth, "The Promised Land" case illustrates the high degree of personal interaction between program representatives and disputants that is a distinctive characteristic of SFCB's approach to case intake and mediation.

A Descriptive Overview of Dispute and Disputant Characteristics

Disputant Characteristics

Of the forty cases included in the Intensive Case Study, the majority (83 percent) involved disputes between persons who were residents of the neighborhoods served by the SFCB. Half of the disputes (48 percent) involved disagreements between "neighbors." More often than not, this term described residential proximity, rather than personal familiarity, since many of the disputants identified as neighbors had never spoken to each other prior to their contact with the SFCB.

The other half of the disputes were nearly equally divided between conflicts between landlords and tenants, roommates, and family members. A small number of disputes involved disagreements between individuals and businesses or other organizations. One dispute was between an employer and a former employee.

Fifty-eight percent of complainants were women, 33 percent were men, and 10 percent were couples. In contrast, men were the subject of complaints almost twice as often as were women or couples. Specifically, men were the subject of complaints in 45 percent of the cases, women were identified as a second party (respondent) in 23 percent of the cases, as were couples.[2]

With regard to race and ethnicity, of 111 disputants, approxi-

---

2. The differential appeal of mediation to women as compared to men, both as mediators and disputants in the SFCB program, suggests the importance of further research on the relationship between gender and disputing (Rothschild 1986a, 1986b). In the Intensive Case Study, the data showed that women contacted SFCB to ask for assistance about twice as often as did men and were almost three times more likely to complain about people with whom they expected to be in continuing contact and ongoing relationships (primarily roommates, family members, and neighbors). A similar pattern appears in statistics about program usage collected as part of the SFCB comprehensive evaluation study (see DuBow and McEwen in this volume).

mately 60 percent were white, 20 percent were Hispanic, 14 percent were black, and 8 percent were Asian.

Of the forty disputes included in the study, 21 involved conflicts between members of the same race. A majority of these disputes (fourteen) were between whites. Of the remaining intra-race disputes, three disputes were between blacks; three were between Hispanics; and one dispute involved the members of a Filipino family.

Sixteen disputes were categorized as involving members of different racial groups. The majority of these cases (n = 14) involved pairings where one of the parties was white and the other party was not.

Data on education was available for about two-thirds of the disputants. Of this group, 29 percent reported attending college; an additional 30 percent reported graduate training or an advanced degree.

Information on income was available for slightly over half of the disputants (n = 55). Fifty-one percent reported their annual household income in 1984 as less than $20,000. Thirty-one percent reported household incomes of $20,000–$40,000, and 18 percent reported household incomes of over $40,000 (in 1984 dollars).

Overall, the cases included in the Intensive Case Study reflected the distribution of dispute and disputant characteristics found in the review of the cases processed by the program from 1977 to 1982 (DuBow and McEwen in this volume; Rothschild 1986a). The small size of the Intensive Case Study sample, compounded by missing data on education and income, precludes a statistical analysis of the study sample's representativeness of the general populations of the neighborhoods where SFCB operates.

Types of Disputes

The cases included in the Intensive Case Study attest to the wide spectrum of complaints that come to the attention of SFCB, and the fluid nature of disputes. Some disputes involved long-standing multifaceted disagreements, while others involved relatively straightforward complaints of recent origin. It was common for one party to refuse to acknowledge the existence of a problem, let alone a dispute, and consequently reject being identified as a disputant. In many disputes, we found that disputants were strangers, and were only "neighbors" by virtue of geographic proximity.

The cases included in the Intensive Case Study were representative of the disputes processed by the program during its history of operation (DuBow and McEwen in this volume; Rothschild 1986a). Disputes between neighbors were about noise, property damage, violence, harassment, theft, zoning ordinances, parking problems, and interpersonal relations. Disputes between landlords and tenants and roommates concerned rental agreements, evictions, building maintenance, and interpersonal relations. Disputes between individuals and businesses involved disagreements about noise, theft, legal violations, and consumer complaints. Other types of "interpersonal disputes" included conflicts between family members and friends about interpersonal relations and harassment.

Table 1 indicates the range of disputes included in the Intensive Case Study. For the purposes of this chapter, disputes are categorized by a primary dispute issue or characteristic. However, it should be noted that disputes often involved more than one issue (DuBow and McEwen in this volume). For example, disputes about noise often involved related complaints about the behavior of the "noisemaker." Similarly, disputes between roommates about rental agreements often involved disagreements about living arrangements and interpersonal behavior, and disputes between landlords and tenants often included complaints about property care.

Case Disposition

Data from the Intensive Case Study attest to the problematic usage of "resolution" and "settlement" as measures of outcome (see Appendix). Interviews with disputants provided ample evidence to show that disputes frequently continued to evolve after written or oral

TABLE 1.   Cases by Dispute Type ($N = 40$)

Dispute	Percentage
Property care / vandalism	28
Interpersonal Relations	28
Landlord-Tenant / Roommate	20
Noise	15
Business	5
Zoning	5

Note: Total percentage greater than 100% due to rounding.

agreements had been forged, settlements declared, and after the SFCB officially closed and recorded cases as resolved. Some disputes ended as a direct result of SFCB's intervention, while in other cases disputing ceased for reasons unrelated to SFCB's involvement. Most importantly, the data indicate that settlements and resolutions did not guarantee final solutions or an end to disputing. Although problems were often diffused as a result of agreements, the potential for future trouble frequently remained a possibility.

SFCB hearings occurred in thirteen (33 percent) of the forty cases included in the Intensive Case Study. In 9 of these cases, disputants reported (in a follow-up interview conducted two months after the hearing) that the hearing or subsequent events had led to an end to the dispute.[3] In two cases, disputants reported partial resolutions of their disputes. In two cases, the disputes continued and were unresolved. In a majority of the mediated disputes, relations between parties had terminated as a result of the resolution, the hearing process, or other unrelated events. (See Appendix for descriptions of these cases.)

Of the twenty-seven cases that were not mediated, when disputants were contacted two months after SFCB had officially declared the case closed, we learned that two disputes had ended, four were partially resolved, and twenty-one were unresolved.

The Promised Land: An Example of Dispute Transformation

I now turn to an analysis of the case of "The Promised Land" to illustrate the interactive nature and dynamic processes that affect dispute transformations in the context of the SFCB experience. Discussion begins by examining how the intake process plays an integral role in the SFCB framing of disputes. I argue that the *mediation* of disputes *begins at the point of case intake,* as program representatives actively encourage disputants to accept and participate in a definitional process that frames disputes and prepares disputants for managing dispute definitions and agreements that emerge during the mediation session.

---

3. A number of disputes settled as a result of disputants moving, assistance from legal authorities or others, or other factors that diminished or eliminated the conflict.

Commencing with the intake process, program staff and representatives direct disputants to attend to interpersonal aspects of disputes. Disputants' acceptance of this definitional orientation, which identifies "talking with one's neighbors" and using the SFCB hearing process as the appropriate method of resolution, depends on a wide range of factors and consequently varies from case to case. However, for disputes to progress to mediation, disputants must agree, at least temporarily, to a framing of the dispute as a problem of communication.

The Intake Process in "The Promised Land"

This case occurred in a lower-middle-class black residential neighborhood, located in the southern part of the city. Most of the residents were homeowners, many of whom had purchased their homes following WWII, in the late 1940s and 1950s. By the mid-1980s, the neighborhood was becoming more integrated, as middle-class whites and Asians moved in as result of rapidly escalating real estate prices in other parts of the city.

The Initial Complaint

In April of 1984, SFCB received a call from Alfred Sands, who asked for assistance in what he defined as a "neighborhood problem."[4] Mr. Sands explained that he and his wife, Gladys Sands, (a black couple in their early sixties), were forty-year residents of their neighborhood and were upset because a young, white couple recently moved across the street and appeared to be operating a business out of their home. Mr. Sands was quick to add that he did not see the issue as a racial problem. Rather, he stated that he and his wife were concerned because they considered their neighbor's home-based business a threat to the residential character of their neighborhood and a violation of zoning laws.

He informed the staff person taking his call that he had already called the mayor's office. They referred him to a local neighborhood economic development organization, who then referred him to SFCB.

---

4. All participants (staff, volunteers, and disputants) are referred to by pseudonyms.

It seemed to him that everyone was "passing the buck." He explained that if SFCB couldn't solve the problem, he'd recontact the mayor's office and the mayor herself, if necessary.

Mr. Sands was encouraged to use SFCB's services. He was advised, however, that he had to agree to not pursue the matter with the formal justice system, including the mayor's office, while SFCB was involved. The staff person explained this policy reflected the SFCB philosophy "that it's best to try and resolve disputes in the spirit of cooperation rather than coercion." Mr. Sands agreed to "give it a try."

He was told that a program volunteer would contact him within the week to schedule a meeting with the Sandses in their home to discuss the dispute and further explain the SFCB hearing process.

The Beginning of the Rephrasing Process: Defining the Dispute Issues and Identifying the Disputants

This initial interaction between SFCB staff and the volunteer intake worker (case developer) marked the beginning of the rephrasing process.[5] Although limited and less visible than subsequent in-person home visits or the hearing, this exchange resulted in the casting of the Sandses as disputants and legitimized the existence of a dispute. The dispute emerged as an officially designated case, and thus a valid occasion for SFCB intervention.

SFCB eschews terms like complainant and respondent when referring to disputants. Instead, the program identifies disputants as first and second parties. This choice of terminology reflects a conscious attempt to assert the equal status of each party and avoid any possible stigma or inequality associated with the terms complainant and respondent.

---

5. SFCB has developed an internal language to refer to program volunteers and activities. Volunteers who provide much of the program's labor force for case intake, mediation, and outreach are referred to as *community members;* the intake of cases is referred to as *case development;* volunteers who do this work are called *case developers;* those who direct hearings are called "panelists"; and SFCB calls their approach to conflict resolution *conciliation,* rather than mediation.

In this chapter, I use the generic terms associated with the field of neighborhood justice and alternative dispute resolution to refer to these tasks and activities. I discuss the SFCB case development process as *case intake.* Case developers are referred to as *intake workers.* Panelists are referred to as *mediators.* The SFCB approach to conflict resolution is referred to as *mediation.* See DuBow and McEwen (in this volume) for further discussion of this topic.

Data from this and other cases included in the Intensive Case Study indicate, however, that subtle distinctions are often made about disputants by staff and volunteers. In this case, by identifying himself as a long-term resident committed to the preservation of neighborhood life, Alfred Sands articulated his complaint in a way that was consistent with values central to the ideology and organizational culture of SFCB. The ensuing analysis of this case suggests how personal characteristics such as verbal skill and length of residence can function as sources of power and authority (for both disputants and program volunteers), and as characteristics that frequently influence mediators' assesments of disputants' claims and credibility. Thus, while all disputants are considered equal, some are perceived as "more equal than others" (Orwell 1946).

Mr. Sands's conversation with SFCB office staff also prompted an initial narrowing of the dispute in scope and content to fit "conventional management procedures" (Mather and Ygnvesson 1980–81). For example, the SFCB consciously avoided the intrinsic legal question of neighborhood zoning regulations. Moreover, the program elected to identify only the Sandses and the neighbors about whom the Sandses were complaining as disputants when the complaint had the potential to be viewed as an issue of concern to a larger audience, that is, other neighbors, other neighborhood associations, the city planning commission, and so forth. Although the staff person who talked with Mr. Sands believed it likely that racial differences were a factor, he chose not to pursue this facet of the dispute. Thus, on the basis of this initial conversation, SFCB set in motion a definitional process that contextualized Mr. Sands' complaint as an *interpersonal* dispute, between two neighbors, about the operation of a business in a residential neighborhood.

In-Person Intake Meetings with the Disputants

Once a complaint is accepted as a SFCB case, it is generally assigned to a two-person team of volunteers for case development, what I refer to in this chapter as case intake. Intake workers (case developers) attempt to meet with the disputing parties to learn more about the dispute and to encourage the use of the SFCB hearing process. Intake meetings usually involve separate discussions with each of the parties to the dispute. The nature of the dispute influences the location of

the intake meetings. Thus, for example, in disputes between neighbors, meetings usually take place at each disputant's residence. In
disputes involving business operations, the setting of the intake meeting for the business operator often occurs at the place of business.
On occasion, intake meetings also take place with SFCB staff at the
local SFCB office.

Meetings with the first party, the party who contacted SFCB,
are generally arranged in advance by telephone. Meetings with the
second party are usually not arranged in advance. SFCB asserts that
the surprise element of the visit assists in getting the second party
to talk about the dispute with a program representative, since "it is
harder to close the door on someone than hang-up the phone" and
it enhances the characterization of the program as an organization
of "neighbors concerned about each other."[6]

Intake with the First Party

In "The Promised Land," SFCB assigned Tom Davis, a veteran program volunteer, to be the intake worker on the case.[7] Tom lives in
a different neighborhood, a couple of miles from the disputants. Both
neighborhoods are serviced by the same SFCB field office.[8] Interviewed before his meeting with the Sands, Tom explained his analysis
of the dispute:

First, there have been major changes in the Sands' neighborhood
over the years. It used to be a predominantly black neighbor-

6. Explained during volunteer training program, 1984.

7. Tom is a white, single, self-employed cabinetmaker, in his midforties. He has
lived in San Francisco for fifteen years. He is one of the program's most active and
experienced volunteers. He has pursued a number of careers. He enjoys discussing
local politics and strongly believes in taking an active role in neighborhood affairs.

8. Community deserves to be approached as a problematic concept in studying
the SFCB program (see DuBow and McEwen in this volume; Ygnvesson in this
volume). SFCB ideology emphasizes the common bond between program volunteers
and disputants as members of the same neighborhood and community. However,
disputants and mediators are often residents of different neighborhoods, and thus
the term community is used in a general, unspecific manner.

In "The Promised Land" dispute, Tom lived about two miles from the disputants'
neighborhood. He traveled by freeway to go to there. One could say he lived in the
same quadrant of San Francisco, in an area that was somewhat comparable sociodemographically. Thus, his "neighbor" relationship to the disputants is similar to the
relationship between mediators and disputants in many other types of mediation
programs that rely on lay mediators.

hood. Now, with the price of homes, a lot of whites are buying there 'cuz it's one of the few affordable, safe neighborhoods in the city. . . . It's also attracting people who are looking to buy second homes as rental property.

I'm betting that the Sands are upset about these changes, maybe not the racial aspect, but seeing renters replace home-owners. I suspect that's an underlying issue. Plus, from talking with Mr. Sands on the telephone, he sounds like he thinks of himself as a "block mayor." . . . He's a longterm resident, and a professional. . . . I'm guessing that he may try to present himself as a neighborhood spokesperson.

Arriving at the Sands's home, Tom is greeted by Alfred Sands, a tall, neatly groomed man. Mr. Sands calls for Gladys, his wife, to join the discussion.

Mr. Sands begins immediately:

I called SFCB because we've lived in this house since 1947. I'm a taxpayer. I've raised five kids in this house. But that's all irrelevant! The point is that I think the people across the street are using their house as a business, and that's inappropriate behavior for this neighborhood. The neighborhood has changed! It used to be all homeowners, but now renters are moving in. If they have a permit, I'm going to fight City Hall! I'm a salesman and I don't run my business out of my home.

I want you to know that it's not a racial thing. I'd feel this way about anyone, even if it was a black cat running a bar-b-que joint. But this guy has inventory in his garage, and parks his trucks right out front. One guy even parks up the street and walks down here. It is just not right! I pay my taxes, so should he! If he has a permit, it could open up the whole block to anyone!

The Sandses describe the offending neighbors as a white couple in their late thirties, who moved into the house across the street about three months ago. The Sandses do not know them by name; they have only said hello in passing. Mr. Sands repeats that race is not an issue.

The Sandses stress how attached they are to their home and their neighborhood. They explain that in 1947 they had to fight redlining to buy their home. Then two years ago they were emotionally devastated when a household fire destroyed a quarter of their home. They rebuilt and plan to enjoy their house "until we die or get too old to care for ourselves. To us, our house is *the Promised Land.*"

Identifying himself as a neighbor familiar with the neighborhood, Tom raises the subject of demographic changes. In response to his probing, the Sandses talk about their experiences in the neighborhood. They reminisce about being among the first black residents in what was originally an almost all-white neighborhood. Nostalgically, they describe the neighborhood as a friendly place, where they and other young families raised their children.

In a more objective tone they detail the changing racial composition of the neighborhood. They have witnessed it go from almost all white to almost all black, and how another turnover appears in the making. Tom agrees and observes that the new residents are often young white families, many of whom are renters rather than homeowners.

The Sandses explain that they are not disturbed by the racial turnover, but rather by watching renters and absentee landlords replace homeowners. To prove their point, they list each house on the block, naming neighbors who have moved, recalling which children have grown and left, and expressing sorrow for the increasing number of widows.

Mrs. Sands adds that nowadays, people seem too busy to care about these things. But neither she nor her husband are going to stand by and watch home-based businesses invade their neighborhood.

Mr. Sands adds that he is angry and offended by the new neighbors' failure to properly introduce themselves. He feels snubbed that they have never come over and seem satisfied to just wave in passing:

> That's just not the way to be neighbors. I'm from the South, there is something called "Southern Hospitality" and those people seem like they have different values.
>
> You know in the South, when you're black, people can put a gun to your head and get away with it. I don't mean to say this is a racial thing, it isn't. But only the police and God have control over my life, and I'm not going to stand by and let people break

the law in front of me and change the neighborhood without my taking control of the situation.

Tom learns that the Sandses have never spoken with their neighbors about their concerns, nor have they contacted anyone else, with the exception of their unsuccessful call to the mayor's office. He commends them for this, and explains the SFCB approach: it offers a nonjudgmental way to resolve disputes and is not in the business of enforcing decisions or behavior. He adds that SFCB has an excellent track record because when people take responsibility for finding a resolution themselves, it normally sticks, and people are much more satisfied with their own resolution than one drafted without their input, which happens when judges or attorneys are involved.

Tom adds that SFCB relies on volunteers, people like the Sandses, to help others resolve disputes. He comments that Mr. Sands appears to have the personality that would make him an outstanding mediator. As an afterthought, he tells Mrs. Sands that she would probably enjoy the program as well.

Tom begins to describe the "hearing," but catches himself and says:

> It's really just a meeting. A meeting where local people try and get a general sense of the dispute and then encourage disputants to trust each other enough to listen to each other's side of the dispute. For example, the panel of mediators might perceive that one issue is absentee landlords.

Tom adds that the "meeting" will allow both the Sandses and their neighbors to learn about how each feels about the situation. Mr. Sands tells Tom he is not interested in this aspect of the hearing:

> What did you say about his feelings? I don't give a damn about his feelings. Wholly and solely I care that he be eliminated; not him, but his business.

Again, Tom tells the Sandses how SFCB is better than court. He explains that in court the strong feelings that are at the bottom of most disputes are ignored: "It's important to recognize those feelings if you want a fair resolution." He gives a number of examples. The Sandses nod in agreement.

Tom concludes by repeating that he is very optimistic that things will work out. He lists his reasons:

First, there has been no direct communication between the parties.

Second, no outside party has been involved.

Third, the neighbors across the street undoubtedly have a vested interest in resolving the matter because they are living where their business takes place. I expect they'll recognize this conflict as a potential threat to their livelihood, and therefore they'll probably want to resolve this problem.

Tom assures the Sandses that by using the SFCB hearing process they will be able to "get all the issues out in the open." The Sandses suggest that since Tom now knows the situation, perhaps he could discuss the matter with the neighbors himself. Tom declines, explaining that as an intake worker his job is to get a sense of the dispute and encourage the parties to use the hearing process. Tom informs the Sandses that he will be talking with the neighbors in much the same way as he has with them, and he is confident they will agree to a hearing.

Mr. Sands asks if Tom would tell the neighbors that the Sandses are speaking for the neighborhood. Tom says he can only say that the Sandses feel they are speaking for others as well as themselves.

Tom and the Sandses agree upon some possible times for a hearing that Tom will suggest to the neighbors.

This marks the end of the intake process with the Sandses. The conversation between Tom and the Sandses lasted forty-five minutes.

Interview with the Intake Worker after His Meeting
with the First Party

I interviewed Tom after the first-party visit about his perception of the dispute and how he planned to complete the intake process with the second party. He was confident that he could get the second party to agree to a hearing for the reasons he discussed with the Sandses. He thought that the second party would be surprised to learn of the

Sandses' concerns, but he felt that as new neighbors they probably wouldn't want to "rock the boat" and might even be grateful for the opportunity to work things out under the auspices of SFCB. He added that he anticipated that the second party might respond somewhat defensively towards him as a result of his unannounced arrival and when they learned of SFCB involvement, since they were probably unfamiliar with the program. He also thought they might be concerned when he characterized the dispute as a potential threat to their business. He planned to use their anxiety, however, "in a positive way," to discuss the benefits of the SFCB hearing process. He strategized that he would present the Sandses' plan to take formal action as another reason why the second party should consider using the SFCB hearing process.

Intake with the Second Party

At 9:25 A.M. on the Saturday following his meeting with the Sandses, Tom arrives at the home of the second party, the Sorensons. He is separated from the front door by a flight of stairs and a security gate. He rings the bell on the security gate. A man in a bathrobe, rubbing the sleep from his eyes, comes to the head of the stairs. Tom announces that he is from the SFCB—"a group concerned with neighborhood-type problems, and I'm here to talk about a problem in the neighborhood that concerns you and your neighbor across the street."

Paul Sorenson agrees to talk after he has had breakfast and dressed. He asks Tom to return in an hour.

Tom returns at 10:30 A.M., and Paul invites him in and introduces his wife, Ann, who by Paul's description is "very pregnant with our first child." She is in her ninth month of pregnancy.

Paul and Ann Sorenson are a white couple in their late thirties. Ann says she is upset by the situation: that Tom, a complete stranger, has arrived at their door on a Saturday morning, without prior notice, to inform them of a problem between themselves and the neighbors across the street, who they don't even know by name. She explains that they are new to the neighborhood and are still adjusting. They were unexpectedly forced to move from their prior residence and have only been in the house three months. She is nervous about her pregnancy, and anxious to know what the problem is, and why Tom is involved.

Tom briefly explains that he is a volunteer with SFCB, "a volunteer neighborhood organization that helps resolve disputes between neighbors without the use of the courts or attorneys." He explains that the Sandses called the SFCB because they are concerned that the Sorensons are running a business out of their home.

Ann acknowledges that they do run a business out of their home, but only because of economic necessity. She quickly explains that she and Paul have been under a lot of stress with the baby's impending arrival, the unanticipated move, and the recent death of Paul's father. They certainly don't want to offend anyone. They are quiet, private people and are still adjusting to their new home and neighborhood.

Paul asks Tom about his role as a go-between:

Why are we learning about this problem from you and not the Sands? Is there any reason the Sands haven't said anything to us directly? Do you know if they've contacted anyone else, like an attorney or some other city agency?

Tom replies that the Sandses have not contacted anyone else as of yet but will if they don't resolve the dispute with SFCB. He adds that SFCB is not a city agency and it "is not in the business of enforcement."

Paul and Ann indicate their willingness to make the business less conscpicuous, if that would help. They suggest that they could store some of their inventory elsewhere, or perhaps park a truck or two up the street.

Ann is becoming flushed and visibly more anxious. She explains that it is a family business. She, Paul, and her brother are commercial electrical contractors. They don't do anything but paperwork at home and store some materials in the garage. She realizes that they have the trucks parked out front, but they are gone most of the day. Her brother doesn't even drive over in the morning. He takes the bus and walks down the street.

Tom asks a few questions about the business:

Do you work in the basement? What kind of hours do you keep? Is there much traffic?

Paul and Ann respond that as commercial contractors almost all of their work is done on-site or downtown. They go to clients' offices, not visa versa. They leave between 7:30 A.M. and 9:00 A.M., depending on the job. They return home in the evening. Ann adds that she has been home more often now because of the pregnancy, but she is inside and quiet.

Accepting the Sorensons' description without comment, Tom begins to describe the hearing process. He relates fewer anecdotes about the program and is less convivial than he was with the Sandses. Instead of talking about his experiences as a program volunteer, he focuses on how he has seen similar problems crop up in his own neighborhood, and how they were resolved when neighbors involved decided to *"talk to* each other, rather than *at* each other." He emphasizes how mediation builds a sense of neighborhood and community by bringing together neighbors—"everyday people like yourself"—to resolve disputes.

He underscores the advantages of the SFCB approach compared to litigation:

> It is less costly, quicker, and can get to the root of the problem. At a hearing you can address issues that you couldn't in court. We help people work out solutions that are personally meaningful to them, and rather than increasing tension, which usually happens when people go to court or involve attorneys, the Community Boards approach diffuses conflict by using a win-win approach.

Tom encourages the Sorensons to agree to a hearing. Persuasively, he comments that he can understand how they would want to resolve things before they escalate since the Sandses' complaint might affect their livelihood. He adds that he is really optimistic about the outcome since it would be a first conversation between the disputants, and since, so far, no other outside parties have been involved.

Ann and Paul reply that they don't feel that they have a choice:

> There's no way we could move at this point in time. Is that what the Sands want? Where do they draw the line? Architects, lawyers, professors are allowed to have offices in their homes. On

what basis are the Sands deciding who can have an office and
who can't?

Tom responds by telling the Sorensons that they would be able
to ask the Sandses these questions directly at the hearing.

Ann asks if they should just go over and talk to the Sandses
directly. Tom discourages them:

> At this point, it might make things worse. It would be really
> difficult to touch upon all the issues that are involved. At the
> hearing, you and the Sands could set up some rules for what to
> do the next time the Sands decide to drop the shoe.

This scares the Sorensons: "all the issues," "the next time." They
want more specifics. What other issues? Tom advises them that the
hearing is the best place to really identify these issues.

Ann asserts that she would really like to attend the hearing
because she is a better listener and speaker than Paul. She asks Tom
whether SFCB could schedule a hearing for the next evening or later
that week, so she could attend, before the baby arrives.

Tom tells her that it would be difficult to contact volunteer mediators and schedule a hearing on such short notice. He adds that Paul
probably won't want to leave her and the baby in the first week after
the baby's birth. He suggests a date two weeks in advance, and says
that he expects that only Paul would attend. Ann is displeased, but
worried that the Sandses might become upset if they think that they
(the Sorensons) are delaying the hearing. With a deep sigh, she agrees
to let Paul participate without her.

Paul asks if the whole neighborhood is involved. Are all their
neighbors opposed or just the Sandses? Tom replies that Mr. Sands
thinks of himself as a "block mayor," but it is a self-appointed position. Both Paul and Ann become alarmed, thinking that Tom has
said that the Sandses were speaking for the neighborhood.

Paul comments that it seems like he is being asked to make all
the changes, what about the Sandses? Tom replies that perhaps they
can work out an agreement about how the Sandses will act the next
time they get upset. Paul is somewhat appeased, but both he and
Ann say that they are quite upset and anxious about the implications
of this unexpected dispute.

Tom thanks them for their time and interest. He advises them that he'll call to check with them about the time and place of the hearing. He repeats that he is confident that they can work things out together. The visit lasted an hour.

Interview with the Intake Worker after His Meeting with the Second Party

I interviewed Tom following his visit with the second party. He described the intake process as a "success." He explained the importance of appealing to people's self-interest to get them to agree to use SFCB. He felt that the Sorensons agreed to participate in the hearing because they were concerned about how the Sandses' complaint might affect their livelihood, and because they had never spoken directly with the Sandses. Tom was convinced that the parties would work out a compromise at the hearing. He doubted, however, that there would be much discussion at the hearing about underlying issues, such as cultural differences or the Sandses' concerns about absentee landlords.

The Disputants' Perspectives: Substantive Issues of the Dispute

Both parties were interviewed, separately, a few days after their meetings with Tom.

The Sandses

The Sandses described the dispute as involving a range of issues, including the negative effect on property values of having the neighborhood become semicommercial, changing demographics of the neighborhood, and hurt feelings about the Sorensons' lack of respect for them and neighborhood standards. The Sandses passionately described how they considered their home a reward for all their years of struggle. They repeated what they had told Tom, that they were planning to stay in their home until "we die or get too old to care for ourselves. . . . To us, our house is *the Promised Land!*"

The Sorensons

The Sorensons reported that notice of their being "disputants" and involved in a "dispute" came as a total surprise, as did Tom's appearance at their door with this news, and his announcement of the involvement of SFCB, an unfamilar agency. The Sorensons explained that they were alarmed by the Sandses' complaint and perplexed by Tom's instructions not to speak with the Sandses directly. They were uncertain about what a SFCB hearing involved but hoped that it would clarify what was troubling the Sandses, and what, if anything, could be done.

The SFCB Perspective: Framing the Dispute as a Problem of Communication

Tom's handling of the complaint and his choice of categories to define the dispute—his "rephrasing" of the dispute—were consistent with program guidelines and his training and years of service as a SFCB volunteer. Looking at this interaction helps to identify the underlying assumptions that direct the SFCB approach to conflict resolution. Moreover, this analysis helps illuminate the practical significance of the program's claims about community and the empowering potential of the SFCB approach to conflict resolution.

Prior to speaking with the disputants, Tom articulated his understanding of a complex array of factors that he thought might be at play in this dispute. Tom's awareness of these factors suggested a number of different ways of defining the dispute that he might have employed in his discussion with the parties. For example, Tom might have suggested that the parties clarify the legal question of zoning. Or he might have approached the complaint as a neighborhood issue and contacted other neighbors about their reactions to the Sorensons' business and the issue of neighborhood change.

Tom chose, however, to frame the dispute as an interpersonal problem involving two parties, the Sandses and the Sorensons. This framing of the problem involved a deemphasis of many of the substantive issues of the conflict. In contrast, Tom attended to, and encouraged the disputants to focus on, the dispute as an interpersonal problem of communication. From this perspective, the conflict was perceived as a problem that could be resolved as a "communication problem" rather than as a legal issue, a neighborhood concern, or a complex conflict about rights, values, interests, behaviors, needs, or the changing composition of the neighborhood.

Tom encouraged the parties to believe that the solution to the dispute hinged on their discussing the dispute within the context of a SFCB hearing. He declined the Sandses' request that he speak with the Sorensons directly. He subsequently advised the Sorensons not to talk with the Sandses prior to the hearing. Instead, he advised both parties that the hearing was the best forum for discussion of this problem. This directive signaled a shift in the "ownership" of the problem, and the balance of power between the disputants and the SFCB. In the language of empowerment, at this juncture in the processing of this dispute, the disputants were for the moment disempowered and SFCB was empowered as a result of SFCB appropriation of the dispute (Christie 1977).

After meeting with both parties, Tom predicted that the Sorensons would modify their activities to avoid further confrontation. Neither he, nor the program staff to whom he reported his intake activity, expressed concern about the justice or fairness of this potential "resolution." Nor was there any discussion about differences in power between the parties as a result of difference in length of residence, age, impinging life events (i.e., birth, death, and moving), or racial or economic differences.

Of the two parties, the Sorensons were seen as the weaker of the two parties. The Sandses commanded respect. They derived authority from initiating the complaint, threatening to pursue further action, and from their age, economic stability, and their status as long-term residents. Moreover, their portrayal of this as a "neighborhood problem" and their interest in solving the conflict "as neighbors," corresponded to SFCB's ideology about the importance of neighborhood and community.

Status differences between disputants and the Sandses' appeal to program values affected Tom's approach to case intake and his strategizing about how the dispute should be resolved. The solution that Tom described and that he hoped would result from the hearing involved encouraging the Sorensons to modify their activities to appease the Sandses.

Dispute Transformation and Case Intake

Data about the intake process attests to the inherent complexities of disagreements and disputes and the problematic meaning of *neighborhood* and *community* in modern urban society. Analysis of data from this and other cases included in the Intensive Case Study demonstrate that the *intake process* is a critcial moment in the process of dispute transformation associated with SFCB's intervention. As illustrated in "The Promised Land," "disputants" may not even be aware of being involved in a "dispute" until contacted by SFCB.

For a dispute to be identified as a SFCB "case," parties contacted by the program must agree that a dispute exists. The parties must also agree that they have some involvement in the dispute, and a role in the genesis and/or resolution of the dispute in order for SFCB to continue to define the dispute as worthy of attention (as a "case"). In other words, parties contacted by the program must consent to be cast as disputants for the intake process to be considered successful. As discussed below, the success of the intake process is ultimately defined by the disputants' willingness to use SFCB and submit their dispute to mediation.

With regard to the specifics of this case, by agreeing to participate in the hearing, the Sandses and the Sorensons accepted a definition of the dispute that focused on the issue of the Sorensons' business practices, even though it appeared that the dispute involved larger issues steming from the changing demographics of the neighborhood and cultural differences. In accepting this definition, both parties, but the Sorensons in particular, agreed to a framing of the events that rendered the dispute amenable to SFCB's interests and method of dispute processing.

The literature on dispute transformation highlights restricting the number of participants as a common form of reframing disputes. In contrast, SFCB has built its reputation on assertions about the empowering potential of mediation, not just for individuals but for communities and neighborhoods. Autonomous from the courts, and with an avowed interest in community empowerment, SFCB clearly has the potential to view disputes in a larger context.

The program asserts that mediation affords the opportunity to process disputes that involve more than two individuals or two parties. Like most ADR programs, it espouses an ideology that is critical of the two-party adversarial system associated with the formal legal system. One might therefore anticipate that the program would process a fair number of disputes that involve more than two parties. Indeed, there is ample evidence to document that disputes spill over and affect the lives of people other than the officially recognized first and second parties. Yet, the overwhelming majority of cases processed by SFCB are defined as two-party disputes.[9]

Given these findings, an important question to ask is, why are disputes processed as problems between two parties when it appears that disputes routinely affect others, in addition to the two parties formally identified as disputants? Approaching this rephrasing critically helps to further identify the underlying, often implicit assumptions that direct the SFCB approach to conflict resolution.

The pragmatic reasons for viewing disputes in a two-party context are the easiest to identify. One such reason stems from the limited demands that can be placed on a volunteer labor force to both contact and process disputes, especially in a program that relies on home visits for case intake. For example, in the "The Promised Land," Tom was fortunate. His prearranged visit with the Sandses occurred as scheduled. He found the Sorensons home on his first try, and they agreed to talk with him. Despite an hour's delay he was able to meet with them the same day. More often than not, intake workers fail in their first surprise attempt to contact the second party and are forced to try a second, third, and sometimes fourth time. Indeed, regardless of his good fortune, Tom spent almost three hours talking with the disputants and an additional two hours preparing for the visits and the hearing. The amount of volunteer and staff time increases exponentially when disputes involve more than two parties.

A second reason sounds equally pragmatic, at least initially. The mediation process itself functions more smoothly when there are only two parties. When more than two parties participate in the mediation session, the process proves to be somewhat unwieldy and certainly more time-consuming. Indeed, in the cases where there are more than

9. SFCB has responded to a number of disputes involving multiple disputants. Group cases often involve a web of ongoing problems. Case intake and mediation in these cases usually requires considerable staff and volunteer attention and represent a challenge to the SFCB framing of disputes as problems of communication. The number of group cases throughout SFCB history of operation has been quite small. The comprehensive evaluation study identified less than thirty group cases for the period of 1977 to 1982.

two parties, or when there are parties who have a collective identity, the SFCB routinely asks the multiple disputants comprising a "party" to appoint a spokesperson to speak for the group at the hearing.

Other reasons that explain why SFCB tends to define and process disputes as two-party problems are more subtle, yet theoretically important. On the one hand, modern American mediation programs including SFCB have emerged in the shadow of the formal legal system. The legal system rests on a political tradition that views struggle and conflict from a two-party perspective. Formal justice is premised upon a dyadic model of confrontation.[10] Judicial intervention introduces an ostensibly neutral third party to help resolve disputes. Western intellectual history concerning the study and interpretation of disputing involves fundamental assumptions that are rarely recognized, considered, or viewed as problematic. These assumptions color the very language used in the study of disputing. For example, by common definition disputes emerge when a grievance is announced to a "third party," and discussion concerning the involvement of a "third party" is routinely employed analytically and linguistically to differentiate between "negotiation" and such "third party" interventions as mediation, arbitration, and adjudication. Culturally and intellectually ingrained in Western society, this tradition profoundly influences the very way people (including disputants, program representatives, and legal scholars) perceive and actively define conflict and disputes. Not surprisingly, although SFCB is critical of the formal legal system's approach to disputing, the program and program participants continue to be influenced by a culturally ingrained two-party approach to disputing.

Underpinning this discussion, however, is the fundamental influence of the communication paradigm of conflict. As mentioned earlier, SFCB representatives elicit the disputants' interest in the hearing process by noting the importance of establishing free and open communication and by describing the hearing process as a unique forum for this exchange. When disputes are seen as communication problems, rather than conflicts over interests, needs, values, behaviors, or rights, then establishing communication is both the method and sought-after outcome of mediation. Limiting the number of disputants to two parties facilitates the mediators' control of the hearing process.

---

10. See Nader (1980) for a discussion of how law, American culture, and economy contribute to and reinforce a dyadic, individualized model of disputing.

Moreover, the goal of a communication model is to establish, re-establish, or otherwise repair the lines of communication between disputants (Silbey and Merry 1982). Not only is it easier to achieve this goal when there are only two disputing parties, but there is no apparent need to expand the definition of the dispute to involve more than two parties.

The Hearing Process

The hearing process employed by SFCB resembles that of other mediation programs in many ways, but also displays a number of distinctive features (DuBow and McEwen, and Shoak and Milner, in this volume). As in other voluntary mediation programs, disputants are informed that the mediators are not judges and they will not render a decision. Disputants are asked to respect each other and the hearing process.

SFCB hearings take place in the program's field offices or space provided by local community facilities (e.g., schools, churches, meeting rooms). The hearing process is directed by three to five mediators. Program staff select mediators on a case-specific basis, attempting to ensure variation in expertise as well as correspondence between disputants' and mediators' sociodemographic characteristics, especially with regards to race and age.

Hearings are bracketed by prehearing briefings and posthearing review sessions. These discussions are directed by either program staff or a veteran volunteer "trainer." Usually one or more of the intake workers attend the prehearing briefing to explain what occurred during the intake process and advise the mediators of their analysis of the dispute. Intake workers may stay for the hearing, but they generally do not participate in the mediation session.

The hearing follows a four-phase process. In the first phase, the disputants explain their understanding of the dispute to the mediators. During this phase, mediators ask questions, but discourage the introduction of "hard" evidence (e.g., written documentation, bills, photographs, etc.), or claims to legal rights.

In the second phase, disputants are directed to talk directly with one another. Mediators ask disputants to reposition their chairs so they are facing each other, rather than the panel. Trained to expect that the emotive component of disputes must be expressed if resolutions are to be durable and satisfying, mediators encourage disputants during this phase to talk about their feelings, as well as the chronology and relational aspects of the dispute. Mediators are trained to use specific techniques such as "active listening" and "role reversals" to help disputants express their feelings and convey their understanding of the feelings and statements of the other party.

The third phase of the process occurs when mediators perceive that the disputants have come to a new understanding of the dispute and their feelings. This phase is usually triggered by a turn in the discussion to possible approaches to settlement. During the data-collection phase of the Intensive Case Study, this phase of the hearing focused on encouraging disputants to acknowledge their responsibility for the events that led to the dispute.[11]

During the fourth and final phase of the session with the disputants, mediators review points of agreement previously expressed and draft a written agreement. One member of the panel writes the agreement. The agreement is signed by the disputants and one member of the mediation panel. Written agreements are not mandatory, but they are encouraged.

In sum, SFCB emphasizes the voluntary nature of mediation. There is a strong emphasis on the use of lay mediators who are "neighbors" of the disputants, their peers, and people concerned about local neighborhood issues. Disputants are encouraged to talk about their feelings and the emotive and relational aspects of their disputes, and to take the responsibility of solving their own disputes. Reference is made to the advantages of mediation over litigation. Consideration of evidentiary materials is limited. Proceedings are public, in the sense that there are no private caucuses between disputants and mediators. Observers may attend if arranged and agreed to by the program and the disputants.

The Hearing in "The Promised Land"

The Briefing

The prehearing briefing of the panel of mediators starts shortly after 7:00 P.M. The hearing is scheduled to begin at 7:30 P.M. One SFCB

---

11. Phase three was modified soon after data collection for the Intensive Care Study ended. The revision introduced a future orientation to this phase that involved asking disputants if they were ready to discuss how things might change in the future, and if they were interested in drafting an agreement.

volunteer fails to arrive. Two other program volunteers, David Owen, a white college student in his early twenties, and Ellen Woods, a white educator in her early fifties and a veteran SFCB volunteer, serve as mediators. Fred Smith, a black SFCB staff administrator and trainer with the central SFCB office, who is in his early thirties, is a third mediator. This is the first hearing for both David and Fred. Tom, the intake worker, agrees to act as the trainer as well, due to the unexpected absence of another SFCB volunteer who was scheduled to serve as the trainer.

Tom asks if David or any of the others have questions about the hearing process. He hands them the case report, which reads:

> Alfred and Gladys Sands, and Paul and Ann Sorenson, are neighbors who live across from each other on Elm Street. Two weeks ago, Mr. Sands called the SFCB with a concern about the electrical contracting business based at Paul and Ann's house. He says that neither Paul nor Ann had mentioned anything about the business to them on the occasions when they greeted each other. They feel strongly that running the business is inappropriate to the residential character of the block.
>
> Paul and Ann say that before they were contacted by the SFCB intake worker they were unaware of the concerns of their neighbors. They are concerned that there be no misunderstanding or hard feelings on the block as they just moved recently and have barely had a chance to settle in.
>
> Both parties have come to the hearing tonight to discuss their concerns with one another, and, with the mediators' help, to arrive at a resolution of their concerns that is mutually satisfactory.

The mediators have no questions. Tom reiterates the same analysis of the dispute that he developed prior to his visit with the disputants. He tells the mediators it is important that they understand that this neighborhood, more so than other neighborhoods in the city, has gone through tremendous social and demographic changes during the past forty years and is presently in the midst of another change. Once a middle-class black neighborhood of family-owned homes, it is becoming more white, and renters are replacing homeowners. He warns the mediators that Alfred Sands considers himself a neighborhood spokesperson. He explains that the Sorensons have agreed to the hearing because their livelihood is involved. He says that Ann Sorenson wanted to attend but just had a baby. (He doesn't mention that he dissuaded her from participating, or that the scheduling of the hearing precluded her involvement.) He notes that the Sandses are a black couple and long-term residents of the neighborhood and that the Sorensons are a white couple who have lived in the neighborhood for only three months.

Tom emphasizes that the Sandses are offended because the Sorensons never introduced themselves, and that this sense of offense has added to the intensity of their opposition to the home-based operation of the Sorensons' business. He clarifies that the Sandses believe that the Sorensons are violating the law and neighborhood standards by running a business out of their home.

Ellen asks if there is something else, some other concern like racism or something generational. Tom replies:

> I think it would be inappropriate for the panel to bring these issues up. Maybe Paul will ask, but Alfred emphasized during the intake visit that it wasn't a racial or personal issue.

Tom is concerned that the disputants may have some time limits that the panel will need to address. Most hearings take about three hours. Unbeknownst to the mediators, Tom told the disputants that the hearing would last about an hour and a half. He advises the panel to congratulate Paul on becoming a father, and to use that as an opening to ask if either party has limits for the hearing.

Ellen advises her comediators to use plenty of active listening and to remember to praise the disputants for the progress they are making throughout the hearing.

Ellen asks if there has been any overt conflict. Her question prompts Tom to tell the panel that the disputants have never talked to each other and don't know each other by name. He advises them:

> Alfred Sands has a plan—he is determined to try and reduce any overt commercial activity in the neighborhood. . . . There is also some emotional baggage here.

Tom suggests that the mediators ask the disputants what they could have done to prevent the conflict. He also advises the panel to ask the disputants to discuss how neighbors should introduce themselves and communicate. He thinks that since they have never talked they might find that they share the same feelings about neighborliness.

At 7:25 P.M., the Sandses arrive and are asked to wait in the hall.

The briefing draws to a close with the panelists discussing how they might respond if the parties don't "budge." The discussion involves strategizing by analogizing to other SFCB cases where impasses occurred. Ellen comments that Alfred Sands sounds as rigid as her father-in-law, and Paul Sorenson reminds her of her son who also runs a business out of his home. She says she will share this information with the disputants if it appears that they need "validation."

Mr. Sorenson arrives at 7:30 P.M. He is asked to wait in the hall together with the Sandses while the panel wraps things up. The panel decides that it will be really important for them to stress similarities between parties, especially similar feelings about neighborhood values, behaviors, and appropriate forms of interaction between neighbors.

The Hearing Begins

The hearing commences at 7:45 P.M.

Fred welcomes the parties. The panelists and Tom introduce themselves. The mediators sit behind a six-foot-long rectangular table. The disputants sit facing the mediators.

Fred begins by explaining the SFCB hearing process. He advises the parties that the panel is not there to decide whether anyone is right or wrong. He reminds them that just as Tom told them, they (the mediators) are not judges or arbitrators but rather concerned citizens and local residents who have been trained by the SFCB to help disputants resolve conflicts like the one between the Sandses and the Sorensons. He thanks them for coming and then proceeds to outline the four phases of the mediation process:

In Phase I, each side will tell the panel about their concerns, without interruption by the other party.

In Phase II, we will ask you to talk to each other directly.

In Phase III and IV, we will work together to resolve the conflict.

He asks both parties to indicate that they will abide by the basic ground rules of the mediation process: they are to talk directly to the panel in phase one and not to each other; disputants are not to interrupt each other; they are to treat each other with respect. He asks if they have any questions. They don't.

He asks David to read the case report (see above). Fred asks the Sandses and Paul Sorenson if they agree with the case report. They nod. Turning to Paul, he says he understands his wife just had a baby. He offers his congratulations, noting that he, too, is a new father. (He does not use this as an opening to ask about time limits). Turning to the Sandses, he asks who would like to start. Gladys volunteers:

> Well, first, I didn't know the other party's name until tonight. I don't want to see the neighborhood change. My feelings is if he starts a business in his home, the next step is something else. We moved here in 1947, because we wanted a quiet neighborhood. We've raised five children here. The neighborhood has been really important to us, and we don't want to see it change. If Paul is allowed to operate a business, then the next thing you know, every house will have a business, and won't be a residential neighborhood any more.

Alfred adds:

> Well, it's the principle. It is a residential neighborhood. We don't want businesses; it's not zoned for businesses; it's zoned residential. I have nothing against this gentleman here. I'd like to add that there's a plumber and a painter who live up the street and they're fine people, and they don't run their businesses out of their homes. I don't know what Paul does, but he shouldn't be allowed to run his business out of his home.

Fred thanks the Sandses, and asks if they have anything to add. They don't. He then asks for Paul's view of the problem. Paul responds:

I didn't even know there was a problem until someone [Tom] came to the house a week ago Saturday to tell me about the Sandses' concerns.

I do have an office in my home. But I don't have a lot of people coming and going. I'm not like the neighbors next door who have parties all the time. I'm quiet. I want to be quiet. I don't want any disturbances in the neighborhood.

In response to questions from the panel, Paul explains that the office is "just a paperwork office." It is where he and Ann write estimates and do their bookkeeping. He and Ann had to move from their last residence unexpectedly, on extremely short notice:

We had the same business there, and had no problems with the neighbors. We had to leave within 30 days. My wife was pregnant. I needed to find a place right away. I want a quiet neighborhood for my daughter. I don't want to have any problems. I'd like to change the situation as soon as I can.

During the next fifteen minutes, the mediators attempts to construct their individual and collective understanding of the dispute. Their questioning is spontaneous and unstructured. During this period, Alfred tells the panel more than once:

You could ask me questions all night, and I'd give you the same answer—I am totally opposed to any commercial activity operating out of a home in a residential neighborhood.

Ellen asks the Sandses to clarify whether their concern is that Paul is setting a precedent, or are they worried about flammable and other potentially dangerous materials being stored in the Sorensons' garage. The Sandses explain that it is neither—they are not worried about materials nor precedent because they don't want a business at all. Ellen states that she can understand their concerns because she knows of a similar dispute in her neighborhood. Her expression of empathy does not appear to have the desired effect of loosening up the disputants.

Fred comments that the conversation is focusing on differences rather than similarities. He asks the disputants to talk about their concept of neighborhood in an attempt to redirect the conversation to what he hopes are commonly held values or interests. He asks Paul to describe what is important to him in a neighborhood. Paul responds to Fred's question:

> I don't know what is important in a neighborhood. I never really thought about it. But, you know, after Tom came over and told us about the problem, my wife talked with our other neighbors. It doesn't seem like our having a business in our home is upsetting them.

Still intent on revealing similarities, Fred asks Paul once again to describe what he wants in a neighborhood. Paul says:

> I guess the only thing that is important to me is that it's quiet.

In what proves to be a futile attempt to point to common concerns, Fred comments that he has heard that both the Sandses and the Sorensons want a quiet neighborhood. He adds that it is important that both parties recognize this as a concern they share. Then, Fred himself rekindles a discussion of differences by asking Paul to describe his daily activities. Paul is somewhat defensive and unsure of Fred's intent. He is also skeptical about the value of this disclosure:

> I am not sure how talking about what I do is going to change anything. The Sands have said it doesn't matter—they are only interested in one thing—getting the business out.

While the Sandses nod in agreement, Fred encourages Paul to continue. Paul does:

> Well, Ann and I get up around 6:30 A.M. Our partners join us by 7:30 A.M. Normally, we leave between 7:30 A.M. and 9:00 A.M., and often don't return until the afternoon or evening, between 3:00 P.M. and 6:00 P.M.

David follows Fred's line of questioning and asks Paul if he has a warehouse for his inventory. Paul replies that he has no specific inventory, occasionally he has leftover materials that he stores in the garage. Fred, David, and Ellen take turns asking about more of the specifics of the business:

> Do people come to you? How long have you been in business? What kind of office do you maintain in your home?

Paul answers their questions succinctly, explaining once again that it is only a "paperwork office, where we write out estimates and do the bookkeeping."

Satisfied by Paul's responses, the mediators try again to identify the specifics about Paul's business that bother the Sandses. The Sandses are resistant. They don't want to talk about specifics. Ellen asks:

> Mrs. Sands, how did it come to your attention that Paul was running a business out of his home?

Alfred Sands angrily interrupts:

> Ellen, is that right? That's your name? Ellen, it doesn't matter how we found out. You can ask us question after question and I'll give you the same answer—It is a residential neighborhood, not a business neighborhood! And that's the way it should stay!

He turns to Paul:

> If Paul, that's your name, isn't it? If Paul can have a business, why can't I? What is to stop everyone? We have to stop it now!

Gladys Sands turns to the panel, subtly apologizing for Alfred's interruption:

> Excuse me, I believe you asked how it came to our attention? [Ellen and the other mediators nod.] Well, the garage door was open one day and I saw what looked like an entire warehouse of electrical supplies. Then, a couple of days later it was open again and I swear I saw twice as many supplies. The place was bursting at the seams.

Ellen asks Gladys:

> Does Paul receive deliveries during the day?

Gladys replies:

> I work from 7:00 A.M. to 6:00 P.M., so I really don't know, but it really doesn't matter because it's the business that's the problem.

Although less aggressive than Alfred, Gladys similarly refuses to identify any specific behavior (which the mediators could then use as a vehicle for discussion and possible compromise). Both she and Alfred reiterate that they are not interested in a modification of Paul's behavior. They want a total halt to his business activities.

Fred tries another tactic to get the disputants to focus on areas of common interest. He explains that he has heard both parties say that the present situation is not ideal. He then asks the Sandses to specify what they would like to have happen.

Gladys obliges the question, but with a fair degree of frustration:

> I want the neighborhood to stay as it is now. We intend to stay. Even though I know things can't always be the same I'd like it to stay as close to the neighborhood we have always known. In the past few years, I've seen many of our neighbors become widows. Kids we've known since they were in diapers have grown up and moved away. But, let me tell you, even if someone offered me a million dollars I wouldn't move. I want families to live in the neighborhood. I welcome Paul and his wife. But NO BUSINESSES!

Paul turns to Gladys and asks her directly;

> How far does that go? Where do you draw the line? Would you feel the same way if it was a professor who had an office, or an architect, or a stamp collector?

Gladys responds that it is the commercial activity that bothers her, not the type of commercial activity.

Fred interprets Paul's direct communication with Gladys as an indication that the disputants are ready to talk to each other. He asks Ellen and David if they have any other questions or if they agree that it is time to begin phase two of the hearing. Ellen and David have no other questions and indicate to Fred that he should proceed. He asks the disputants to turn their chairs so that they face each other and suggests that they start by having the Sandses tell Paul specifically what's bothering them.

Gladys is more amenable to following the panel's directives than Alfred, but she is starting to resent this line of questioning. Instead of talking to Paul, since Fred is the one who asked the question, she turns back to the panel to explain that "what bothers and upsets me is ANYTHING that denotes business activity." Fred tells her to talk to Paul. She shifts her focus to Paul:

> Okay. For example, there are three trucks that come and go, and are parked on the street. There is the material that I can see in your garage. There are your "partners" who are in and out.
>
>   I am opposed to commercial activity in a residential neighborhood. I'd feel the same way if there was a beauty parlor being operated out of another neighbor's house.

Alfred is quick to add:

> Why can you run a business and I can't? My tax base is going to be affected by your commercial activity.

Paul asks the panel if he might say something in response to the Sandses' "allegations." Breaking from the phase two convention of direct communication between parties, they invite Paul to tell them what he has to say. In a very serious tone, he begins:

> The Sands seem concerned about my trucks and my partners. One of the men they see is my brother. The other is my nephew— who I am being nice to by giving him a job for the summer. They are the only people they see, they're the only ones involved in the business besides Ann. It is a family business—not a big commercial enterprise.

Fred perceives that the hearing is starting to stall. The parties seem immobile. He tries to move things forward by thanking the disputants for their interest in using the SFCB. Next, he reminds them that they are at the hearing not to fight but to try and work out a resolution. He tries to reintroduce the phase two process by telling his fellow mediators and the disputants that before moving on he wants to summarize the disputants' concerns and congratulate them on the progress they have made thus far:

> I heard Paul say that under ideal conditions he wouldn't want to have his business in his home. I heard the Sandses say that they really wished for a totally residential neighborhood. I am not sure about the gray areas that the Sandses would find tolerable, but I realize that Mr. and Mrs. Sands believe that specific boundaries about activity in the neighborhood are not being observed. All of us [the mediators] would like to thank you for discussing your concerns with us, and I think we all agree that we are moving in the right direction.

Fred asks if the disputants have any questions. Alfred doesn't have a question but makes use of the opportunity to restate that it's not important to him what materials Paul stores, all he wants is for Paul to cease those activities that constitute his commercial business. Fred asks the other mediators if they have any further questions for the disputants. Ellen says she would like to know how long Paul has been in business. He tells her five years. She nods empathetically and comments that it is a tough business. She asks if he would be willing to move his business, in the next few months. He says that's a possibility.

As she indicated during the prehearing discussion, Ellen informs the disputants that she knows the situation is upsetting to them both because she has been involved in a similar dispute in her own neighborhood where one neighbor is uncomfortable with a younger neighbor's home-based entrepreneurial activities. She comments that she "can see both sides, and feel for both sides." Fred adds that he, too, can understand that it is hard to watch a neighborhood change, and that when you are new to an area it is difficult to demonstrate that you want to be a good neighbor.

Since there are no further questions, Fred repeats his earlier explanation of phase two, emphasizing that this is the chance for the disputants "to talk to each other and begin to work on a resolution to the dispute."

Paul interrupts:

> Is there really any reason to go on? It seems to me that Alfred is not interested in changing his position. Continuing seems like a waste of time.

Ellen responds:

> Oh, it is always important to go ahead. It's important to talk with each other to find out how the situation is affecting both parties.

Exasperated, Paul replies:

> You know, I've been working sixteen hours a day, my wife was expecting and overdue, and I truly haven't had any time to think about the Sandses, or how the problem is affecting them!

Ellen, Fred, and David discourage Paul from ending the hearing. Each stresses how important it is for both parties to talk to each other at this time. They emphasize that Paul's and the Sandses' attendance at the hearing indicates their interest in resolving the dispute, and that to stop now would not only preclude an immediate resolution but would probably inhibit further communication and thus limit the chance for an amicable and mutually satisfying resolution.

Reluctantly, Paul agrees to continue. He asks the panel to repeat their summary of the concerns. This time Ellen responds. She focuses on how both parties seem equally concerned with living in a quiet, family neighborhood. She suggests that they begin phase two by discussing what constitutes a "good neighborhood." Ellen suggests that they move their chairs so that they face each other fully (they never really accomplished this task when previously instructed).

Alfred turns to Paul and outside of the panel's instructions reintroduces himself with a handshake, and asks for Paul's name again. It seems a ceremonial move, designed to put Paul on the defensive and allow Alfred a sense of control. Alfred then takes up on the panel's invitation for direct communication:

Well, since I'm sitting in the middle I'll start. I want to preface this by telling you about this neighbor who was growing a marijuana plant. This has nothing to do with you, Paul. Well, I told him not to grow it because it wasn't right. I didn't call the police. He removed it. Now, if you were the President, I'd do the same thing. I'd call the Planning Commission, just like I did in this case. I called them and they referred me to a local community agency who then referred the SFCB. But, if we don't work it out tonight, I'll go back to the Planning Commission.

I've said hello to you. This is nothing personal. It is the commercial venture we are opposed to, that's the only reason we are here tonight. Nothing personal, okay?

Fred attempts to diffuse any tension prompted by Alfred's comment about the marijuana by suggesting that Alfred was using this incident merely as a way to express his concerns about neighborhood standards of behavior. The panel ignores Alfred's statement about prior contact with the Planning Commission, as well as his overt threat of further action against Paul.

After nearly twenty minutes of back and forth, Paul turns to the panel and questions the utility of continuing:

I can't see continuing. The situation is intractable. Nothing has changed from when we started. . . . It wouldn't matter if in six months the inventory was gone. Alfred has called the Planning Commission, and is threatening to call them again. Obviously, I'll have to do something.

Fred indicates that he is not sure the Sandses responded to the question about using the home office for estimate writing. Paul corrects him, saying that the Sandses indicated that they refuse to accept any commercial activity at all. The Sandses nod.

The mediators persist in efforts to get beyond this impasse but are uncertain about what to do. The disputants are quite polarized and it is difficult to identify common concerns. Alfred counts the change from his pocket.

Since Alfred has been so recalcitrant and has dominated the conversation, Fred, in a last attempt to move the hearing forward, asks Gladys to tell Paul her concerns. She has no problem turning to Paul and repeating her opposition to his having any kind of business. She adds that it is not the individual issues that the mediators have enumerated, but rather the business in general that concerns her.

Paul asks her if it would make any difference if he removed all the inventory from the garage. Still fiddling with the change from his pocket, Alfred replies:

Nope, 'cuz you'd still be violating the zoning ordinance—And that can only be corrected if you move the entire business.

At this point (approximately an hour and a half from the start of the hearing), both parties ask the mediators if they can stop. Paul observes that he now knows where the Sandses stand, and that the only resolution they are willing to accept is for him to move his entire business. The Sandses nod in agreement. Paul concludes that there is no reason to continue. The Sandses nod again.

Fred turns to the other mediators and asks if they have anything to say. David, who has been fairly quiet, comments that it seems to him that by contacting the SFCB the Sandses demonstrated that they would prefer not to take legal action.

Paul interrupts:

But they have a fixed position. The next step is filing a complaint. And that's what they've said they'll do. So, what's the point of going on with this?

The following dialogue ensues:

Fred: The SFCB is designed to give neighbors an alternative, to let them talk to each other. As neighbors we can deal with anything, we're not restricted like the legal system. Plus, this is not an adversarial process.
Paul: That's fine, but what is there to discuss as neighbors? They [the Sandses] are not interested in specifics.
Gladys: That's absolutely right. Just moving the inventory, or parking the truck somewhere else is not the issue.
Fred: The spirit of the process is resolution. Is there any room

for resolution? The next step is to have a third party intervene who doesn't care about you as neighbors.

Gladys: Well, I want Paul to know that we TOTALLY object to his business. I'm happy to have him live there, but if you say that you can't afford to move the business, then there is nothing further to talk about here.

Paul: That's what I said.

Ellen thanks the disputants for expressing their feelings. She informs them that sometimes hearings don't result in resolution, although in this case she thinks there might have been some misunderstandings about the purpose of the hearing. After commending Gladys for speaking so clearly about her commitment to the neighborhood she turns to Paul and asks him how he came to pick this neighborhood. He explains he had no choice, he had been served a thirty-day eviction notice and had to find something he could afford, especially with the baby on the way.

Fred notices that Gladys is nodding her head as Paul speaks. Perceiving this as a sign of "softening," he asks Gladys to repeat back what Paul has just said. She repeats it verbatim. Fred then asserts that "what's important is not what you do, but how you feel."

Although a few minutes ago it seemed that the panel was about to oblige the disputants' request to stop the hearing, Fred tries again to get the Sandses and Paul to talk about their feelings. He asks Gladys how she would feel in Fred's place.

Gladys replies:

I haven't the foggiest. Besides, Paul could NEVER understand my feelings. How could he? We had to fight to get here. We succeeded! We've been here since 1947, and we're not going to move now!

At Fred's request she describes how in order to buy their house she and Alfred had to fight redlining and other forms of racial discrimination. She repeats the account of the fire that they discussed with Tom during the intake visit, but this time around she displays much more emotion and anger than before. She describes the fire "as the worst experience of my life—it was a terrible and devastating experience to see our dreams go up in flames."

David acknowledges the Sandses' struggles and their success at survival. He then adds that it seems like Paul is trying to survive as well, "trying to make it with a business and a new baby."

David's comparison infuriates Gladys. She agrees that Paul is struggling but she doesn't think it is fair to assess the trauma as equal. With an innocence that Gladys finds insulting, David comments that perhaps Paul's loss of his business might be more traumatic than the Sandses' fire. With a raised voice, Gladys tells the panel:

> There is NO COMPARISON! When your house goes up in flames, you don't have options! When you have to fight to get a loan because you're black, you don't have options! Paul has options, he can move his business!

The panel turns to Paul and asks him what he sees as his options. He replies:

> None. I guess we will have to move. I don't have time to go to Planning Commission meetings. Besides, I probably wouldn't win, and I'd have to move sooner or later.

Tom signals to the mediators to call for a short recess. Fred notices and suggests that before they abandon the hearing they take a five-minute break. The other mediators endorse his suggestions. The disputants reluctantly agree.

The disputants are asked to wait in the hallway. They position themselves at opposite ends of the corridor.

The Mediators' Caucus

Outside of the presence of the disputants, the mediators express their dismay with the hearing. They are frustrated by the Sandses' inflexibility. They ask Tom if he provided an accurate description of the hearing process to the Sandses. They question if Alfred Sands is taking advantage of the hearing merely to theaten Paul Sorenson with legal action. This exchange lasts for five minutes.

Alfred knocks on the door to ask if they are ready yet. He is told that the hearing will resume in a few minutes.

Ellen suggests that they reopen discussion by asking what will happen the next time the "shoe drops again." She thinks it might be helpful to encourage the disputants to think of the hearing as a learning experience. The others agree and the disputants are called from the hall.

The Hearing Resumes

Ellen reconvenes the hearing, explaining:

> In terms of experience, every one of our hearings is a learning experience—just even in terms of what will happen next time.
> What have you learned from the problem, from being here tonight? What might you do differently next time a vacant house becomes occupied?
> What would you do differently Gladys?

Gladys replies:

> If it was the same situation? Well I'm not very out-going so I'd probably ask Alfred if he has met the other people.

Fred turns to Alfred:

> What about you, Alfred?

Alfred responds:

> I have a question? Fred, that's your name, right? [Fred nods, but appears perplexed by this turn in questioning.] Where did you go to school?

Fred:

> Howard University.

Alfred:

Ask me your question again. That's a salesman's ploy.

Ellen repeats Fred's question, to which Alfred replies:

I'd do the same thing. I'd introduce myself and see if the guy is interested in the neighborhood. And if something was wrong, a business thing, or like the guy with the marijuana plant, I'd work to put a stop to it.

Ellen turns to Paul and asks him what he would do differently the next time he moves. Paul says:

I was in a hurry to find housing. I introduced myself to the neighbors on both sides but not across the street. . . . Next time I'd look for a neighborhood that's part commercial.

The mediators are thrown off by the disputants' responses, especially Paul's. They had hoped the disputants had come to recognize the value of friendly communication and negotiation.

Acknowledging the futility of proceeding further, Ellen asks the Sandses and Paul what they are planning to do next. Alfred responds:

My understanding was that as neighbors we could work things out. You're admitting defeat. I'll call City Hall—the Planning Commission. [Turning to Paul] I want you to know it's not personal.

Ellen suggests that Alfred inform Paul of when he is planning on contacting the Planning Commission. But Paul interjects that it doesn't matter because he is not in a position to do anything until he and Ann get settled with the baby.

As the hearing draws to a close, Paul comments that he's sorry that "you people have hearings when the other party is planning to go the next day to the Planning Commission."

This prompts Ellen to ask Paul if he would have made any compromises if the Sandses had not been so firm. Paul tells her that her question is "too hypothetical," since the Sandses refused to negotiate.

Fred concludes the hearing with the following remarks:

Thank you for coming tonight. We try to bring people together. People are what's important. I personally believe that the impasse was not necessary. What's important is people trying to understand each other and each other's viewpoints. We hope this can be accomplished through the hearing process, and I believe we've all done our jobs to try and have that happen. If you change your mind, and want to discuss the dispute further, you can contact the SFCB and schedule a second hearing. Sometimes that's necessary. Anything to add Ellen? David?

As he leaves, Alfred turns to Paul and states:

I'm 63 years old. I think it takes a big man to say he's wrong. Thank you. Nothing personal, right?

He extends his hand. Paul, with a bewildered shake of his head, accepts Alfred's outstretched hand, and both men shake hands.

The hearing with the disputants ends at 9:45 P.M., two hours after it began.

The Post-Hearing Review

After the disputants leave, Tom initiates the posthearing review. The mediators are frustrated and disappointed. At the same time, they compliment each other on their efforts, briefly discuss the effectiveness of specific questions and their sensitivity to various interpersonal dynamics between the disputants and themselves.

The mediators also want an explanation of the impasse. They are anxious to assign responsibility to persons other than themselves. Attention turns to the disputants and the quality of the intake work. They question whether the hearing was scheduled prematurely. Ellen, Fred, and David are perturbed with the Sandses and Tom. Ellen, who joined the SFCB at the same time as Tom, relies on her status as his peer and friend, to casually confront him on his intake work. As she puts on her coat, she asks him if he really explained the mediation process to the Sandses, because it seems that they were only there to complain and weren't interested in working out an agreement. Fred agrees, but softens Ellen's direct question by noting that perhaps Tom hoped they wouldn't be so stubborn at the hearing.

Tom avoids answering Ellen's question. Asserting himself, in his role as the trainer, he instructs the mediators to take a few minutes to discuss what they might have done to encourage more cooperation during the hearing. The responsibility for the failed hearing falls back on the mediators, although Tom mentions that as the trainer he wishes that he had caught their attention sooner, so they might have averted the polarization that occurred. He adds that maybe things would have moved forward if they had succeeded earlier in the hearing in getting the parties to talk about what they would have done differently.

David disagrees and says he thinks Alfred Sands (as opposed to intake work, or the panelists) was the problem because he refused to discuss anything except a total end to the business. It bothers him that the Sandses refused to indicate where they drew the line (i.e., why could professors and accountants have offices at home, and not the Sorensons?). He contends that the hearing stalled because they were being unfair and unrealistic. Fred and Ellen are also willing to blame the Sandses, but Ellen notes that they probably should have done more active listening. She reminds the others:

> We have to remember how important active listening is—people need to feel like they're being heard. That's the key to getting a good resolution.

Tom agrees, and reflects that they could have also tried some "role reversals"—getting Alfred to express how Paul must be feeling and vice versa. This prompts further comment on how difficult it was to get the Sandses to do anything but complain.

The mediators resign themselves to the impasse by wondering if the disputants will decide to return for a second hearing, and by categorizing the hearing as a "good experience," even though the case might not have really warranted a hearing.

Tom informs the mediators that he would like to recontact the disputants. He thinks the Sandses might "loosen up" if he talked to them, and he asserts that he thinks Paul is "pretty repressed" and might need some psychological counseling to become more expressive about his feelings.

Ellen tells Tom that she thinks he might be overstepping the duties of an intake worker. She cautions him not to become too involved, but if he chooses to recontact the disputants, maybe he should do it on his own and not as a program representative. He accepts her warning.

Tom ends the review by telling the mediators that they all did a good job. The mediators and Tom leave at 10:05 P.M. The hearing with the disputants lasted two hours. The entire process, including the briefing and review, lasted nearly three hours.

Follow-up Interviews with the Disputants

Follow-up interviews were conducted with each party on two occasions: in the week following the hearing; and two months after the hearing.

The Sandses

Although disappointed by the outcome of the hearing, Alfred and Gladys Sands viewed the hearing positively, immediately after the hearing and when they were interviewed two months later. They found the mediators fair and impartial, although Gladys Sands doubted whether they (especially the younger mediators) fully understood the Sandses' concerns. The Sandses reported that they had hoped that the mediators would have had the power to render or enforce a decision. Despite their disappointment, they indicated that they would gladly use the program again for other disputes, and they expressed an interest in joining the program as mediators.

Dissatisfied with the outcome of the hearing, the Sandses explained that they had called their city supervisor the very next day. In the two months between interviews, they had taken no other action, and their contact with the supervisor's office appeared to have no direct effect on the dispute.

When asked about the status of the dispute, they reported (at both interviews) that the dispute had worsened. Paul Sorenson was now leaving his garage door open, an action that the Sandses considered purposefully offensive—as Gladys explained: "They're flaunting their business, rubbing our noses in it, just to show they can get away with it." She added that she valued the hearing for showing her the true depth of her opposition to the Sorensons' business.

At the second follow-up interview, she and Alfred talked at some

length about their fears of a commercial invasion of their neighborhood, and how such a change threatened the appreciation of their
home and neighborhood that they are depending on for financial
security in their retirement years.

Thus, from the Sandses' perspective, not only had the problem
worsened, but distrust and dislike had come to replace expectations
about an amicable relationship with the Sorensons.

Paul Sorenson

Paul Sorenson also offered a positive evaluation of the hearing process, the mediators, and indicated his willingness to use the process
again. Specifically, he approved of the hearing because it allowed
him to meet the Sandses, hear their complaint, and talk with them
in a safe environment. Unlike the Sandses, he thought the mediators
fully understood the situation and he was not disappointed by their
lack of coercive authority.

Consistent with his statements at the hearing, Paul continued
to have few expectations about the Sandses as neighbors. He had
however taken seriously Alfred's threats about contacting the Planning Commission, and consequently decided to contact the Commission himself. He learned that he was legally allowed to store 25
percent of his inventory at home and maintain a "paperwork office"
at home.

At the second interview, he reported that he was in the process
of moving his excess inventory to comply with the Planning Commission's directive. Thus, as far as he was concerned, the dispute
was resolved.

He noted that he hoped one day to move the business fully but
did not anticipate such action in the near future. He did not expect
to have any further contact with the Sandses, and was unaware of
their perception that the dispute had worsened.

Dispute Transformations and the SFCB
Hearing Process

The Briefing

The briefing represents the backstage of the hearing and is much like
a warm-up and last-minute rehearsal. How did Tom as intake worker

and trainer describe the case during the briefing, and how did this information shape the collective construction of the dispute?

Tom began by contextualizing the dispute in relation to the changing demographics of the neighborhood, in particular the changing racial composition and homeowner-renter mix, yet he then directed the mediators to attend to distinctly personal and interpersonal aspects of the dispute rather than social or legal dimensions. Avoiding the legal dimension of the complaint, and deciding to remain silent about underlying racial and cultural differences (and issues associated with the differential degree of power and authority associated with homeowners and renters, and long-term versus recently arrived residents), the mediators chose a strategy that emphasized communication techniques such as the need to use "plenty of active listening" and saw their task as facilitating a discussion between the disputants about business specifics and normative assumptions about how neighbors hoped to encourage the disputants to talk about feelings about "neighborliness," since they anticipated that the Sandses and the Sorensons would subscribe, as they themselves did, to similar beliefs about neighborhood values, behaviors, and appropriate forms of interaction.

These choices reflect values central to the SFCB. The program emphasizes the importance of cultural diversity, and the practice and ideology of mediation is premised on a particular view of "community," a view that I believe is apolitical despite the rhetoric of empowerment associated with community mediation. It is a view that inspires program volunteers by relying on an ideal, nostalgic vision of neighborhood as a place of friendly, peaceful, harmonious social interaction and coexistence, where neighbors are friends who engage in amicable forms of communication. Indeed, the mediators' strategy involved stressing similarities about expectations of neighborhood life even though the essence of the dispute stemmed from a disagreement about the validity of this vision.

The Hearing: The Task of Sustaining the Definition of Disputes as Problems of Communication

To staff and program volunteers, the hearing is the climax event in the mediation process. This may be less true for disputants. For as noted previously, disputes often continue to evolve even after being "resolved" by mediation. It is during the hearing, however, that mediators make important, strategic decisions about what and how to respond to issues. Generally speaking, mediators focus attention on those issues they hope will lead to the resolution of the dispute.

In discussing the hearing, I am interested in how the panel of mediators sought to maintain the definition of the Sandses' complaint as a communication problem, building upon Tom's work in shaping the issues during the case-development process. Discussion of this topic helps to illuminate the underlying normative assumptions of the SFCB approach to community-based, nonjudicial mediation.

Prior to the hearing, and as a result of the intake process, disputes that go to mediation have already, to some degree, been shaped to conform to the paradigmatic expectations of disputes as communication problems. Even so, the fluid nature of disputes presents mediators with the central and often difficult task of sustaining this definitional framework. Thus, the success of the SFCB hearing process, like that of the intake process, requires the disputants' willingness to view their conflict as involving an interpersonal problem of communication. As noted, the SFCB viewed the Sands-Sorenson dispute as ripe for mediation precisely because there had been no previous communication between the parties. This absence of communication was particularly responsible for fueling Tom's enthusiasm about the likely resolution of the dispute, an enthusiasm for which he was later chastised.

The mediators began the hearing assuming that the dispute would dissipate once the Sandses clarified the aspects of the business that perturbed them and communicated their concerns to the Sorensons. Although they wondered about the Sandses' initial inflexibility, they took the Sandses' willingness to discuss their concerns with the Sorensons to mean that this was primarily a communication problem that would be settled once the two parties discussed their concerns with each other directly. Indeed, the willingness to discuss a complaint in the context of the hearing underpins the SFCB operational definition of mediation.

Seeing their role as facilitators of this process of communication, the mediators were unprepared for the Sandses' refusal to rephrase the dispute in terms of specific objectionable aspects of the business operation. They were similarly confused and frustrated by the Sandses' refusal to alter their position in light of the information about Paul and his business that they learned as a result of their interaction. It seems that communication, in this case, further distanced the parties.

Failing in their efforts to get the Sandses to identify discrete aspects of the business that they found objectionable, the mediators turned their attention to the only other topic of the dispute that they felt they had the authority to address, and the only other topic of discussion amenable to a communication paradigm—that is, the disputants' feelings about what constituted a good neighborhood and good neighbors. Expecting to find agreement, they were surprised and dismayed by the disputants' responses, since they were not only unable to elicit agreement about shared values, but Paul Sorenson seemed indifferent to the concepts of neighborhood and community— the very concepts that the mediators saw as essential to the dispute, key to their own involvement as mediators, and, perhaps most importantly, as integral to the ideology of community-based mediation.

I argue that this impasse occurred because the dispute could not be managed as merely an interpersonal problem of communication. That is, the Sandses refused to oblige this rephrasing, indeed they maintained throughout the hearing that the problem was not a "personal" problem in any way. The mediators were thus unable to rely on a communication paradigm of disputing as a vehicle for compromise. Consequently, they were unable to mediate the dispute in the form in which they had sought to construct it.

One of the consequences of the hearing was its effect on the Sandses' assessment of the Sorensons as neighbors and people. The hearing succeeded in personalizing the dispute, but with an unexpected twist. The hearing had shown the Sandses that Paul Sorenson was, as Gladys described, "not the kind of person I would welcome as a neighbor, I don't think he can be trusted." The hearing did not foster a sense of friendship and respect between people as individuals or "neighbors." Instead it led to an acknowledgment of personal and social differences that contributed to a distancing and sense of dislike between disputants.

This response runs counter to fundamental ideological claims that assert the restorative effects of mediation in relation to sustaining relationships and building and empowering communities. Moreover, findings from this study indicate that disputants often turn to mediation not because they want to improve the quality of their relations with "the other party," but rather because they want to put an end to their interactions. The data suggest that for some disputants the SFCB hearing process provides an important, somewhat ceremonial, quasi-official process that allows for the termination of relations between disputants. This study suggests the need to further explore the connection between mediation and disputants' interest in "flight" as opposed to their desire to fight, and how issues of trust and appropriate standards of "neighborliness" affect disputes between neighbors, and similarly inform the normative assumptions of community-based mediation.

The Post-Hearing Review

Officially, the goal of the posthearing review is to "gather information and express feelings to improve the quality of work done in future hearings" (San Francisco Community Boards 1984). The trainer's job is to assess the panel's strengths and weaknesses and provide each mediator with individualized feedback. Each mediator is also expected to contribute to the group learning process by reporting on how they "felt" as a mediator, highlighting aspects of their and other mediators' performance that they found particularly effective, as well as aspects of the hearing and their interaction that they found confusing or dissatisfying.

When mediation sessions lead to settlement agreements, the review is marked by uplifted spirits and positive comments about the mediators' skill and performance. In hearings that do not produce agreements there is an overriding sense of frustration and often fatigue. The trainer and mediators search for reasons for the lack of settlement. In "The Promised Land," the mediators faulted the intake work (i.e., Tom) and the Sandses for scheduling the hearing without assurances of a sincere interest in compromise and mediation. As the trainer, Tom hinted that perhaps resolution would have been achieved had the mediators used a wider range of communications techniques (e.g., role reversals), or more rigorously followed through on the various stages of the hearing process.

At present, it is important to note that when a dispute cannot be handled as a communication problem, it does not lead to a change in the normative framework of mediation. The reasons why this change does not occur are discussed in the concluding section of this chapter.

Conclusion

This chapter offers a detailed account of how "The Promised Land" dispute evolved in relation to interactions between SFCB program volunteers, staff, and disputants. The intake process was highlighted as the first stage in a process of rephrasing whereby instances of conflict come to be defined as disputes and attempts are made to define issues and identify disputants in ways that conform to the SFCB communication model of disputing.

Analysis of the forty cases in the Intensive Case Study indicate that the SFCB approach to conflict resolution focuses on defining disputes as personalized, individualized instances of conflict. Disputes are primarily approached as problems of interpersonal communication, although program volunteers, staff, and disputants are often cognizant of other social, legal, and economic dimensions.

The choice to attend to disputes as problems of interpersonal communication is neither arbitrary nor accidental. On the one hand, as a service-delivery program that relies primarily on volunteer labor, SFCB has not been designed to provide the training necessary to enable volunteers to respond to the range of legal, political, and economic issues that underlie many disputes. Decisions about program structure, however, are directly related to the program's approach to and philosophy about conflict resolution.

In approaching SFCB's ideology as problematic, as I have tried to do in this chapter, attention has focused on some of the implicit assumptions about the nature of social organization and conflict that underlie SFCB's claims and ideology. I assert that the SFCB approach to "community-based justice" is premised on an idealist vision of community and neighborhood as places of social harmony and shared values. The program's approach to conflict resolution presumes societal consensus about rights and values. SFCB is able to operate as an *informal justice* program precisely because of this presumption that allows mediation, as practiced by the SFCB, to operate without explicit procedural, substantive, or distributive guidelines. In other words, the SFCB approach to mediation operates without explicit standards of justice. Absent these standards, the

SFCB method of conflict resolution operates essentially as a process of communication, rather than a process of justice. Justice and fairness as concepts, let alone as measures of performance, receive little attention in the SFCB context precisely because program intake workers (case developers), mediators (panelists), and other program representatives see themselves as communication facilitators rather than decision makers.

The success of the SFCB rests not on its ability to effect justice or fairness per se, but rather stems from its ability to encourage a sense of community and neighborhood, primarily among program volunteers. Volunteer case developers, panelists, outreach workers, trainers, and members of the program's internal governing structures derive a sense of "empowerment" both from their involvement in program activities and their active participation in other people's lives and conflicts. This is not a minor achievement and warrants considerable attention, for it is the members of the internal community of the SFCB program who I argue experience empowerment as a result of the program's approach to conflict resolution, to a far greater extent than individual disputants or the external community at large.

In contrast, the empowerment of disputants is a problematic project in the context of the SFCB experience. Few disputants understand the SFCB hearing process prior to participation in a hearing, and there is little follow-up with this community afterwards to evaluate or encourage the empowering potential of community-based mediation. What disputants find as a result of their participation in the program is an opportunity to talk, to communicate, in a SFCB-managed setting. For many disputants, this is a valuable forum that would be difficult to find without the SFCB intervention. Thus, the SFCB succeeds in providing some disputants with a safe forum for communication. In many situations, this is in and of itself a major accomplishment. Data from the Intensive Case Study also suggest that this is the primary service SFCB provides disputants.

While the simple provision of a safe forum for communication falls short of the program's promotional promises, the SFCB deserves credit for this achievement. Data from the Intensive Case Study and other components of the comprehensive evaluation project indicate that many complainants turn to SFCB because they are afraid or otherwise reluctant to initiate contact with their neighbors to announce even the most mundane, easily remedied concerns. And, in many instances there are no other forums for complainants to turn to for assistance in dealing with a range of difficulties, many of which stem from the exigencies of life in a densely populated urban environment.

The findings of this research highlight that the SFCB approaches conflict from an apolitical perspective; and that a political perspective about social change and social control is absent, if not antithetical to the normative framework that informs the SFCB approach to conflict resolution. This, I believe, is the fundamental reason why disputes are processed as personalized, attenuated events. The absence of a political perspective on social change and social control limits knowledge about local conflicts, disputes, and mediation to a narrow audience of disputants and program representatives. The opportunity for disputants to develop a "class" consciousness, in the sense of a collective identity with others who have, are, or might voice similar complaints (e.g., in disputes between landlords and tenants), is effectively denied by the program's approach to conflict resolution. Among political observers and organizers, it is generally accepted that a class consciousness is a usual prerequisite for the political organization necessary to "empower" a local community or neighborhood. In the continuing debate about the liberating potential of informal justice, an understanding of the SFCB approach to disputing suggests the limitations of neighborhood-justice programs (such as the SFCB) to operate as forums for popular justice, if popular justice is defined in relation to politically progressive social change and justice for those historically denied power in society.

Appendix

Provided below are examples from the Intensive Case Study of cases that were recorded by SFCB as resolved following SFCB participation in the disputing process. These examples suggest the range of disputes that are handled by SFCB and indicate the problematic nature of "resolution" as a measure of outcome.

Section 1 includes summary descriptions of five disputes that were "resolved" as a result of a SFCB hearing.

Section 2 includes summary descriptions of two cases that were "resolved" without hearings.

Section 1:

Examples of Disputes Defined by SFCB as Resolved
after a Hearing

The Noisy Fans

This dispute involved a complaint by a man who lived in a second-
story apartment next to a grocery store and was bothered by noise
from the refrigeration fans on the store's roof.

Both parties had discussed the matter with each other before
deciding to involve SFCB. They agreeed to mediate because they
wanted to structure a time and place for their discussion, they liked
the idea of mediation as a process, and the store manager was friendly
with a SFCB volunteer.

The hearing lasted an hour (quite short by program standards).
The disputants drafted an agreement stating that they would work
together to build a box around the fans, and that the store owner
would pay for the necessary materials.

The second party (the store manager) was the only one who
agreed to the first follow-up interview, conducted a week after the
hearing. He reported that after the hearing, he chose to ignore the
aspect of the agreement that called for the two of them to work
together, deciding it would be simpler and more expedient for him
to build the box alone. He completed the project on his day off, a
week after the hearing. He reported that the first party seemed
pleased.

At the second follow-up interview, conducted two months after
the hearing, the first party could not be located by telephone or mail.
The store manager was contacted, and he reported that there had
been no further complaints about the noise. He added that he had
not seen the first party recently and thought he might have moved.

Splattered Paint

In this case, an elderly Hispanic woman called SFCB to complain
that her Chinese neighbor had splattered paint on her house while
painting the exterior of his house. She explained that the second

party, her Chinese neighbor, was a middle-aged man who lived up the block. The second party owned the house next door to hers as a rental property.

The first party, the elderly woman, attended the hearing with her forty-year-old grandson. The second party (the homeowner) was accompanied by his wife. The disputants drafted a resolution that called for the second party to repaint the splattered side of the first party's house. The first party's grandson was to help the second party paint, on a Saturday two weeks from the hearing. The mediators and staff were particularly pleased because they felt they had overcome a number of cross-cultural barriers to communication during the hearing.

Inverviewed a few days after the hearing, the disputants reported their satisfaction with the agreement. Interviewed two months later, the first party reported her displeasure with the color of paint, the quality of the painting, and the second party's refusal to work with her grandson. She reported that she never wanted to have anything to do with the second party again. The second party refused to be interviewed.

Time to Move

This dispute involved a married couple and a single woman who shared a two-bedroom apartment. All three were in their late twenties and employed part-time. Prior to sharing this apartment all three had lived together with other friends in a larger collective household. The married couple had contacted the SFCB at the suggestion of the second party, the single woman.

The second party had found the apartment and invited the first party (the couple) to share it with her. The couple thought the single woman was planning to move in the near future, but that did not happen. All three liked the apartment, especially the low rent. The couple felt increasing strain over sharing what they thought was too small an apartment for three adults. The couple and the single woman agreed that someone had to move; each thought the other party should be the one to move.

The dispute was settled after two hearings. At the first hearing, the man suggested they settle the issue of who should move by flipping a coin. He proposed that the winner of the coin flip compensate the loser for the costs of moving and having to find a more expensive apartment. The single woman started crying and said she was not comfortable with that approach. She argued that if they improved their communication they could continue sharing the apartment. The parties could not agree about who should move but agreed to have a second hearing a week later.

At the second hearing, the couple began by noting that the situation was intolerable, someone had to move, and they would move if the second party would agree to contribute to their moving costs. The second party agreed that someone had to move. She did not think she could or should be the one to move but said she might. She suggested they open a joint account and each contribute to a "moving fund" that would be used by whomever moved. The couple agreed. They said they didn't want to move but would do so and would try to move as soon as possible. They then used the hearing to inform the second party that they had recently learned that they were expecting a baby.

Working together, the two parties drafted a settlement agreement that called for opening a joint "moving account" to which each party would make a set monthly deposit. In addition, the agreement included solutions to other issues of contention, specifically to spell out behavioral changes about noise, the use of shared space, and jointly purchased groceries.

At the two-month follow-up, the couple reported that they had found an apartment. Both parties had made two contributions to the joint account. The couple said they were perturbed about losing the apartment and that they felt manipulated by the second party. They believed they had "lost" at the hearing because they agreed to give up the apartment but they saw no other option in dealing with the second party.

The single woman reported that she had upheld her end of the agreement. She was pleased with the agreement and the hearing process.

Both parties reported that their friendship had cooled but they were thankful that civility had been restored to their daily interactions. Both parties expected their relationships with each other to continue after the move, but the couple expected far less involvement with the second party than she did with them.

The Moving Business

The police referred this case to the SFCB after receiving repeated requests from the first party, a single, middle-aged, professional woman, to ticket the moving vans belonging to her neighbor for illegally parking on a residential street. She had also filed numerous complaints with the Planning Commission about her neighbor (the second party), who operated a commercial furniture-moving business from his home. She was opposed to what she believed was a zoning violation and upset by the parking of commercial moving vans on her street. As a single mother of a teenage daughter, she was scared by the number and character of the men who "hung around" her neighbor's house and business.

The second party, a middle-aged man, readily acknowledged that his business violated the area's residential zoning. He agreed to mediate specifically because the hearing was not a legal proceeding and he wanted to stop getting tickets. The second party did not know who was responsible for calling the police. The disputants had never spoken to one another before the hearing.

The two parties drafted a settlement agreement at the hearing that called for the first party to rescind her complaints to the Planning Commission and stop calling the police if the second party stopped parking his trucks on the block where the disputants lived.

Interviewed a week after the hearing, the first party reported that the second party continued to park his vans on the block. Consequently, she had not withdrawn her complaints to the Planning Commission. Interviewed the same week, the second party reported that the agreement was in effect, although he found it a nuisance to park his vans on adjacent streets. He believed that the complaints had been withdrawn.

Two months later, the first party refused to be interviewed. The second party remained unaware that the complaints had not been withdrawn. He was pleased to report that he thought the dispute was over, not because of the SFCB hearing, but because in the month after the hearing he had been presented with the opportunity to relocate his business out of the neighborhood. He had not informed the first party of this change. There had been no further contact between the two parties since the hearing.

Mysterious Harassment

This dispute involved three people. A fourth person also participated in the hearing. The first party was a former SFCB volunteer. He contacted the program to complain about being harassed by two of his neighbors. His neighbors, the second party, were a gay couple. The third party was a person who had recently bought the second party's house and was planning to assume occupancy shortly.

The first party did not know his neighbors by name but believed they had called the police to ticket his car on numerous occasions for being illegally parked and had called the SPCA to report him for animal abuse after he had rented a goat to clear his backyard of weeds. He also reported they had "publicly maligned" him by coming to his garage sale and talking with other neighbors about the insanity of "anyone who would keep a goat in his backyard." The first party described the situation as intolerable. He planned to retaliate by contacting the city building inspector to report improvements that the second party had made to their house without a building permit.

The second party lived two houses away from the first party. They had recently sold their house. The second party denied any responsibility for the acts of harassment claimed by the first party. They were surprised when they learned from the SFCB volunteer about the complaint because they said they did not know the first party and had never spoken to him in the seven years they had been neighbors. They agreed to come to the hearing, even though they were moving, because they did not want to be falsely accused.

The second party told the new owner about the complaint and the upcoming hearing. The new owner attended the hearing because he thought the accusations against the second party were wrong, and he wanted to meet the first party to avoid any future confrontations that might arise from what he believed to be misconceptions by the first party.

The first and second parties quickly reached an agreement at the hearing that specified that the second party was not responsible for the harassment and that the first party would not attempt to solicit an apology from them. Everyone, including the new owner and the mediators, agreed that better communication was central to improving the situation. All were pleased with the agreement.

At the follow-up interview, the second party had moved as planned, the first party had experienced no further harassment, and there had been no further contact between the first party and his new neighbor.

Section 2:

Examples of Disputes that were "Resolved" without Mediation

Please Move the Clothesline

This case involved two families and was prompted by a complaint about the location of a clothesline that was fastened to their adjacent houses. The first party did not want her neighbor's clothesline tied to her house. She had never spoken to her neighbors and did not know their names.

The second party was unaware of the first party's objection to the placement of the clothesline until informed of the dispute by the SFCB intake worker. Following this conversation, the second party promptly removed the clothesline. Two months later, both parties were satisfied with the changed placement of the clothesline. There had been no further communication between the neighbors.

Bad Pistons

This case involved a consumer complaint about engine pistons purchases at an auto parts store. The first party, a middle-aged Hispanic man, contacted the SFCB after he had bought a set of engine pistons that he said were the wrong size. He had checked the size of the pistons with the salesperson before buying them. He had attempted to return the pistons but the store had refused to give him a cash refund. The intake workers spoke to the store manager who told them that he had already offered the first party a store credit for the pistons. After speaking with the store manager, the intake workers went directly to the first party's home (located two blocks from the auto parts store) to tell him of the store's response. They found the first party in his garage, having just installed the pistons. He informed them that he had decided to use the pistons anyway and was in fact quite satisfied with the fit. Two months later he was still pleased and reported that he was a steady customer of the auto parts store.

REFERENCES

Beer, Jennifer E. 1986. *Peacemaking in Your Neighborhood: Reflections on an Experiment in Community Mediation*. Philadelphia: New Society Publishers.

Christie, Nils. 1977. "Conflicts as Property." *British Journal of Criminology* 17:1–15.

Felstiner, William F., Richard L. Abel, and Austin Sarat. 1980–81. "The Emergence and Transformation of Disputes: Naming, Blaming, Claiming." *Law and Society Review* 15:631–55.

Glaser, Barney. 1978. *Theoretical Sensitivity*. Mill Valley, Calif.: Sociology Press.

Glaser, Barney G., and A. J. Strauss. 1970. *The Discovery of Grounded Theory: Strategies for Qualitative Research*. Chicago: Aldine.

Harrington, Christine B. 1985. *Shadow Justice: The Ideology and Institutionalization of Alternatives to Court*. Westport, Conn.: Greenwood Press.

Mather, Lynn, and Barbara Ygnvesson. 1980–81. "Language, Audience, and the Transformation of Disputes." *Law and Society Review* 15:775–822.

Merry, Sally E., and Susan S. Silbey. 1982. "Social Disputes or Legal Disputes: Dispute Dimensions and the Convergence of Legal Forms." Photocopy.

Nader, Laura, ed. 1980. *No Access to Law: Alternatives to the American Judicial System*. New York: Academic Press.

Nader, Laura, and Harry Todd, eds. 1978. *The Disputing Process: Law in Ten Societies*. New York: Columbia University Press.

Orwell, George. 1946. *Animal Farm*. New York: Harcourt, Brace, and Jovanovich.

Rothschild, Judy H. 1986a. "Mediation as Social Control: A Study of Neighborhood Justice. Ph.D. diss. University of California, Berkeley.

———. 1986b. "The Feminization of Conflict." Paper presented at the annual meeting of the Law and Society Association, Chicago.

San Francisco Community Boards. 1984. *Training Manual*.

Police and "Nonstranger" Conflicts in a San Francisco Neighborhood: Notes on Mediation and Intimate Violence

Fredric L. DuBow with Elliot Currie

The reconciliation of disputes between people in close relationships—spouses, lovers, parents, and children—would seem to have a particular affinity with the values and aims of a program like San Francisco Community Boards. Given the program's emphasis on intervening in conflicts before they escalate into violence that threatens individuals and tears the fabric of communities, the idea of moving preventively to resolve potentially explosive disputes between intimates has an obvious appeal.

That appeal is strenghthened because intimate violence is both frequently devastating and often recurrent—and enormously widespread (U.S. Bureau of Justice Statistics 1986). And it is given particular urgency because of the often-documented failure of the formal criminal justice system to deal with "nonstranger" conflict in ways that provide even minimal protection to the threatened parties, much less any resolution of the underlying problems that the immediate

---

The data presented in this paper were gathered during 1983 by the team of evaluators of the San Francisco Community Boards program under the direction of Fred DuBow. Other than organizing the data and editing them, I have presented them here generally as they were written in early drafts of the section of the evaluation devoted to the police. Neither Fred DuBow nor the other evaluators should be held responsible for the more analytical reflections on domestic violence and the role of mediation in addressing it, which I've added—E.C.

conflicts reflect. Here the criticism leveled by San Francisco Community Boards—and by much of the alternative dispute-resolution
movement—at formal criminal justice seems most solidly on the
mark.

That failure has been most spectacularly apparent in the case
of violence within the family. It was dramatically exposed, beginning
in the 1970s, largely through the efforts of the women's movement.
Advocates for battered women argued that from the stage of police
intervention through the court process, abused women were systematically denied the equal protection of the law. Domestic violence
was typically treated as a minor crime at most, often as a "private"
family matter that the justice system ought to leave alone, leaving
abusers undeterred and victims vulnerable to repeated injury (U.S.
Commission on Civil Rights 1982).

Formal social-science research into the police and court response
to domestic violence drove home the criticism with hard and increasingly predictable findings. It was repeatedly shown that police tended
to regard domestic conflicts as inherently frustrating and of generally
low priority; that they often regarded them as private disputes best
settled within the family; and that what intervention they offered
was usually quite superficial, aimed most often at simply restoring
an immediate semblance of order to the scene. On the relatively rare
occasions when domestic conflicts were launched into the formal court
system, the response was equally minimal. Most studies suggested
that cases involving "intimate violence" were much more likely to be
dropped before prosecution than other crimes of violence, and that
even where they were prosecuted, the resulting sanctions, if any, were
unusually light (Morash 1986; Elliot 1989; Bowker 1982; Berk et al.
1982; Black 1980).

Research suggested not only that police and prosecutors were
less than eager to move hard against family violence, but also that
victims themselves often had a complex and ambivalent response to
the formal and adversarial character of the justice system. That system
required complainants to be ready and willing to invoke the formal
power of the state against people close to them. Their frequent reluctance to do so in part reflected the widespread sense among victims
that the justice system could not effectively protect them against
retaliation by their victimizers if they took them to court. But it also
stemmed in many instances from the nature of the underlying rela-

tionships themselves—long-standing ones in which complainants, while they wanted *something* to happen to prevent their further victimization, did not necessarily want to jeopardize the relationship itself or could not see a realistic alternative for themselves outside of it.

These understandings helped fuel the movement to provide better alternatives—for shelter, support, and assistance toward independence—for women outside the criminal-justice system. At the same time, they also led to a partly successful effort to reorient the criminal-justice response to domestic violence itself. Across the country, many police departments—close to half of the big-city departments, according to one estimate (Elliot 1989:434)—formally adopted policies directing officers to treat domestic violence as a serious violent crime. A number of departments adopted mandatory or presumptive arrest policies. This development was importantly stimulated by the well-known Minneapolis Domestic Violence experiment, in which social scientists were able to document on the basis of a highly regarded research design that women were less likely to be assaulted in the future if their abusers were arrested, with or without going to court, than if the police responded in a more superficial way through on-the-spot crisis intervention or simple maintenance of order (Sherman and Berk 1984; Lempert 1989; Sherman and Cohn 1989).

But while the movement for a stronger criminal-justice response has garnered widespread support, it is much less clear that it has made as much difference as hoped, in practice, in the way cases of domestic violence are handled "on the ground." More recent studies of the handling of domestic violence by police in departments that have formally adopted tough policies have found a discouraging continuity in the day-to-day realities of the police response. Kathleen Ferraro's research in the Phoenix police department, for example, which adopted a presumptive arrest policy in 1984, found that police officers still managed to make considerable use of the inevitable margin of discretion in cases of domestic violence, with the result that less than a fifth of police calls to family fights resulted in an arrest, a proportion very similar to that found in earlier studies done in departments *without* mandatory arrest policies. The Phoenix police often failed to arrest even when women clearly expressed the fear that violence would be repeated (Ferraro 1989:64, 67).

Part of the problem may be that in Phoenix, as in other cities, presumptive or mandatory arrest policies have been adopted without substantial corresponding changes in the practices of courts and prosecutors. Thus one reason police may continue to avoid arrest is the sense that it will be futile anyway once the batterer reaches the court system. Hence, the research could be read as simply pointing to the need for a tougher response in the courts. But studies of the effects of formal court sanctions on the recurrence of violence in domestic-abuse cases do not yet inspire great confidence about the ability of the courts to protect women from victimization, even if the sanctions are applied. Jeffrey Fagan's research, for example, suggests that conviction and punishment may work to some extent to deter less-serious batterers from recidivism, but not more serious offenders; if anything, prosecution and conviction may increase the risks of violence (1989: 383–84). In addition, some research suggests that any observed reduction in violence after formal sanctions may mainly reflect a "displacement effect" in which the batterer simply continues the same behavior in a new relationship. Moreover, given the short follow-up time in studies of the deterrent effect of arrests, it is not clear that such deterrent effects as have appeared in these studies last much beyond a few months (Elliot 1989:455; Tauchen, Tauchen, and Witte 1981).

On the surface, at least, these limitations would seem to support the ADR movement's view that relational conflicts, including those involving violence or its threat, are better handled in a setting outside the formal system that is more explicitly attuned to the realities of the parties' long-term relationships and to a *preventive* intervention that can address the roots of the conflict itself. And indeed another consequence of the growing critique of the justice system's response has been the extension of ADR, already in widespread use in other family-law matters, like divorce and custody, to family violence (see Bailey 1989).

But that development itself has not gone without strong criticism—again, most consistently from within the feminist movement. The U.S. Commission of Civil Rights, in its 1982 report *Under the Rule of Thumb: Battered Women and the Administration of Justice,* took the position that mediation and arbitration "should never be used" as an alternative to formal prosecution in cases involving physical violence against women, and that view was adopted by others as well (1982:96). For one critic, diversion from prosecution to mediation amounts to the "tacit decriminalization of wife abuse" (Lerman 1984:92).

The heart of the critics' argument is that in several interrelated ways mediation may serve to lock victimized women, if anything, more tightly into subordinate and vulnerable roles. This is partly, in this view, because mediators tend to define such cases as disputes in which both parties are in some sense equally implicated and to which each contribute: "Instead of emphasizing that the husband/batterer has engaged in criminal behavior," writes another critic, "such mediation programs imply that the problem is mutual. Although compromise and negotiation are necessary if a couple hopes to stay together and improve their relationship, they are an inappropriate response to criminal battering behavior" (Eppler 1986:791). Critics also argue that the dispute-resolution process tends to individualize the dispute and take it out of the context of the larger gender inequalities in which domestic violence is embedded, thus in effect calling on the abused to "make peace with oppression" (Lerman 1984:94). Finally, in this critique, by deliberately removing the "dispute" from the formal justice system, mediation works to take away such (admittedly limited) protection as that system is able to offer—or can be forced to offer—to women at risk.[1]

In this paper we want to discuss those issues, using, as a backdrop, a set of data on police and court responses to "nonstranger" cases gathered as part of the San Francisco Community Boards program (hereafter SFCB) evaluation during 1983. We say "as a backdrop" advisedly, for the data can only be suggestive: the research was not designed specifically to address these questions. Initially, the evaluators sought data on police responses to "prior-relationship" cases with the aim of determining whether there existed in San Francisco a large pool of cases routinely dealt with by the police that were unknown to SFCB but that might be suitable for referral to the program if, in fact, police officers and their leadership could be brought to appreciate the potential of the program to deal with them.

---

1. This critique gains force from the evidence that *serious* batterers tend to be violent outside intimate relationships as well as in them—in a generalized pattern of criminality that extends beyond the confines of the relationship itself. Thus the violence is arguably not simply the reflection of some underlying family dispute that can be negotiated (see for example Fagan 1989:382–83).

As we shall see, the evaluation turned up a vast number of non-stranger conflicts, including a very substantial proportion involving violence or the threat of violence between intimates (a proportion much higher than that found in SFCB's own caseload). The research therefore provides some valuable information reaffirming both the vast extent of domestic violence in low-income communities in urban America and the relative failure of the formal justice system to offer effective protection to its victims. By itself, the research cannot provide much help in answering the implicit question that underlay the police research in the first place—whether alternative dispute resolution would constitute a more effective response to these cases. Still, the data, along with data from other research on domestic violence, can provide one part of the background for a broader discussion of a more effective community strategy against intimate violence and of the potential role of mediation within that strategy.

In what follows we will first present the data gathered in the evaluation in what became known as the "freestanding police study" and then use it as a springboard to return to the issue of the appropriate community response to domestic violence and the potentials and pitfalls of alternate dispute resolution within it. In this, perhaps even more than in other discussions of the evaluation material, the discussion must remain only evocative and provocative.

The Data

In order to determine the depth of the pool of prior-relationship cases, the evaluators gathered several kinds of police data. All were drawn from the Potrero District, one of San Francisco's nine police districts, during 1983. The Potrero District was the one that most overlapped with the Visitacion Valley neighborhood, where SFCB had its oldest and strongest local office. (At the time of the study, the program fielded three separate neighborhood offices; at this writing, it has consolidated its operations into one that offers services city-wide.) About a third of Potrero District lies within Visitacion Valley. The Potrero District covers some of the most crime- and drug-ridden areas of the city, including several high-crime public housing projects with large minority populations. These were tough areas in 1983; they have become more so since.

The evaluators looked first at data from two types of police records: (1) daily logs of police dispatches and (2) more detailed incident reports. In 1983, the Potrero police recorded, in a logbook, each call to which one of their patrol officers was dispatched. (In 1984 this function was computerized.) For each logged call, the logbook records the time of the dispatch, the nature of the call, the type of action taken by the responding officer, and the time at which the police response was terminated. (Note that these logs only cover the activities of the patrol force; specialized tactical, detective, vice, or juvenile activity was not recorded in the log.) These were examined for four selected months (January, April, July, and October) in order to include possible seasonal or cyclical variations in the data.

In about 20 percent of the logged calls, the responding officer wrote an *incident report*. All Potrero District incident reports for the same four months of 1983 were read and coded. These reports contained significantly more information about the nature of the problem, the characteristics of the parties involved, and the actions taken by the police than was available in the logs.

For each log entry and incident report, a judgment was made as to whether the incident involved the kind of prior relationship that the evaluators believed characterized the incidents typically handled by the SFCB. The chief criterion was whether the complaining party had some kind of relationship with the accused party that went beyond the immediate incident. Such relationships could be (and often were) familial, but also included unrelated persons living together, friends, or neighbors; less frequently, employers and employees, landlords and tenants, ex-lovers or ex-spouses. Cases that involved very serious offenses (like murder, rape, or assault with serious injury) were not included.[2] In addition to the police logs and incident reports, court and police records were examined to determine the final disposition of those cases—about 20 percent of the prior-relationship incidents—in which an arrest was made.

These official records were supplemented by direct observations and interviews, in order to throw light on the police response to

---

2. The evaluators originally called these cases "CB-like" on the premise that they resembled the usual Community Boards caseload. But this seems to beg the question of whether the distribution of the nonstranger cases in the police reports— relatively heavy on assaults and incidents between intimates—actually *were* like the typical SFCB caseload, which included a higher proportion of cases involving disputes among neighbors. I've therefore renamed them.

prior-relationship incidents and on the working attitudes of police officers and commanders toward the suitability of these cases for alternative dispute resolution. During July and August of 1984, ride-along observations and interviews were conducted, on all three shifts, with patrol officers in Potrero. Over a four-hour period, the evaluators observed any calls the officers answered, paying particular attention to incidents involving parties with ongoing relationships. When they were not actively answering calls, the officers were asked about their experience with, and attitudes toward, prior-relationship cases (and other relevant matters). Finally, interviews were conducted with the present and former commanders of the Potrero station, as well as three watch commanders, focusing on departmental policies regarding prior-relationship cases.

The Prevalence of Prior-Relationship Incidents

During the four months studied, over twelve thousand entries were made in the dispatch log (table 1). From these, those that involved traffic matters or calls for service were subtracted, to come up with a rough count of what the evaluators termed "crime" calls (5,541). For each log entry, the evaluators attempted to determine whether a relationship existed between the complainant and the accused beyond the incident about which the call was made. Because the log entries were very brief, they did not always provide sufficent information to

TABLE 1. Percentage of Logged Crime Calls and Incident Reports Involving Prior Relationships

	Calls and Reports	Percentage
Total Logged Calls, 4 months 1983	12,356	
Total "Crime" calls—logged calls minus calls for service or traffic matters	5,541	
Total "Prior relationship"	645	11.6%
Total Incident Reports, 4 months 1983	2,507	
Total "Prior relationship"	383	
"Prior-relationship" incidents not recorded as such in logs	285	
Total logged calls involving prior relationship when additional calls included	930	16.8%

make a judgment about the parties' relationships; as we will see, the analysis of the incident reports suggested that many prior-relationship calls were not recorded as such in the logs. But the logs themselves produced an estimate that a little less than 12 percent of crime calls involved parties with a prior relationship.

The evaluators expected to find a similar proportion of prior-relationship cases in the survey of incident reports. As it turned out, they found many more. There were an additional 285 prior-relationship incidents for which there was no clear indication in the logs that such a relationship existed. The proportion of prior-relationship cases among the logged crime calls was at least 17 percent—and may have been considerably higher, since an unknown number of logged cases in which no incident report was filed may also have involved prior relationships. All told, there were 930 clear prior-relationship incidents among the four months' worth of police calls, suggesting that the yearly total of such incidents in the Potrero District alone may have been in the neighborhood of 2,800.

The sheer number of these incidents may be surprising; but the general pattern is not unexpected. Many other studies of routine police work have shown that a substantial proportion of police activity is spent on cases involving parties who know one another (Elliot 1989:427). On the basis of (admittedly limited) direct observations of patrol officers' responses to these incidents, the evaluators estimated that prior-relationship calls took up perhaps 10 to 16 percent of the patrol officers' active work time.

There is little question, then, that police in Potrero, as elsewhere, spend a significant proportion of their time on cases that involve prior relationships. But what specific *kinds* of incidents were involved in these calls? Most of the prior-relationship calls recorded in the logbooks involved personal or public order crimes (and those involving a missing juvenile) (table 2). What the reports describe as "fights"—fistfights or family fights—are by far the most frequent of them, comprising over half of the prior-relationship calls and more than a quarter of *all* police calls not involving vehicles.

The incident reports provide a more detailed and accurate characterization of these cases. Two-thirds of the prior-relationship incidents for which a report was written involved crimes against persons, almost another third crimes against property. A more detailed breakdown (table 3) shows that battery is the single most common offense among the prior-relationship cases, followed at considerable distance by malicious mischief, family and other fights, and assaults.

As the right-hand column in the table shows, crimes against a person are much more likely to involve a prior relationship between the parties than are crimes against property. We estimated that about a third of all crimes against a person in Potrero were prior-relationship, versus less than 10 percent of crimes against property. An especially high proportion of battery and family and other fights involved prior relationships. *Importantly, then, the category of prior-relationship cases includes an overrepresentation of those in which some personal harm is present or threatened.* These are incidents that may be expected to cause considerable fear and potential danger to the parties, as well as a negative impact on the quality of community life.

Relationships Between Parties

Who were the parties involved in these cases? Analysis of the incident reports found a wide range of relationships. The largest percentage (about 27 percent of prior-relationship incidents) involved people who lived with each other, which the evaluators termed "domestic" relationships. As table 4 shows, about half of these involved husbands and wives, or people living together, and nearly half involved parents

TABLE 2. Types of Crimes among "Prior-Relationship" Log Entries ($N = 645$)

Type of Crime	Percentage of Prior-Relationship Calls
Fist or Family Fight	58.7
Missing Juvenile	13.4
Noise	8.3
Juvenile Beyond Control	3.6
Assault	2.0
Senile, Mentally Ill Person	1.4
Drunk	1.4
Juvenile Disturbance	.3
Malicious Mischief	.3
Other	10.4
Total	100.0

and children. The next largest category was noncohabiting lovers, followed by friends and acquaintances, neighbors, and relatives. Put in another way, about a third of cases recorded in the incident reports involved adults who are spouses or lovers. (This contrasts with informal comments by the patrol officers we interviewed, in which most cases involving prior relationships were characterized as domestic. It may be that domestic cases were a larger proportion of total calls than they were of those written into incident reports, or it may be that police selectively define these incidents.)

Who Is Involved?

What kinds of people were typically involved in these cases? The parties in prior-relationship police cases were especially distinctive along lines of gender, race, and age.

Gender Women were much more likely than men to be the complainants in prior-relationship calls, and more likely to be complainants in prior-relationship (72 percent) than in other kinds of police calls (42 percent). Men, on the other hand, were the typical *suspect* in these cases, regardless of the sex of the complainant. Women were

TABLE 3.   Most Frequent Crimes among Prior-Relationship Cases in Incident Reports

Type of Crime	Percentage of All Prior Relationship	Percent of Crimes in This Category That Involve Prior Relationships
Battery	28.7	65
Malicious Mischief	13.6	30
Family Fight	7.8	70
Assault	7.3	32
Other Fights	5.2	57
Grand Theft	3.9	6
Harassment	3.9	39
Juvenile Beyond Control	2.9	73
Burglary	2.6	3
Assault with Deadly Weapon	2.6	13
Petty Theft of Persons	2.3	15
Robbery	1.6	6
Juvenile Malicious Mischief	1.3	28
Eviction	1.3	100
Trespassing	1.3	29

four times as likely to name a male suspect as a female one; indeed, *female complaints against male suspects comprise 60 percent of all prior-relationship incidents for which the gender of both parties was known.* Men, too, were more likely to accuse other men. This pattern appeared in all types of complaints, but was strongest for those involving spouses or noncohabiting lovers.

Race   The prior-relationship cases were also importantly structured by race. Blacks were much more likely to be complainants in these cases than in others; they were 74 percent of the complainants in prior-relationship incidents, but only 38 percent in other types. As is true for serious crime generally, most prior-relationship incidents are intraracial; indeed, black against black conflicts comprise a very high 73 percent of those prior-relationship incidents in which the race of both parties was known.

Age   Both the complainants and, especially, the suspects in prior-relationship cases were young; 44 percent of complainants and 54 percent of the suspects were twenty-five years or younger. The age distribution of the *suspect* matches, roughly, that found in police incidents generally, but the *complainants* in prior-relationship cases are on average considerably younger than in other police cases.

Overall, the most common relationship in these conflicts was between a young, black, female accuser and a young, black, male accused. Black women were 58 percent of all complainants; black

TABLE 4.   Relationships between Victims and Suspects in Prior-Relationship Incidents ($N = 364$)

Type of Relationship	Percentage
Domestic	26.9
Husband-Wife	10.4
Parent-Child	12.6
Roommates	1.4
Live together	2.5
Noncohabiting Lovers	19.8
Friends/Acquaintances	10.7
Neighbors	9.9
Relatives	6.0
Other[a]	8.8
Unspecified relationship	17.9
Total	100.00

[a]Landlord-tenant, merchant-customer, employer-employee, coworkers

men were the second most frequent complainants, but far behind at just 16 percent. On the other hand, black men were almost two-thirds (64 percent) of *suspects*, with black women a distant second at 15 percent. Blacks, whether accusers or suspects, tended to be younger than whites, with 47 percent of black complainants and 56 percent of black suspects twenty-five years old or younger.

Moreover, significant connections between race, gender, and specific types of incidents emerge in the incident report data. Blacks were much more likely to be complainants in cases involving greater amounts of physical violence; including over 80 percent of the assaults, batteries, and family fights. By contrast, whites were more likely to be complainants in incidents of trespassing, juveniles missing or beyond control, harassment, and violations of public order. Women were disproportionately complainants in almost all incidents involving physical assaults, burglarly, and juveniles beyond control. *Blacks and women, in short, were not only generally overrepresented as complainants but even more so in some of the most harmful, or potentially harmful, incidents.*

The Recurrence of Incidents

Other studies have often found that nonstranger crimes are frequently recurrent in nature; violent episodes between spouses or lovers, for example, are typically preceded by other similar incidents, and there is often a pattern of escalation from less to more serious encounters (U.S. Bureau of Justice Statistics 1986:5). The evaluators were therefore especially interested in whether and how often the prior-relationship incidents in this sample were preceded by others of a similar kind.

Since the police are primarily concerned with the specific events at hand when they write an incident report, such reports are not an accurate source for the history of these disputes; prior occurrences are probably significantly underreported in them. Nevertheless, in 40 percent of the prior-relationship incident reports—versus only 7 percent of the other incidents—a prior occurrence was mentioned. In 20 percent of the prior-relationship cases, there was evidence in the incident report of a *long-standing* conflict between the parties.

In general, the tendency for these conflicts to be recurrent was also supported in interviews with patrol officers. All of the officers interviewed could recite half a dozen or more addresses to which they had been dispatched frequently because of relationship conflicts. (Moreover, this probably underestimated the recurrence of conflict, since an occurrence on another officer's shift would most likely have escaped their attention.)

The Police Response

A pattern, then, does emerge in the numerous incidents we have characterized as prior-relationship cases in the Potrero District. The parties involved knew each other, often as spouses or lovers but also as parents and children, neighbors, and others; they were drawn disproportionately from the young, the black, and women; and they often suffered repeated incidents of victimization. For our purposes, the next key question is, how do the police respond to these incidents? What services do they provide to the parties in these conflicts?

Consistent with most other studies of the police response to nonstranger incidents, Potrero District officers were much less likely to take formal action in prior-relationship cases than in other (non-vehicular) crimes. They wrote a report in 15 percent of prior-relationship incidents, versus 66 percent of other crime incidents; and they made an arrest in just 3 percent of the prior-relationship cases, versus 17 percent of other crime incidents (table 5). A person accused in a prior-relationship incident was only one-sixth as likely to be arrested as an accused in another crime call—even though the victims in the former cases are more likely to be able to identify the suspects, which, as other studies show, is a key factor in increasing the likeli-

TABLE 5. Frequency of Actions by Police in "Prior-Relationship" versus Other "Crime Calls"

Action Taken	Prior Relationship (N = 645)	Other Crimes (N = 870)
Report written, no arrest	12.4	48.7
Arrest and report	2.9	16.9
Resolved by responding Officer	48.8	17.6
No action: parties resolve	14.4	8.8
No action: gone on arrival	8.5	1.1
Other	13.0	6.9
Total	100.0	100.0

hood of apprehensions. Similarly, police are only one-fourth as likely even to write a formal incident report in prior-relationship cases.

The most frequent action, reported in almost half of the prior-relationship log entries, was for the police officer to "resolve" the conflict at the scene. Such resolutions were three times as common in prior-relationship cases as in other nonvehicular crimes. What did resolution entail in these incidents? Most often, according to the interviews, resolution meant that the officers abated, or defused, the conflict. The aim was generally to remove the immediate threat of violence and to calm—or threaten—the parties sufficiently so that the dispute would not flare up again during their shift. Officers used a variety of responses to deal with specific cases, but they agreed that their impact was typically superficial:

> You don't do much besides stop the violence. That's not really dealing with the problem.
>
> We give advice about how to get a "stay-away" order, about separating and things like that. There isn't much we can do in these situations, so we handle the immediate violence and go away.
>
> If it's clear that they aren't going to solve the problem tonight we see if one or the other has someplace they can go to spend the night. And we finally say that we'll arrest them the next time we have to come out.
>
> It would be totally out of line for us to go to a house the next day and say "now about that fight you had last night." Yet that is what is needed.

In these limited observations of police interventions in prior-relationship incidents, there were few attempts to solve problems except in this most immediate sense, and no efforts at serious mediation. Sometimes, indeed, the police left the situation barely changed at all. In one case, according to the observer, the parties

> were more or less oblivious (to) the police intervention. The parties just kept screaming at each other as the police left. The police officer just radioed in "418 abated" when the people were screaming just as loud if not louder when we left than when we had arrived.

Occasionally, the officers lectured one of the parties, but in no instance did they attempt to work with the parties to find a longer-term solution to the problem.

Similar limits to police intervention in prior-relationship conflicts have been described in earlier studies. Donald Black, for example, reports in a 1980 study that police generally tried to dispense with such cases quickly, acting indifferently toward the parties' legal, medical, or interpersonal needs:

> A striking feature of dispute settlement by police is that in most cases the officers do little or nothing to help the parties reach a lasting resolution of the conflict. They function at best as pacifiers, dealing only with the facts on the surface, rarely inquiring into the underlying causes of the complaints they hear. Their solutions are situational and temporary, and have little bearing on what happens after they leave. In this sense it can hardly be said that the police settle disputes at all. (1980:7)

These calls were often described as uncomfortable and frustrating by the Potrero officers:

> We look stupid. People won't prosecute so we make sure no one gets hurt. We take guns away, separate people, and try to de-escalate the situation. Sometimes we take women to a shelter. . . . We almost always feel like unwanted outsiders.

Officers were more comfortable in situations where they can easily tell who is right and who is wrong; in these prior-relationship conflicts, they said it was often difficult to know whom to believe. They felt caught in the middle, often feeling that they had become the "bad guys" toward whom both parties vent their emotions. Most officers agreed that familial conflicts in particular were dangerous and frustrating; answering such calls meant going into settings in which the parties are familiar but the police are strangers.

The racial makeup of many such incidents, in the Potrero District, clearly influenced the response of at least some officers; more than one referred to domestic disputes in the district as "TNBs"—"typical nigger beefs." That kind of stereotyping of many domestic disputes

as characteristics of, or normal in, low-income or minority communities has turned up in other studies as well.[3]

The special problems of prior-relationship calls were also
acknowledged by the Potrero police leadership. Noting the frustrating
character of these calls on the one hand, and their unpredictability
and potential danger on the other, they agreed that alleviating problems through temporary abatement or restoration of the peace was
all that could be expected of their patrol officers. They did not accord
a high priority to arrest and other formal sanctions.

Even when responding officers did decide to write an incident
report in a prior-relationship case, they were less likely to take further
action than they were in other types of incidents (table 6). In both
these and other cases, the police response was hampered most of the
time by the fact that the suspects were gone when the police arrived,
making arrest or citation at the scene impossible. But even when
suspects *were* present, police were less likely to make an arrest (22
vs. 35 percent) and much more likely to merely admonish the parties,
or do nothing. (In general, if the suspect was not present when the
officers arrived on the scene, they usually did little more than listen
to the complainant's story and suggest that they contact the district
attorney's office if they wanted to press charges.)

The level of the police response varied, however, according to
the type of dispute and the relationship between the parties. Police
were much more likely to make arrests in domestic conflicts and
especially disputes among relatives; arrests or citations, indeed, were
made in almost all of the domestic conflicts that resulted in an incident
report. On the other hand, police almost never made arrests in con-

TABLE 6.   Actions Taken by Police in Cases with Incident
Reports

Action Taken	Prior Relationship	Other
Arrest/Citation	22.0	34.5
No Action Taken/Admonish	9.7	1.1
Other	.9	1.7
Gone on Arrival	67.4	62.7

---

3. "Officers on patrol often referred to Mexicans, Indians, gay men, and people
in housing projects as 'low lifes,' 'scum,' or 'these kind of people.' Officers believed
arrests were a waste of time and meaningless for these people because violence is a
way of life for them" (Ferraro 1989:67).

flicts between neighbors. Recurring problems, especially if they were long-standing, had higher rates of arrest than did "first time" calls. Arrests were also more common when females accused males than when males accused suspects of either sex or women accused women. Police were more likely to take no action when both accuser and suspect were of the same sex.

These differences may be explainable in large part by the greater degree of violence associated with domestic conflicts and with male victimization of women. They suggest that the police response, though uneven, was by no means simply indifferent to the well-being of the complainants. But what *happens* to the minority of cases that result in arrest and are thus launched into the formal justice system?

Postarrest Disposition

Studies suggest that the police response to prior-relationship incidents is also influenced by what typically happens after arrest. Police sometimes adopt a passive role in such conflicts in part because they think nothing will happen beyond arrest in any case. The evaluators attempted to determine the court outcomes of the eighty prior-relationship cases in the Potrero sample which in fact led to an arrest. This was difficult, because court and police case-management systems yielded information on less than twenty percent of the cases—partly because misdemeanor cases were often purged from the system after six months, especially if the case was dismissed. Accordingly, the suspects' "rap sheets" were also checked to determine the disposition of the incident in question. This strategy increased the proportion of cases with known outcomes to 53 percent.

In only seven (about 17 percent) of cases was there a finding of guilt with a sanction imposed on the suspect. Almost two-thirds of these cases ended with a dismissal. The remaining cases ended with suspects being exonerated or diverted from the criminal-justice system. Of those suspects convicted, four were imprisoned and three given probation.

The most frequent reasons for the dismissals were lack of sufficient evidence or the noncooperation of the victims; the frequency of both of these was often mentioned by the patrol officers we interviewed as strong disincentives for them to take formal action in the first place. Similar reasons for "dropping" prior-relationship cases have appeared in other research on the court processing of nonstranger crimes (Vera Institute of Justice 1977).

Summing Up

This study, then does clearly reaffirm that the police deal routinely with a very substantial pool of prior-relationship cases. Moreover, the most common police response—though not the only one—was some attempt at a temporary "abatement" of the immediate conflict. In the majority of cases, little was done to address the underlying causes of the conflict. More than in most other kinds of police calls, the typical response was informal and often minimal. Even when police did decide to initiate some further action, it usually ended with the filing of a report on the incident. Few such cases were brought to court; even fewer resulted in a formal sanction against the accused.

Given the limits of the typical criminal-justice response, it seems clear that the formal system, in this neighborhood as elsewhere, is not providing much protection to the complainants in nonstranger conflicts. We have no way of quantifying the extent of the social and personal damage this may cause; but given what we know about the tendency of domestic incidents in particular to recur and even to escalate, it is safe to assume that in the absence of stronger intervention, many people will be hurt; and they are, as the data suggest, likely to be disproportionately young, minority, and female.

Discussion

What is clear from this rather fragmentary data is that a huge volume of domestic violence cases exists in communities like the Potrero District, and that the victims typically get little relief from the formal criminal-justice system. To anyone familiar with the wider literature on the criminal-justice response to domestic violence, this should come as little surprise. By itself, data such as these might lend themselves simply to an argument for toughening the criminal-justice response through mandatory arrest, "no-drop" policies in the courts, and other measures. That has been the approach of many proponents of what Lisa Lerman calls the "law enforcement critique" of the diversion of domestic violence cases to mediation (1984:98). But the shards of evidence we have from other studies suggest that the issue is more complicated. Again, the evidence from research in other cities suggests that formal policies aimed at getting tough on domestic crime remain limited in their capacity to offer consistent protection to its victims, much less to address in any serious way the underlying imbalances of power and fundamental vulnerabilities that put so many women at risk of abuse.

Does it follow that, as some have suggested and as the initial research presumed, the answer is to bring these cases into alternative dispute resolution in general or a program like SFCB in particular? "The question raised by feminists," writes Lisa Lerman, "is whether the 'soft' remedy of mediation can be effective in stopping domestic violence" (1984:81).

One concern has often been noted by critics of ADR approaches to family violence; while the formal justice system at least offers the *possibility* (and today often the mandate) of providing immediate protection to battered women, and arguably some modicum of deterrence against future assaults, the mechanisms for accomplishing this in mediation programs are unclear.

More subtly, but perhaps even more importantly, the current operating ideology of much of the ADR movement may militate against women's claims being taken with appropriate seriousness. As other contributors to this volume note repeatedly, ADR often tends in practice to downplay the very real structural inequalities that shape the real-life relationships among the participants; the "ideology of harmony," as Laura Nader puts it, does tend to obscure what are in reality often harsh and long-standing patterns of domination and subordination and the presence of vastly unequal resources. With the possible exception of child-protection cases, this is nowhere more true than in intimate violence between women and men. In addition, the tendency in ADR to individualize and balance conflict—to adopt some tendency to view both parties as contributive and to view resolution as involving both parties' willingness to compromise—could serve to (and does in some instances) create an atmosphere of undue tolerance for assaultive behavior on the part of men (Lerman 1984:86–87). (It is worthy of note that some family-violence research finds that lower-income women spontaneously chose shelters as a response to victimization much more often than they choose interventions that involve some sort of "counseling" [Saunders and Azar 1989:494–95]). Indeed the very definition of violent family assaults as disputes can be seen as part of the problem, not part of the solution; a physical attack may take place in the *course* of a "dispute," but the attack itself is a crime and ought to be treated as such, not as a matter for bargaining or compromise. In SFCB and programs sharing its unique view of conflict in particular, this issue may be aggravated by the emphasis on individuals' "taking responsibility" for the conflict and its resolution. The obvious response must be, why should it be in any sense the victimized woman's responsibility to resolve the conflict? Isn't there a more basic claim of wrongdoing at issue in these cases—one that ought in the last analysis to be upheld forcefully by the community as a whole?

Our own sense is that these caveats do not tell us that there should be no role for mediation in these cases—only that (1) the character of mediation should be rethought if it is to be applied in domestic-violence cases, and relatedly (2) mediation should be viewed as only one part of a broader, community-based strategy against domestic violence that takes as its central task the relative empowerment of at-risk women on several interrelated fronts at once.

In thinking through the elements of that kind of strategy, it is important to look back at the lessons that emerge from the evaluation data here as well as from other research. In the Potrero study, the women who were the most frequent complainants in prior-relationship cases tended to be triply disadvantaged—by gender, income, and race. Victims like these have few reliable resources, public or private, to call on in response to abusive relationships. We have seen that they are underserved by the criminal-justice system. But they are also underserved by the conventional social-service agencies that might offer aid and assistance, including the public income support and mental-health systems. This is, of course, even more true because of the devastating impact of federal and state budget cuts on communities like Visitacion Valley during the 1980s. Given the frequently atomized and disrupted character of these low-income communities, it is also unlikely that these women can consistently call on stable informal networks of kin and friends to provide assistance and shelter, which, as research shows, can be of crucial help in reducing the threat of repeated violence and establishing a new life outside the abusive relationship (Saunders and Andrews 1989). This, too, has become ever more true in many low-income urban communities by the 1990s, given the overall rise in poverty, the disruptive effect of drugs and alcohol on family stability, and intensified geographical mobility in search of affordable and safe housing. The women who appear so prominently in the Potrero data are among the most devastated casualties of the savage rending of what passed for a safety net in urban America in the past decade.

What this most clearly suggests is the need for a comprehensive and sustained response to the threat of violence these women face. Within that response, ADR could have a place. But it should be embedded in a broader effort to provide options and supports for low-income women and families that are now under siege in the broader arena of social policy as well as in the intimate sphere of the home. We could conceive of a family mediation program closely connected with a community-based strategy that worked simultaneously on several fronts to address the fundamental imbalances of power, lack of viable options, and cultural tendencies that both help promote domestic violence in the first place and simultaneously render conventional mediation a problematic means of dealing with it.

In order to maximize the chances for protection of women at risk, that strategy should involve a close working relationship with the formal justice system, rather than simply removing the conflict from its purview. This means actively educating, prodding, and sensitizing police and courts on domestic violence. The police could be brought to adapt the notion of problem-oriented or community-oriented policing to domestic violence—taking a more proactive and preventive role that involves, among other things, delivering a clear educational message to the community that violence against women is a serious crime that will not be tolerated.

A comprehensive strategy should also include expanded shelter options for women and children at risk. These in turn should be linked closely with opportunities for training, education, job placement, and housing and child-care assistance in order to enhance women's realistic options to leave threatening relationships. In one recent study, 70 percent of abused women who remained in relationships with their abusers cited a financial reason for staying, including lack of a job or of child care (Caputo 1988). Such a broad strategy should also involve visible and vigorous advocacy in the public and legislative arena for more consistent policies toward batterers and more resources for abused women and children, and for family-supported programs generally.

At the same time, it should work toward the tougher goal of trying to change the culture of violence and domination in which— as research affirms—specific incidents of domestic violence are often embedded (Fagan 1989:408). Part of this necessarily complex task could go on within the mediation process itself. Several papers in this volume raise the issue of the problematic and somewhat vague definition of "community" in the ADR movement. This is a particularly important issue in thinking through the appropriate role of ADR in intimate violence. In many communities in urban America today the dominant norms are at least lenient toward, and often explicitly supportive of, male domination and exploitation of women generally, and the male exercise of violence against women in the home specifically. Efforts at conciliation or mediation, therefore—if they are not to encourage, subtly or blatantly, the persistence of those norms—cannot assume the existence of consensual community standards in the light of which the conflict will be effectively resolved, but must actively challenge the dominant norms themselves. Reconciliation in this context would mean working to reframe the relationship on the basis of explicit values of mutual dignity, equality, and nonviolence.[4] In a comprehensive strategy against domestic violence at the community level, this sort of mediation as political education and normative reconstruction would be backed by the provision of the best supportive options for the complainant that could be mustered, including access to a sensitized criminal-justice system and assistance in establishing, if necessary, economic and social independence outside the abusive relationship. Without those linkages, with all of the existing inequalities of resources left intact, it is doubtful that this sort of mediation could work.

All of this is a tall order, to be sure. But the urgency of the need for such a comprehensive approach is apparent, from these and other data. As Merry and Milner note, the most distinctive claim of San

---

4. Lisa Lerman suggests a number of additional considerations for maximizing the effectiveness of mediation in protecting women against further violence; they include, among others, screening out cases in which violence has been recurrent; encouraging victims to seek more formal remedies *concurrent* with mediation; meeting separately with each party before beginning mediation to insure that women have an opportunity to disclose the level of abuse in the relationship without having to worry about the abuser's presence; monitoring the abuser's compliance with resulting agreements; and training mediators to a better understnading of the nature of domestic violence (1984:100–111).

Francisco Community Boards is to be in some sense transformative, striving not merely to resolve individual disputes but to empower individuals and the community as a whole. These are fine aims. But the difficulty is that they may become vague or contradictory aims in the context of long-standing structural inequalities that rend the community into victims and victimizers, the powerful and the powerless (or in the case of low-income urban communities, the powerless and the more powerless). Faced with those structured inequalities, civic work that aims to be truly transformative must explicitly challenge those inequalities in the name of a larger, more humane community that does not yet exist; must accept the task of working to build, over the long haul, something like real community where fear and exploitation ruled before.

REFERENCES

Bailey, Martha J. 1989. Unpacking the "rational alternative": A critical review of family mediation. *Canadian Journal of Family Law* 8, no. 1:61–94.

Berk, Richard A., Sarah Fenstermaker Berk, Donileen R. Loseke, and David Rauma. 1982. Throwing the cops back out: The decline of a local program to make the criminal justice system more responsive to incidents of domestic violence. *Social Science Research* 11, no. 3:245–79.

Black, Donald. 1980. *The Manners and Customs of the Police.* New York: Academic Press.

Bowker, Lee. 1982. Police services to battered women. *Criminal Justice and Behavior* 9:476–94.

Caputo, Richard K. 1988. Managing domestic violence in two urban police districts. *Social Casework* 69:81–87.

Elliot, Delbert S. 1989. Criminal justice procedures in family violence cases. In *Family Violence,* ed. Lloyd Ohlin and Michael Tonry. Chicago: University of Chicago Press.

Eppler, Amy. 1986. Battered women and the equal protection clause: Will the Constitution help them when the police can't? *Yale Law Journal* 95:788–809.

Fagan, Jeffrey. 1989. Cessation of family violence: Deterrence and dissuasion. In *Family Violence. See* Elliot 1989.

Ferraro, Kathleen, J. 1989. Policing Woman Battering. *Social Problems* 36, 1:61–74.

Lempert, Richard. 1989. Humility is a virtue: On the publicization of policy-relevant research. *Law and Society Review* 23:145–61.

Lerman, Lisa. 1984. Mediation of wife abuse cases: The adverse impact of informal dispute resolution on women. *Harvard Women's Law Journal* 7:57–113.

Morash, Merry. 1986. Wife Battering. *Criminal Justice Abstracts* 18, 2:252–71.

Saunders, Daniel G., and Sandra T. Azar. 1989. Treatment programs for family violence. In *Family Violence. See* Elliot 1989. University of Chicago Press.

Sherman, Lawrence W., and Richard A. Berk. 1984. The specific deterrent effects of arrest for domestic assault. *American Sociological Review* 49:261–72.

Sherman, Lawrence W., and Ellen G. Cohn. The impact of research on legal policy: The Minneapolis domestic violence experiment. *Law and Society Review* 23:117–44.

Tauchen, George, Helen Tauchen, and Ann D. Witte. 1981. *The Dynamics of Domestic Violence: A Reanalysis of the Minneapolis Experiment.* Washington, D.C.: Police Foundation.

U.S. Bureau of Justice Statistics. 1986. *Preventing Domestic Violence against Women.* Washington, D.C.: U.S. Government Printing Office.

U.S. Commission on Civil Rights. 1982. *Under the Rule of Thumb: Battered Women and the Administration of Justice.* Washington, D.C.: U.S. Government Printing Office.

Vera Institute of Justice. 1977. *Felony Arrests in New York City.* New York: Vera Institute.

Part 3

Contested Words: *Community, Justice, Empowerment,* and *Popular*

The Paradox of Popular Justice: A Practitioner's View

John Paul Lederach and Ron Kraybill

In the past decade mediation and other forms of alternative dispute resolution have emerged as a challenge to the prevailing modes of resolving conflicts. In their efforts to capture a legitimate space many proponents of the community- or popular-justice movement engage in a rhetoric of community empowerment and social transformation. The question posed by the current set of essays is whether a transformation toward popular justice and social empowerment is indeed taking place. As practitioners in some aspects of this movement we respond to that question from an insiders' view. Based on our experiences we argue that the movement faces external and internal paradoxes that militate against its success, unless they are explicitly embraced by the movement in creative ways.

There are two ways we might approach such an assignment. We could paint a broad picture based on our extensive but largely impressionistic view and experience throughout the United States, reflecting what we think is happening out there. Or, we could narrow our reflection to our own network and the mostly religious context in which we theorize and practice. In this chapter we have chosen the second for several reasons. First we have a clearer understanding of key concepts like popular, justice, community, and empowerment in the context of our practice and network. Second, to consider the definitions, tensions, and successes of popular justice in our more immediate circles grounds the discussion in concrete terms and provides a useful comparison and contrast with other settings like the San Francisco Community Boards (SFCB).

Specifically, we will begin with a description of how we understand the use and evolution of these terms in Mennonite Conciliation Service (MCS). Such a discussion addresses several aspects of a dialectic process: (1) What do concepts like popular, justice, community, and empower mean to us? (2) How do they inform and shape our work? (3) And simultaneously, how does our work inform and shape our understanding of these concepts? This reflection will highlight the inevitable tensions we experience and provide an inside view and assessment of the success and potential of the movement toward popular justice in a broader context.

Background and Definitions

The establishment of the Mennonite Conciliation Service is recent, 1979, but a four-hundred-year-old tradition precedes it. We see the strategic application of peacemaking skills to human conflict as a central expression of that tradition.

The tradition originates in the sixteenth century during the Reformation. Mennonite leaders, named after Menno Simons, a Dutch ex-Catholic priest, have commonly been described as the "left wing" of the Reformation because they felt other reformers of their day were not going far enough. Broadly known as the Anabaptists (those who rebaptized themselves), the early Mennonites stressed separation of the church and state, rejection of violence, and the voluntary nature of faith. They felt that following in the footsteps of Jesus, or discipleship, was the key to faith and called for living a life reconciled with all, including one's enemies. Oddly enough, one consequence of this conviction about peacemaking is most often articulated in a primarily negative stance: "We will not participate in taking human life." Refusing to bear arms and preaching love of enemies is a countercultural act in any setting, and Mennonites have paid a price with their lives in every century, including the early 1900s in the United States. But the theological understanding of Christian faith as a Gospel of peace and Jesus as a bringer of peace on earth remains. Thus when discussion about establishing a Mennonite Conciliation Service began in 1975—inspired in part by Methodists Jim Laue and John Adam—it fell on ready ears.

The Mennonite Conciliation Service (MCS) represents a movement in the Mennonite tradition: a movement from the abstract to the practical and a proactive response to conflict. The MCS has two major thrusts. First, since our beginning we have recognized that our historic peace church little resembles the outpost of the "peaceable kingdom" we theologically proclaim, as our splits into various conferences illustrates. Thus a major portion of MCS work is to provide training and intervention services to our own constituency. Of the ten locations where MCB "chapters" or affiliated agencies operate, eight are in communities where numerous Mennonites reside. The second thrust is contributing to the emergence of more effective dispute resolution within the larger society. MCS has aimed persistently to inject questions of values into settings in which we operate, but we avoid creedal approaches to dispute resolution. Thus we have been able to handle cases, provide training, and contribute to dialogue among practitioners in a wide variety of religious and secular settings.

It is in the context of the local congregation that MCS is most often invited to mediate interpersonal and group conflicts. The issues at the root of congregational conflicts are often forms of worship, use of budget, and leadership styles and roles. With this brief background we want to define several terms that are at the core of the current set of essays on community mediation as they are understood in the Mennonite context.

Community

In our setting, *community* refers to a group of people who share a common vision for corporate life and are accountable to each other to live in accordance to that vision. They are not simply linked by geographic proximity or common interest, but through a myriad of connections that may include family, congregational membership, shared work setting, and friendship ties. Thus our understanding of community is similar to common understandings of the term, but differs in its scope and intensity. For example, in the SFCB model, community appears to mean the aggregate of individuals living within a geographic area. To us, community means people bonded by a common core of values and accountable to each other in decision making regarding those values.

Popular and Empowerment

We see *empower* as a verb and *popular* as an adjective form of the same concept. That concept is participation in and accountability for decisions regarding one's own life. We have learned that a great deal of conflict is due to the fact that many people are disenfranchised. Disenfranchised people are identified as antagonists and troublemakers in many conflicts because they often react in ways that appear childish, irresponsible, or terroristic. Part of the challenge for mediators is to get the focus of attention away from the cycle of action/reaction between disputing parties and onto the issues of structure that triggered and perpetuated the antagonistic interaction. Enabling thoughtful, proactive participation of people who are normally omitted from decision-making processes to participate in discussions of their situation is one of the most effective strategies for accomplishing this. Empowering is more than establishing an open process, it is a matter of enabling people to function coherently and purposefully.

Empowerment in the fullest sense is inseparable from community. It is essentially participation in decisions that affect one's life. In this sense empowerment is popular, the people's participation. This is possible only when one is integrated into and accountable to community. True empowerment is impossible to create around isolated issues or individuals. It has to do with the integration and quality of people's lives together.

Justice

For purposes of this discussion we define *justice* to be the restoration of right relationships, the healing of broken relationships. This implies economic fairness in regards to basic human needs, a concern for redress of wrong, protection of the innocent, and the spiritual dimensions of repentance, forgiveness, and accountability. It goes beyond a restoration of balance or mere application of legal principles. An example of the former is "eye for an eye," reflecting an understanding of justice that more accurately is defined as vengeance. An example of the latter is trial and punishment in the current American legal system. We have no quarrel with the application of social values codified in legal principle to selected conflicts. But we believe this should be an avenue to justice of last resort. Unfortunately, much of our society sees justice as synonymous with the application of legal principle. Thus the legal system functions not only as the avenue of last recourse, but also as that of the first and only recourse.

There are dangers of subjective and arbitrary justice, to be sure, in locating standards of justice within relationships rather than in external standards. But locating justice solely in mechanisms external to the relationships (i.e., in legal principle) is equally problematic. The first casualty is erosion of participation and empowerment. Where community members experience abstract principles as the arbiter of disputes, the fabric of community ultimately suffers. Community is no longer a vital, ever-unfolding encounter with diverse others. Rather it is a static location for imposition of values defined by one's predecessors.

To us justice is doing what is necessary to establish right relationships. Right relationships are those that honor mutual human worth, that redress past wrong so far as injuries are able to be redressed, and in which steps have been taken so that neither fear nor resentment play dominant roles.

From Orthodoxos to Orthopraxis: The Paradoxes of Justice

The question naturally emerges: But what does all this mean and how do we apply it? How does our understanding of popular, justice, community, and empowerment shape what we do? How does it relate to the SFCB and the movement toward popular justice in the United States? We can respond to these questions by reflecting on our strategy as mediators in congregational conflicts.

Commonly we mediate conflicts in Mennonite congregational settings. A word about the nature and organization of the Mennonite faith communities is useful for understanding how and in what ways MCS intervenes in this context. Worldwide, Mennonites number nearly 800,000 with 250,000 in the United States. Mennonites are a congregational rather than a hierarchical community. At the beginning of the Anabaptists movement in the sixteenth century was a belief in the "priesthood of all believers." The statement refers to the direct access each person has to God and the need the believers have to share in a common process of discernment with each other in making decisions of faith. In North America a congregation, often referred to as "church" in everyday parlance, is the modern local association of members that share regular worship and mutual accountability, usually ranging from fifty to several hundred members. Each congregation is responsible for its own theological practice and administrative and organizational structure.

Congregations link together in broader church bodies or what in some cases are referred to as "conferences." These are usually defined by theological similarities. Currently in North America there are some four thousand congregations grouped in twenty-two of these church or conference bodies. The divisions represent the historic schisms that have been experienced in the broader Anabaptist movement since the sixteenth century. Thus between conferences there exists diversity in faith, belief, and practice, while the congregations within a given conference are relatively similar. There are some national and international Mennonite projects and institutions that bring together different church bodies and conferences, but each usually has its own set of independent service and mission activities. One such interconference institution is the Mennonite Central Committee, which brings together seventeen of the twenty-two Mennonite and Brethren of Christ church bodies and conferences. It is under the auspices of Central Committee that Mennonite Conciliation Service finds its institutional home.

At the local level in the United States Mennonite congregations are traditionally rather homogenous groups, particularly in rural settings, where European descendency has created a mostly white, Germanic, but English-speaking middle-class constituency. This is changing as Mennonites have become increasingly present in urban and suburban settings. Typically, the congregation elects a pastor or a pastoral team—a group of elders and deacons. While these persons play special roles in the local church leadership, decision-making about the expression of faith and broader theological issues lies with the body of the congregation.

In congregational settings parishoners typically have an inherited fear of conflict, perceive signs of sin, and usually engage in patterns of avoiding, blaming, and, in extreme cases, splitting. Often little attention has been paid to the structure of decision making, with a few spiritual "fathers" wielding a great deal of authority in spite of a long-standing tradition of community discernment and process. In this context, people almost always are looking at the question of right and wrong and assessing whom to blame. Several people or a minority are targeted as the antagonists. Generally, people seek to understand what is wrong with these folks, get frustrated and eventually exasperated with their "shenanigans." As mediators we get called in when there is imminent threat of separation and people are about to give up trying to deal with each other. The context, the network of relationships in which conflicts like these develop, and our entry and intervention in them each provide insight into the themes of this paper.

The Entry: Trust-Based and Neutrality-Based Models of Mediation

In the last ten years MCS has evolved as a Mennonite resource for conflict resolution in the Mennonite Church. Being comparatively small in number and a homogeneous body, Mennonites have a strong sense of identity and networking. This generally means we know each other. The checking of pedigree known as the "Mennonite game" at times frustrates newcomers. In conflict, however, this means that more often than not the Mennonite mediators are known and connected to Mennonite disputants in ways other than through their role as mediator. We enter and work at conflict resolution with characteristics of both a trust- and a neutrality-based model of mediation (Lederach 1988), which creates its own special tensions and differentiates it from the primarily neutrality-based models practiced in North American mediation circles. A discussion of these ideal types is useful for exploring this difference.

In North America, mediators point to neutrality and impartiality as key elements of the third-party role. Mediation is the work of third-party neutrals. Training emphasizes impartiality. Proposed ethical codes bind mediators to these principles in their work (Moore 1986). In North American mediation, legitimacy and authority are created primarily through the role, position, and function of the mediator as a professional. This is a rational-legal type of authority as Weber (1947) described it.

entry	1. distance	legitimacy
through	2. anonymity	fairness
professional→	3. connected through→	efficiency
role	function	effectiveness
	4. connected through conflict	

The characteristics of a neutrality-based model are numerous. The mediator maintains a certain distance from both parties. He or she is chosen precisely because there is no formal connection of that person with either disputant, or because it is obvious to the disputants that such prior connection if it exists will not affect the outcome. The mediator is therefore judged to be unbiased. Impartial intervenors, then, are connected to the disputants only where their mediator role is being played. Mediators relate to the disputants because of and through the conflict alone. They are connected only during the process and in ways relevant to the functions of conflict mediation.

Neutrality and impartiality help create the necessary perception of legitimacy, professionalism, and fairness to both sides. The mediator works hard to present a self, to give a performance that promotes this role of neutrality and the definition of the situation in which it is staged (Goffman 1959). Of particular interest, however, is the fact that both neutrality and impartiality are defined negatively, in terms of what the mediator *is not*. The third party is *not* connected to, is *not* biased for either side; has *no* investment in the outcome; and does *not* expect any special reward (Moore 1986:15–16).

In contrast, in a recent ethnographic study of conflict management in squatter villages in Costa Rica (Lederach 1988) a different form of providing informal mediation was observed, coined in the study as a trust-based model. In that setting, the primary concern of people when they consider getting help for conflictive situations is related to their notion of *confianza*, or trust. At the folk level, this relationally based concept is understood as circular and cumulative. *Confianza* builds through interactive levels, proceeding from an "acquaintance" to "friendship," then to "being like family" and finally to "being bosom buddies," or the closest of friends. At different levels different kinds of problems can be shared, and more intimate concerns can be revealed. Sharing "personal problems," for example, is reserved for the latter two categories. This is the level where help is sought for resolving interpersonal and family conflicts. Thus the ability of sharing and dealing with problems depends on the level of trust people have with the go-betweens.

In the *confianza* model, legitimacy and authority for the helper to act is invested in the person through a personal relationship, as opposed to a functionary role. This corresponds to what Weber (1947) called traditional authority.

entry   1. personal relationship   legitimacy
through→   2. closeness to→   tradition
trust   3. knowledge of   connections
                       4. wholly connected   fairness

The *confianza* and neutrality models of intervention differ in
several respects. *Confianza* is based on accumulated and usually
rather intimate knowledge of each other. *Confianza* is used by all
involved to bring helpers into the conflict and maintain their presence.
The community and network are both the context and resource for
resolution. A *confianza*-based model depends, not on the performance
of impartiality, but rather through and because of connectedness.
Confianza is used to assure sincerity, openness, and revelation, as
well as a channel for opening negotiations. Third parties are often
chosen because they are connected, that is, are recognized as having
confianza of all sides. Such intervenors are chosen for their positive
impact: they are *close* to, *known, with* and *for* each side. Concern
for the appearance of impartiality and neutrality is replaced with
concern for the ability to know, get to, and "get into" the world of
the other.

MCS mediation in Mennonite circles is built on elements of both
trust-based and neutrality-based models. Crosscutting relationships
connect us across several planes, including family, friendship, church
committees, and profession. We often connect to those involved in
ways other than our roles as professional mediators. Yet people view
us as impartial professionals entering a volatile situation. Put sociologically, we gain entry and legitimacy through a combination of
traditional and rational-legal mechanisms, which create unique tensions and dynamics in our work and may shed light on the tensions
experienced in community mediation.

Congregational conflicts often involve a combination of interpersonal disputes between individual members and group decisions
that must be made by broader consensus. In our interventions, rather
than separate out the individuals for one-to-one mediations, we often
mediate aspects of the multiple interpersonal disputes in the presence
of a broader group from the congregation or at times in the presence
of the entire congregation. Thus, mediation moves from the primarily
individual and private process prevalent in the mainstream United
States model to one based in the community and the broader network

it represents. In this sense the network, or the relationships in the congregation, serve both as the context where the conflict is expressed and as a resource for resolving it.

These comparative models may provide an explanation of the difficulties facing community mediation. The movement faces the paradox of introducing a traditional form of providing help in a modern complex society. Specifically, the San Francisco Community Boards and popular justice in general propose a movement from a legal-rational model of conflict resolution (court, institution, and bureaucracy) to a modern form of traditional authority in offering help. The paradox and ensuing tension emerges when the model is applied to geographic communities that are not traditional, extended-family networks. Thus, while the model is neighbor helping neighbor, the neighbors are still only connected through the conflict and the function of resolving it rather than in a myriad of other ways. The paradox is created by attempting to apply a trust-based model in a community functioning in a modern bureaucratic society. The result is a movement that espouses an ideology approximating a trust-based model of popular justice but in practice represents a neutrality-based model.

This is a paradox we experience in our congregational mediation, although we have the advantage of working in a community defined by crosscutting relationships and common values, permitting a trust-based approach to be more fully engaged. Likewise, in other settings we suspect that the overall paradigm of popular justice would be most effective in areas where strong ethnic, religious, and family ties are already established—in other words, where people's lives are more wholly connected. We also suspect that the descriptions of SFCB in other chapters (see DuBow and Currie; Thomson and DuBow; and Yngvesson) indicate the limited ability of a trust-based model of conflict resolution to create community in areas where that is not happening by other means. In this sense, the movement toward popular justice, in the ideological terms expressed by SFCB literature, is not and will likely not be fully realized. The places where we see more potential are those areas where community is not defined strictly by geographic proximity but by elements of traditional society, particularly connectedness in ways other than professional specialization.

Moving the Problem: Trust- and
Neutrality-Based Approaches

In congregational fights parishoners tend to frame the conflict as an
issue of substantive justice, of right and wrong, or in the spiritual
definition, as sin. This happens both in a substantive and retributive
sense. In other words, people look for who is to blame, who needs
to be disciplined. Our MCS strategy has been to reframe the conflict
initially as a systemic procedural issue. In other words, we do not
approach the conflict as lodged between isolated individuals. Instead
we look at the systemic concept of powerlessness as a key in producing
the antagonists. More often than not they are a vocal minority who
have little recourse to decision making affecting the life and direction
of the congregation. They feel they have no voice and do not count.
Correspondingly, many of their antagonistic actions are aimed at
finding a way to be heard and counted.

Our intervention is thus aimed initially at the community system
and at achieving process agreements. In other words, *empowerment*
takes place through *participation* and the validation of diverse voices.
The process is no longer static and taken for granted, but popular
in the sense that it is the people's. Here then, justice is first pursued
by creating fair and participatory processes before we pursue justice
of substantive right and wrong on the issues. To put our congregational strategy in a nutshell: *Community* is built when *people* are
empowered to pursue *justice* through direct *participation.*

However, in many cases the issues of right and wrong, or substantive justice, remain salient and pose a paradox for the mediation.
Where ethical principles and (in this case) accepted Mennonite values
have been infringed (e.g., inappropriate financial or sexual behavior
by a member or pastor), then the frame of sin and wrongdoing
requiring repentance and disciplinary action dominates over the frame
of negotiation or accommodation. The problem lies not only in deciding which frame of reference is appropriate but also in the fact that
people involved in church conflicts tend to view their antagonists as
displaying non-Christian attitudes at best and sin at worst, independent of the issue. This means they enter the process of resolving
the conflict from the viewpoint that the issues are nonnegotiable.
The paradox lies with the power of reframing these issues from "non"

to "negotiable" and in deciding whether we pursue procedural empowerment or substantive justice. In other words, if we choose to empower the process we bracket for a time the ultimate question of right and wrong; if we proceed, as many participants often desire, directly to the question of justice, we diminish the ability of the participatory process to run its course.

For example, the ordination of women is not accepted as a matter of biblical principle in many Mennonite church bodies. The MCS approach would reframe that issue as a procedural one that renders it negotiable and up for discussion through a process based in dialogue. Our experience suggests that only a small percentage of issues are indeed nonnegotiable and that the facilitated procedure of dialogue produces new insight into biblical principle and into past misunderstanding and interactions. We find the mediation process inappropriate when the process affects a nonrepresented populace outside or inside the congregation, and when there is evidence of actual or imminent psychological and/or physical violence. But otherwise, we recognize that the difficulty of determining when and where the line is drawn (what is and is not mediable) is the weakest aspect of our model and that we tend to rely on subjective evaluations. Our rather fluid criteria suggest we mediate when there is a relative balance of power, when representation of affected parties is assured, and when a safe environment can be established.

As a result we measure success by rather fluid standards. In our context, it is measured not by the number or significance of final agreements, but rather by the degree to which people feel they have an impact, that they have been treated fairly, that they have understood each other, that they have better mechanisms for making decisions and handling their differences, and that their key issues have been addressed. In particular we try to assess whether there is an enhanced level of participation in decision-making that affects people's lives. If successful, the participants feel that they are a valued part of their community.

Measuring such success is not easy. Realistically we are struck with the monumental task we face in fostering procedural justice in our own context and the small steps of progress we make, even though this context comes with four hundred years of participatory decision making and dedication to peacemaking. We are thus even more overwhelmed by the difficulties faced by advancing popular justice in "communities" that are not bound by a common vision and values that deal with issues of injustice that go beyond face-to-face relations.

Coming to an End: Justice as Restoration and Forgiveness

We view justice not primarily as punishment or retribution but as restoration of broken relationships. This involves the paradox of working on accountability and forgiveness. Such an approach assumes that conflict resolution goes beyond settlement or agreement. For MCS, that includes the dimension of relational reconciliation, the creation of something new.

To elaborate on this point we wish to consider the experience of our colleagues in the Criminal Justice section of Mennonite Central Committee who helped initiate the specialized form of mediation know as the Victim Offender Reconciliation Program (VORP), which since has spread to broader circles throughout the United States and Canada. The current status of criminal law in the United States is based on a purely restitutive system at best, and a punishment system at worst. To manage and control the volatility of conflict, it has evolved into an objective, distant, anonymous, and almost totally depersonalized mechanism for resolving broken relationships. The courts look to establish right and wrong by objective fact, discarding for the most part the emotional, subjective, interpretive elements. They virtually eliminate the victim's participation by establishing that the crime is committed against the state. They sentence retribution through punishment of seclusion, monetary exchange, and work for the community. Rarely does this process heal the brokenness in the community or between the principle protagonists. In many instances they never see each other.

The VORP model, on the other hand, attempts to work at the restoration and the rehumanization of the conflict. As outlined by Zehr (1985), it views justice as right relationships judged not by the rules but by the outcome; the restoration of both parties rather than imposition of pain to deter; the repair of social injury and the encouragement of mutuality and reconciliation. In this model the victim's rights and needs are recognized and the offender is encouraged to understand the impact of his/her action and to take responsibility for it. Finally, the community is not on the sideline, abstractly represented by the state, but is the active facilitator of the restorative process.

It is in the growth and spread of the VORP movement that we see the most direct move toward the implementation of popular justice, as we have defined it, in a broader secular context. At the same time we see an inherent contradiction that militates against its truly being popular justice. According to Umbreit (1988), VORP-type models, which began in 1978, are not operating in more than one hundred jurisdictions around the country. They increase at about fifteen to twenty per year. Such growth points to the genuine need for an alternative system of handling victim-offender issues and to the success of a primarily volunteer, community-based program. The contradiction emerges when the program is attached to or funded by the current justice institutions. As Zehr notes, the VORP programs then tend to become add-ons rather than alternatives. "Part of the problem is VORP's dependence on the system" he notes. "That creates the dangers of co-optation and subversion" (1988). To put it in other terms, accountability becomes the primary agenda (establishing restitution) and the relational elements of reconciliation and forgiveness are lost. For the alternative process to survive it must emulate the system it wishes to change.

The Paradoxes of Popular Justice

In this section we have endeavored to demonstrate the paradoxes facing popular justice from the viewpoint of the MCS model, both in Mennonite settings and in criminal-justice applications. We can suggest several general observations based on these ideas. First, we note that community mediation has moved to incorporate a more traditional, trust-based model of resolving conflicts. To do so presupposes the existence of a trust-based network. Without such a network, as is the case in many urban neighborhoods, the movement is faced with the paradox of needing to create both the model of conflict resolution and the community that uses it, a difficult if not impossible task. Second, the movement must legitimate its activities. It has done so by articulating a space parallel to, or adjunct to, the current legal system. It thus faces the paradox of a relationally oriented mode of conflict resolution housed in a legal-rational organizational framework that tends to place higher value on substantive settlement than on relational restoration. Both of these difficulties may explain why other articles in this volume (e.g., DuBow and McEwen) indicate that most mediated cases end a relationship rather than sustain them on new ground. Finally, the movement faces the paradox of justice as process and substance. The emphasis on process may tend to overshadow or at times simply miss the substantive issues at stake, resulting in the creation of inappropriate forums incapable of adequately handling the underlying issues.

From Praxis Back: The Essential Tensions

How has a decade of practice and experience at MCS affected our understanding of popular justice and community empowerment? What are the essential tensions, as Kuhn (1979) would call them, that we experience, and how have they changed the conceptualization of our work? Two areas stand out as examples.

Professionalization

It is no secret that the relatively new and evolving field of conflict resolution is experiencing the pain of a budding new specialization and profession. We envision this tension along a continuum. At one extreme are the neighborhood centers espousing volunteerism, self-help, and peer relationships. At the other end are highly trained professionals who want to make a decent livelihood carving out a niche in the professional world of help somewhere between career diplomats, organizational consultants, lawyers, and therapists. Clustered along both ends are differing views of charging and fees (for free or minimal charge as community service vs. the accepted professional rates) and differing perspectives on credentials (minimum training vs. licensing).

volunteerism	professionalism
no charge	professional rates
basic training	licensed
peer help	specialized help

We find ourselves, as we suspect others do, operating simultaneously at both ends and all points between. This produces a constant form of organizational and personal cognitive dissonance. Take, for example, the question of fees. MCS is housed and partly funded in the broader Mennonite Central Committee budget. However, each year we raise over half of our budget through fees for service rendered. As an organization our policy has been to respond to requests for training and intervention whether or not persons asking for help can reimburse us adequately. We also are dedicated to high-quality service in terms of materials, techniques, and personnel. Our recent "Compensation" document reflects this inherent contradiction. On the one hand we go to great lengths to explain why we charge forty dollars an hour or three hundred dollars a day. On the other, we say that we make our "skills available to others whether they can pay or not."

Credentials and licensing represent another example. We are fully given to the goal and principle that everyone be empowered with better conflict and mediation skills. We hope for a church constituency and a society in general that has learned alternative and more responsible ways of resolving conflicts. We are dedicated to a popular movement in that direction. We also recognize that not everyone nor just anyone can adequately respond to conflicts at different levels. For the sake of our integrity and the field in general we must maintain some quality control. We are uncomfortable with the movement toward credentials and elitism. We are also ill at ease with people mediating in our network who are not adequately prepared and create more conflict and pain than they resolve.

We have tried to address this dissonance by drawing on the concept of discipleship. In the Mennonite tradition, discipleship is the path of mentoring, following, and accompanying. Rather than elitism, it is the model of choosing to walk together on the same path, but recognizing that some have been walking longer and can accompany those who have recently arrived. The model presupposes a certain fluidity and a high degree of mutuality.

Our internal tensions highlight our concern for the larger field and the movement toward popular justice in the United States. If this tension is not handled creatively, it has and will militate against the success of popular justice, even though it originated with that goal in mind. If the field of conflict resolution chooses the route of professionalization, specialization, and inevitably elitism, it will cease to be popular or just. If it chooses not to set standards or tackle the complexities or quality control, it will be denigrated, viewed as inferior by other professions, and inevitably cease to be a viable and serious alternative to the current systems. We believe that the challenging and creative alternative is to embrace the paradox and work at both ends simultaneously.

Training

We have also discovered an essential tension around the model, purpose, and content of training. Training more than anything else represents the doctrine of any given field. It is the formal accumulation of practice and knowledge to be transferred. Training is the institutionalization of a specialized language and paradigm that distinguishes a profession. It is the movement from art to science, from experiment and experience to prescription. Invariably, the formalization of knowledge for purposeful transfer is packaged overtly as a model, in this case a mediation or conflict-management model, but one that is built on implicit assumptions and values rooted in the cultural context in which the model emerged.

The cultural context in which most conflict-resolution models have emerged in North America is Western, modern, industrial, bureaucractic society (Lederach 1986, 1988), educated professionals, and twentieth-century social sciences (Merry and Silbey 1984). Thus, in general, conflict is viewed in linear, rational terms best handled by specialists using formalized, linear, and rational models of intervention. Training programs tend to present a basic model with adaptations according to different settings and specialties (divorce, environmental, neighborhood justice, etc.), while rarely raising to an explicit level these underlying values and assumptions on which the model is built.

Our experience in radically different cultural contexts (Ireland, Central America, Europe, Africa) has raised some fundamental questions about the prescriptive model of mediation training. We have found that the simple transfer of the mainstream North American model of mediation to other settings can exacerbate conflict rather than help transform it constructively. Although not the intention, the transfer of this model with its unspoken values can easily represent a form of cultural imperialism. It tends to assume the trainers know what the target population needs. It assumes the model need only be translated and adapted to local cultural nuances. It assumes the target population will be empowered if they learn the model and necessary skills to implement it. It assumes that the expertise about conflict and its management lies with the trainer.

In recent years and through the slow, at times painful baptism of experience, we have moved through a paradigmatic shift in our approach to training in other cultures, and to a serious questioning of our training in the United States. The movement has been toward an elicitive rather than prescriptive model of training. An elicitive model assumes the local receiving population are already creators and managers of conflict in their context. They are the experts, although their knowledge is taken for granted and implicit. Elicitive training assumes that the participants' natural, everyday knowledge about conflict, how it works and how it is handled, is the single most important resource for creating appropriate models responsive to their context. From this perspective the trainer is not the expert or prescriber, but rather a catalyst for reflection. The power of creation, Freire (1970) once suggested, lies in discovery and naming. In our approach, we reframe training in mediation as an exercise in participatory creation that fosters such discovery and naming. This suggests the possibility of an appropriate technology of help in conflict, rooted in the context and culture of those who create the conflict.

This question points to an essential tension in the movement toward popular justice. There is a general tendency in the institutionalization of a profession toward formalization and ossification (Weber 1947). We see that happening in the field of conflict resolution, most evident in the way we conceive and carry out training and the dissemination of our models. Creation and participation is replaced with prescription and the transfer of knowledge—in other words, the promotion of a new, albeit alternative institution. As practitioners we must take seriously Laura Nader's critique (in this volume) that the means have overtaken the ends. If our conceptualization is aimed at alternative institutions rather than popular empowerment, we will witness more of a common trend: conflict resolution will become institutionalized largely by co-optation by the current justice system, thus further expanding the legal apparatus with a host of legal professionals and paraprofessionals, and creating a dual-track system of justice (Matthews 1988; Zehr 1985).

Conclusions

An assessment of the movement toward popular justice in the United States must be based on a clear definition of what is meant by popular and justice and community empowerment. From our perspective justice is ultimately aimed at restoration of right relationships more than retribution. Popular means direct participation. Community is more than geographic location. It signals integration and connection of peoples' lives around common goals and values. Empowerment assumes that people have influence on the decisions that affect their lives. Based on such a definition, we view the movement toward popular justice as minimal and slow, for reasons external and internal to the alternative dispute-resolution movement.

Externally, we recognize the immensity of the current justice system. Not only is it based on generations of institutions and bureaucracy, but also it represents the institutionalization of the widely accepted and unquestioned norms and values of mainstream America. While there are increasing signs of system overload and inefficiency, the task faced by the popular alternative is not simply revamping the system nor convincing those currently in power. It is, in the end, the challenge of reorienting the basic normative assumptions about handling conflict in the mind of the person in the street. These challenges are widely recognized by most people in the alternative movements. Less explicit are the internal contradictions that militate against the success of the popular justice movement, which we have attempted to delineate in this paper by reflecting on the tensions we experience in our own network.

First, popular justice models like SFCB represent sociological forms for handling conflict more closely akin to traditional society orientations, yet they are placed in the context of modern bureaucratic society. We find the differences between a neutrality-(anonymous, professional) and a trust-based model of help (connected, known) to be particularly salient in highlighting these inherent tensions and contradictions. In a more traditionally oriented society the mode of handling conflicts emerges from the context of the social network, relationships, and common values. In the popular-justice movement community is supposed to emerge from a new way of handling conflicts. The contradiction and inherent tension enters when the alternative mode, to be successful, must simultaneously assume as present and create a sense of community, participation, and empowerment, in a context where these do not exist. Thus success is high among those who are in the movement because they sense a new community and common values, but limited in the geographic community where these people practice. The local mediation program tends to become increasingly professional (a new, quicker, and less formal way of helping) or becomes a form of anonymous peer help.

Second, professionalization of the alternative creates another inherent contradiction militating against the success of popular justice. Professionalization occurs because of a need for legitimacy, credibility, and the need to support the growing number of practioners. The movement is trying to find a niche in a modern, bureaucratic society. The implications are numerous.

Increasingly, professionalization creates formalized models, prescriptive training, and expert elitism. To a large degree this is already taking place in the growing field of alternative dispute resolution. While the values and goals of the movement, that is, the desired end-state, is participatory empowerment, that *end* is undermined when the *means*, the delivery and training structures, are increasingly professional and prescriptive, or co-opted as a part of the current system in order to gain legitimacy.

These observations suggest two directions community-justice programs might consider. First, redirect the target away from geographic communities and toward communities that represent already established relational networks. For example, ethnic networks in many urban settings that are connected through extended ties of family, language, work, and friendship suggest unique resources. With such a reorientation the goal of the project is not to create a community where it does not exist, but to empower the natural network's ability to serve as resources of justice. Second, as a necessary complement the training should not be conceived as a prepackaged model to be delivered and emulated but as a catalyst for building appropriate procedures.

Finally, after reflecting on our own internal tensions and weaknesses, and on the other essays in the current volume, one last observation about the movement toward popular justice in the United States is in line. Success, in our mind, is contingent upon the implementation of a radical social critique that goes beyond rhetoric. It is a critique of institutional mechanisms for handling conflict, of the strengths and excesses of professionalism, and in particular of the societal assumptions and norms about community and justice. To implement such a critique implies that the movement itself has found creative approaches of delivering services and preparing people in ways that respect the positive values of participation, restoration, and integration. It also demands that the movement engage in serious self-evaluation not merely about ways to improve the technique but also about the possibilities of contributing to an increase in procedural and substantive justice in this society. In particular this necessitates more in-depth evaluation of the criteria by which an increase in justice is measured, and about the ways the organizational structure of the movement contributes to it. Ultimately, the movement must recognize that legitimacy lies not with the acceptance of the current system but with the level of contribution toward constructive and just systemic change. We must face the reality that paradoxically some of the directions we have chosen to gain access and legitimacy in this society may be contradictory to the ultimate goals we espouse.

BIBLIOGRAPHY

Freire, Paulo. 1970. *Pedagogy of the Oppressed.* New York: Seabury Press.
Goffman, Erving. 1959. *The Presentation of Self in Everyday Life.* Garden City, N.Y.: Anchor Books.
Kuhn, Thomas S. 1979. *The Essential Tension: Selected Studies in Scientific Tradition and Change.* Chicago: University of Chicago Press.
Lederach, John Paul. 1986. "The Cultural Assumptions of the North American Model of Mediation." Akron, Pa.: Mennonite Central Committee.
———. 1988. "Of Nets, Nails, and *Problemas:* A Folk Vision of Conflict in Central America." Ph.D. diss., University of Colorado.
Matthews, Roger, ed. 1988. *Informal Justice?* London: Sage Publications.
Merry, Sally Engle, and Susan S. Silbey. 1984. "What do Plaintiffs Want? Reexamining the Concept of Dispute." *Justice System Journal* 9: 151–78.
Moore, Christopher. 1986. *The Mediation Process.* San Francisco: Jossey-Bass.
Umbreit, Mark. 1988. "The Mediation of Victim Offender Conflict." *Journal of Dispute Resolution* 1:85–105.
Weber, Max. 1947. *The Theory of Social and Economic Organization,* trans. A. M. Henderson and Talcott Parsons. New York: Oxford University Press.
Zehr, Howard. 1985. "Retributive Justice, Restorative Justice." In *New Per-*

spectives on Crime and Justice: Occasional Papers of the MCC Canada Victim Offender Ministries Program and the MCC U.S. Office of Criminal Justice. Issue no. 4. Akron, Pa.: Mennonite Central Committee.

———. 1988. "The State of the VORP Movement." *Network Newsletter,* July–September.

Local People, Local Problems, and Neighborhood Justice: The Discourse of "Community" in San Francisco Community Boards

Barbara Yngvesson

"Individuals" create "communities" by congregating with other individuals whom they decide to consider similar to themselves.
—Hervé Varenne 1977:15

By devoting 26 hours to training over two successive Saturdays and five weeknights in a two week period interested people could become "community members."
—DuBow and McEwen 1990:43

I don't think that we should consider the "modern state" as an entity which was developed above individuals, ignoring what they are and even their very existence, but on the contrary as a very sophisticated structure, in which individuals can be integrated, under one condition: that this individuality would be shaped in a new form, and submitted to a set of very specific patterns.
—Foucault 1982:214

The story of community told in the San Francisco Community Boards literature is one in which the involvement of local people in mediating local problems will create a moral order of neighbors, and in this way produce a political and moral alternative to an increasingly expansive state (Shonholtz 1984). The discourse of voluntarism (of individual choice, intent, and commitment) is a key term in this story, shaping both the political project of the San Francisco Community Boards program and the strategy of mediation through which it is realized. Volunteer mediators, who are also described as "neighborhood residents" or "community members" in program literature, are trained in techniques for resolving conflict. These techniques are oriented towards facilitating communication and the sharing of feelings. Shared feelings, in turn, along with the "shared work" of participating in mediation sessions, are envisioned as empowering, and as giving neighbors greater control over the resolution of conflicts that divide them.

I argue in this paper that the discourse of voluntarism blurs the distinction between volunteers who act as mediators in the program, on the one hand, and those who voluntarily participate by having their problems mediated, on the other, suggesting that they are the same and that volunteers *are* community members participating in a locally based movement. In this way the mediation practice of San Francisco Community Boards produces an ideology of community that is simultaneously local (constituted in opposition to a state that is imagined as alienating, distant, and separate from neighborhoods of people living contiguously) and translocal (constituted in opposition to the parties whose conflicts are brought to the program for mediation).

The referent for the local "community" is itself a complex concept, including the immediate parties to a conflict (who are in principle brought together through a training process in which they are taught to share feelings during a mediation hearing), as well as a broader community of neighborhood residents of which these parties are a segment. Resolving a conflict between parties is seen as instrumental to the construction of shared values and commitment among a broader localized community of residents.

The referent for the translocal "community," by contrast, is the volunteers, whose training, civic work as mediators, and involvement in other social and governance activities of the program set them apart from the program's clients and constitute them as what DuBow (1987) and DuBow and McEwen (1990) describe as an "internal community" distinct from the "external community" of parties. In the ideology of SFCB, the internal community of volunteers is understood as a utopian model for a localized, but more inclusive, "community as a whole" of neighborhood residents (DuBow 1987:chap. 5, 6).[1] At the same time, the community as a whole should be produced by the increasing involvement of local neighborhood residents in the mediation process, as volunteers and/or as disputants.

This complex discourse of community is shaped by an ethos of individual choice and by assumptions about the potential for individual empowerment through collective action that have deep roots in the ideologies of liberal legalism and republican humanism,[2] and this may account for the support of the program by both public and private funding agencies, as well as for its popularity among the career-oriented, middle-class professionals who serve as volunteers. "Community" appears as a symbol of mutuality and emotional intimacy for volunteers in the SFCB program, as a symbol of voluntary citizen participation in civic work (and the assumed relevance of this to neighborhood regeneration and crime control) for funding agencies, and as a symbol of collective action to solve structurally based conflicts for at least some of the parties who come to the SFCB for assistance (see below). At the same time, the bias of the program towards an interpretation of community as like-mindedness (moral consensus) produced by enhancing communication, rather than building on the potential for collective action grounded in collective experience, has skewed the forms of community that are produced towards the internal community of volunteers rather than the external community of parties or their neighbors. Indeed, I suggest that far from creating communities in which local people are empowered, the SFCB program empowers mediators at the expense of the parties to conflict, producing forms of community that *exclude* the parties to conflict while generating relationships of control that expand (rather than undermine) diffuse mechanisms of power in the modern state.

1. My two primary sources in describing the practice of the Community Boards are Fred DuBow's manuscript, "Conflicts and Community: A Study of the San Francisco Community Boards" (11 July 1987) and Judy Rothschild's Ph.D thesis, "Mediation as Social Control: A Study of Neighborhood Justice" (1986). Revised versions of both of these manuscripts are included in this volume, but I include citations to the originals, as well as to the revision of the DuBow manuscript (cited here as DuBow and McEwen 1990). Because the pagination in the DuBow manuscript is not continuous (each chapter is numbered separately), references in the text are to chapter and page.

2. For a discussion of these traditions see Bellah et al. 1985 and Tocqueville (1966), part 2. For a critique of liberal legalism, see Mensch 1982.

I focus in particular on the politics involved in the production of an ideology of community empowerment that is grounded in a notion of community produced voluntarily by autonomous individuals, and I note the connection between this understanding of community justice and another central symbol of the neighborhood-justice movement, consensual justice, in which voluntarism also is a key theme (Harrington and Merry 1988). The assumption that *both* community and consensus are grounded in a voluntary agreement between individuals who share a geographical space (i.e., they are "neighbors") but little else and must learn to communicate their feelings, marks a key difference between the approach to social transformation of the SFCB, and the approach in revolutionary contexts (e.g., Cuba, Nicaragua, Portugal). In these settings, popular tribunals have been used as vehicles for creating shared understandings of order at the local level, but the basis of community or of the "popular" is understood to be located in structural commonalities (e.g., a common working-class history or shared experiences of powerlessness in the context of class difference), rather than in the intention or will of alienated individuals whose only similarity is a specific instance of conflict and who "choose" to participate in order to resolve this.

Neighborhood: The Landscape of Community

The discourse of community in the literature of and about Community Boards is complex and contradictory, including notions of community as a physical space, as moral order, and as heightened forms of communication. The words *neighborhood, locality,* and *community* are used interchangeably and capture some of the slippage between topography and moral order. DuBow and McEwen, for example, define the neighborhoods served by the program as "geographical areas whose residents had some sense of shared identity" (1990:5). More specifically, neighborhood is used to imply a spatially bounded area of contiguous streets in which residents may experience problems of noise, notice the maintenance of homes, the presence of abandoned vehicles, hear neighbors' quarrels, and be offended by garbage or graffiti (Shonholtz 1987:49). At the same time, *neighborhood* is used by studies of the Community Boards to refer to ethnically defined enclaves, as in the description of San Francisco as "a city of neighborhoods" (Rothschild 1986:60). The concept may refer as well to geographical areas with populations of widely differing socioeconomic status (Rothschild 1986:61). Finally, in descriptions of field offices established by the Community Boards program, neighborhoods are grouped into six "neighborhood areas." These areas are quite extensive (populations range from 8,000 to 105,000) and may contain populations that differ in terms of class, ethnicity, age, and so on (Rothschild 1986:61–67). For example, in one such "neighborhood area," with a population of over 50,000, "The majority Hispanic population included people from over twenty-six countries, living alongside whites, blacks, Filipinos, Samoans and Native Americans" (DuBow and McEwen 1990:8).

It is in this multireferential framework that the Community Boards are described as "neighborhood-based" (Rothschild 1986:69). The six field offices (one per neighborhood area) are described as "centrally located within the cluster of neighborhoods serviced by each office" (Rothschild 1986:70). Volunteers associated with each office are required to be residents of the neighborhoods serviced by the program, and on this basis present themselves to parties as "local people" (Rothschild 1986:149), as "community member[s] concerned about the neighborhood" (Rothschild 1986:142), or as "members of the same neighborhood" (Rothschild 1986:180 n. 7). "Mediators routinely describe themselves to the disputants as 'people like yourselves'—that is, residents of the neighborhood and 'people who care about the neighborhood and believe that neighbors can work together to solve local problems'" (Rothschild 1986:78–79). As Rothschild notes, however, volunteers may, at best, "live . . . in the same quadrant of the city, in an area . . . somewhat comparable sociodemographically" and they may have to travel on the freeway to reach the residence of disputants (1986:180).

The suggestion that comparable sociodemography is as important to community as geographical proximity suggests a more complex understanding of this concept. In this view, likeness (i.e., shared social space, based on historical experience in sociopolitical contexts where specific kinds of difference shape social life) rather than shared physical space becomes significant. The significance of likeness in this sense is supported by literature that notes the commitment of program staff and leaders to a diverse pool of volunteers, and to selecting mediators who "match" parties as much as possible (DuBow and McEwen 1990:30, 40–43).

At the same time that the volunteer recruitment practice of the program assumes that community is based on likeness constructed in demographic terms, the emphasis in the mediation process itself is on techniques for *constructing* like-mindedness between individuals who are assumed to be alienated, living irretrievably separate lives. The program is described as "neighborhood-based" (i.e., located in a particular residential area), but it is civic work, in the form of program activities, that will create (or renew) neighborhood as community (i.e., shared values and feelings) in the lives of participants. The program "focuses on *developing neighborhoods* and the capacity of their residents to be engaged with each other in resolving conflicts before they reach the formal justice system" (DuBow and McEwen in this volume; emphasis added).

Civic Work: The Practice of Community

Community conflict resolution provides people a unique opportunity to perform civic work, reduce community and individual alienation, and prevent violent and potentially violent situations from escalating. . . . It is this very work that serves to build new alliances and relationships at the community level. . . . In disorder and community decline studies, the issue of civic participation and bonding is identified as an important factor in what determines whether a community can maintain forms of informal social control or not. (Shonholtz 1987:51–52)

The vision of community built through civic work proposed by Raymond Shonholtz, the founder of the San Francisco Community Boards in the 1970s, echoes the discourse of community found in the work of early twentieth-century communitarian social thinkers such as Charles Horton Cooley, Jane Addams, and John Dewey. Addams founded a settlement house for neighborhood poor in 1889 in Chicago, and this became the focus of community-based social-reform activities (Addams [1910] 1961). Dewey also advocated the importance of local communities as a source of vitality in modern society. "Face-to-face intercourse" would create "likeminded" individuals, and in this way local communal life could play a significant role in resolving problems of identity in the modern world (Dewey 1927:216, 1966:4). Similarly, the boards were envisioned as a basis for creating community through engaging citizens in "civic work." Shonholtz argues that "[c]ivic work is the means through which citizens come to know and understand one another and develop social networks" (Shonholtz 1987:47).

This understanding of civic work as creating social bonds through "commonality of work interests" (1987:52) is grounded in a tradition of republican humanism in which virtue was located in devotion to the public good through exercise of their "active ruling quality" by equal citizens (Pocock 1985:41: Bellah 1985:38). The tradition has provided the impetus for a number of important reform movements in the late nineteenth and early twentieth centuries (see Harrington in this volume), all of which share assumptions about the location of disorder *in* social relations, and the dependence of social order (and thus of moral consensus) on the voluntary acts of individuals who can choose to engage in cooperative work. By this account, the causes of disorder are sought in the family or in the community, and the remedy for disorder in the "engineering of a proper family and community life" (Wolf 1982:9). As Wolf (1982) and Bender (1978) argue, this is part of a more general paradigm in which the atrophy of an imagined (past) community characterized by densely knit social relations and value consensus is used as a basis for explaining modern disorder and for prescribing its cure. Internal cohesion—and specifically social cohesion within a particular locale—is defined as a social good; the absence of this is defined as community breakdown.

For Shonholtz, community conflict resolution "is not a program. It is a long-term social investment in the health and stability of individuals and communities" (quoted in DuBow and McEwen 1990:2). The long-term social investment, more important than "the actual delivery of conflict resolution services," involves recruitment, organization, and training of volunteers to "take on local issues and problems" (DuBow and McEwen 1990:4).

The assumption that the community of volunteers and the neighborhood community are (or will become) overlapping communities justifies the heavy investment of the program's resources in volunteer training:

[F]or Community Boards the effects of recruiting and training volunteers have always been imbued with larger significance. Because of its neighborhood orientation the people who were recruited and trained were not merely volunteers; they were also "neighbors" and members of a community. In this light training volunteers who came from the same neighborhood was not just the training of individuals, but the upgrading of a "neighbor-hood's" capacity to deal with conflicts in a new way.[3]

In keeping with the premise that volunteers were neighbors, train-ing became synonomous with civic work and has come to include a broad array of activities beyond the mediation of conflicts: large numbers of meetings in which planning and policy decisions are made (DuBow 1987:chap. 4, 21, 34); other social activities that increase the interaction of volunteers with one another (DuBow 1987:chap. 4, 24, 33); and substantial amounts of time devoted to conciliation training, aimed in part at increasing skills, but viewed equally as *build[ing] commitment to Community Boards as an organization, to its goals, and to its way of doing things* (DuBow 1987:chap. 4, 41, emphasis added). As this implies, it is the San Francisco Com-munity Boards program itself that becomes the relevant community in these practices, a shift that is unproblematic only if no distinction is made between parties and volunteers, between neighbors and serv-ice providers, between community as shared historical experience and community as building communication between people who are by definition separate in that they *lack* shared history.

An important dimension of the civic work of volunteer "commu-nity members," (and an aspect of mediator training that distinguishes the San Francisco Community Boards from other neighborhood justice programs) is the development of separate tracks involving training for community "outreach," for "case development," and for concili-ation (DuBow and McEwen 1990:45). A Trainer's Institute has been developed to sharpen these skills for volunteers, but the ongoing work of "community building" (typically involving the pairing of less with more experienced volunteers in various roles) is at least as important as more formal training processes and is described as "an integral and substantial part of the continuing Community Boards experience" (DuBow and McEwen 1990:46).

Outreach—"educat[ing] the neighborhood about the program and how to use it"—and case development—a personal visit by a volunteer to the complaining party and the other (second) party—

---

3. DuBow (1987:chap. 1, 20); and see Shonholtz 1987:45–47.

are emphasized by the program as crucial to its central goal, that of "broadening the scope of civic work" (DuBow 1987:chap. 4, 18; DuBow and McEwen 1990: 24–25). In particular, "in-person, in-the-field case development" (DuBow 1987:chap. 4, 18), a labor-intensive process involving several hours of home visits with the parties, is key in persuading parties to "voluntarily" participate as well as providing a basis for familiarizing the volunteer with the context in which a conflict developed. At the same time, volunteers are explicitly *discouraged* from attempting to resolve a conflict at this stage (DuBow and McEwen 1990:28). Rather, case development is seen as a vehicle for engaging parties in the hearing process to follow, and as a means to keep the conflict "fresh" so that people are "still emotionally committed" by the time of the hearing (Rothschild 1986:144). Strategies for achieving these goals include surprise visits to parties as a way of catching them off guard, and explicit efforts to discourage parties from contacting one another or from attempting to resolve the matter on their own (Rothschild 1986:149, 154–56, 180 n. 10).

As this suggests, then, civic work "in the neighborhood" is preliminary to the "real" work of conciliation and community building during the hearing process, in a setting distanced from that in which the conflict developed. Privileging of the hearing itself over case development is apparent from the regular attention given to successful panel hearings in the program newsletter, by contrast to the passing recognition given to successful case development. Just as the emphasis on case development as a way of keeping conflicts fresh and parties emotionally committed separates volunteer community members from the parties who are persuaded to "voluntarily participate," the privileging of the hearing process over case development separates the experience of the volunteer community from that of local people "engag[ing their] fellow citizens in the informal discussion and settlement of differences" (Shonholtz 1987:46). These distinctions, evident in the practice of SFCB but blurred in the discourse of community and neighborhood found in the literature of and about the program, produce an empowered translocal community of volunteers while undermining the potential for collective action among parties.

The Four-Phase Process: Building a Community of Love

The most valued work of Community Boards, the hearing, is a social activity in that it is not performed by a lone mediator, as in many other programs, or even a pair of mediators. Rather there are three to five panelists accompanied by a case developer, a trainee, and often a staff member. The focus of the hearing process is, in many respects, on the Comunity Boards group. The disputants are given little attention immediately before the hearing, to the point sometimes of making them wait outdoors or in situations with uncomfortably close proximity to the other party. After the hearing, too, the emphasis is on letting the volunteers debrief—release tensions and get feedback. The disputants are sent off alone. (DuBow 1987:chap. 4, 31–32)

The hearing, as "the focus of most Community Boards training and the activity most celebrated by the Program in its internal and external publicity" (DuBow and McEwen 1990:30), is distinctive in its use of multiple mediators, in its prohibition of private caucuses between panelists and parties, and in its emphasis on the use of proper techniques for developing "new modes of communication" through the hearing process (DuBow 1987:chap. 4, 22; DuBow and McEwen 1990:30–31). Proper technique, and specifically what is known in the program as the four-phase process, is viewed as key to the success of the hearing and particularly to achieving a form of intersubjective relationship in which "pretenses are abandoned and deeper issues and feelings are expressed" (DuBow 1987:chap. 4, 28).

The four-phase process was so central to training and to practice that many panelists kept a summary of the phases in front of them during a hearing. . . . By having each party talk in turn about their perceptions and feelings, the first phase was supposed "to help the parties define the problem and express how they feel about it." . . . The goal of the second phase was to help the parties understand "how the other experiences the problem." Panelists were directed in this phase to "select one issue or concern and encourage the people to talk about it." . . . *In this phase the parties were supposed to be interacting with each other, and expressing their feelings about one another and the problem at hand. That fact was symbolized by the request that they turn their chairs toward one another.* In phase three, the panelists were directed to help "the parties understand that to solve the problem, each must be willing to acknowledge what new understanding they have about the dispute." . . . The panelists tried in phase four to help the parties reach agreement by asking each in turn what they thought would be a fair solution, and by using questioning and listening techniques to help the parties find a specific agreement. (DuBow and McEwen 1990:32–33, emphasis added)

Central to the four-phase process, indeed its key strategy for "getting the feelings out," is the *en face* positioning of parties in the second phase (DuBow 1987:chap. 4, 38; Rothschild 1986:80–83, 125 n. 17, 195). According to program philosophy, this is an effective strategy for "[g]etting disputants to see their own responsibility in the conflict and to become actively involved in finding a resolution" (DuBow 1987:chap. 4, 32).

The emphasis on voluntarism—on owning the conflict, and thus on more authentic involvement in resolving it (DuBow 1987:chap. 2, 5)—is a key to the individual empowerment that the program promises. Empowerment is contingent on self-transformation through communication with others (i.e., by abandoning pretenses and expressing deeper issues and feelings), while maintaining the capacity for free choice and voluntary engagement. In this way "free" individuals are able to build "community" while at the same time maintaining autonomy.

This emphasis on voluntary engagement as a process of self-transcendence in order to build relationships with others echoes themes found in mainstream American culture, in which community is dependent on the continued autonomy of the individuals who create it, and where community must be "a matter of choice on the part of the 'I'" (Varenne 1977:34). In this account, communities and individuals are restatements of each other (Varenne 1977:159), existing in an uneasy tension in which the one does not destroy the other. The problematic here, as Varenne notes, is the tenuousness of community, a notion that (for North Americans) has no substance in itself and must continually be renewed (1977:204–6). To do this (while maintaining authenticity through the autonomy of the "I") it is necessary "to enter into a direct relation with one other person and exchange equally, communicate" (1977:164). This form of communication produces "one-mindedness," or love, "a total giving away of oneself to somebody else who must answer in kind and equally, and thereby 'save' himself and the originator of the exchange" (Varenne

1977:204). Similarly, the political goals of the San Francisco Community Boards involve personal and social change through "meaningful" and "consequential" encounters where emotions are bared and pretenses abandoned" (DuBow 1987:chap. 4, 27–28). Social transformation is accomplished by "getting people to express their differences and to improve their communications" (DuBow 1987:chap. 4, 32; Rothschild 1986:153, 300–302).

Analyses of the work of the San Francisco Community Boards by DuBow, Rothschild, and others point to a number of problems in these assumptions, both in terms of the capacity of the four-phase process to build community among parties, and in the assumed link between this approach to conflict management and the transformation of neighborhood order (Rothschild 1986:138–226, DuBow and McEwen 1990: 53–55). At the same time, these studies point to the key role of this process (together with other program activities) in building community among the generally white (as is the city-wide population), typically female, middle-class volunteer mediators the program has been so successful in recruiting. I discuss these issues in turn in the final two sections of the paper.

Resistance to Community

DuBow and McEwen's study of the San Francisco program (in this volume) notes that 91 percent of the cases that went to mediation were successfully resolved, and that disputants in these cases reported satisfaction with their experience (1990:38–39). They also note, however, that surveys of the experience of residents in the neighborhoods served by the program evidence no "increase or decrease in sense of attachment to the neighborhood, confidence in neighborhood improvement, involvement in civic work with neighbors, or [in fear] of crime" (DuBow and McEwen 1990:54). While they note that the failure of the program to develop neighborhoods may follow from an ideology that directs publicity towards the alienated individual rather than to existing networks (DuBow and McEwen 1990:17), they raise questions about the program's celebration of a hearing process that assumes the goal of conflict resolution (and of community building) is to respond to alienation, rather than focusing on the potential for strengthening common interests among networks of people linked by common experiences of discrimination along lines of race, gender, or class. By contrast, Rothschild's analysis of the hearing process, and particularly of the management of one case in which the complaining parties resisted the efforts of panelists to have them "share feelings" with the responding party, points to the ways that the ideology of community in Community Boards works to inhibit goals of local neighborhood development. This case suggests, rather, that the communities produced in community mediation will be shaped not so much by individuals sharing feelings during a hearing but by interests and values (those of the volunteer mediators as well as those of the parties) defined in historical and relational contexts that extend well beyond the hearing both in time and space.

The case on which Rothschild focuses ("The Promised Land" dispute) involved a middle-class black family in a conflict with white renters across the street.[4] The neighborhood in question had once been predominantly white, had gradually been occupied by black homeowners, and was now perceived (by the black family) as subject to pressure from white families moving in. In this case, the white family was operating a small business from their home, and this became the focus of the black family's complaint. While racial, gentrification, and quality of life issues in this case were clearly articulated by the parties, mediators defined the conflict as a communication problem between families, discouraged either of them from involving others, and attempted to focus the mediation hearing on a discussion of feelings rather than on the conflict of values and behavior that seemed paramount to the parties themselves (Rothschild 1986:188–208, and see Rothschild this volume).

While the case was revealing of differences between parties and mediators relating to the substance of the complaint and to appropriate strategies for resolving it, it also underscored the contradictions in an ideology of authenticity (of noncoerced participation by citizens engaged in civic work, rather than by professionals engaged in career work) that is at the heart of SFCB practice. The tensions in the hearing of "The Promised Land" dispute emerged from mediation practices in which volunteers controlled the process through approved therapeutic techniques and other intervention strategies endorsed by the program, while establishing themselves as community members, local people with interests and concerns similar to those of the parties to

---

4. Portions of the following five paragraphs are taken from Yngvesson 1989: 1706–7. See also Rothschild's discussion of this case in the present volume.

conflict. Particularly important as a control strategy, and a focus of
Rothschild's research, was the narrowing of this conflict by volunteers
in such a way that collective issues were eclipsed in favor of the
interpersonal exchange of feelings (Rothschild 1986:141, 300–304).[5]
This involved an interrelated process of restricting the number of
participants and narrowing of issues (Rothschild 1986:164–68, 210–
11). The premise that community is about meaningful communication, rather than about interests and values, requires this form of
narrowing, since as Varenne observes, "love . . . cannot be for eve-
rybody, since there is no way one could get into direct contact with
more than a few people." Large groups more easily disintegrate "as
internal diversity becomes so great that even the mildest and most
insubstantial forms of superficial one-mindedness become impossible
to maintain" (1977:205).

The efforts to control the mediation process by volunteers contrast noticeably with the discourse of party control that is used during
hearings and in case development. Thus the hearing process was
described to complainants in this case as "a meeting where *local people*
try to get a general sense of the dispute and then encourage disputants
to trust each other enough to listen to each other's side of the dispute"
(Rothschild 1986:149, emphasis added). The volunteer who visited the
complainants during the case-development phase described the philosophy of the program by explaining that "when people take responsibility for finding a resolution themselves, it normally sticks; and
people are much more satisfied with their own resolution than one
drafted without their input" (Rothschild 1986:149). A key point here,
as suggested above, is the ambiguous meaning of "local people."
Mediators, who typically differ along a number of dimensions from
parties (Harrington and Merry 1988:724; Rothschild 1986:180 n. 7)
nevertheless emphasize their social similarity and like-mindedness to
parties. Rothschild notes further that while mediators may indicate
to parties that they have some training, "they often make explicit
that this is not . . . 'expert skill,' but rather that anyone, including the
disputants, could be a mediator were they to attend the Center's
training program" (Rothschild 1986:78–79).

These efforts to produce community through the construction of

5. See Mather and Yngvesson (1980–81) for a discussion of narrowing in dispute
transformation, and the relationship of this strategy to the reproduction of social
order.

likeness during the mediation process may come up against barriers to communication shaped by historical processes through which different kinds of individuals, located differentially in societies structured by relations of inequality (of race, gender, class, etc.), are produced. Both families in this case resisted the efforts of mediators to focus on communication and emotions. For example, one of the complainants, a middle-aged black man, responded to the volunteer's suggestion that a hearing should provide an opportunity for each side to learn about the feelings of the other by exclaiming: "I don't give a damn about his feelings. Wholly and solely I care that he be eliminated; not him, but his business" (Rothschild 1986:149). Describing his understanding of what "neighborhood" means, this complainant continued:

> We moved here in 1947, because we wanted a quiet neighborhood. We've raised five children here. The neighborhood has been really important to us, and we don't want to see it change. If Paul [the defendant] is allowed to operate a business, then the next thing you know, every house will have a business, and it won't be a residential neighborhood any more. (Rothschild 1986:190)

By contrast, the defendants in this case, a white couple in their thirties, were struggling to keep a family business going and had been evicted from their previous home a few months earlier. When asked by the mediators about neighborhood values, the younger man replied: "I don't know what is important in a neighborhood. I never really thought about it" (Rothschild 1986:192).

Mediators in this case repeatedly sought to impose their definition of neighborhood and community (as a process of open communication about feelings) on the parties. For the black complainants, however, feelings could only be understood in the context of shared history and shared struggle. The wife in the black family responded to the mediators' efforts to have the parties share their feelings by saying, "Paul [the defendant] could never understand my feelings— How could he? We had to fight to get here, we succeeded, we've been here since 1947 and we're not going to move now!" (Rothschild 1986:202).

By persisting in a definition of this conflict as a matter of failed communication, mediators undermined their capacity to work more effectively with the parties to this case. But their stance was revealing as well of assumptions about the nature of social order shared by mediators and San Francisco Community Boards staff, but rejected by at least some of the parties served by the program:[6] assumptions about society as "a purposeful, individualistic process" (Varenne 1977:157) that could be created by attuning individuals to one another so that they might achieve consensus about "common" problems, rather than shaped by less rational processes to which SFCB hearings, neighborhood struggles over gentrification, and other relations of power and inequality in a much broader field contribute.

Internality and Exclusion

While the community practice of San Francisco Community Boards is rejected by some parties and has not been successful in producing more socially cohesive neighborhoods in the areas where the program operates, DuBow and McEwen's work points to the importance of the program in the lives of its volunteer mediators. Here, unlike the "loosely organized, large and heterogeneous urban areas" where the program operates (DuBow and McEwen 1990:53), the program seems to have generated a translocal community of volunteers, linked by a common culture, maintained by shared practices, and produced (in part) through the private and public funding that has made the San Francisco Community Boards program possible. By contrast to the relatively small caseload, which remains small several years into the program's operation (case intake peaked at 387 in 1979, and has not grown since then [DuBow and McEwen 1990:16]), the policy of recruiting "widely and almost continuously" (DuBow and McEwen

---

6. See DuBow and McEwen (1990:34) for another example of party resistance to sharing feelings during a San Francisco Community Board hearing. Similar examples of party resistance to efforts by mediators and other conflict-management personnel to handle disputes in ways that obscure issues of value and of order are documented in other literature (Yngvesson 1988a, 1988b; Merry 1990), suggesting that Rothschild's example is not unique, and that mediator strategies may generate opposition as well as the more widely reported satisfaction reported in the literature on the neighborhood-justice movement. Indeed, it might be argued that reports of satisfaction and of the experience of mediation as "fair" (McEwen and Maiman 1981) are examples not so much of empowerment through involvement in a more participatory process, but of disempowerment through a procedure that produces an experience of control in a context of unequal power.

1990:40) to develop a pool of volunteers has been successful. At any one time there are typically 350 to 400 people available to act as mediators, and attrition rates are low (DuBow and McEwen 1990:47).

As this suggests, volunteers are enthusiastic about the program. For these predominantly female, predominantly white, relatively young, well-educated, aspiring professionals, the program provides an opportunity both for personal growth and for what is experienced as meaningful engagement in shaping neighborhood life (DuBow and McEwen 1990:52). Indeed, the two are inseparable: meaningful intervention in the emotionally charged encounters of others becomes a vehicle for personal growth, and volunteers report using the techniques of conflict management learned in the program to handle problems in their own lives, as well as teaching them to friends or coworkers (DuBow and McEwen 1990:51).

Central to the appeal of the program for volunteers is what DuBow and McEwen describe as their own desire for "attachment in the face of urban isolation" (1990:17):

> Many volunteers expressed a deep longing to be part of communities that were highly interactive and mutually supportive. The sense of community that they felt within Community Boards was the single most satisfying part of their volunteer role for veteran volunteers. They involved romantic images of neighborhoods where people knew each other and took care of one another.... They interpreted their actions on behalf of Community Boards as contributing to the restoration or creation of such conditions. (DuBow 1987:chap. 4, 16)

DuBow and McEwen note that for several volunteers, participation in the program "was viewed as the turning point in their lives" (1990:52). Many reported the use of skills learned in the program to handle their own problems, and more than half taught the skills to friends, family members, and coworkers. "Forty percent of the volunteers said that they had used the four phase process for conflict resolution in disputes outside of the Community Boards context" (DuBow and McEwen 1990:51).

The appeal of the discourse of community to alienated middle-class volunteers is complemented by the commitment of the program to activities that develop an internal community among them. These include governance and social activites (see above), but the training process itself, which transforms "interested people" into "community members" (DuBow and McEwen 1990:43), plays a key role in the construction of a volunteer community. In addition to the formal twenty-six hour training process, volunteers can participate in "institutes" and workshops that "provide understanding, skills and models necessary to train community members in the three essential roles of a neighborhood-based conflict resolution program" (DuBow and McEwen 1990:45). Training is not simply a matter of learning skills, however, but "an integral and substantial part of the continuing Community Boards experience" (1990:46). The hearing itself becomes an additional forum in which the experience of the volunteers is the primary focus. Indeed, the *exclusion* of the parties at certain key points "while the volunteers focussed attention on one another" (DuBow and McEwen 1990:49, and see in this volume) has been noted as a unique characteristic of San Francisco Community Boards hearings.

The privileging of this internal community of volunteers over the external community of parties is underscored in program terminology, which has "excise[d] the term 'volunteer' from the SFCB literature and replaced it with 'community member'" (DuBow and McEwen 1990:48). Thus, "One never hears or reads the word 'volunteer' in Community Boards" (DuBow 1987: chap. 4, 31). Volunteers are transformed into "community members" through the training process, and in this context (but *not* when addressing parties to a conflict)[7] "the reference to community is not to the larger neighborhood, but to those who work within the organization" (DuBow 1987: chap. 4, 31). It is striking that the discourse of community in SFCB *excludes* the participants to a conflict. Participants are officially referred to as "the parties," by contrast to volunteers, who are the official "community members."

The slippage between the meaning of community as *volunteers* engaged in the civic work of the boards and "community" as *local citizens* engaged in the early identification and prevention of conflict in their neighborhood is central to the philosophy of San Francisco Community Boards. Yet it masks key differences in structure between these two forms of community order and blurs an inherent tension

---

7. Rothschild (1986:144) notes that "the term has a specific meaning to volunteers, and a fairly ambiguous meaning to disputants."

between the production of an internal community of volunteers and the production of local neighborhood communities of citizens engaged in civic work. This may (in part) explain the strength of the translocal volunteer community and the failure of this to operate as a utopian model for civic work in local neighborhood arenas.

Conclusion: Voluntarism and Empowerment in Community Justice

The slippage from one community referent to another facilitates assumptions by members of the SFCB and by some researchers that this is a neighborhood movement, staffed and led by local people at their own initiative (i.e., intervention and participation are voluntary). At the same time, the voluntary involvement of mediators who constitute the internal community is somewhat different than the voluntary participation of the parties in the external community.

DuBow's and Rothschild's research suggests that for mediators, the experience of engagement and of control is compelling, and that the program has not had difficulty recruiting volunteers. By contrast, the small caseload of the program suggests that it is less compelling to potential parties. The program underscores its independence from the judicial system, so that a significant proportion of the caseload is self-referred (DuBow 1987:chap. 1, 5). But participation in the process is heavily monitored by volunteers, whose practices in securing the continued participation of parties may be quite controlling. The social, geographical, and power differentials between the community of volunteers and the community of parties, and more specifically, the investment of program resources in developing the former rather than the latter, suggests the central problem of an ideology of community empowerment that is dependent on the assumed identity of volunteers with "neighbors" or "local people," and on the potential for passing on transformations of the one (from volunteer to community member) to a transformation of the other (that is, of local people into a local community).

The notion that the boards are a neighborhood movement is also in some tension with program practices that embody key elements of a "feeling culture" (DuBow 1987:41), most familiar in the ideology and practice of the therapeutic professions. The production of an ideology of community justice in which community is ambiguously located *both* within a translocal helping culture *and* in the civic work of neighborhood citizens is suggestive of what Foucault (1982:214–16) has described as the simultaneous totalization and individualization that characterizes "pastoral power" in the modern state.[8] Through an ideology of personal growth that is accomplished in mediator training and specifically in learning the four-phase hearing process for managing conflict, individual mediators are transformed into community members; at the same time, the practice of mediation in Community Boards contributes to a form of disciplinary regulation and normalization in which individuals learn to construct themselves (and their relationships with others) through a specific form of truth that displaces structural considerations in the construction of shared experience and of community. These structural considerations, in which class, ethnicity, gender, and a shared history of struggle, rather than voluntarism, are seen as the basis for community, challenge the notion that social transformation is likely to be produced through shared feelings, empathy, and voluntary engagement in mediation as civic work.

The ethos of voluntarism that underpins the San Francisco Community Boards approach is a key feature linking the participation of individual mediators and disputants to a voluntary process that is suffused with the practices of a powerful professional group in our society, of which the San Francisco Community Boards is a local outgrowth. This, in turn, raises questions about the nature of the empowerment that the SFCB produces, and about the potential for social change in a movement where local power is contingent not on collective action by diverse communities that share common histories, but on effacing these histories to create communities where everyone is free to belong as long as they are properly trained.

The notion of community as freely chosen appears to be empowering, but in practice "this form of freedom cannot be escaped" (Varenne 1977:158), since it requires continual reaffirmation of likeness for its maintenance and is threatened by the expression of difference. By contrast, when community is understood as developing

---

8. In a similar way, Harrington and Merry (1988:731) argue that the ideology of "consensual justice" locates "consensus" ambiguously in the voluntary agreement of parties as well as in the neutral stance of mediators, contributing to the production of a professional culture of mediators that submerges the "community" in community justice, even as the notion that community justice is consensual is perpetuated.

over time through the positioning of subjects in similar relationships of dependence and inequality, empowerment must also be viewed relationally, rather than as a matter of choice and of learned techniques for sharing feelings in the absence of shared experience. Explanations of community and of empowerment must look beyond an ideology of voluntarism to examine the relational context of community mediation, and consider the implications for local autonomy of a practice that reproduces dependence and which requires the intervention of specialists to hold community together.[9]

REFERENCES

Addams, J. [1910]. 1961. *Twenty Years at Hull House*. New York: Signet.

Bellah, Robert N., Richard Madsen, William M. Sullivan, Ann Swidler, and Steven M. Tipton. 1985. *Habits of the Heart*. New York: Harper and Row.

Bender, T. 1978. *Community and Social Change in America*. Baltimore: Johns Hopkins University Press.

Dewey, J. 1927. *The Public and Its Problems*. New York: Holt.

———. 1966. *Democracy and Education: An Introduction to the Philosophy of Education*. New York: Free Press.

DuBow, F., 1987. "Conflicts and Community: A Study of the San Francisco Community Boards." Photocopy.

Felstiner, W. L. F., and L. Williams. 1979–80. *Community Mediation in Dorchester, Massachusetts*. Washington, D.C.: U.S. Government Printing Office.

Foucault, M. 1982. "The Subject and Power." in H. L. Dreyfus and P. Rabinow, *Michel Foucault: Beyond Structuralism and Hermeneutics*. Chicago: Chicago University Press.

Harrington, C., and S. E. Merry. 1988. "Ideological Production: The Making of Community Mediation." *Law and Society Review* 22:709–37.

McEwen, C., and R. Maiman. 1981. "Small Claims Mediation in Maine: An Empirical Assessment." *Maine Law Review* 33:237–68.

Mather, L., and B. Yngvesson. 1980–81. "Language, Audience, and the Transformation of Disputes. *Law and Society Review* 15:775–822.

Mensch, E. 1982. "The History of Mainstream Legal Thought." In *The Politics of Law*, ed. D. Kairys. New York: Pantheon.

Merry, S. E. 1990. *Getting Justice and Getting Even: Legal Consciousness among Working-Class Americans*. Chicago: University of Chicago Press.

---

9. The significance of structural and value concerns to parties in mediation cases is documented in Felstiner and Williams (1979–80) and in Merry and Silbey (1984).

Merry, S. E., and S. S. Silbey. 1984. "What Do Plaintiffs Want? Reexamining the Concept of Dispute." *Justice System Journal* 9:151–78.

Pocock, J. G. A. 1985. *Virtue, Commerce, and History.* Cambridge: Cambridge University Press.

Rothschild, J. H. 1986. "Mediation as Social Control: A Study of Neighborhood Justice." Ph.D. diss., University of California, Berkeley.

Shonholtz, R. 1984. "Neighborhood Justice Systems: Work, Structure, and Guiding Principles." *Mediation Quarterly* 5:3–30.

———. 1987. "The Citizen's Role in Justice: Building a Primary Justice and Prevention System at the Neighborhood Level." *Annals of the American Academy of Political and Social Science* 494:42–52.

Tocqueville, Alexis de. [1850] 1966. *Democracy in America.* 13th ed. Vol. 1. Trans. G. Lawrence. New York: Vintage.

Varenne, H. 1977. *Americans Together: Structured Diversity in a Midwestern Town.* New York: Teachers College Press.

Wolf, E. R. 1982. *Europe and the People without History.* Berkeley and Los Angeles: University of California Press.

Yngvesson, B. 1988a. "Making Law at the Doorway: The Clerk, the Court, and the Construction of Community in a New England Town." *Law and Society Review* 22:409–48.

———. 1988b. "Disputing Alternatives: Settlement as Science and as Politics." *Law and Social Inquiry* 13:113–32.

———. 1989. "Inventing Law in Local Settings: Rethinking Popular Legal Culture." *Yale Law Journal* 98:1689–1709.

Community Organizing through Conflict Resolution

Christine B. Harrington

In this chapter I examine the politics of community conflict resolution projects, such as the San Francisco Community Boards, by locating their activities in the larger historical context of community and neighborhood organizing. Where does the use of dispute resolution as a means for developing community fit into the array of American community organizing strategies? How is "community" understood in relation to "law" by organizers who adopt conflict resolution strategies and by organizers who do *not* turn to dispute resolution as a means of organizing communities? By asking these questions I argue that we can break away from the paradigm and language of dispute processing, which has been a dominant framework for analyzing mediation, to explore variations in community organizing strategies and locate community conflict resolution services within the larger context of community and neighborhood organizing.

In the mid-1970s, newly emerging mediation programs were categorized as "court-based" or "community-based" by practitioners who created them (McGillis and Mullen 1977) and by scholars who studied dispute processing reform (Hofrichter 1977). This classification distinguished programs that were dependent on courts for their clients from programs that only accepted noncourt referrals. It was used to indicate that under certain circumstances different kinds of coercion

I would like to thank Peter Fitzpatrick, Bill Lyons, Neal Milner, Ray Shonholtz, Douglas Thomson, and Barbara Yngvesson for their helpful comments on an earlier version of this paper. I am particularly grateful to Sally Merry for her editorial ideas. I am also grateful to Kelley Bevans for her research assistance. Portions of this paper appeared in *Social and Legal Studies: An International Journal* 1:177–99.

(Harrington 1980) and different levels of compliance (McEwen and Maiman 1984) correspond to institutional design. The terms *court-based* and *community-based* were also surrogates for describing case-load volume (high and low respectively).

By the mid-1980s the court-based/community-based distinction, while less prominent in the literature, continued to organize debates in the field. The central debate then focused on whether community mediation was becoming an "entrepreneurial industry" and moving away from its social-reform roots (Nader 1988). Many practitioners in community-based programs echoed this criticism and forcefully argued that the push towards professionalization (e.g., training of lawyers, certification of mediators) undercut goals of community organizing, such as extending participation in decision making to lay citizens, community groups, and other underrepresented people (National Association for Community Justice 1986). Court-based programs were the targets of this attack as they were leaders for the "multidoor" courthouse reform (Goldberg, Green, and Sander 1985; Roehl 1986), the late-twentieth-century model of courts as all-pur-pose department stores.[1] Criticism of this model appeared to over-shadow earlier concerns with insuring that alternative dispute processes were voluntarily agreed to by the parties (Harrington and Merry 1988). Practitioners added a new dimension or layer to the debate by articulating an antiprofessional stance toward mediation. Within their discourse a shift away from the earlier concern—whether referrals from courts and mediation programs coerce parties to par-ticipate in an ostensibility voluntary dispute-resolution process—was evident. New concerns over the consequences of professionalizing and institutionalizing alternative dispute resolution (ADR) appeared (Har-rington and Merry 1988).

However, when this discourse is examined more closely, it is evident that these new issues are in fact modern remnants of the old debate. As concerns about state coercion to participate in mediation

---

1. The department store conception of lower courts was first implemented with the creation of the municipal court movement in 1905 and the development of the branch courts (small claims, domestic relations, etc.) in the 1910s and 1920s. The multidoor concept is a more highly rationalized adaptation of this approach to organization and management. For a discussion of the application of business man-agement concepts to court reform and dispute-processing reform during the Pro-gressive period and in contemporary times, see Harrington (1985), chap. 2, "Judicial Management and Delegalization."

questioned the institutional autonomy of ADR in the late 1970s, so too do current debates about training, certification, and regulation of mediators. The new concern with licensing mediators and establishing more formal and mandatory links between courts and ADR processes is a contemporary manifestation of the continuing political tension embodied within and constitutive of this reform movement: To what extent is mediation autonomous from or dependent on state institutions? How "popular" is the "popular justice" produced by mediation programs that are organized by and dependent upon the state?

Today, as we move into the second decade of alternative dispute-resolution reform, the court-based versus community-based perspective is still alive and serves as the prevailing way of conceptualizing a new strata of dispute institutions in American society. Those who disagree with the critical research on state-sponsored informalism still embrace the court-based versus community-based perspective, charging that critical research "understates the important role played in the ADR movement by community organizers, volunteers, independent professional, and service sector entrepreneurs" (McEwen 1988:251). In the search for ways to interpret the politics of community-mediation programs like the San Francisco Community Boards (SFCB), the court-based–community-based perspective stands out as an option, indeed an invitation. Yet I think it is an invitation we should decline if not resist. Although we know far less about the "community-based" projects than we do about the "court-based" programs, the issue for me is not merely a matter of articulating the "other side." Indeed, empirical research on the formation of the alternative dispute-resolution movement demonstrates that there is a striking degree of interdependence between court- and community-based ideologies and institutions. Thus in some sense there is not an "other side" to this movement, rather conflict within it, as described above, and a consensus on political and legal symbols mobilized to attract resources and establish legitimacy (Harrington and Merry 1988).

The intellectual and political history of community organizing in the United States is the context I have chosen for interpreting community mediation. This context has been absent from studies of community mediation in part because community organizing is not a history of dispute-processing reform, and dispute-processing reform has been the context for describing and analyzing community mediation.[2] The literature on SFCB clearly speaks the language of dispute processing (e.g., case referrals, case files, disputant interviews); however, goals other than conflict resolution services are also mentioned: SFCB "seeks to *develop a neighborhood's capacity to respond to neighborhood disputes*" by getting disputants to "assume a greater degree of responsibility for the resolution of their conflict" (DuBow 1987: "Uniqueness," 1). Fred DuBow's study of SFCB also suggests that "Community Boards bears many of the characteristics of a social movement rather than a service delivery organization" (DuBow 1987: "Volunteer Development," 1). Just as other community organizers "have an entity against which to struggle," so too does SFCB according to DuBow; for SFCB "it is the justice system and its attendant professions" (1987: "Volunteer Development," 35; see DuBow and McEwen in this volume).[3] SFCB engages in grass-roots organizing and training of volunteers for the purpose of expanding citizen participation as an alternative to professional interventions in the arenas of conflict resolution. Its involvement in community organizing stands out in its appeals to foundations for funding, even though scholarly attention to SFCB often centers on its capacity to handle disputes. Thus one of the most distinctive characteristics of SFCB is its emphasis on developing a neighborhood's capacity to respond to conflict. Building this capacity is not conceived of as opposed to the provision of dispute services. Rather, SFCB claims to engage in community organizing *through* the delivery of conflict-resolution services.

In this chapter I develop an analysis of strategies for organizing communities and argue that the politics of mediation reforms, such as SFCB, might be better understood in relation to other community-organizing strategies than in relation to dispute-processing models or typologies.[4] As other chapters in this book have struggled to pin down

---

2. Auerbach's (1983) historical treatment of "non-legal dispute settlement" is an example of what I am calling the dispute-processing paradigm. His study tells us more about the existence of informal dispute processes throughout American history than about their relevant importance to organizing communities.

3. Interviews with SFCB volunteers revealed that most believed the "justice system does not work well and the actions of legal professional[s] are often not in the best interest of disputants" (DuBow 1987: "Volunteer Development," 35; see also Thomson and DuBow in this volume).

4. The court-based–community-based perspective comes out of a traditional dispute-resolution paradigm (Fuller 1971; Goldberg, Green, and Sander 1985), which builds topologies and classification systems for different *mediation forums* (e.g., nego-

the concept and content of "popular justice," I too must begin by clarifying the subject matter that constitutes the scope of this inquiry. The first part of this analysis is an argument for examining SFCB within the context of community-organizing movements in the American populist tradition. The second compares conflict resolution with three other approaches to community organizing (policing, governance, and direct action). My main concern is to articulate a comparative framework for analyzing how "community" is understood in relation to "law" across these different kinds of community-organizing strategies. The last section focuses on the politics of the late twentieth-century neopopulist empowerment ethos that I argue constitutes the SFCB strategy—community organizing through conflict resolution.

The Community Organizing Context

At a conceptual level, the boundaries of community organizing are in many respects as difficult to articulate as the boundaries of popular justice, largely because of the vague political appeals and complex power relationships that underlay such movements. Historically, community organizing has been concerned with a return of political and economic power to the local level. This concern recalls the citizen advocacy tradition of American, small p populism.[5] Citizen organizations appeal to the communitarian values of populist movements in their focus on the "people" being in some way exploited by the powerful. As Reissman argues, the "essence of populism is ordinary people getting involved with others to collectively control their lives" (1986:54).[6]

American populism flourished among agrarian movements in the

---

tiation, mediation, arbitration). If we are interested in politics, however, this paradigm is of little use because "forums" are abstracted from the conditions, experiences, and ideologies that constitute them.

    5. I use the phrase "small p populism" to distinguish the activities of community organizers from the third-party Populists of the late-nineteenth century (e.g., the Farmers Alliance created in the 1870s and the People's party, 1892–96). While both populisms have in common certain ideological positions, the community organizers I am talking about here were less concerned with forming an alternative political party (national, state, or local) than in preserving social order within a community or mobilizing to change it. For an analysis of populism see Wright (1974), Goodwyn (1976, 1978), and Pollack (1967, 1987).

    6. "Opinion polls indicate that some two-thirds of the American people feel powerless and ignored, buffeted by big institutions" (Reissman 1986:54).

South and West (e.g., in the 1930s), and its themes were activated in movements that had right-wing racist overtones as well as in progressive movements challenging the concentration of political power in the state and economic power in the hands of industrial capitalists (see Goodwyn 1976; and Pollack 1987). The most noted themes of American populism have been the "emphasis on traditional values like family, neighborhood, religion, and patriotism," along with a peculiar mixture of communitarianism and individualism that led to organizing movements that were self-initiated activities from the grass-roots level (Reissman 1986:54).

On the one hand, a bottom-up participatory approach has been a central theme of American populism, yet on the other hand there has been a strong emphasis placed on individualism. This is not to suggest that participatory-community politics and individualism are polar opposites; on the contrary, populist individualism shapes the meaning of community participation, as individualism in this tradition is shaped by the nature and scope of populist participation.[7] As Robert Bellah notes, the tension between communitarianism and individualism "poses both opportunities and dangers for those who would espouse a new populist politics" (1986:100). He also argues that a "degree of anti-institutionalism, in the sense of dissatisfaction with the way institutions are operating, may be effective in mobilizing people for political action," but "where anti-institutionalism becomes a pervasive orientation, as it does in the ideology of American individualism, it hinders the development of the counterinstitutions that are the only vehicles for substantive change" (1986:103). This tension is a well-noted characteristic of the American liberal tradition as well (Hartz 1955; Norton 1987; Dolbeare and Medcalf 1988).

Despite the difficulty scholars have had in articulating concepts, such as "community" and "individual," implicated in populist appeals, there is agreement that these concepts are themselves ambiguous, and thus that the political actions inspired by populist appeals are volatile (see Boyte and Reissman 1986). The political ambiguity and volatility of populist movements are in fact why we should *not* locate

---

7. C. B. Macpherson's discussion of the concept of liberal individualism is useful because he articulates tensions within the liberal tradition over the concept of "individualism" while also showing how these tensions shape the political meaning of "liberalism" (1962).

SFCB in the same tradition with state-sponsored dispute resolution reforms, such as the Neighborhood Justice Centers.[8] Elsewhere I have argued that the Neighborhood Justice Centers developed in the late-1970s are part of the Progressive Era tradition of institutional reform, noting the close ties between reforms focused on informal procedures and judicial management strategies during the twentieth century (Harrington 1982). In contrast, as I will elaborate later, the community-organizing activities of SFCB are an integral part of recent citizen movement attempts to rediscover the American populist tradition and reflect the political instability of those movements.[9]

This is not to suggest, however, that community-organizing movements are autonomous projects, independent from state-organized reforms. Community-organizing efforts are linked to larger social movements, and thus the "interactions between official power holders and people claiming to represent a constituency that is not formally represented" are a defining characteristic (Tilly 1984). The repertoires of community organizing convey a "group image" that is important in terms of legitimating a social movement and in the interaction between the state and representatives of community groups.

Often, however, the precise nature of this interaction is where much of the debate begins and ends. For example, in the critical literature on community justice, attention has centered on whether informal justice can have a transformative effect on the wider structure of the state-sponsored legal system (see Santos 1979; Fitzpatrick 1983, 1988; Henry 1983). These works reject both the view that community justice is a wholly independent alternative to the legal system and

8. Peter Fitzpatrick raised an important point in an earlier draft about why we tend to see popular-justice movements as being so diverse, marginal, waning and waxing. He noted that when we look for a sustained tradition to associate popular-justice movements with, we find that they are marginal simply because other sites of power in society marginalize them. These sites (e.g., state power) are in the historical position to create that definition of the tradition. I agree with Fitzpatrick on this point. Indeed, the dispute-resolution literature, written from a court-based–community-based perspective, is a site of power able to define the dispute-resolution tradition such that Community Boards is marginal.

9. Whether any of these movements come out of or are representative of an "authentic community" raises issues that are not addressed in this chapter (but see Yngvesson in this volume). Rather, here my interest is in the strategies of those movements that claim to be engaged in community organizing and in particular the connection between community-organizing movements and SFCB.

the view that community justice functions solely in the interest of the dominant legal and social structures. Instead they view the relationship between the official legal system and community-justice alternatives as an ambiguous one, which allows the alternatives to have a transformative effect on the wider structure of the state-sponsored legal system (Henry 1985, 1987; also see Harrington and Merry 1988). This relationship can be simultaneously supportive and oppositional (Cain 1985; Fitzpatrick 1988).[10]

In the literature on community and neighborhood organizing, particularly from the early 1960s to the mid-1970s, these same debates are played out as well (e.g., organizational co-optation by the state versus bottom-up social transformation). Different sets of issues, however, are raised by community organizers.[11] Community organizers tend to focus on how to mobilize political action through the enhancement of neighborhood or community *identity*. Unlike the dispute-processing analyses of community-justice alternatives, which center on the relationship between alternative and conventional forums of dispute processing, community organizers have been occupied with the problem of stimulating and rebuilding a sense of community and neighborhood. The most prominent American community organizer in the postwar period, Saul Alinsky, proposed commmunity organization (People's Organization) as an *agent* to activate community identity. Community organizations, he argued, could fill the "structural void created by the bureaucratic pressures to centralize authority and increase the scale of institutions" (Reitzes and Reitzes 1987:19).

Community organizers, like Alinsky, recognized what political scientists and sociologists discovered in their research on informal

---

10. In related discussions, several scholars have argued that contrasts between informal and formal justice fail to grasp the interdependent character of legal ideology (Abel 1981; Nader 1988; Santos 1979; Harrington 1985; Henry 1987). Both lines of debate (relationship between community alternatives and state institutions; relationship between informal and formal justice) are more useful for their insights on interdependency, or the relational character of legal power, than for predicting or determining which form of justice is more likely to prevail over the other.

11. In the community-organizing literature the debates are more often among activists who are theorists for community organizations and social movements than among social scientists, as in the case of community-justice alternatives. Examples of community organizers who worked as activists and theorists are Saul Alinsky (Industrial Area Foundation), Frances Fox Piven and Richard A. Cloward (National Welfare Rights Organization), and Gary Delgado (Association of Community Organizations for Reform Now).

organizing in neighborhoods: that identity is also a key agent for mobilizing political action. Studies of unofficial forums of neighborhood organizing reveal that a sense of community need not depend on the existence of a political consensus or personal solidarity among neighbors (Crenson 1983:143). In other words, there is little to no connection between neighborhood identity and shared values or "neighborly intimacy" (1983:144). While geographical areas may be important markers, signifying some fixed boundaries of a neighborhood, identity with neighborhoods need not conform to geographic jurisdictions either. Instead, numerous studies of neighborhoods suggest that awareness of and discussion of neighborhood problems are key in constituting a sense of neighborhood identity. Crenson's survey of twenty-one neighborhoods in Baltimore in the late 1970s, for example, found strong relationships between neighborhood discourse (informal talk about neighborhood problems) and heightened neighborhood identity.[12]

Whether talk about local problems leads to a stronger community identity or whether people talk more about community problems because they identify with a community is difficult to untangle. In general, the problem community organizers face is how to strengthen the spontaneous sense of community identity that is formed in everyday life and sustain it over the course of direct political actions (Boyte 1980:44). Law may or may not play a strategic or central role in this effort. Yet in most community organizing there is some attention to the role of state power, legal or political. For organizers who see conflict resolution as an avenue for strengthening community identity, the problem is how to build community identity in conflict resolution, given what we already know about the interdependent relationship between alternative and official legal orders. Other forms of community organizing have different perspectives on the place of law in preserving or transforming community identity. This brings us to the issue of what kinds of strategies community organizers use to organize neighborhoods and communities, and how community is understood in relation to law across different kinds of community organizing.

---

12. Crenson's study examines the "flow of spontaneous political talk among neighbors" (1983:143). He asked residents if they "had spoken with neighbors during the past year or so 'about any neighborhood problems or needs'" or participated in community discussion about community matters that "took place without the sponsorship of formal organizations or official political leaders" (1983:144).

Orientations toward Community Organizing

As noted above, there are different political traditions associated with populist movements and their appeal to local control and the values of communitarianism and individualism (e.g., those with a progressive, participatory, democratic potential and those that have a reactionary, narrow, parochial, racist, and sexist agenda). This political diversity might suggest that the category itself is so vague as to be meaningless. Rhetorical appeals to popular justice and claims of popular support are well-known ways in which movements seek to legitimize themselves in a liberal democracy. Separating those who really have popular support from those who do not is outside the scope of this chapter, however. Instead I will suggest that we can identify orientations within populist community-organizing movements that are evident in both progressive and reactionary movements.

Populist community movements are constituted by a mixture of historical, political, legal, social, and economic constraints and opportunities that at times belie efforts to categorize. The particular histories of these movements cannot be ignored, nor is it obvious from reading case-study narratives that people doing community organizing conceptualize their work in terms of well-established traditions or strategies. Yet after reading volumes of such narratives, one learns that in some cases there are common orientations across organizations and time. I will discuss four general orientations I have identified from the literature on American community organizing: policing, governance, direct action, and conflict resolution.

Policing

Policing is predominantly a strategy for maintaining and preserving values that are under attack from the outside. In fact the creation of an "inside" and an "outside" is typical of how community boundaries and identities are forged. This is particularly evident among community organizing that uses policing as its key strategy. These efforts are characterized by a defensive orientation toward an outside, and they also presuppose the existence of a community under attack. Surveillance and policing are the primary methods for maintaining community identity. Within this form of community organizing, however, the relationship between official police and community policing activities varies greatly.[13] In the variations as well as the mode of organizing itself (policing), "community" and "law" are constructed.

Patrols are the main kind of community organization that have historically had a policing strategy. Unlike vigilantism, the subject of signficant historical work,[14] community and neighborhood patrols are not well documented and often omitted from discussions of protectionist organizations because they are not seen as vigilante groups. Self-protection activities of vigilante organizations are usually carried out for the purpose of preserving a community from the outside,

---

13. Vigilantism is both an extreme version of populism and an example of self-protection movements that often employ violence. After considerable debates with colleagues, I decided not to include vigilantism in this analysis of community organizing through policing because it expands the scope of "community organizing" to incorporate activity that is loosely connected with efforts to forge "community identity" and more concerned with establishing effective law and order. For example, historians define the vigilante tradition in the United States as "organized, extralegal movements, the members of which take the law into their own hands" and date these movements back to 1767 with the South Carolina Back Country Regulators (Brown 1979:153). An heir of the Regulators that served as a model vigilante organization during the mid-to-late nineteenth century was the San Francisco Vigilance Committee (most active 1856–60). It has been described as organizing citizens to respond to the lack of effective law and order in frontier regions (Coblenz 1957). Many of its members were leading businessmen from the upper class of San Francisco who maintained standing in the community through other civic organizations and actions (Williams 1921; Kennedy 1987). It had a written constitution developed by the organizers, and the committee received a high degree of public support in its initial years. Williams argues that their actions were often responses to immediate situations; and therefore like many other vigilantes, the committee did not effect lasting reforms in local politics or courts. In fact this form of self-help law emerged more often in parts of the country where weak official systems existed (Friedman 1975).

14. Brown distinguishes the "old" (self-protectionist) from the "new" (violent) vigilantism, suggesting that the defensive character of their organizing turned into a paramilitary offensive. This distinction may not be useful, however, because it combines the *tactic* of an organization with its *purpose*. In his own description of the early vigilante movements he points out that 511 people were killed by vigilantes between 1860 and 1909 (1979:162). Others have documented the lynching and holding of prisoners by the San Francisco Vigilance Committee (Nolan 1987). The Ku Klux Klan, probably the most studied vigilante organization, exemplifies the nativism and racist extreme of populism that used violence to protect its values. Scholars distinguish the Klan of the 1920s from the resurgence in Klan activity in the 1980s, arguing that during the former period the Klan was a vigilante organization, whereas today it is a paramilitary organization (Gerlach 1982). I would argue that the law-enforcement tactics (policing, lynching) may be means of achieving a common purpose—defending "community," and thus the level of violence is not a useful way of distinguishing vigilante organizations from contemporary paramilitary styles.

and the internal order of that community is not the primary focus of their attention.[15] Neighborhood and community patrols have a similar purpose, yet instead of systematically attacking the lower class, as did or do most vigilante organizations (Brown 1975), patrols tend to focus on protecting the order of a community or neighborhood by protecting its people and property from outside forces.

The youth, neighborhood, and ethnic and racial patrols developed in the 1960s—some remaining active today—all function to maintain order within their communities.[16] They share the defensive posture associated with vigilantes but take a distinctively different position on whom to watch. The neighborhood-watch groups of the 1960s work closely with local police and reinforce the values of law and order (Rosenbaum 1986). Youth patrols developed in the late 1960s work in their own neighborhoods "as a buffer between their community and the civil authorities" (Knopf 1969).[17] Many of these patrols dissolved when the crisis atmosphere began to wane, and this then led to a reduced willingness on the part of municipalities and citizens to fund the groups. In addition, several youth patrols had confrontational relationships with the police over racial issues (many of the people in the patrols were black).

These citizen-staffed organizations formed the basis for a neighborhood strategy for control of crime later developed and funded by

---

15. There are three main components to the ideology of vigilantes: self-preservation as their "first law of nature"; the "right to revolution" to protect basic rights; and popular sovereignty (Brown 1975). Vigilantes organized to defend private property and establish order. Despite their view that officials of the established order were ineffective law enforcers, they did not oppose them but rather worked to strengthen their forces. These organized vigilantes and much of the vigilantism in the twentieth century (rural and urban) were conservative, seeking to maintain or reestablish the status quo. Conservative politics are also evident in today's urban vigilante organization, such as the Tampa Citizen's Committees, which organized in Florida largely to end labor strikes by cigar rollers. The strikes were not only aimed at improving working conditions but preserving the idea of craftsmanship in cigar rolling. The Tampa Citizen's Committee was supported by many in Tampa's "free Cuba" community and directed its efforts against workers, labor organizers, immigrants, blacks, socialists, and communists (Ingalls 1988).

16. See Wilson's (1968) distinction between law enforcement and order maintenance and Harrington (1985) for an example of the application of this distinction to state-sponsored dispute-processing reforms in the twentieth century.

17. Youth patrols were formed throughout the U.S. in towns and cities as diverse as Tampa; New Rochelle, New York; Grand Rapids; Providence; Boston; Newark; Pittsburgh; Tork, Pennsylvania; Cincinnati; Toledo; Kansas City, Missouri; Nashville; Los Angeles; and Louisville. See Knopf (1969).

the Law Enforcement Assistance Administration (LEAA) in the early 1970s. Several city police departments received LEAA funding to set up Crime Prevention Bureaus (CPB) run by volunteer citizens. CPBs identified "several high crime target areas for door-to-door canvassing of residents. This effort was followed by neighborhood meetings, usually sponsored by local residents, in which the program was explained, engraving equipment distributed, and decals signifying participation were given to those who attended" (Rosenbaum 1986: 69–70). Protection of property, information about "suspicious behavior," and training on how to "watch out for the safety of each other" were their primary concerns (1986:70). These programs even brought community groups in closer contact with the community patrol experiences in several "reform" police departments (Pate 1986; Trojanowicz 1986).

In addition to patrols that have been closely linked to if not formed by the police, there are patrols that have been more autonomous. DeSena's study of citizen neighborhood watch patrols in Greenpoint, Brooklyn concludes that the patrols were part of a larger community defensive movement organized by white ethnics against incoming Hispanics (1985). These patrols engaged in surveillance through informal neighborhood-watch activity and formal block patrols, called the Civilian Observation Patrol (COP). They also urged that potential owners/tenants be screened to keep out Hispanics.

The Guardian Angels in New York City are yet another example of community organizing through the establishment of citizen patrols. Some scholars argue that the Angels are firmly in the American vigilante tradition, noting the growth of Guardian Angel undercover operations (dressing like winos almost to invite criminal action) and conflict with the police over the lawfulness of their tactics (threatened violence, chasing people believed to be drug dealers out of neighborhoods). Their training focuses on physical development, self-defense skills, CPR, first aid, making citizen's arrests, and familiarity with the municipality's penal code. One public opinion survey found largely positive perceptions of the Angels, suggesting that what the police call unlawful is not objectionable to the public (Kennedy 1987).

Patrols do not always function to assist law enforcement officials; in some instances they are formed in order to protect their community *from* the police. Examples of such organizations include the Deacons for Defense and Justice, a black organization protecting the black community against white harassment and violence, formed in 1965 in Louisiana. This was an armed patrol that protected blacks and civil rights workers from the police, Klansmen, and rednecks. The Deacons at its height claimed seven thousand members in Louisiana, with sixty loosely federated chapters in five states (Mississippi, Alabama, Florida, and both Carolinas) (Kennedy 1987). The Black Panthers' "Shotgun Patrols," formed in 1969, is another example of a citizens' patrol not concerned with maintaining or restoring police authority but seeking to defend the black community from police brutality (Knopf 1969).[18]

Similarly, the American Indian Movement (AIM) created a citizens' patrol, known as the Indian Patrol, in 1968 in Minneapolis (Cohen 1973). Initially, it was a foot patrol that combed neighborhoods on Friday and Saturday nights, watching out for the police and helping intoxicated Indians get home safely. AIM believed that the number of police cars in the area was not to be understood as protection for Indians; they argued that most police arrests of "drunken Indians" were acts of discrimination. Later the patrol, which had non-Indians participating in it, used cars to survey police activity and kept logs of their actions. They objected to the high concentration of squad cars in their area and filed complaints against police brutality and discrimination with the chief of police. Following these complaints, the police, who had previously given tacit support to the patrol, backed away from the antipolice sentiments of the patrollers. Cohen convincingly argues that the Indian Patrol did not function as a law-enforcement agency and therefore should not be viewed as part of the vigilante tradition.

Community organizing through policing strategies places law at the center of forming community identity. In the case of youth and neighborhood patrols, the official legal order is either too weak to protect a community from "outsiders" or lacks the necessary connections to the local community to effectively do the job. The LEAA-sponsored citizen patrols represent a critical shift from patrols formed at the grass roots (which had links to police, but were not initiated by the state) to community organizing by local police. These organizing efforts, to one degree or another, ally their conception of community order with the official system. In opposition to the official

---

18. See Oberschall (1973) for an analysis of organizations with a Maoist orientation (e.g., CORE, SCLC, SNCC, and the Panthers). Also see Foucault (1980) on "popular justice" and Maoist politics.

order are ethnic and racial patrols that also employ defensive policing strategies. These patrols mobilize a defensive community identity without support from official law, indeed often directly against it.

Governance

Community organizing that demands community control and participation in *governance* has historically worked towards expanding access to services, including legal service, and hence is orientated more toward constructing or building community than using law (official or unofficial) to protect community from "the outside." The roots of twentieth-century community governance are traced to the early settlement houses and community centers that were formed by private charities in the late 1880s. Neighborhoods were the "unit of organizing," which meant largely the development of relief and welfare resources for poor and working-class neighborhoods. Settlement houses began using public schools as community centers after the turn of the century, and it is reported that by 1913, 629 schools in 152 U.S. cities were serving as community centers (Hallman 1973). At the same time the focus shifted from a relief service for neighborhoods to a program for community revitalization. Throughout the early decades of the twentieth century precinct committees began to serve as a forum for bringing together different communities and centralizing governance. Notwithstanding attacks on the machine politics that provided resources and other forms of political support for such centralization, precinct committees began to mobilize communities to engage in broader city-planning fights. Hallman argues that the New Deal accelerated the centralization process with funds for public works projects and later federal funding for urban redevelopment after the war (Hallman 1973:11).

The Great Society program of the Economic Opportunity Act of 1964, Community Action Program (CAP) and its slogan of "maximum feasible participation," was the largest citizen governance effort by the national government in the postwar period. After numerous battles over the structure of community representation, an amendment to the act in 1966 required that at least one-third of community-action programs be neighborhood groups. CAPs were tripartite coalitions made up of representatives of the poor, community leaders, and welfare-agency officials. The community-organizing philosophy focused on how to organize the poor so that they could function effectively within the political system. While organizers were focused on the issue of governance, they also perceived the poor as consumers of government services. This led to a tension between efforts to stimulate citizen participation and at the same time provide services to the poor. Neighborhood organizations struggled to mediate tensions within CAPs between the provision of services (e.g., legal services; see Stumpf 1975) and the political and educational roles of community governance. Conflict arose over whether participation was anything more than "clientele feedback" (Kramer 1969).

In addition to CAPs, the Office of Juvenile Delinquency and Youth Development and the Office of Economic Opportunity sponsored demonstration programs that also gave a prominent place to the role of neighborhood organization for community action. The National Association of Social Workers, through its Commission on Community Organization and its Council on Social Work in Community Planning and Development, surveyed neighborhood-action programs in order to examine the problem involved in motivating poor people to take group action on their own behalf. This led to the Project on Neighborhood Organization for Community Action and a series of workshops on community action that took place in Ann Arbor, Michigan; Bryn Mawr, Pennsylvania; Durham, North Carolina; and New York in 1968. In many respects these workshops reflected the overall dilemma of the governance orientation toward community building: how can the nonpoor organize the poor so as to increase poor people's participation in community control and national politics? Most of the workshops focused on how to prevent neighborhood organizations from being co-opted. Rather than challenging the system fundamentally, CAPs were described by their organizers as attempts to implement the dominant value system (Turner 1968).

Local political leaders involved in CAPs were distinguished more by their activism (level of involvement in community affairs), than by their political beliefs (Lamb 1975). Grass-roots organizing in the governance programs was structured by a professionalized staff and not local community leaders. Some critics argue that the main problem with neighborhood organizations that are primarily social-service programs is that they are not based on grass-roots participation, but rather come out of a welfare system and merely adopt the language of community governance as a method of administrating services.

Direct action

Community organizers working to establish governing structures and maximize representation of the poor crossed paths with organizers doing *direct action* organizing. Predating the OEO governance program, settlement workers continued to do "what little neighborhood organizing there was" in the fifteen years after the war, and the "profession" of community organizing was underway with the leadership of the charismatic Saul Alinsky. Alinsky is credited as having developed community organizing as a new profession; transforming it from a loosely used term to describe the activities of single-issue community struggles (housing) and social movements (civil rights, women's rights) to refer to people trained in the skills of mobilizing neighborhoods and communities for the purpose of strengthening their identity. Alinsky used "local organization as a catalyst to purposely create cohesiveness and local attachments . . . challenging local elites and creating new, diverse centers of power and influence" (Reitzes and Reitzes 1987:3).

The Industrial Area Foundation (IAF), Alinsky's only national organization, was formed in 1940. It was established with funding from churches (Bishop Bernard Sheil) and a foundation (Marshall Field Foundation in Chicago—department store heir and philanthropist). Foundation support was less stable during the 1950s and 1960s. In the later 1960s and early 1970s IAF was funded through Alinsky's lecturing, fund-raising, and the 10 percent IAF got from grants received for local community-organization projects. By the 1980s many of Alinsky's original community organizations were no longer in existence (e.g., the Chelsea Community Council in New York, FIGHT in Rochester, and the Organization for the Southeast Community and the Citizens Action Program in Chicago).[19] Alinsky

---

19. See Lancourt (1979) for an overview of various community-organization efforts by Alinsky, including The Woodlawn Organization (TWO), Chicago; FIGHT, Rochester; BUILD, Buffalo; Council for United Action (CUA), Kansas City, Missouri; Northwest Community Organization (NCO), Chicago; Chelsea Community Council (CCC), New York; Community Action Training Council (CATC), Syracuse; and Citizen's Action Program, Chicago.

equated his direct-action approach to building community with the "unfolding of a play: '. . . the first act introduces the characters and the plot; in the second act the plot and characters are developed as the play strives to hold the audience's attention. In the final act, good and evil have their dramatic confrontation and resolution'" (as quoted by Reitzes and Reitzes 1987:34). During the first two acts, as it were, community organizers seek to win local acceptance and create interest in communitywide participation. In the final act, confrontation with external adversaries is heightened to win outside acceptance of the community organization as a bargaining agent to press the claims of the local community organization for participation in external decision making.[20] Alinsky's organizations were designed to be umbrella organizations made up of smaller ones. Thus the organizer calls a meeting of local groups or their representatives and the organization is then formed by ratifying a charter or constitution, which establishes how the organization is to be governed (usually through an elected executive board and president). The organization's executive board reports to a senate formed from delegates from the member organizations. The senate appoints members to chair standing committees that focus on specific community issues. This structure is periodically reaffirmed (usually at annual conventions). The organization also retains a *professional staff* to implement decisions and to run daily operations. IAF's staff has never exceeded six to ten full-time professional organizers. Alinsky's organizers were "outside organizers" who received "formal invitation[s]" from local leaders (Reitzes and Reitzes 1987:34). Alinsky's groups insist that they receive one year of financial support before they are to be invited into a community.

In contrast, when Caesar Chavez was involved with Alinsky and Fred Ross in barrio Community Service Organizations (CSOs), there were few preexisting neighborhood organizations for Chavez to use as a basic structure. The lack of Mexican-American political power and involvement in organized labor further undercut the standard "transmission belts" Alinsky's methods used (Finks 1984). In the bar-

---

20. Examples of Alinsky's confrontational tactics include confrontation with a large national department store in Back of the Yard; with the University of Chicago and the city of Chicago in Woodlawn; and Eastman Kodak in Rochester to force external organizations to recognize their responsibility to the community and negotiate with the community organization (Reitzes and Reitzes 1987).

rios, considerable use was made of the house meeting. Organizers listened to residents by hanging around and making contacts with potential organizers in the farm workers' community. Then a series of meetings in people's houses would be scheduled where Chavez would describe activities of other CSOs and ask for the community's response on issues. People at the meeting would sign a pledge to contact others and return for more meetings. Then temporary committees would form. Only months later would an organizing convention be held (Finks 1984).

Unlike Chavez's methods, Alinsky's approach was far more structured and formal; he believed in on-the-job training. Alinsky's ideal training program was envisioned as a "15-month, intensive program to which communities would send students (and pay their tuition) and the IAF would train them to apply organizing strategies and principles to their own communities" (Reitzes and Reitzes 1987:14). Alinsky wanted about 30 percent of each training group to be white middle class in order to integrate community-organizing efforts. Some describe Alinsky's training of organizers as a combination of learning by doing and "Alinsky's Socratic questioning" (Finks 1984).

Despite the fact that Alinsky had a formal approach to training and maintained that professional organizers were an essential resource for community building, he claimed that his community-organizing tactics were situational and not programmatic. For him, inevitable changes in daily life and political situations demand that radicals be wedded only to the idea of empowering the people. Radicals must not hold any principle that constrains their ability to act in ways that will further democracy (Alinsky 1971). Thus tactics varied according to the circumstances. For example, Alinsky organizers helped organize the Butte Citizens Project in Butte, Montana, in 1959. Over a five-year period "the organization *mediated* strikes, conducted an immunization survey to improve the quality of health care for school children, established a mental health hygiene clinic, sought to bring new industry and employment to Butte" (Reitzes and Reitzes 1987:11, emphasis added). Butte Citizens Project became inactive in 1964. In Chicago, TWO mobilized the community "gradually through a variety of activities, including picketing and boycotts against the exploitative practices of local landlords and merchants. TWO then applied pressure on the university [of Chicago] and the city to stop their urban renewal plans for Woodlawn" (Reitzes and Reitzes

1987:13). Voter registration, pressuring city officials to appoint community representatives to school boards and antipoverty programs, and using stock proxies are other examples of Alinsky's situational tactics.

In all of this organizing, Alinsky cautioned "organizers to stay within the experiences of local residents" and continually argued that it was "counter-productive to go beyond the communities' experiences" (1971). As several of his biographers note, Alinsky's training in anthropology and sociology at the University of Chicago (1926) may have contributed to this notion of organizers "staying within the experience" of community members. Alinsky's own experience in labor organizing with John L. Lewis and the CIO also had an important impact on his approach to community organizing.[21]

In terms of political ideology, Alinsky's direct-action community organizing was self-proclaimed as "non-ideological." "He stated flatly that he was not a Marxist and even a cursory reading of Alinsky's work highlights that he traced his beliefs and orientation to the American founding fathers and not to the tradition of European socialism." He "fervently maintained that the role of the organizer is not to change people's values but to convince them that if they join together they could generate the power to effect change and achieve their goals" (Reitzes and Reitzes 1987:16). Alinsky anti-ideology ideology was not only extemely critical of the old Left, but during the 1960s he strongly attacked student radicals, arguing that they had doctrinaire values that were not part of his approach to community organizing. "He firmly believed that through the process of coming together in a community organization residents discover, 'that their individual problem is also the problem of others, and that furthermore the only hope for solving an issue of such titanic proportions is by pooling all of their efforts and strengths'" (Alinsky [1946] 1969:115 as quoted by Reitzes and Reitzes 1987:31–32).

Critics question whether Alinsky's community organizer was a political organizer or merely a "community organization tactician" (Reitzes and Reitzes 1987:21). Although he clearly wanted to attack the sense of alienation and powerlessness within communities, he insisted that these goals should never be out in front of the com-

---

21. He also had a fellowship in criminology at the Institute for Juvenile Research in Chicago, and he taught at Joliet state prison in Illinois.

munities' own sense of injustice.[22] Fainstein and Fainstein (1974) link Alinsky's philosophy to the broader problematic of urban political movements: transforming the way Americans think about politics. Alinsky in many respects was part of the American tendency to equate "good" politics with nonpoliticized issues treated professionally. Indeed, the nonideology ideology of Alinsky is not unlike the ambiguities of populism that led some Alinsky-organized groups, such as the Back of the Yards Neighborhood Council in Chicago, to overwhelmingly support George Wallace for President—a position Alinsky himself deeply opposed.

After Alinsky's death in 1972, Edward Chambers became IAF staff organizer.[23] Chambers has continued to institutionalize and professionalize IAF, such that now IAF retains involvement in local community affairs even after the initial organizing period. The organization contributes funds to IAF under its service contract. Chambers has also decentralized leadership of the IAF, which is now divided among him and four regional associates. Training has also been systematized. New organizers now apprentice under more experienced organizers and attend training sessions regularly. Organizers'

---

22. In contrast, ACORN organizers argue that the "point is not *just* to build a machine that can win concessions from this complex socioeconomic system. The real challenge is to create an institution that can collectively validate an alternative view of social reality and redefine appropriate behavior and collective social action" (Delgado 1986). ACORN was formed in 1970-72 with a focus on the development of local infrastructure and separation from its predecessor—the National Welfare Rights Organization (NWRO). In 1973-75 it became a statewide organization. In 1976-79 it expanded to nineteen states through mergers and affiliations. About that time, the United Labor Unions Organization (ULU) was established. In 1979-81 its membership began working with the Democratic party. By the mid-1980s ACORN began building coalitions around electoral campaigns, merged with the Service Employees Union of the AFL-CIO in efforts to unionize, and returned to an adversarial/disruptive role and its original constituency, the poor, using militant squatting and 'Jobs for Residents' campaign in twelve cities.

23. Chambers organized tenants associations in Harlem for two years before joining IAF. He organized community action in Lackawanna, New York for his first two years with IAF. Then he established the Organization for the Southwest Council in white working-class Chicago. Here action focused on protesting explosive real-estate practices and peacefully achieving integration. Chambers became IAF staff organizer for TWO after Nicholas von Hoffman resigned in 1963. In 1965 Chambers went to Rochester, New York, to become lead organizer for FIGHT, which was engaged in a proxy battle with Eastman Kodak. In 1969 Chambers became the director of the IAF Institute. With Richard Harmon, Chambers established a training program based on Alinsky's methods for local organizations.

salaries have also been raised. Chambers has been critical of single-issue and charismatic organizing (i.e., the civil rights movement, the feminist movement, and the antiwar movement), and he is also critical of the limitations of small civic associations. But Chambers is perhaps most critical of any political problem solving that does not enhance citizen participation and community empowerment (i.e., machine politicians or anyone who must intervene personally to correct a given situation).

The direct-action strategy of Alinsky did not turn to law as a means for organizing community. Mediation, as in the case of the Butte Citizens Project, or taking landlords to court, were tactical decisions often separate from the process of defining community or building community identity. In Alinsky-type organizing, law appears as one instrument among many for pursuing the goals of a community. In this sense, law may or may not be useful to a community, and it was clearly not the main resource for mobilizing direct-action campaigns.

Conflict Resolution

Community organizing through conflict resolution shares much of Alinsky's ideology about the relationship between organizers and "the community." Yet it differs from Alinsky in tactics. Rather than building community through direct action, programs like SFCB provide a conflict-resolution *service* for the construction of community identity. The "community" of SFCB is formed in and through the practice of dispute resolution. The focus is on training, case development, and the mediation process, without a notion of confronting "good and evil" as in Alinsky's community organizing play. That is, SFCB does not have a final act that engages the community and outside organizers in direct action. Yet the absence of direct-action tactics is perhaps the only aspect of an Alinsky organizing approach not present in SFCB. Both the Alinsky approach and SFCB organizing take a pragmatic and situational stance towards building and "empowering" the community.[24]

24. For a discussion of the "neutral stance" mediators take in Community Boards see Harrington and Merry (1988). As other chapters in this book demonstrate, SFCB sought to be nonideological in its positions about "good" and "evil," to use Alinsky's phrases. Yet like Alinsky's pragmatic politics, SFCB has a pragmatic view on the function of mediation in community organizing. It is interesting to note that Alinsky-

Predating Alinsky organizing and SFCB were ethnic and religious conflict-resolution tribunals in the early twentieth century. Similar to the policing form of community organizing, these tribunals had a defensive posture. They were established to maintain cultural values and preserve ethnic and religious identity, often seen as being under attack from the "outside." The best-documented examples of conflict resolution as a defensive community-organizing strategy are the immigrant tribunals Jerold Auerbach writes about (1983). He describes the arbitration tribunals in Chinatown as a means of maintaining traditional authority and resisting assimilation. Similarly, the Jewish conciliation boards (also formed in the 1920s) located in New York City's Lower East Side were primarily geared toward preserving religious and cultural values. The Jewish Conciliation Court was established after the Arbitration Court began attracting attention as a less than reputable group of ambulance chasers. In 1939 the Jewish Conciliation Court changed its name to the Jewish Conciliation Board.[25]

Auerbach argues that the "retention of disputes within the Jewish community was not merely a defensive response to external hostility. It expressed deep desires for religious and cultural autonomy in exile" (1983:77). Preservation of community is of course hard to separate from the desire for cultural identity, or as Auerbach calls it, "autonomy." In both the Chinese and Jewish immigrant communities, conflict resolution was seen as a way of holding the community together. Instead of taking conflict between members of the community to the police or city courts, community resolution, like the youth patrols, was a buffer between religious and ethnic values and the Anglo-American institutions that seemed ever more to press against those values. Indeed, as Auerbach himself notes, once the "community of common interest transcended individual self-interest," the informal dispute tribunals of the Scandinavians, Chinese, and Jews "dissolved," and the "immigrants were American" (1983:94). This suggests that their capac-

---

type organizing occurred in one of the SFCB's neighborhoods prior to its establishment (see Thomson and DuBow in this volume). The first community board developed in Visitacion Valley, California, was in an area where Alinsky-type anticrime organizing had been going on. This broke up as the SFCB came into the area, but some of the same people who organized the crime project came to the SFCB meeting.

25. Also see Auerbach (1983) for a discussion of the *Kehillah*, which focused primarily on resolving religious issues until the clothing industry strikes of 1909–10. The Kehillah ended after World War I.

ity to maintain and defend these traditional values through community conflict-resolution services was overwhelmed by the forces of assimilation and the values of individualism (see also Merry in this volume).

In the 1960s the federal government also developed "community" conflict-resolution services; here too the language of empowerment was not central to the programs they funded. Related to the OEO-CAPs and also in response to the racial unrest and the intensification of urban disorder in the 1960s, the federal government created the Community Relations Service under the authority of the 1964 Civil Rights Act, Title X. The purpose of the Community Relations Service was to "organize local advisory panels of citizens in some forty localities to alert the agency to potentially serious disputes and to intervene in conflicts involving public housing, economic development, education, and police conduct" (Ford Foundation 1978:4). Disputes between ethnic groups over the control of community programs, such as the antipoverty programs, and conflicts over the administration of government contracts and the regulation of housing authorities are the kinds of conflicts the Community Relations Service was established to mediate. The courts are authorized to refer cases in which they believe that voluntary compliance with the Civil Rights Act can best be achieved through mediation.

Following this effort by the federal government, a number of privately funded community-mediation programs were established. In 1968, the Ford Foundation began funding local advisory panels to develop alert systems at the local level and to establish mediation services. Similar to the federal government's program, these panels were concerned with mediating racial disputes before they escalated into highly explosive situations. The Ford Foundation funded mediation and arbitration programs, such as the National Center for Dispute Settlement (1968), sponsored by the American Arbitration Association. The Center later became known as the Community Dispute Service. The principal tasks of the Community Dispute Service were to train community mediators and arbitrators and mediate community conflicts. In 1970 the Institute for Mediation and Conflict Resolution (IMCR) was established with Ford Foundation support. IMCR also trained community interveners, though it placed greater emphasis on mediation than on arbitration. These citizens were trained in the philosophy and techniques of labor management.[26]

---

26. See Harrington (1985:89–90) for a discussion of the debate over using labor-management techniques to mediate community disputes.

The American Friends Service Committee, a Quaker community organization based on the East Coast, established a committee on community mediation and developed several programs during the mid-1970s (Wahrhaftig 1982). One such program, the Friends Suburban Project, established in 1976, is an organization imbued with the Quaker philosophy of conciliation and civil disobedience. Jennifer Beer, a member of this organization, argues that its primary role is to strengthen community bonds through addressing conflicts within the community in nonadversarial settings such as mediation (Beer 1986). Her perspective on mediation, as well as Paul Wahrhaftig's, comes close to that of SFCB (Wahrhaftig 1978, 1982). Paul Wahrhaftig was an actor in the national alternative dispute-resolution movement during the late 1970s and through the 1980s. He worked to establish a National Community Mediation Clearinghouse but was defeated not only because Congress failed to provide funding for the Dispute Resolution Act of 1980, but also because foundations put their resources into the National Institute for Dispute Resolution (NIDR) instead of a more community-focused mediation clearinghouse, and the American Friends Service Committee decided to commit its resources in other directions.

Foundations have been the main supporters for SFCB, despite the fact that community-mediation groups have often been critical of the leading national institution these same foundations funded, NIDR.[27] Alinsky's IAF also relied heavily on foundations for funding. Indeed, both IAF and SFCB received over 80 percent of their support from foundations (see Delgado 1986; DuBow and McEwen in this volume).

SFCB put forth its training strategy as an innovative scheme for enhancing voluntary participation, a project many foundations found very attractive. Training was treated as the primary method for building the capacity of communities to handle their own conflicts (Shonholtz 1977, 1978, and in this volume). This is in fact what SFCB means by "empowerment." Citizen volunteers are the key aspect to community building for SFCB. DuBow notes that while "in most programs volunteers are primarily a means to provide low cost conflict resolution services to private citizens, in SFCB the development of volunteer skills is an end in itself. SFCB, within the limits of its resources, 1) seeks to maximize the number of neighborhood residents

---

27. See DuBow and McEwen in this volume.

who receive training in conflict resolution skills; and 2) provides opportunities for volunteers to develop organizational skills beyond those needed to conduct conflict resolution sessions" (DuBow 1987: "Volunteer Development," 1). DuBow's study tends to support the view that SFCB was able to mobilize around these aspirations. He notes that in the volunteer survey, the "most prominent motivation [given by respondents] is a desire for *personal development through acquiring a greater understanding of mediation and the development of better communications skills.* This was the primary motivation given by over half of the trainees" (1987: "Volunteer Development," 15).[28] There are also some indicators that SFCB had gained a fair amount of community recognition. DuBow reports that in the community residents survey, he "found a high degree of recognition for SFCB within Visitacion Valley. Over forty percent of the respondents were aware of its existence. This is an unusually high recognition rate for a volunteer community program" (1987: "Conflict Resolution: The Primary Service," 7; see also DuBow and McEwen in this volume).

The relationship between "law" and "community" is conceptualized differently in these four strategies of community organizing (policing, governance, direct action, and conflict resolution). It is first striking to note that law plays only a minimal role in governance and direct-action organizing. Surely the governing structures and legal support for the institutions that are challenged by governance and direct-action organizers have some effect on the formation of tactical and perhaps even ideological stances taken by organizers.[29] However, in terms of staking out an identity for a community and determining what is good and bad for communities, governance and direct-action community organizing appear less likely to turn to the law. Law is either a resource for getting community services (governance) or tactic for achieving a specific community goal (direct action). In this sense law's relationship to community organizing for these kinds of organizers is instrumental in achieving a particular goal.

---

28. DuBow also found that getting to know their neighbors and helping them were two other motivations volunteers expressed. This seems to have been the case with veteran volunteers who also expressed an even stronger interest in *self-development* through acquiring new skills (Ibid, 157).

29. See John Brigham's 1987 analysis of how different forms of law constitute different kinds of social movements.

In contrast, both the policing and conflict-resolution strategies rely heavily on law in their conception of the community to be protected (policing) and the community to be formed (conflict resolution). Beliefs about law's authority to regulate "outsiders" (youth and neighborhood patrols) and the law of a community (ethnic and racial patrols) that will protect it from the official legal order (read "outsider"), as well as beliefs about law's capacity to create a community by conflict resolution (SFCB), constitute the character of certain community-organizing strategies (policing and conflict resolution).

Community Conflict Resolution as a Neopopulist Movement

Whether community conflict resolution leads to or is a form of empowering neighborhoods and mobilizing support for social transformation is, of course, the question that scholars and program evaluators often ask about SFCB. I think that rather than assess this issue solely in terms of whether SFCB is "more empowering" than say a court-based mediation program (Neighborhood Justice Centers), we should alter the basis for comparison and ask what kind of empowerment this *form of community organizing* produces. By comparing conflict resolution to other community-organizing strategies I hope to have shown that it (along with policing) is more closely tied to and reliant upon law than other forms of community organizing. But what is the political significance or meaning of this particular connection to the law?

In terms of politics, SFCB is part of the American populist tradition of home rule and local participation. Those who have written more generally on the emergence of neopopulism claim that new social movements based on a vision of an active citizenry play an important role in rebuilding community as well as refueling mistrust of large institutions (Boyte 1980). Others have raised questions about the scope of coordinating activities by organizations working on a citywide versus national basis, doubting whether Alinsky-inspired approaches to community organization can mobilize and sustain a progressive populist movement given their self-proclaimed lack of ideology (Lancourt 1979; Castells 1983). These questions may be a useful starting point for discussing the politics of SFCB organizing strategy.

The ideology of SFCB embodies three aspects of a neopopulist citizen movement: voluntarism; empowerment; and opposition to experts. Voluntarism depends on the moment-to-moment feelings of individuals to sustain an organization. While personal motivations would seem to be important in any organizing effort, organizations like SFCB depend heavily on the excitement and vitality of volunteers, which can lead to a fragile and volatile organization and politics. As Bellah has pointed out, what is "missing is some commitment to principles in a social context where one can count on others to be similarly committed so that together it will be possible to sustain long-term political engagement" (Bellah 1986:101).[30]

The desire for empowerment is reflected in a wide range of social movements over the past twenty-five years (e.g., civil rights movement, women's movement, consumer and environmental movements, and the self-help and neighborhood movements). There is, however, a new dimension to this ethos that emerged most clearly in the 1980s: an ethos that emphasizes self-actualization through participation (see Reissman 1986:55). The ideology of mediation in SFCB is an example of this dimension. It uses psychology in the design of its training and mediation programs to emphasize the individual's ability to grow in the context of community conflict resolution. This emphasis, like the reliance on volunteers, places the larger issues of social transformation and struggles over economic and social justice at a distance from the concerns of empowering individuals.

The third theme of neopopulism that some have argued was not as prominent in previous populist movements is the attack on experts and professionals. Reissman argues that a focus on independence from professionals emerged from the progressive critique of the expanding and dominating welfare state, with alternatives viewed as free from professionalism. Programs not oriented to conflict resolution that reflect this opposition to expertise are numerous, such as self-help mutual aid groups, natural helpers, neighborhood groups, and peer groups (Reissman 1986:58). SFCB, of course, is clearly within this tradition of viewing conflict as a resource (if not property) that pro-

---

30. He also argues that the strength of American voluntarism "(perhaps just another name for populism) seems to be correlated with the weakness of our political parties, for in many other industrial societies with less involvement in voluntary associations there is a concomitantly higher participation in political parties on the part of ordinary citizens" (Bellah 1986: 101).

fessionals take away from individuals and communities. In their rhetorical statements about the dangers of professionals, community organizers (particularly those from the Alinsky line) place themselves at risk of having this very same critique turned on them.

Conclusion

Although some observers would argue that populism runs throughout the history of American politics, others have pointed out that there is now a new version of populism flourishing in citizen movements like SFCB. The neopopulism of the 1980s tends to be conservative because it treats community as a "residual category—that which is not reserved to the individual" (Boyte 1980). To the extent that the ethos of individualism replaces that of empowering a community for the purpose of redistributive social change, neopopulist movements like SFCB will break from "authentic" or "genuine" populism. Since SFCB espouses neutrality, it fails to advocate group interests and therefore is unable to mobilize an "inside" or an "outside" vision of "community," which is fundamental to constituting a sense of community in other organizing strategies, such as governance and direct action. The conservatism of this neopopulism may, in part, help explain why it has emerged at a time when both liberal and radical visions of community and law have come under severe attack.

BIBLIOGRAPHY

Abel, Richard L. 1981. "Conservative Conflict and the Reproduction of Capitalism: The Role of Informal Justice." *International Journal of the Sociology of Law* 9:245–67.
———, ed. 1982. *The Politics of Informal Justice.* Vol. 1: *The American Experience.* Vol. 2: *Comparative Studies.* New York: Academic Press.
Alinsky, Saul D. [1946] 1969. *Reveille for Radicals.* Reprint. New York: Vintage Books.
———. 1971. *Rules for Radicals: A Practical Primer for Realistic Radicals.* New York: Random House.
Auerbach, Jerold S. 1983. *Justice without Law: Resolving Disputes without Lawyers.* New York: Oxford University Press.
Beer, Jennifer E. 1986. *Peacekeeping in Your Neighborhood: Reflections on an Experiment of Community Mediation.* Philadelphia: New Society Publishers.
Bellah, Robert N. 1986. "Populism and Individualism." In *The New Popu-*

lism: The Politics of Empowerment. See Boyte and Reissman 1986. Philadelphia: Temple University Press.

Boyte, Harry C. 1980. The Backyard Revolution: Understanding the New Citizen Movement. Philadelphia: Temple University Press.

Boyte, Harry C., and Frank Reissman, eds. 1986. The New Populism: The Politics of Empowerment. Philadelphia: Temple University Press.

Brigham, John. 1987. "Right, Rage, and Remedy: Forms of Law in Political Discourse." Studies in American Political Development 2:303-17.

Brown, Richard Maxwell. 1975. Strain of Violence: Historical Studies of American Violence and Vigilantism. New York: Oxford University Press.

————. 1979. "The American Vigilante Tradition." In Violence in America: Historical and Comparative Perspectives, ed. H. D. Graham and T. R. Gurr. Beverly Hills, Calif.: Sage Publications.

Cain, Maureen. 1985. "Beyond Informal Justice." Contemporary Crisis 9:335-73.

Castells, Manuel. 1983. The City and the Grassroots: A Cross Cultural Theory of Urban Social Movements. Berkeley and Los Angeles: University of California Press.

Coblentz, Stanton A. 1957. Villians and Vigilantes: The Story of James King of William and Pioneer Justice in California. New York: Thomas Yoseloff.

Cohen, Fay G. 1973. "The Indian Patrol in Minneapolis: Social Control and Social Change in an Urban Context." Law and Society Review 7:779-86.

Crenson, Matthew A. 1983. Neighborhood Politics. Cambridge: Harvard University Press.

Delgado, Gary. 1986. Organizing the Movement: The Roots and Growth of Acorn. Philadelphia: Temple University Press.

DeSena, Judith Noel. 1985. "The Dynamics of Neighborhood Defense: A Sociological Account of Greenpoint, Brooklyn." Ph.D. diss., CUNY.

Dolbeare, Kenneth M., and Linda J. Medcalf. 1988. American Ideologies Today: From Neopolitics to New Ideas. New York: Random House.

DuBow, Fredric L. 1987. "Conflicts and Community: A Study of the San Francisco Community Boards." Photocopy.

Fainstein, Norman I., and Susan S. Fainstein. 1974. Urban Political Movements: The Search for Power by Minority Groups in American Cities. Englewood Cliffs, N.J.: Prentice-Hall.

Finks, P. David. 1984. The Radical Vision of Saul Alinsky. New York: Paulist Press.

Fitzpatrick, Peter. 1983. "Law, Plurality, and Underdevelopment." In Legality, Ideology and the State, ed. D. Sugarman. New York: Academic Press.

————. 1987. "The Rise and Rise of Informalism." In Informal Justice, ed. Roger Matthews. London: Sage Publications.

Ford Foundation. 1978. Mediating Social Conflict. New York: Ford Foundation.

Foucault, Michel. [1971] 1980. "On Popular Justice: A Discussion with Maoists." In *Power/Knowledge: Selected Interviews and Other Writings, 1972–1977,* ed. Colin Gordon. New York: Pantheon.

Friedman, Lawrence M. 1973. *A History of American Law.* New York: Simon and Schuster.

Fuller, Lon L. 1971. "Mediation—Its Forms and Functions." *Southern California Law Review* 44:305–39.

Gerlach, Larry R. 1982. *Blazing Crosses in Zion: The Ku Klux Klan in Utah.* Logan: Utah State University Press.

Goldberg, Stephen B., Eric D. Green, and Frank E. A. Sander, eds. 1985 *Dispute Resolution.* Boston: Little, Brown.

Goodwyn, Lawrence. 1976. *Democratic Promise: The Populist Movement in America.* New York: Oxford University Press.

———. 1978. *The Populist Movement: A Short History of the Agrarian Revolt in America.* New York: Oxford University Press.

Hallman, Howard W. 1973. *Government by Neighborhoods.* Washington, D.C.: Center for Governmental Studies.

Harrington, Christine B. 1980. "Voluntariness, Consent, and Coercion in Adjudicating Minor Disputes: The Neighborhood Justice Center." In *Policy Implementation: Penalties or Incentives?* ed. J. Brigham and D. Brown. Beverly Hills, Calif.: Sage Publications.

———. 1982. "Delegalization Reform Movements: A Historical Analysis." In *The Politics of Informal Justice,* vol. 1. *See* Abel 1982.

———. 1985. *Shadow Justice: The Ideology and Institutionalization of Alternatives to Court.* Westport, Conn.: Greenwood Press.

Harrington, Christine B., and Sally Engle Merry. 1988. "Ideological Production: The Making of Community Mediation." *Law and Society Review* 22:709–37.

Hartz, Louis. 1955. *The Liberal Tradition in America.* New York: Harcourt Brace.

Henry, Stuart. 1983. *Private Justice: Towards Integrated Theorizing in the Sociology of Law.* Boston: Routledge and Kegan Paul.

———. 1985. "Community Justice, Capitalist Society, and Human Agency: The Dialectics of Collective Law in the Cooperative." *Law and Society Review* 19:303–27.

———. 1987. "The Construction and Deconstruction of Social Control: Thoughts on the Discursive Production of State Law and Private Justice." In *Transcarceration: Essays in the Sociology of Social Control,* ed. J. Lowman, R. Menzies, and T. S. Palys. London: Gower.

Hofrichter, Richard. 1977. "Justice Centers Raise Basic Questions." *New Directions in Legal Services* 2:168–71.

Ingalls, Robert P. 1988. *Urban Vigilantes in the New South: Tampa, 1882–1936.* Knoxville: University of Tennessee Press.

Kennedy, Dennis Jay. 1987. *Crime, Fear, and the New York City Subways: The Role of Citizen Action.* New York: Praeger.

Knopf, Terry Ann. 1969. *Youth Patrols: An Experiment in Community Participation.* Waltham, Mass.: Brandeis University Press.

Kramer, Ralph M. 1969. *Participation of the Poor: Comparative Community*

Case Studies in the War on Poverty. Englewood Cliffs, N.J.: Prentice-Hall.

Lamb, Curt. 1975. *Political Power in Poor Neighborhoods.* New York: John Wiley and Sons.

Lancourt, Joan E. 1979. *Confront or Concede: The Alinsky Citizen Action Organizations.* Lexington, Mass.: Lexington Books.

McEwen, Craig. 1988. "Differing Visions of Alternative Dispute Resolution and Formal Law: A Review Essay." *Justice System Journal* 12:247–59.

McEwen, Craig and Richard J. Maiman. 1984. "Mediation in Small Claims Courts: Achieving Compliance Through Consent." *Law and Society Review* 18:11.

McGillis, Daniel, and Joan Mullen. 1977. *Neighborhood Justice Centers.* Washington, D.C.: U.S. Government Printing Office.

Macpherson, C. B. 1962. *The Political Theory of Possessive Individualism.* Oxford: Clarendon Press.

Merry, Sally Engle. 1979. "Going to Court: Strategies of Dispute Management in an American Urban Neighborhood." *Law and Society Review* 13:891–92.

The Mooter. 1977–80 Pittsburgh: Grassroots Citizen Dispute Resolution Clearinghouse.

Nader, Laura, ed. 1980. *No Access to Law: Alternatives to the American Judicial System.* New York: Academic Press.

———. 1988. "The ADR Explosion—The Implications of Rhetoric in Legal Reform." *Windsor Yearbook of Access to Justice* 8:269–91.

National Association for Community Justice. 1986. Presentation at the National Conference on Peace Making and Conflict Resolution, St. Louis, Mo.

Nolan, Patrick B. 1987. *Vigilantes on the Middle Border: A Study of Self-Appointed Law Enforcement in the States of the Upper Mississipi from 1840 to 1880.* New York: Garland Publishing.

Norton, Ann. 1987. *Alternative Americas.* Chicago: University of Chicago Press.

Oberschall, Anthony. 1973. *Social Conflict and Social Movements.* Englewood Cliffs, N.J.: Prentice-Hall.

Pate, Anthony. 1986. "Experimenting with the Foot Patrol: The Newark Experience." In *Community Crime Prevention: Does It Work? See* Rosenbaum 1986.

Pollack, Norman. 1967. *The Populist Mind.* Indianapolis: Bobbs-Merrill.

———. 1987. *The Just Polity: Populism, Law, and Human Welfare.* Urbana: University of Illinois Press.

Reissman, Frank. 1986. "The New Populism and the Empowerment Ethos." In *The New Populism: The Politics of Empowerment. See* Boyte and Reissman 1986.

Reitzes, Donald C., and Dietrich C. Reitzes. 1987. *The Alinsky Legacy: Alive and Kicking.* Greenwich: JAI Press.

Roehl, Janice A. 1987. *Multi-Door Dispute Resolution Centers. Phase I:*

Intake and Referral Assessment. Washington, D.C.: American Bar Association and U.S. National Institute of Justice.

Rosenbaum, Dennis P., ed. 1986. *Community Crime Prevention: Does It Work?* Beverly Hills, Calif.: Sage Publications.

Santos, Boaventura de Sousa. 1979. "Popular Justice, Dual Power, and Socialist Strategy." In *Capitalism and the Rule of Law,* ed. B. Fine et al. London: Hutchinson.

Shonholtz, Raymond. 1977. *Review of Alternative Dispute Mechanisms and a Government Proposal for Neighborhood Justice Centers.* San Francisco: San Francisco Community Boards Program.

———. 1978. "Testimony before the Subcommittee on Courts, Civil Liberties, and the Administration of Justice, Committee on the Judiciary Dispute Resolution Act, S.957." H.R. 95th Congress, 2d Session, 27 July and 2 August 1978.

———. 1987. "The Citizen's Role in Justice: Building a Primary Justice and Prevention System at the Neighborhood Level." *Annals of the American Academy of Political and Social Sciences* 494: 42–52.

Stumpf, Harry. 1975. *Community Politics and Legal Services: The Other Side of the Law.* Beverly Hills, Calif.: Sage Publications.

Tilly, Charles. 1984. "Social Movements and National Politics." In *Statemaking and Social Movements,* ed. C. Bright and S. Harding. Ann Arbor: University of Michigan Press.

Trojanowicz, Robert. 1986. "Evaluating a Neighborhood Foot Patrol Program: The Flint, Michigan Project." In *Community Crime Prevention: Does It Work?* See Rosenbaum 1986.

Turner, John B., ed. 1968. *Neighborhood Organization for Community Action.* New York: National Association of Social Workers.

Wahrhaftig, Paul. 1978. "Citizens Dispute Resolution: A Blue Chip Investment in Community Growth." *Pretrial Services Annual Journal* 1978:1–8.

———. 1982. "An Overview of Community-Oriented Citizen Dispute Resolution Programs in the United States." In *The Politics of Informal Justice,* vol. 1. See Abel 1982.

Williams, Mary Floyd. 1921. *History of the San Francisco Committee of Vigilance of 1851: A Study of Social Control on the California Frontier in the Days of the Gold Rush.* Berkeley and Los Angeles: University of California Press.

Wilson, James Q. 1968. *Varieties of Police Behavior.* Cambridge: Harvard University Press.

Wright, James E. 1974. *The Politics of Populism.* New Haven: Yale University Press.

When Is Popular
Justice Popular?

Laura Nader

In this paper I will argue that "popular justice" movements are not usually popular, in the sense of being locally controlled or bottom-up in origin, but rather movements that originate in centers of power and then try to connect with local populations for purposes of control (Yngvesson 1989). I will distinguish San Francisco Community Boards (SFCB) as a movement of control different from local popular-justice movements, such as those described for San Francisco Community Action (SFCA) by Wilson and Brydolf (1980), whose purpose is to gain control over powerful adversaries. Community justice such as described for the early United States by Auerbach (1983) or those described by Rose (1992) for contemporary Swaziland also have as their purpose holding control and maintaining autonomy. Even though popular-justice organizations of top-down and community origins may share similar features, such as community mediation, and may resist contact with state law, the point of origin and their purpose may render them as different as apples and oranges.

The themes that emerge as central to my argument require a recognition of San Francisco Community Boards as part of a broader strategy of minimizing conflict and maximizing order by managing interpersonal conflicts—rather than root causes—in specific locales. An opposing strategy requires, in addition to dealing with conflict, an examination of root causes of social problems and an address of those causes as central to the strategy of preventing social conflict. The gradual emergence of an ideology of harmony that overruns attention to root causes indicates a preference for harmony, or what Barbara Yngvesson has called "a professional therapeutic culture in the guise of a popular culture developed from existing community values" (1989:1703).

Several issues provide the background for this paper: (1) the close relationships over time between styles of disputing processes and the political conduct of governments and economic and religious institutions (Chanock 1985; Greenhouse 1986; Nader 1988, 1989, 1990), and (2) the manner in which such relationships have influenced domestic U.S. legal policies (Nader 1988) as well as international policies of dispute settlement (Nader 1989), and (3) the consequence for real and potential litigants of state and private "justice" systems (Abel 1982; Nader 1980).

The growing emphasis on harmony and compromise in the legal and social-science policy literature, and the value placed on harmony behavior in a variety of institutions over the past two decades was preceded by an emphasis on social injustices in which litigation and court access predominated in the discourses over legal politics or policies. While a good deal has been written about the possible consequences of what may be regarded as a shift in discourse since the 1970s, we understand less about the actual processes by which change in discourse and instrumental innovations came about. Understanding an organization such as the San Francisco Community Boards in the national context may allow us to maximize integration of interest and cross-fertilization between varieties of discourse. Hybrid vigor is badly needed in this area of an increasing microinterpersonal, alternative dispute-resolution perspective. A comparison of two San Francisco-based "justice" organizations—San Franscisco Community Boards and San Francisco Consumer Action—allows us a comparison of local-level organizations that were inspired by different models of achieving justice.

Comparing San Francisco Consumer Action with San Francisco Community Boards

Analyzing discourse is useful in revealing basic value orientations. At the inception of San Francisco Community Boards I was serving as a trustee and advisor. I was simultaneously studying another justice-oriented organization in San Francisco with the help of two researchers (Wilson and Brydolf 1980), who called their study "Grass Roots Solutions: San Francisco Consumer Action." In their introduction

(1980:417–18) the authors state, "Our description of SFCA illustrates the evolution of the organization from a complaint switchboard to a much larger consumer organization involved in a broad range of activities." The organization did not emerge from a preconceived blueprint. Rather, through a process of learning, the group repeatedly sought to address problems of increasingly broader scope. From the beginning the organization was responding to its constituents, and not to a preconceived structure.

San Francisco Consumer Action was founded by an activist, middle-class housewife, who along with other middle-class house-wives handled consumer complaints from their homes. The young organization started by helping to resolve consumer complaints, each complainant being counseled individually. Only later did it evolve into a set of staff grievance committees, and finally to consumer-run complaint-resolution committees, based on models developed in other U.S. cities. SFCA never had any formal or informal ties with government regulatory bodies and operated mainly with broad-based support (both individual and other) and heavy use of volunteers from the community, one of whom was a professional lawyer. The organization was dedicated to building a powerful consumer constituency; they explicitly did not want to be "holding people's hands and become a passive information receptacle" (Wilson and Brydolf 1980:421). SFCA was not focused on the interpersonal, nor was it therapeutically inclined. When a former deputy attorney general joined the staff, SFCA had articulated its goal as "an alternative mechanism for regulating business behavior" (1980:422). Although initially a consumer-grievance organization, SFCA had by now gained a reputation as a force in consumer matters leading, for example, into investigations of banking and finance, into lobbying efforts for consumers and block handling of grievances. They worked in three specific areas: food, utilities, and the media, each of which had a consumer task force. In 1975, SFCA had the distinction of being the first private organization ever to be reimbursed by a federal agency for participating in agency hearings as a representative of the public interest. Through its existence SFCA "evolved a philosophy of dispute settlement that recognizes disputing as an activity related to broad economic and political structures in this society" (Wilson and Brydolf 1980:459). Among its innovations was the use of complaint mobiles in poor neighborhoods that later became the work of the Consumer Fraud

Division of the San Francisco district attorney's office. SFCA shifted in its lifetime from handling complaints one by one toward "block solutions and prevention, and toward the exercise of consumer power through the use of shoppers' guides and self-help complaint committees" (1980:458). SFCA lasted over a decade in its activist function.

In the meantime the political environment was changing. A student with experience in neighborhood justice summarized the difference this way:

> For the white middle class, the therapy decade of the '70s took love and peace and community and unity and put them all on individual shoulders. The answers were to be found in healthy bodies, in solitary wilderness, in relationships . . . the "personal" began to overshadow the "political." Why? . . . the rhetoric of personal therapized harmony which pushes anger and intimacy back into the household have all combined to relegate massive outpourings of discontent into buckshot complaints. (Beer 1987)

San Francisco Community Boards was started by a lawyer with the idea of "building a primary justice and prevention system at the neighborhood level" (Shonholtz 1987). Lawyer Shonholtz argued, "Interpersonal violence in the United States can be dramatically reduced if cities adopt such neighborhood justice like that pioneered by the Community Board Program. So defined, the concept of prevention is a community responsibility maintained by citizens exercising their civic rights" (1987:42). The goals of love, peace, and community were to be shouldered by individual citizens.

The language of Community Boards is particularly revealing of a blueprint that was, however, hardly popular or grass roots. In fact, as the following selections from Shonholtz (1987) indicate, the tone is distinctly managerial: "community-based conflict resolution by *trained* citizen volunteers"; or "with such a public policy, it is possible to *place* citizens in a preventive role"; or "citizens can be *trained*" (46–47; emphasis added). Nobody who knows anything about what constitutes community would dare to call such a system *community* mediation. It would be more like indirect rule in the colonial context, a means to create local peace by the use of local peoples.

In the proposal for the conference held in 1989 out of which this volume grew, Neal Milner and Sally Merry define popular justice as "referring to a wide range of informal judicial reform *implemented* at the grass-roots level to serve the legal needs of average citizens" (3; emphasis added). They also note that the "political import of community mediation is more subtle in the United States than it is in popular justice reform in other countries." The political import of community mediation may be more subtle because, as Judy Rothschild notes, when mediation is a process of communication, justice is defined "not in relation to rights or explicit standards, but rather in relation to implicit standards of conformity" (1986:16). The institutionalization of the ideology of mediation *is* subtle.

If language is a fruitful indicator, so too are patterns of use. Studies of use of SFCB indicate low frequency of use (DuBow and McEwen in this volume), while SFCA, with much less money, had a broader self-generated constituency (Wilson and Brydolf 1980). More generally, conference efforts to multiply use of alternative dispute resolution (see Nader 1984) is also indication that such "popular" justice mechanisms are not popular or community based. Analysis of the discourse has indicated that we are dealing with double-talk or denial and use of words such as *popular* or *community* may mislead our analyses. In this context, comparisons between two ideal types such as SFCA and SFCB are instructive.

Although mediation forums may have been less successful at solving the problems that their proponents articulate, we would have to concede that the *ideas* represented in alternative dispute-resolution organizations such as SFCB have multiplied in a dozen directions in what I call an *ideology of harmony*, within which conflict is controlled, not resolved. Denial of social problems becomes personalized and solvable by good-naturedness (listen to Bobby McFerrin's song, "Don't Worry, Be Happy"), or by the construction of courses on consensus taught to sixth graders. Under such conditions confrontation and anger have not disappeared; rather they have been suppressed (Greenhouse 1986; Baumgartner 1988). M. P. Baumgartner uses the term *moral minimalism* to describe a daily life "filled with efforts to deny, minimize, contain, and avoid conflict . . . the pervasive moral minimalism found in the surburbs contrasts sharply with claims that American society is particularly violent or litigious" (1988:127). The suburbs have come to the San Francisco Community Boards.

What Shonholtz (1985) calls prevention is possibly suppression of conflict between individuals and is characteristic of an American tendency to blame the victim as part of the attempt to contain conflict. In order to elaborate upon this point I will step away from the oppositions mirrored by Consumer Action and Community boards to add a historical perspective on the same oppositions as they appeared at the national level. Opposing positions are illustrated by the discourse of idealistic young advocates and establishment members of the American bar.

Opposing Harmony and Adversarial Law Models

In 1970 a group of lawyers published a book entitled *With Justice for Some: An Indictment of the Law by Young Advocates*. In the introduction to the volume Ralph Nader observed, "[T]he paradox of a wealth of abuse (consumer fraud, for example) and a poverty of access by individuals grows more acute as society grows increasingly complex" (Wasserstein and Green 1970:ix). The articles in the book address a wide variety of legal problems pertaining to the young, soldiers, students, women, blacks, poor people, consumers, the crimes of the courts, the corporate industrialists, the regulators, and the beginnings of a decade of repression. What is interesting for our purposes is the range of solutions that were included in these papers of young advocates, "determined to make the law a force in reducing the institutional injustices and in shaping an *initiatory* democratic system of active and skilled citizens" (1970:xi). They put forth several recommendations: it is not wise to respond to peaceful protest with repression; military justice reforms would expand the powers of military judges so that they more closely resemble federal court judges—the civilization of military law; women must organize politically to achieve legal change through legislative change, and through suing in cases of discrimination; blacks called for reparations; the poor can have legal representation through government-provided legal services or judicare in order that "the powerful . . . can be made accountable" (1970:189). They recommended that the "adversary process" that is being diluted by "continuances" and "plea bargaining" should be strengthened, and that the corporations should be tamed through structural reform. Additionally, they argued for democratizing the corporations and they encouraged a grass-roots consumer movement to challenge oligopolistic market structures. The response to injustices for these young advocates was legal action—the public interest law firm. The last chapter is called "The 1970s: A Decade of Repression?" They knew it would be a fight, but I do not believe they realized it would be a subtle fight, one that was akin to mind colonization.

While these young advocates were writing, the alternative dispute-resolution movement was being constructed. The movement was spearheaded by the then chief justice of the United States Supreme Court, Warren Burger. Early in the 1970s, the chief justice began to deliver a series of speeches in which he argued that American society had too much conflict, that Americans were too litigious and that what was needed was "a better way." The chief justice's chief aide was Mark Cannon, a man of Mormon background, whose philosophy reflects the Mormon idea of community and consensus and the Mormon dislike of courts and lawyers (Dredge 1979; Cannon 1986). This dislike of courts and lawyers was expressed time after time in Warren Burger's speeches, which touched on harmony and efficiency, on the incompetency of lawyers, on what it meant to be civilized—and rarely on subjects of injustice. Chief Justice Burger was to become a prominent leader of an antilaw movement.

The Roscoe Pound Conference, "Perspectives on Justice in the Future" was held in St. Paul, Minnesota, in 1976 (Levin and Wheeler 1979). I attended this conference and watched as the so-called litigation explosion was replaced by the alternative dispute-resolution explosion (Nader 1988). The concerns were not with justice, but with harmonious relations, with community, with removing "garbage cases" from the courts. Nonjudicial means were suggested as a means for dispute handling. Law schools shifted their training in the adversarial methods and began to include training in the alternative dispute-resolution mechanism of mediation, or "med-arb," a combination of mediation and arbitration. The concern with harmony was accompanied by the silencing of disputes; Americans were repeatedly described as too litigious. The production of harmony was to be achieved by the movement against the contentious, the movement to control the disenfranchised. The loss of concern with rights created a model of law intolerant of conflict, its causes and its expression. An intolerance for strife seeks to rid the society of those who complain, and by various means—sometimes coercive—attempts to create consensus, homogeneity, and agreement.

At the Pound Conference a way of thinking about the structural problems of inequality, about social relations more generally, and about solutions to these problems *by cultural means* was dramatized. In order to be more civilized Americans had to abandon the centrality of the adversary model. The solution that emerged was a procedural reform whereby the harmony law model would come to replace the adversarial, and mediation and compromise were to replace no-win solutions of the adversary process. The rhetoric at the conference extolled the virtues of alternative dispute mechanisms. Alternative dispute resolution would provide access, help resolve overcrowded courtrooms, and decrease American litigiousness. There were plentiful assertions, not much data (Nader 1988). Alternative dispute agencies were described as agencies of reconciliation, and people who stood in the way of such procedural reforms were said to suffer from "status quoism."

Because of his authoritative position as chief justice, Warren Burger carried considerable weight in setting the tone that characterized the speeches and writings of the movement. The language was formulaic (Bloch 1975). Generalizations were repeated without grounding. Authority and danger were invoked, and values were presented as facts (see Nader 1988). Justice Burger warned that adversarial modes of resolving conflict were tearing the society apart and that alternative forums were more civilized (1982). He insisted that Americans are *inherently* litigious. He argued that lawyers should serve as "healers of human conflicts" (1982:7). In such a model plaintiffs are patients needing treatment (Claeson 1987). In spite of evidence and arguments presented to the contrary (see, for example, Galanter 1983, 1986; Fiss 1984), the chief justice proceeded relentlessly with his solution, the privatization of law, arguing that we must move toward taking a large volume of private conflicts out of the courts and into the channels of arbitration, mediation, and conciliation (1985). Relationships, not root causes, interpersonal conflict-resolution skills, not power inequities or injustice, are the crux of the ADR movement.

In this context it is useful to return once again to SFCA and SFCB. In SFCA activism is based on shared consumer injustices, which provide the impetus to organize. Common complaints came from a lay public that understood power differential by personal experiences. Their remedy was to be found in organizing pressure on the political and economic forces that generated their disputes. The SFCB impetus to participate, however, was generated around values of consensus settlement, and the declared aim: to manage social disorder in geographical locales (that the social managers call neighborhoods or communities) by means of training in conflict-resolution skills.

Both San Francisco–based organizations are local reflections of expressions at the national level. The first is an example of the legal-action model; the second emanates from the "healers of human conflict" school. The healers were dominated by a professional expertise that ignored power differentials and articulated the dominant assumption that disputes are generated in relationships, that is, generated by failure of individuals to act as they should. The opposition between conflict and harmony law models is not unique to the United States.

The Politics of Law

Changes from harmony to confrontation or adversarial law models and back have been documented by historians for a number of societies. Over the past decades anthropologists of law and legal historians have observed that with the development of colonialism, harmony models replaced feuds and wars, and with the development of nation-states the harmony model, so commonly associated with communities under colonialism, was being replaced by the adversary model (Nader and Todd 1978; Abel 1979). In imperial Japan between 1922 and 1942 formal conciliation was used as a substitute for trials (Haley 1982). In the old nation-states the situation appeared to be moving in the opposite direction. Vilhelm Aubert (1969) reported that Norway had moved toward the harmony model and away from the adversarial one with the development of the welfare state. A decade later the harmony model was also center stage in the United States, competing with the adversary process. Such observations indicate that cultural values underlying disputing processes change over time and circumstance and that they are *profoundly political.* Any evaluations of alternative dispute resolution must take note of this observation first and foremost, and of the use of disputing styles in relation to controlling processes.

Anthropological studies of non-Western law in the 1950s and 1960s in Africa (Gluckman 1955; Gulliver 1963; Holleman 1974; Shapera 1959; Bohannan 1957) had little patience with questions of origin and spent little or no time examining historical documents.

As a result their ethnographic studies conveyed the impression that native systems of law were indeed native, and the term *customary law* came to refer to studies of native law that centered around compromise models. Often peoples were studied as if they had not been radically affected by colonial governments and administrations and as if untouched by ideologies and structures introduced by Christian missionaries of a variety of sects (Beidelman 1974). There are of course some exceptions like Sigfried Nadel (1947). Nadel wrote about the role of Christianity in radically changing the law in its zeal to reconstruct African society and culture "rather than lend strength to a slowly emerging new morality" (1947:512).

More recently, however, in the tradition of global theorists such as Wallerstein (1974) and Wolf (1982), both legal historians and anthropologists have turned their attention to the influence of world economics, politics, and religions on the construction of law. The most brilliant exposition using African materials belongs to legal historian Martin Chanock (1985). Chanock brings together the data on the missionary presence in Africa from the 1830s onward, thereby revealing the original connection between local law, the presence of Christian missions, and the spread of harmony models, models that emphasize compromise, reconciliation, and turning the other cheek. Chanock uses the term *missionary justice* (1985:79) to call attention to the fact that from the early 1860s English missionaries were heavily involved in the settlement of disputes according to a Victorian interpretation of biblical law they had brought with them, disputes they generally fit into English legal procedures as they knew them.

Although there were regional variations between mission groups, mission justice suffered from contradiction. On the one hand, the hearing between disputants was supposed to be a discussion; on the other hand, missionaries resorted to harsh punishment. Missionaries found it difficult to respect the separation of religion from law, so much a part of law in the West. They found this separation especially difficult to maintain in relation to the law of marriage and divorce, which they saw through the lens of mid-Victorian Christian law. Indeed, some missionaries promulgated the Ten Commandments as the law of God, and according to Chanock, the missionaries were glad to be peacemakers and hand down Christian judgments, while the colonial courts evolved customary law, which emphasized conciliation and compromise, operating on the principles of the Christian ideology of harmony.

The history of African customary law is rich on the origin and modern consequences of harmony ideology. A law that focuses on compromise or mediation to the exclusion of other forms of resolving disputes reflects a politics of adjustment. In colonial times community courts became places where people engaged in the discourses that establish possibilities for dealing with indirect rule. African peoples used harmony at different points in their contact experiences—when war and raiding were being routed as part of colonial policy, when African courts were designated as maintainers of social order under colonial conditions, and when nationalists sought to protect their communal bonds from developers under postcolonial conditions (Rose 1988). In all these settings harmony ideology—which was part and parcel of government or religious policy to begin with—controlled African native peoples, as well as controlling processes in the post-colonial period.

Disputing processes cannot be explained as a reflection of some predetermined set of social conditions; rather they reflect the processes of cultural construction that may be a response to demand, a product of ruling interests, or a result of class conflict. SFCB's ideology of mediation as a general conception for life should be scrutinized in relation to the construction of law, much as conflict has been scrutinized in relation to the development of law.

In this regard, it is useful to look at some of the recent literature promoting mediation. For example, in *Getting Disputes Resolved: Designing Systems to Cut the Costs of Conflict* (Ury, Brett, and Goldberg 1988) the authors wish to minimize "costly lawsuits or power struggles." Their book is described: "Introducing a new approach to dispute resolution design the authors define three types of dispute resolution and arrange them in order of efficiency and cost: reconciling the interests of both parties using problem-solving negotiation; determining who is 'right' by relying on the courts and arbitration; and letting power decide the issue, using strikes, lockouts, or physical violence" (from the advertisement). Their concern is with valuing reconciliation: "To be sure, reconciling interests can sometimes take a long time. Generally, however, these costs are pale in comparison with the transaction costs of rights and power contests such as trials, hostile corporate takeovers, or wars" (14). They describe themselves as conflict managers; when used in the San Francisco schools, the label *conflict manager* is worn on bright T-shirts by children who work on school playgrounds to try to mediate emerging disputes. The authors are concerned with anger:

> When faced with the decision of a state agency to place unwanted waste facilities in their community some local residents have obstructed highways, threatened to dynamite existing facilities . . . all to vent their anger about policy making processes that failed to adequately address their concerns. (1988:44)

The phrase "vent their anger" rather than a phrase like "in an attempt to block the waste facilities," further underscores the concern with emotion (anger) and not the cause of emotion—the proposed waste facilities. The designers of disputing systems are also aware of providing motivation for and overcoming resistence to "low-cost" dispute-resolution designs:

> designing a dispute is not just a technical task of making the best changes; it is also a political task of garnering support, dealing with resistance, and motivating people to use the changed procedures. . . . In working with the parties, the dispute systems designer plays the roles of coach, evaluator, and evangelist. (1988:xvi, 83)

"Loop-back" procedures turn disputants away from contests of power and rights contests to negotiation, all designed to achieve a negotiated order and to rid ourselves of "the turbulent environment" (1988:xiii). A collaborative approach leads to consensus agreement. The environment they describe fits well with the conditions noted elsewhere as important to creating "group think" (see Janis 1972:chap. 8). Furthermore, the components of a harmony ideology resemble the conditions found in Judy Rothschild's key observations about the ideology of mediation at SFCB (1986). Rothschild notes that at Community Boards disputes are shaped as communication problems; that unequal power does not enter the paradigm; that disputes about facts and legal rights are transformed into disputes about feelings and relationships; and that conflict is personalized and problems are localized in the realm of emotion. In addition, at Community Boards conflict is viewed as dysfunctional and threatening to the social order. Harmony is believed to be inherently good, and the issue of justice is not apparent. These new disputing ideologies have been rediscovered in studies of worker's-compensation claims (Claeson 1987), in studies of arbitration (Dart 1987), and in studies more broadly gauged (see Harrington and Merry 1988; Yngvesson 1988). The social meaning of the alternative dispute-resolution movement is now being understood in relation to the expansion of state and corporate control (Abel 1982), but to understand managerial movements of popular justice a theory of harmony as control is in order.

Discussion

When is popular justice "popular?" Probably not when it is implemented from above. The dispute-resolution movement was inspired by an awareness of the increased need for access to justice for the poor, for "minorities," for consumers—for those that do not have general access to law. There were many conferences during the 1960s, and populist input was important. However, there were also other motivations. For example, corporations wanted to reduce their legal fees, and others wanted to unclog the courts. But what gave the movement its moral push was the attempt to address the question of access to justice for the masses, for the many. Today, very little is said about the underlying issue—requiring that kind of class access—except in generalities.

Instead, the initiative today is to develop new organizations for dispute resolution, to expand the dispute-resolution movement, to train people in dispute resolution, and to credential people. The whole has taken on a professional style that is increasingly coercive, and that increasingly values means over ends.

> ... from a cost benefit perspective the establishment of such a procedure (mediation) might be a very worthwhile investment. It not only would help reduce unemployment compensation expenditures and promote harmony and productivity in the work force but would also reduce court caseloads. (Bierman et al. 1985)

From a professional point of view, it means new jobs for people and new domains of control by means of alternative dispute resolution. The prime focus on organizational expansion and the implications for profitable new jobs for professionals is part of what leads to moral decay. Means have become ends. In this context few people notice that alternative dispute-resolution mechanisms are "justice" mechanisms that are unregulated and uncontrolled. There is little concern with what it means for potential users of the system to have alternative systems; what it means to privatize judicial functions; what it means to move in the direction of a privatized legal system with no written records.

There should be a backlash on the alternative dispute-resolution movement, for the same reason that there was a backlash on the judicial system: ADR is not relevant to most people's substantive concerns. In addition, it promises what it cannot deliver. The dispute-resolution movement is not providing the kind of alternative justice systems that originally motivated the public-interest community's critique. In fact, ADR is becoming coercive and increasingly mandated by law (Nader 1992).

There could be an effort from within the movement to reform the goals, the organization, and the professional spirit that presently governs dispute resolution, one that moves in the direction of prevention. I am not talking about microprevention, where you get two neighbors to talk to each other so they don't kill each other. I mean macroprevention, where you find out where the number and seriousness of disputes occur in society in order to look for some kind of structural, organizational, or productive means of preventing those disputes. As I said in *No Access to Law:* "The assumption that change is to be achieved preeminently through individual reformation is so deeply embedded that there has developed a cultural blindness to the importance of the social and cultural structure that produces the problem in the first place" (1980:59–72).

"Popular justice," we will find, is popular when justice is fashioned after the needs of the potential litigants. Where is this to be found with the ADR movement?—in the settling of corporate cases where time, money, and the privatization of justice have benefited the litigants.

Over the past two years, 400 corporations, many of them Fortune 500 companies, have signed a pledge to mediate or arbitrate before pursuing litigation. . . . Recently, 60 corporate signatories announced a two-year savings of nearly $50 million in legal fees and costs. . . . Unlike litigation, these alternatives resolve our disputes quickly so we can get on with business. (Wiehl 1989)

Mediation works when parties are of equal bargaining strength and sophistication.

In the San Francisco Community Boards, mediation works to promote harmony, and to socialize citizens to the new justice forums where the focus explicitly ignores power differentials. Similar approaches have appeared, for example, at Union Carbide, which has experimented with minitrials, presided over by a company executive. In product-liability cases involving workers injured by accidental exposure to toxic chemicals, the potential defendant becomes the judge. At Ford Motor Company, for over a decade it has been possible to complain to Ford about Ford in mediation hearings.

The question Marc Galanter (1989) asks is one I am left with: "What's so good about settlements?" The uncritical celebration of harmony is at the base of acceptance of philosophies that undergird SFCB. Such celebration has more to do with religious or ideological belief than with justice (Nader 1992).

REFERENCES

Abel, R. L. 1979. "Western Courts in Non-Western Settings: Patterns of Court Use in Colonial and Neo-Colonial Africa." In *The Imposition of Law*, ed. S. Burman and B. Harrell-Bond. New York: Academic Press.
———, ed. 1982. *The Politics of Informal Justice*. Vol. 1: *The American Experience*. Vol. 2: *Comparative Studies*. New York: Academic Press.
Aubert, V. 1969. "Law as a Way of Resolving Conflicts: The Case of a Small Industrialized Society." In *Law in Culture and Society*, ed. L. Nader. Chicago: Aldine.
Auerbach, J. 1983. *Justice without Law? Resolving Disputes without Lawyers*. New York: Oxford University Press.
Baumgartner, M. P. 1988. *The Moral Order of a Suburb*. New York: Oxford University Press.
Beer, J. 1987. Personal communication.
Beidelman, T. O. 1974. "Social Theory and the Study of Christian Missions." *Africa* 44:235–49.
Bierman, L., J. C. Ullman, and S. A. Youngblood. 1985. "Making Disputes over Dismissals." In *Harrow Business Review*, January–February, 160.

Bloch, M., ed. 1975. *Political Language and Oratory in Traditional Society.* London: Academic Press.

Bohannan, P. 1957. *Justice and Judgment among the Tiv.* London: Oxford University Press for the International African Institute.

Burger, W. E. 1982. "Isn't There a Better Way? Annual Report on the State of the Judiciary." Midyear meeting of the American Bar Association, Chicago, 24 January.

————. 1985. Year-End Report on the Judiciary by Warren E. Burger, Chief Justice of the United States. Washington, D.C.: Supreme Court.

Cannon, M. 1986. "Contentious and Burdensome Litigation, A Need for Alternatives." *Phi Kappa Phi Journal,* 10-12.

Chanock, M. 1985. *Law, Custom, and Social Order: The Colonial Experience in Malawi and Zambia.* Cambridge: Cambridge University Press.

Claeson, B. 1987. "The Privatization of Justice: An Ethnography of Control." B.A. honors thesis, Department of Anthropology, University of California, Berkeley.

Dart, S. 1987. "Closing the Door on the Public: Controlling Processes in Arbitration." B.A. honors thesis. Department of Anthropology, University of California, Berkeley.

Dredge, C. P. 1979. "Dispute Settlement in the Mormon Community: The Operation of Ecclesiastical Courts in Utah." *Access to Justice.* Vol. 4. *Anthropological Perspective,* ed. K. Koch. Milan: Dott A. Guiffre, Editore Mulan.

Fiss, O. 1984. "Against Settlement." *Yale Law Journal* 93:1073–89.

Galanter, M. 1983. "Reading the Landscape of Disputes: What We Know and Don't Know (and Think We Know) About Our Allegedly Contentious and Litigious Society." *UCLA Law Review* 31:4–71.

————. 1986. "The Day after the Litigation Explosion." *Maryland Law Review* 46:3–39.

————. 1989. "Judges and the Quality of Settlements." Working Paper, Center for Philosophy and Public Policy, University of Maryland, March.

Gluckman, M. 1955. *The Judicial Process among the Barotse and Northern Rhodesia.* Manchester: Manchester University Press.

Greenhouse, C. 1986. *Praying for Justice: Faith, Order, and Community in an American Town.* Ithaca, N.Y.: Cornell University Press.

Gulliver, P. H. 1963. *Social Control in an African Society: A Study of the Arusha, Agricultural Masai of Northern Tanganyika.* Boston: Boston University Press.

Haley, J. O. 1982. "The Politics of Informal Justice: The Japanese Experience, 1922–42." In *The Politics of Informal Justice.* ed. R. L. Abel. Vol. 2. *Comparative Studies.* New York: Academic Press.

Harrington, C. B., and S. E. Merry. 1988. "Ideological Production: The Making of Community Mediation." *Law and Society Review* 22:709–37.

Holleman, J. F. 1974. *Issues in African Law.* The Hague: Mouton.

Janis, I. L. 1972. *Victims of Groupthink.* Boston: Houghton Mifflin.

Levin, A. L. and R. R. Wheeler, eds. 1979. *Proceedings of the National*

Conference on the Causes of Popular Dissatisfaction with the Administration of Justice. St. Paul, Minn.: West Publishing Company.

Nadel, S. 1947. *The Nuba.* London: Oxford University Press.

Nader, L. 1980. *No Access to Law: Alternatives to the American Judicial System.* New York: Academic Press.

———. 1984. "A Study of Barriers to the Use of Alternative Methods of Dispute Resolution." Vermont Law School Dispute Resolution Project.

———. 1988. "The ADR Explosion—The Implications of Rhetoric in Legal Reform." *Windsor Yearbook of Access to Justice* 8:269–91.

———. 1989. "The Crown, the Colonists, and the Course of Village Law." In *History and Power in the Study of Law,* ed. June Starr and Jane Collier. Ithaca, N.Y.: Cornell University Press.

———. 1990. *Harmony Ideology: Justice and Control in a Zapotec Mountain Village.* Stanford: Stanford University Press.

———. 1992. "From Legal Process to Mind Processing." *Family and Conciliation Courts Review* 30, no. 4:468–73.

Nader, L., and H. Todd, eds. 1978. *The Disputing Process: Law in Ten Societies.* New York: Columbia University Press.

Rose, L. 1992. *The Politics of Harmony: Land Dispute Strategies in Swaziland.* Cambridge: Cambridge University Press.

Rothschild, J. 1986. "Mediation as Social Control: A Study of Neighborhood Justice." Ph.D. diss., University of California, Berkeley.

Shapera, I. 1959. *A Handbook of Tswana Law and Custom.* New York: Oxford University Press.

Shonholtz, R. 1987. "The Citizens' Role in Justice: Building a Primary Justice and Prevention System at the Neighborhood Level." *Annals of the American Academy of Political and Social Science* 494:42–52.

Ury, W. L., J. M. Brett, and S. B. Goldberg. 1988. *Getting Disputes Resolved: Designing Systems to Cut the Costs of Conflict.* San Francisco: Jossey-Bass.

Wallerstein, I. 1974. *The Modern World-System: Capitalist Agriculture and the Origins of the European World-Economy in the Sixteenth Century.* New York: Academic Press.

Wasserstein, B., and M. J. Green. 1970. *With Justice for Some: An Indictment of the Law by Young Advocates.* Boston: Beacon Press.

Wiehl, L. 1989. "Private Justice for a Fee: Profits and Problems." New York Times, 17 February 1985.

Wilson, G., and E. Brydolf. 1980. "Grass Roots Solution: San Francisco Consumer Action." In *No Access to Law: Alternatives to the American Judicial System,* ed. L. Nader. New York: Academic Press.

Wolf, E. 1982. *Europe and the People without History.* Berkeley and Los Angeles: University of California Press.

Yngvesson, B. 1988. "Disputing Alternatives: Settlement as Science and as Politics." *Law and Social Inquiry* 13:113–32.

———. 1989. "Inventing Law in Local Settings: Rethinking Popular Legal Culture." *Yale Law Journal* 98:1689–1709.

The Impossibility of Popular Justice

Peter Fitzpatrick

Unorganized innocence: an impossibility.

—Blake

My argument is that in the West popular justice, as it is currently understood, is impossible. To illustrate the argument I draw on the experience of the San Francisco Community Boards program. This program represents the most rigorous commitment to popular justice in the U.S. and is immensely influential (Harrington and Merry 1988:718; Shonholtz 1984:17; Wahrhaftig 1982:88–90). As such, it provides a significant and strong claim to the possibility of popular justice, a claim against which to set my argument.

Popular justice, I suggest, can be seen as a mythology accommodating a conflict—a not unusual thing for mythology to do. In terms of a myth of origin, popular justice sets itself against a formal and an alienated realm from which it is essentially different and apart. With its constriction and artifice, this realm is contrasted with the more spontaneous, naturelike, intrinsically human characteristics of popular justice. Such a realm is occupied by formal law and state administration. But closer observation of popular justice reveals compatibilities, even similarities between it and these formal modes of regulation. We could explain this, as in so many accounts, by reducing popular justice to these formal modes. Popular justice is but an extension of formal regulation, its mere mask or agent. In terms of

Reprinted from *Social and Legal Studies: An International Journal* 1 (1992):199–215.

my argument, there is a point to seeing popular justice as both opposed and integral to the formal. The conflict between these views is accommodated within an encompassing set of mythological figures that inhabit and unite popular justice and formal regulation, the figure of the individual being perhaps the most significant. Within this set of mythic figures, popular justice can oppose the grand, formal modes of the regulation even whilst being identical with them. The challenge then becomes to extract elements of opposition in popular justice from its subordinating identity with formal modes in such a way as to give effect to its foundational aspirations. Somewhat perversely, I see law as one way of doing this. I argue for the possibility of an alternative legality within popular justice instead of a peremptory rejection of law in the constituting of popular justice as its opposite. In advocating this seizing of the law, I also address the seeming disenchantment with popular justice and with the variants of informal and private justice (cf. Matthews 1988:1), and I delineate a way in which law could sustain a revival of popular justice, if not a reenchantment.

The Constitution of Popular Justice

Popular justice takes identity through the not uncommon mythic mode in which binary oppositions provoke and produce positive contents. The great figure of opposition and rejection is the state. "Alternative" justice, including popular justice, is set in a dynamic of opposition to the formalized and centralized power of the state. Alternative justice exists in the denial or partial dissolution of state power, or it exists in the operative affirmation of the limits of such power. That is, where alternative justice works specifically in conjunction with state power, it does so on the basis that such power is limited and that alternative justice makes good this deficiency. Alternative justice does what the state cannot.

As a type of state power, formal law has proved the most productive affront to popular justice (cf. Nader 1988). Formal law focuses on delimited and predefined types of behavior separated from any extensive context. Existential involvement of the subject is absent or restricted to straitened conceptions of responsibility. Popular justice takes identity in positive contrast to all this. It is concerned with the whole person, and no case is specifically confined at the outset in its social relations. Being so unconfined, popular justice can make its characteristic claims to reflect, or strengthen, or even create a holistic "community."

Turning to the San Francisco Community Boards, a considerable literature on them or providing their foundational ideas abundantly attests to their being conceived as profoundly "alternative" to the state, especially to state law (DuBow 1987c:35). The boards stand opposed to the alienating professionalism of the state, to its formality and its "record-keeping apparatus," to its insensitivity in the face of the real needs of individuals and communities, and to its illimitable arrogation of conflicts and other matters that can only be dealt with adequately by individuals and neighborhoods (Shonholtz 1984:5-7, 15, 21-22; Wahrhaftig 1982:89-90). Resort to the state "suppresses and evades" conflict "in its full interactive dynamic," drastically narrows the range of matters considered relevant to it and renders these matters manipulable; in doing all this, the state undermines the responsibility of the individual and the neighborhood for conflict and destroys "the vitality of individual and community life" (Shonholtz 1984:2, 4, 8, 13). So, individual and communal self-reliance oppose the intrinsic assumptions of state regulation (Shonholtz 1984:17, 21).

These mythic assertions are reflected in the practice and strategies of the San Francisco Community Boards. The responsibility of individuals for their conflict and its resolution is to be inculcated and in this way the authenticity of the disputing process will be secured. Thus, the boards claim a significance that sets them apart from other forms of alternative justice in their refusal to accept cases where an agency of the legal system retains jurisdiction: the continuing pressure of the legal system can produce a "less authentic" result (DuBow 1987c:5). Comparable pressure from the panels that hear disputes must of course also be avoided. The "defined passivity" of the panels, their eschewing "active intervention" leaves space for the authenticity of the parties to operate (DuBow 1987c:50). There is a "practice of minimal intervention based on the principle that the disputants are responsible for resolving their own dispute" (DuBow 1987c:53). Again, "the conflict belongs to the disputants; any resolution is of their own making" (DuBow 1987c:50). Disputants are considered holistically and only the authentic resolution of their conflict promoted, even if this may mean having authenticity thrust upon them. The prime emphasis of the panels is to extract the feelings of the parties, so much so that there is a "functional tendency to concentrate on the feelings of the parties rather than on the facts in the dispute" (DuBow 1987c:56). Thus, in one case, there was a "pronounced attempt by the Panel to concentrate on the feelings of the parties when both of them . . . were more concerned about the issues of money and responsibility" (DuBow 1987c:58). So, the handbook for training conciliators to serve on panels contrasts their role with that of mediators in other programs in this way:

> if racism or sexism became apparent on the part of the disputants, a mediator might de-emphasize these issues to avoid inflaming hostility and to reach an agreement more efficiently. The conciliator, on the other hand, would identify these attitudes and encourage their expression, to promote greater understanding, since these factors can significantly affect the quality of a relationship. (Hawkins 1986:6; cf. DuBow 1987c:68)

The responsibility and the vitality of the neighborhood are less precisely articulated in strategies and in practice than those of the individual. "Neighborhood building" is a "central goal" of San Francisco Community Boards, as is "developing a neighborhood's capacity to respond to neighborhood disputes" (DuBow 1987b:1). There would seem to be nothing assuredly linking the boards' core activity of dispute handling with these desiderata.

Formal Compatibilities

Bare and preliminary as it is, my account of popular justice begins to show that it is not constituted only in opposition to the characteristics of formal power. Panels seem to exercise a formal power that is inextricable to and yet more basic than the informal or the popular, more fundamental than the authentic participation of the parties. There would appear to be an unresolved conflict between opposition to the formal and compatability with it. I will now develop this intimation of conflict. I will then show how myth takes its characteristic part in the accommodation of unresolved conflict.

It is hardly novel to suggest that there are compatibilities between formal justice and informal or popular justice. The academic implications drawn from this are by now quite standard if diverse (see

Fitzpatrick 1988:179–82). The distinct identity of informal justice is extinguished in its subordination to, for example, the state. Or formal and informal justice remain distinct and different yet mutually influential. A variant on this sees a bit of the formal in the informal, and vice versa. The difference and integrity of each in the face of some similarity between them is not infrequently secured by seeing the relation as dialectical. Following the cogent insight provided by Bottomley and Roche (1988:90–91), I will explore a contrary possibility: that they are distinct but the same, that what is involved here is a homology. I shall look, firstly, at the configuration of power within popular justice. Then I shall move out from that location, taking popular justice with me to set it in the homologous configuration of power within the formal.

In mapping the operation of power within popular justice, an exemplary beginning is provided by Harrington and Merry in their telling observations of alternative justice (1988:726–29). As I interpret these observations, mediators see their own purposive strategies as the prime impetus and basis for their activity. So, although responsiveness to the parties is emphasized, it is a responsiveness contained within such strategies, within modes of manipulation and direction that operate beyond the knowledge of the parties. Thus, parties can be induced to engage with each other through the maneuvering of eye contact. Or the confidence of the parties is to be purposively created. They are to be made to feel that they are being listened to and that their concerns count. In a "successful" case, parties are brought to accept, to take on themselves, a reality of which the mediator is agent. Yet the parties are seen as ultimately responsible. The door through which they can depart the scene remains open. But this standard picture ignores what is waiting outside the door— a reality of coercive aspects that is invoked by the mediators in order to promote "agreement." I do not mean this egregious interpretation to say more than it does. It does not, for example, impute ulterior motives to mediators. What it says about the orientation and dynamics of informal dispute resolution is just the way things are, and I am extracting from it a certain "nature of things" or a certain "order of things."

I will look at one such thing indicatively (and consider it in more detail later)—the figure of the individual. In mythic terms, the individual is the fount of the informal and of the popular in alternative justice. The individual's voluntary participation and willingness to adapt and enter into agreements are the foundation of the whole process. Everything else in the process—the efficacy and role of the mediators or conciliators, its very success—depends on and springs from that involvement. Formal elements in the process can only be secondary to the thrust of this informal, popular element. My analysis would reverse this mythic account. The individual is an effect of the power exercised in processes of popular justice (cf. Foucault 1980:98). In that revelatory picture of mediators presented by Harrington and Merry (1988), we can discern a disputing individual who is to be maneuvered into certain defining modes of engagement with the other party and with the mediator, an individual who is responsible yet responsive to a preset reality. The individual that emerges from the story-so-far of the Community Boards is not of a completely different kind. Indeed, even greater depths of individuality, extending to the very feelings of the parties, are to be appropriated and shaped in terms of the power being exercised. It is a "basic value" of the boards' processes "that it is of prime importance to probe for the underlying feelings that disputants have about each other" (DuBow 1987c:50). Feelings are elevated over facts and aspirations, even over a resolution of the dispute. The primacy of feelings disconnects the disputants from the social forces encapsulated in their conflict. At best, what is relevant is how they feel about such things. The primacy of feelings inculcates an acceptant attitude in the parties, one in which they are to be fully responsible for "their" conflict—all of which must be heightened in the mutuality entailed in the baring of feelings. If I bare my feelings and become vulnerable to you, almost in return you should become vulnerable to me. The vulnerability of the parties and their induced readiness to take on responsibility leaves the ground clear for the most effective power that can occupy it. I now describe the immediate occupants.

In DuBow's predominantly sympathetic evaluation, a panel derives power from identifying with the process used in hearings:

> However neutral it may be with respect to the dispute that it hears, it is an advocate of CB and its process. When it is most faithful to its advocacy of that process, thereby avoiding the kind of control that professional mediators, lawyers, or courts might

exercise, the Panel unwittingly employs coercion through its unyielding implementation of the process. (DuBow 1987c:69)

And he asks,

What is the essential makeup of the CB Panel? What is the core of its identity? First, it is a group of neighbors who carry the four-phase CB hearing process, and it is very self-conscious about upholding that process, sometimes to the point of being legalistic. (DuBow 1987c:49)

In the first two of these four set phases, the parties express their perceptions of the issues and their feelings. They are thus encouraged to communicate with each other. In the third phase—"sharing responsibility for the conflict and its resolution"—"the parties are now guided through an understanding of their responsibility in both the existence of the conflict and the resolution." Finally, the resolution "is clearly spelled out," "an agreement form between the parties" is concluded, and, "the hearing is closed" (Shonholtz 1984:18).

Informal and responsive as parts of the process may appear to be, it does have, in all, powerful, defining and organizing effects. Thus, in one case:

The Panel was so taken with its responsibility to the CB process that it tended to ignore the attitudes of the parties, and it tended to miss opportunities to use information from the hearing to advance toward resolution of the conflict. (DuBow 1987c:58)

And in another case:

As a proxy for the CB process, the panel seemed at first to be trying to prevent a resolution from coming too soon, since there are three Phases prior to the resolution. In that sense it tended to break off communication between the parties when they wanted to discuss the technical details of the plan they could agree to. It also tried to get the Parties to communicate about underlying feelings and issues when there evidently were none. (DuBow 1987c:61)

An "intervention technique" used in training panel members in a mock hearing tells the trainer,

> To make sure that people are clear that what they are trying to do coincides with the purpose of the phase, ask team members what phase they are in and what are its objectives. (Hawkins 1986:55)

An effective technique, apparently, for

> The common occurrence of panelists trying to identify which Phase the hearing is in, is a major instance of the form of a process displacing the demands of a dispute itself. (DuBow 1987c:71)

It is beside my point to suggest, as DuBow does, a solution in loosening the procedure by relying more on "the Panel's demonstrated potential for ingenuity" (DuBow 1987c:71). The four-phase process is only one of a number of inevitable organizing elements that constitute this mode of popular justice as a formed site of power, and as one that creates and subordinates its own integral element of the "informal" in, for example, the figure of the feeling individual.

No matter what its unique virtues, the Community Boards hearing does share with other types of alternative justice organizing elements contributing to an operative core of formal power. Its quasi-litigious focus and its "defined passivity" accord a formal equality of power to the parties that can deny significant inequalities between them (see, e.g., DuBow 1987c:53, 58). That same focus means that a panel has "no mechanism for engaging the program in a larger social issue unearthed by a two-party dispute" (DuBow 1987c:50). There is even an understandable tendency to avoid such issues and to confine the dispute to the modes and forms in hand (see DuBow 1987c:54). These forms and modes are reinforced by what can loosely be described as a professional orientation on the part of members of panels and by their general cohesion. As Shook and Milner aptly remark, the training program of Community Boards emphasizes "skills . . . familiar to those who have studied inter-personal communication, or have been trained in any of the helping professions" (this volume). Their training and their work are often seen by panel members in professional terms and as beneficial to their careers (DuBow 1987c:16, 35). Training, the encouragement of "teamwork," involvement together in the hearing process, identifying favorably with the neighborhood, all these build up a sense of a distinct "internal" or "exclusive" community (DuBow 1987c:69, 1987d:13, 32, 41; Hawkins 1986:39).

The foundational role of members of panels is heightened in their being "agents of reality." The neutrality of panels in the disputing process positions them to respond to a general reality, beyond yet brought to bear on that process. Thus, an old woman who complains about noise can be put in perspective as either "'crazy' or . . . overreacting" (DuBow 1987c:62). Further, "the Panel, with its three to five persons, is literally and symbolically a public entity" (DuBow 1987c:52). The panel dominates the table—that most potent figure that posits a shared reality on the basis of which a dispute is resolvable. The neighborhood provides a like figure linking the parties and the panel. The panel takes on a "representative role as neighbors of the parties" embodying "community norms and values" (DuBow 1987c:69):

> Whatever authority and control it is able to command over the disputants it accomplishes by way of the CB process which it strongly advocates, and by an empathetic and persuasive identification as a neighbor with experience similar to [that] of the disputants. The latter is usually expressed in subtle ways, such as a panelist identifying his address when he lives a few doors down or around the block from the disputants. At times the identification is made very directly with reference to an actual issue in dispute. In looking at particular hearings we can see that the Panel has the capacity to exert considerable control and even coercion when it chooses to use it. (DuBow 1987c:51)

Indeed, and in terms of myths of origin, the "community board model advances a community-based normative justice system. The model is premised on a community perspective," and "the neighborhood should exercise responsibility for a conflict" (Shonholtz 1984:13–14).

As with the individual, that other constituting basis of popular justice, neighborhood and community are rendered and ultimately created in the formed terms of this site of power. It is, of course, a

common and continuously ineffective charge that alternative justice
is not grounded in a true or real community, or some such. In one
way this sort of criticism may now seem beside the point. In terms
of my account of Community Boards, neither the community nor
the individual has an intrinsic, holistic content. Theirs is a constrained, attenuated content, created and bound within the operation
of a specific type of power. Why, then, should their failure to match
a utopian wholeness be a cause for criticism? But in another way,
the criticism is the point. For the very quality of wholeness, of the
popular and the informal, is generated by and within the exercise of
the power. So, the whole in-dividual is created and maintained in
"popular" terms as informal, as an in-finite repository of effects produced by popular justice. Myths, as Lévi-Strauss has it, are "in-
terminable" (Levi-Strauss 1986:6). In its voluntarism and assumption
of limitless responsibility, the figure of the individual takes on itself
and accepts as its own the effects of popular justice—effects the origins
of which lie in constricted, preformed processes and relations of
power. Likewise with community and neighborhood. These provide
an infinite source of standards and legitimations invoked and given
effect by and within the operation of popular justice. Community
and neighborhood lay claim to an in-finite disciplinary domain where
power can respond to such vast and expansive imperatives as the
"potential" for "disorder," the need for "control," "precriminal" and
"problematic" activities, and community "ideas" and "fears" (Shonholtz 1987:42–45). Indeed, in Shonholtz's definitive account, such
categories can encompass community and neighborhood. Thus, community is equated with "social control," and as "the area of prevention
[of conflict] is extended . . . thereby the scope of community is
extended as well" (Shonholtz 1987:47, 52).

The maintenance of the specificity of formed processes and relations of popular justice depends on the in-finite, the unbounded capacities and natures of the individual and the community. These exist
in a mythically elevated, depoliticized realm of original innocence.
As free-floating entities, not compromised by inexorable ties to the
specific, they can supportively accommodate the widest range of
effects produced by popular justice. And they can do this in a way
that does not challenge the formal sources of these effects or call such
sources to account. The formal elements of popular justice are presented as operating within and in the cause of these whole, unalien-

ated entities. The acceptant, responsible individual and the protean community absorb any elements of popular justice, including elements that would otherwise be incompatible with its defining, informal attributes. So, ultimately, the informal, itself an effect of processes and relations of power within popular justice, seemingly comes to encompass and define those processes and relations. Hence, informalism is to entail the "liquidation of the formal element which separates legal institutions from community life" (Galanter 1980:16).

The identity of alternative justice as informal or popular is both secured and constantly challenged in its relation to types of power usually taken to be formal. There is, of course, a large literature on the deep-seated connections between formal and informal justice (notably Abel 1982b and Harrington 1985). This literature usually emphasizes the reduction of the informal to the formal in two related dimensions. In one, the informal is seen as serving the purposes of the formal (e.g., Cohen 1985). In the other, there is "a gradual infiltration of legal concepts and actors into non-legal reforms" and "a subtle transformation of language, personnel and procedure" (Harrington and Merry 1988:109–10). My analysis would suggest that this is not only or even predominantly a subordination from without. Rather, the "formal" elements operating outside of alternative justice call for and amplify those already operating within. But if those operating within become over-developed, if they become so conspicuous and pervasive that they set explicit limits on the essentially boundless realm of the informal and the popular, then this realm would be undermined.

There is an opposed, if largely unremarked, tendency here. If the formal is to operate through the informal, then the informal must be maintained as such. In Habermas's terms, if it loses its "living," naturelike quality, the informal would cease to legitimate the administrative system (Habermas 1976:68–75). Or as Donzelot concludes, with a more convincing historical specificity, in his account of the constitution of the modern family:

It could even be said that this familial mechanism is effective only to the extent that the family does not reproduce the established order, to the extent that the juridical rigidity or the imposition of state norms do not freeze the aspirations it entertains. (Donzelot 1980:94)

Not only that but, as Donzelot shows for the family, the formal operates to create and sustain the informal. It can do this in obvious ways. Sites of alternative justice are often explicitly created and empowered through state law. The formal legal system provides them with sustaining business. Yet, as the reductionist criticism of alternative justice so often shows, this relation tends also to the undermining of alternative justice.[1]

Mediating Mythologies

The informal or the popular is created and maintained and its corrosive conflict with the formal is mediated through powerful mythic figures. Myths give content to the informal and the popular in their opposition to the formal. Yet as "in-terminable" (Lévi-Strauss 1986:6), myths can extend responsively to the operation of the formal. They exist in a transcendent realm that abstracts from and yet absorbs the effects of power. As meta, myths cannot be brought into a definitive relation with any particular site of power. For example, the individual is formed into different identitites in different sites of power. As a conciliated subject within Community Boards it takes one form. As a legal subject another. Or as the effect of a particular disciplinary field of administration, yet another. The mythic figure of the individual absorbs these indistinguishably. It is this mythic, indeterminate figure of the individual that provides a basis for popular justice. But this transcendent quality of the individual is itself an effect of the sites of power from which it is abstracted. This transcendence, at its broadest, corresponds to the specific Western construction of reality as unitary, exclusive, and objectively knowable and the construction of the individual as the presocial, the ultimate, and the sufficient site of knowing and mastering that reality.

I will look at those two fundamental figures from the mythological charter of the San Francisco Community Boards—the responsible individual and the community. I will weave into them cognate mythic figures that have proved significant in the organizing of alternative justice in its relation to the formal.

---

1. Both the reduction of the informal to the formal and the attribution to them of mutual yet distinct influence tend to be sociologically functionalist in character. My somewhat oblique reliance on these perspectives does not share that character. I use the dissonance between them to point toward a further perception, one of myth.

The Western figure of the self-realizing, responsible individual takes identity through the internalizing of control that accompanies and gives effect to modern systems of administration. New imperatives of internal control elevated a highly individuated self. The connection has been most cogently elaborated by Foucault (see Fitzpatrick 1987). Modern administration provides modes of creating an individuality that is distinctive and notable, responsible and responsive. In short, "the subject" is created as an infinitely self-responsible, self-reflective being with an autonomy necessary for these attributes, a being who acts positively in the cause of her or his own normalization or self-realization as normal. Subjectification is a condition and an effect of subjection (cf. Foucault 1981:60). Power in an administered world operates in the most general dimensions yet through techniques of an intimate and pervasive kind that rely on and imbue all social relations. Such power is indefinite in its scope and unbounded in its ranging over the whole person, the whole "soul." Its manifestation in types of alternative justice has already been instanced. Mediation, as observed for example by Harrington and Merry (1988:726–29), is indistinguishable—in, for example, its instrumental modes and its inculcation of unbounded responsibility—from such foundational administrative strategies as those described by Tuke in 1813 in his account of the first psychiatric asylum in England (Tuke 1964:esp. 131–86).

This self-responsible, self-ordering individual is yet the individual "as posited by nature" (Marx 1973:346). The modern myth of nature is an invention nearly contemporaneous with the formation of the modern individual. Nature exists apart from the artifices of form and culture. It can be acted on and subordinated by form and culture. It lacks purposive power and a project of its own. It simply is. It is spontaneous, an unbounded, authentic realm, a realm of Edenic and unsullied wholeness, where we can be "truly," naturally, ourselves. The rule of law, as the ultimate mode through which a posited determination can seek to appropriate nature, becomes negatively the basic definer of the natural. It is here that we can locate another contemporary invention, that of the private sphere that is marked out by law but not regulated by it (O'Donovan 1985:2–3). This is where the new individual can be left to assume responsibility for her or his own actions (O'Donovan 1985:9). So, in his theorizing about law and "private justice," Henry relies on an "informal, spontaneous level"

(Henry 1983:61). Or an article can be about "alternative dispute resolution and divorce: natural experimentation in family law" (Teitelbaum and DuPaix 1988). And the natural, the authentic individual has
long been situated integrally in the natural, the authentic community
(Turner 1987). "The new community justice system recruits from the
neighborhoods the natural dispute resolvers" (Shonholtz 1987:47). It
is in the vacuity of the natural and the authentic that we find "what a
dispute is all about" and "actual substantive relationships in ongoing
communities" (Lempert and Saunders 1986:478).

Tenuous traces of community supporting this mythic foundation
of alternative justice have failed to survive critical explorations of
their substance. But such deficiencies are hardly to the point. The
dynamic of identity does not come from mundane empirical corre-
spondences. It is a mythmaking dynamic of rejection, of negativity.
It can be readily encapsulated in the mythic figure of utopia, of no
place. The true community of informalism is a vacuous utopia constituted in abrupt opposition to the perceived inauthenticity of certain
existent sites of power (cf. Delgado 1987:312–13). Like the figure of
the spontaneous, unregulated individual, utopian alternatives to the
administered world prove to be modes of further implicating us in
it (Minson 1985:111–12). Through its identity in negation, the free-
floating figure of community is able to range temporally and geographically in search of substance, absorbing, as we have seen, imperatives of control, discipline, and preemptive surveillance. In one
version, community is meant to provide a "modern analogue to the
historical experience of community" in the European colonization of
North America (Shonholtz 1987:46). But the colonized, at least elsewhere, are not left out of the picture. A voracious ethnography
provided accounts of "different cultures" in which "the apparent
naturalness . . . of informal dispute processing" provided ideate origins
for alternative justice in the United States (Matthews 1988:2–3; cf.
Merry 1982). The savage and the savage community have always
been akin to nature, with its mythic, precivilized origins. Such a
primal community was a simple, consensual, and natural whole.
Confirmations of its historical existence were found in similarities
with the "primitive" communities studied by anthropologists. And
these similarities correspond to those attributed to the premodern
community in general. But this idea of community is a construct of
the colonial experience and of the degradation of community in transi-

tions to capitalism. The result is a reduced and contained "native" or "peasant" community whose diversity and organizational complexity have been denied (see Fitzpatrick 1985). And it was precisely this decadent type of community that provided origins for alternative justice.

This adoption of a solidary wholeness, of a consensual commonality, provides an essence for the informal and transforms the merely populist into the popular. Foucault could tie the destruction of revolutionary popular justice to its attempting to operate through the figure of the table (Foucault 1980:chap. 1). The table is an effective symbol importing the myth of law into processes of popular justice. It serves to subordinate competing claims to shared standards of universal applicability. With alternative justice, the community provides a shared, consensual domain, and the table continues to bring it to bear on competing claims. The figure of community also imports a unity and a distinct integrity. This specific identity of community sets it in potential opposition to the world beyond its bounds, but this conflict is preempted in the reduced figure of the modern community whose effects are contained within its own sphere. Community establishes a proportion with and subordination to a wider reality. It is small-scale, decentralized, and qualitatively different to the alienated, formal world beyond it. It cannot, therefore, challenge or disrupt the wider world in the terms of that world. In these terms, operative embodiments of the wider world, such as law, are left in a clear field to dominate community.

Law as myth is implicated with and sustains alternative justice. Law is a metasocial entity seeking to dominate social relations from a point that transcends them. This domination, as the rule of law, asserts a competence to do, potentially, anything. Yet law is bound and constrained in its acting on social relations. If the integrity of law is to be maintained, these limits on its universal competence must be kept apart from it. This is done in several significant ways. One involves the denial of explicit form to such limits. Limiting form is denied or dissipated in the ideas of the informal and the popular. Henry's studies of law and labor discipline provide an example (Henry 1982). The divide between law's universal pretensions and its limited purchase on the labor relation was obscured and mediated by an anodyne "private justice" in the workplace.

As with other formal modes, law is found associated supportively, with the limits on which its formed integrity depends. Negatively, it relates constitutively to those limits by standing in continual opposition to what they contain and affirming its essential alterity. In the utopian response to this rejection, the popular and the informal are self-constituted in opposition to law. Positively, law creates such limits by providing forms of the informal and of its mythic contents, and these forms are integrated into or subordinated to law. There results a penetration by law that continually undermines the popular and the informal and thus undermines a protection of law's own integrity. Hence the constant observation of the constant renewal of popular and informal justice. In this complex of relations to law, alternative justice occupies a position little different from that of other informal limits such as the official discretion characteristic of the modern form of law and the procedural informality of administrative tribunals.

The Politics of Law and Informalism

In the sketching of this complex of relations, I am not reducing the informal and the popular to law or to other formal powers. The relations within the complex are interdependent but mutually and specifically resistant. I have presented a more extensively theoretical account of these relations elsewhere (Fitzpatrick 1988). I will look now at that dimension of these relations that has been my predominant concern here—at how the very terms constituting alternative justice in opposition to certain types of formal power not only dissipate that opposition but reverse its flow into channels of complicity and support. I concentrate more particularly on the potentiality of law, as an alternative legality, for countering that situation. This is neither to claim any particular efficacy for alternative legality nor thoroughly to explore the availability of a politics supporting it. I am concerned to extricate law as an available resource from an opposition that denies its integral relevance to popular justice and to show how law could confront the mythic underpinnings of this opposition.

What has been involved in my account is a denial of the assumptions of authenticity invoked by the popular and the informal, but to question the unorganized innocence of the informal and the popular is not to gainsay the popularity of an alternative justice that "is advocated by reformers and embraced by disputants precisely because it expresses values that deservedly elicit broad allegiance" (Abel 1982:310). Such values make up the original aspirations of alternative justice. They are to do with popular participation in justice on the basis of equality, not just an equality between those in dispute but between them and the people charged with resolving the conflict. These aspirations have not been met, and it is the in-finite nature of the popular and the informal that mutes this failure and prevents its palpable appearance. Yet it cannot be denied that aspirational infinities are politically significant in generating support for and involvement in alternative justice. The challenge is to render these aspirations operationally tangible and assessable. The means of doing this would have to be capable of engaging not just with these aspirations but with their mythic underpinnings in the figures of the individual and the community, nature and utopia. What is more, such an engagement would have to encompass and render accountable the uses to which aspiration and myth are put in the obscuring of the operation of formal power, both within sites of alternative justice and without. More positively, if the subversion of the popular and the informal can be countered by making them more operationally tangible— constituting a popular record—and by making them subject to account, this outcome could be a step in making their contents available for that liberating political practice so readily and yet so elusively associated with alternative justice.

To suggest that law is what is needed to give effect to this ambitious prospectus may induce a certain incredulity, and what is worse, weariness in my readers. After all, the resort to the popular and the informal has been in opposition to law. And those who rightly find a source of their oppressions in a utopian informalism would advocate formal law as a counter to the informal and the popular (see, e.g., Delgado 1987:312–15, 319). But, if my earlier analysis is accepted, it does not seem likely that formal law would move decisively against the informal and the popular, that it would render them more tangible and subject to account, since to do this would expose limiting conditions on its own identity as the rule of law. The problem lies in the alternation. As I have shown, the constitution of the popular and the informal in peremptory opposition to law is a first and essential step in subordinating alternative justice to a wider configuration of power. Formal law, or state law, is integral to that wider power. And popular or informal justice is characteristically seen to fail, to require renewal the more it becomes similar to or absorbed into state law. But to leave law there is to cede the terrain before entering it. Even if we accept the oppositional premise—the denial of state law in the constitution of alternative justice—this need not extend to the denial of all law. But it does so extend in practice because the utility of the informal and the popular for formal sites of power is incompatible, I now argue, with their operating through any legal modes, since such modes would reveal their limited and organized nature and reveal the formal powers that limit and organize them.

Let us consider law's perverse virtues. For the proponents of alternative justice, law is the epitome of that alienation to which it is foundationally opposed. Its asserted aims "of informality, of solidarity, of overcoming distance" stand sharply opposed to the abstraction from social relations, to the distancing between people that law effects, and to the appropriation of law by professionals that this makes possible (Williams 1987:409). Yet, in the sentimentality of informalism, the virtues of alienation are too readily ignored. In its origins, modern formal law opposed old informal power through the production of "visibility, accountability and clarity" (Mohr 1973:14). To render social relations, literally, in this light entails an alienating, reflective distance from them. It is important, I would argue, to separate these sources of alienation from that other alienating dimension of Enlightenment which would lay claim to a transcendent rationality. Although this metaquality is integral to modern law, it has existed in tension with an older and continuing dimension of law— with law as embodied in particular practices and traditions and as sustaining the tradition or practice by ensuring its continuity whilst acting to evaluate and transform it. Of course, the persistence of localized legal orders—"living law" and such—has been much commented on, as has the opposition of modern state law to these legal orders. The opposition is well founded. Alternative law of this kind has the potential for making visible, for subjecting to account the claims of the informal and the naturelike, and these claims, as I have shown, protect a transcendent rule of law from its limiting connections with particular social relations.

Such a law against law is not simply a speculative prospect. The efflorescence of alternative justice and alternative social action of the 1970s was but a part of a larger and persisting tradition of popular radicalism. Within it, people—"ordinary," nonprofessional people—

have competently operated locally based but extensive legal orders
(see e.g. Garlock 1982). The spread of popular justice is indicative
of this competence, and so is what Matthews, referring to "various
surveys," sees as

> a surprisingly high level of satisfaction (75–95 percent) with the
> experience of neighborhood courts by those who actually par-
> ticipated. This may be due to the fact that, regardless of the
> shortcomings of the process and the pressures involved, the par-
> ticipants were encouraged to participate actively in the process
> and the outcome. (Matthews 1988:12)

Although presented as informal and alternative to law, these
processes do have lawlike qualities. They incorporate legal values.
They adopt casuistic modes of argument, and through them conflicting interests are addressed in a disinterested evaluation. Henry's
account of private justice provides an abundance of illustrations
(Henry 1983). But, as with his account, these lawlike elements are
usually seen as borrowings from state law, as intrusions into the
essentially different realm of alternative justice. But in my argument,
such elements can be indigenous. Law is ordinary and everyone has
the law. Elsewhere I have argued that there is a popular competence
in legal ordering integral to the constitution and self-ordering of the
modern individual (Fitzpatrick 1987:15–18, 1988:196–97). I would
derive support for this also from studies of an extensive legal consciousness and of the social pervasion of legal discourse (see Merry
1988:881–82 and references there cited).

But the legal mentality is far from homogeneous. It can accommodate a diversity of conflicting aspirations and contents (e.g. Williams 1987:417). The very transcendence of law makes it potentially
responsive to a diversity of interests. Law gives an effective form to
interests, making them visible and more clear. It brings interests into
evaluative relation to one another and makes them accountable. It does
prefer and identify with particular interests, but that is an outcome
reached through some explicit consideration, and as an outcome it is
always subject to reevaluation in relation to later configurations of
interests. Law can be thus opposed to naturalist or informal domination. The discovery and formulation through this process of values and
standards could provide a content for that community which seems so

necessary yet proves so elusive in the operation of popular and informal justice. With Community Boards, for example, alternative legality
could provide those "internal structures and processes" that DuBow
sees as necessary if SFCB is to bring about "neighborhood cohesion"—
"one of the major goals [SFCB] has aspired to but has not achieved"
(DuBow 1987c:70). Such structures and processes cannot emerge in the
dissolution effected by the informal and the popular.

Conclusion

I shall draw together the lineaments of my argument in a questioning
of standard distinctions between formal and informal justice, between
state law and alternative justice. We saw that alternative justice takes
mythic content negatively by being set in opposition to law. But the
terms of this opposition themselves conflicted with similarities and
compatibilities between alternative justice and law. The organization
of power within state law and within alternative justice was distinct
but homologous. With each, there was a core of "formed" power
that operated through and depended on informal or popular elements. But even these elements of the informal or popular could not
be seen as truly informal or popular. For one thing, their very identity
as informal or popular resulted from their relation to the core of
formed power. For another, they took positive identity from a combination of mythic figures, the figures of the individual and the
community for example, which were themselves formed, historical
constructs.

This dissection of the informal and the popular was accompanied
by an account of how these categories operated in ways contrary
to the aspirational aims invested in them. They did not found a
justice that was alternative. They were not the product of a supportive community or an autonomous individual as these entities
are evoked in popular and informal justice. Rather, the categories of
the informal and the popular secured the integrity and efficacy of
state law and other sites of power usually considered as formal. I
then argued for an alternative legality as a potential means of meeting
the original aspirations of informal and popular justice. This alternative legality could fundamentally challenge formal law by countering the elements on which it was shown to depend, those elements
of the informal and popular and their seductive mythic contents.

REFERENCES

Abel, R. L. 1982a. "The Contradictions of Informal Justice." In *The Politics of Informal Justice*, vol. 1. See Abel 1982b.

———, ed. 1982b. *The Politics of Informal Justice, Vol. 1: The American Experience. Vol. 2: Comparative Perspectives.* New York: Academic Press.

Bottomley, A., and Roche, J. 1988. "Conflict and Consensus: A Critique of the Language of Informal Justice." In *Informal Justice? See* Matthews 1988.

Cohen, S. 1985. *Visions of Social Control, Crime, Punishment and Classification.* Cambridge: Polity Press.

Delgado, R. 1987. "The Ethereal Scholar: Does Critical Legal Studies Have What the Minorities Want?" *Harvard Civil Rights–Civil Liberties Law Review* 22:301–22.

Donzelot, J. 1980. *The Policing of Families: Welfare versus the State.* London: Hutchinson.

DuBow, F. 1987a. "Overview of Community Boards." In *Conflicts and Community: A Study of the San Francisco Community Boards* Draft. Center for Research in Law and Justice, The University of Illinois at Chicago: Chicago.

———. 1987b. "Uniqueness and Impact." In *Conflicts and Community. See* DuBow 1987a.

———. 1987c. "Conflict Resolution." In *Conflicts and Community. See* DuBow 1987a.

———. 1987d. "Volunteer Development." In *Conflicts and Community. See* DuBow 1987a.

Fitzpatrick, P. 1985. "Review Article: Is It Simple to be a Marxist in Legal Anthropology?" *Modern Law Review* 48:472–85.

———. 1987. "A criação do sujeito de Direito nas genealogias de Michel Foucault." *Revista do Ministério Público* 30:7–24.

———. 1988. "The Rise and Rise of Informalism." In *Informal Justice? See* Matthews 1988.

Foucault, M. 1980. *Power, Truth and Strategy.* Sydney: Feral Publications.

———. 1981. *The History of Sexuality. Volume 1: An Introduction.* Penguin: Harmondsworth.

Galanter, M. 1980. "Legality and Its Discontents: A Preliminary Assessment of Current Theories of Legalization and Delegalization." In *Alternative Rechtsformen und Alternativen zum Recht, Jahrbuch für Rechtssozologie und Rechtstheorie, Band VI,* ed., E. Blankenburg, E. Klausa, and H. Rottleuthner. Westdeutscher Verlag. Opladen.

Habermas, J. 1976. *Legitimation Crisis.* London: Heinemann.

Harrington, C. B. 1985. *Shadow Justice: The Ideology and Institutionalization of Alternatives to Court.* Westport: Greenwood Press.

Harrington, C. B., and Merry, S. E. 1988. "Ideological Production: The Making of Community Mediation." *Law and Society Review* 22:709–35.

Hawkins, K. 1986. *Handbook for Conciliation Trainers.* San Francisco: Community Board Center for Policy and Training.

Henry, S. 1982. "Factory Law: The Changing Disciplinary Technology of Industrial Social Control." *International Journal of the Sociology of Law* 10:365–83.

———. 1983. *Private Justice: Towards Integrated Theorizing in the Sociology of Law.* London: Routledge and Kegan Paul.

Lempert, R., and Saunders, J. 1986. *An Invitation to Law and Social Science: Desert, Disputes, and Distribution.* New York: Longman.

Lévi-Strauss, C. 1986. *The Raw and the Cooked: Introduction to a Science of Mythology.* Harmondsworth: Penguin.

Marx, K. 1973. *Grundrisse: Foundations of the Critique of Political Economy.* Harmondsworth: Penguin.

Matthews, R. 1988. "Reassessing Informal Justice." In *Informal Justice?,* ed. R. Matthews. London: Sage.

Merry, S. E. 1982. "The Social Organization of Mediation in Nonindustrial Societies: Implications for Informal Community Justice in America." In *The Politics of Informal Justice,* vol. 2. *See* Abel 1982b.

———. 1988. "Legal Pluralism." *Law and Society Review* 22:869–96.

Minson, J. 1985. *Genealogies of Morals: Nietzsche, Foucault, Donzelot, and the Eccentricity of Ethics.* Basingstoke: Macmillan.

Mohr, J. W. 1973. "Law and Society: From Proscription to Discovery." *Canadian Bar Review* 51:6–14.

Nader, L. 1988. "The ADR Explosion—The Implications of Rhetoric in Legal Reform." *Windsor Yearbook of Access to Justice* 8:269–91.

O'Donovan, K. 1985. *Sexual Divisions in Law.* London: Weidenfeld and Nicolson.

Shonholtz, R. 1984. "Neighborhood Justice Systems: Work, Structure, and Guiding Principles." *Mediation Quarterly* 5:3–30.

———. 1987. "The Citizens' Role in Justice: Building a Primary Justice and Prevention System at the Neighborhood Level." *Annals of the AAPSS* 494:42–52.

Teitelbaum, L. E., and DuPaix, L. 1988. "Alternative Dispute Resolution and Divorce: Natural Experimentation in Family Law." *Rutgers Law Review* 40:1093–1132.

Tuke, S. 1964. *Description of the Retreat, an Institution near York for Insane Persons of the Society of Friends.* London: Dawsons of Pall Mall.

Turner, B. 1987. "A Note on Nostalgia." *Theory, Culture and Society* 4:147–56.

Wahrhaftig, P. 1982. "An Overview of Community-Oriented Citizen Dispute Resolution Programs in the United States." In *The Politics of Informal Justice,* vol. 1. *See* Abel 1982b.

Williams, P. J. 1987. "Alchemical Notes: Reconstructing Ideals from Deconstructed Rights." *Harvard Civil Rights–Civil Liberties Law Review* 22:401–33.

Contributors

Peter S. Adler is executive director of the Hawaii Bar Foundation and formerly director of the state's Center for Alternative Dispute Resolution. He is also a member of the Accord Group. He has had extensive experience mediating, facilitating, and training in the United States and in Australia. His published research includes work on the practices and ideologies of alternative dispute resolution. His book *Beyond Paradise: Encounters in Hawaii Where the Tour Bus Never Runs* will be published in the fall.

Eliott Currie is a sociologist in Berkeley, California. His latest book is *Reckonings: Drugs, the Cities, and the American Future.*

The late Fredric L. DuBow was Professor of Criminal Justice at the University of Illinois at Chicago and the principal investigator of the original Community Boards evaluation study. He was one of the early analysts of the contemporary mediation movement in the United States.

Peter Fitzpatrick is Professor of Law and Social Theory at the University of Kent, England and has taught at universities in Europe, North America, and Papua New Guinea. His latest book is *The Mythology of Modern Law.*

Christine B. Harrington is an Associate Professor of Politics at New York University. She is the author of *Shadow Justice*, coauthor of *Administrative Law and Politics*, coeditor of *Lawyers' Work* and *The Presidency in American Politics*. She has published articles on legal ideology, constitutive and interpretive sociolegal theory and empirical methods, dispute processing, alternative dispute resolution and informalism, and the relationship between law and state formation. She is currently writing a book on the role of American legal ideology and the legal profession in forming the twentieth-century administrative state.

Ron Kraybill holds a Ph.D. in Religious Studies from the University of Capetown and currently is the director of training at the Centre for Intergroup Studies in Capetown, South Africa. He is the founding director of the Mennonite Conciliation Service, a position he held for ten years. He has trained extensively throughout Southern Africa, Europe, and Ireland. He is the author of numerous books and articles, and is now completing his dissertation on the mediation of the Zimbabwean independence at the Religious Studies Program at the University of Capetown.

John Paul Lederach holds a Ph.D. in Sociology completed at the University of Colorado in the specialized program on social conflict and currently is director of the International Conciliation Service of the Mennonite Central Committee and Associate Professor of Sociology at Eastern Mennonite College. He is former director of Mennonite Conciliation Service, has served as a trainer in over 20 countries, and a consultant or mediator in conciliation efforts at the highest levels in Nicaragua, Ethiopia, Somalia, Spain, and the Philippines. He is the author of numerous books and articles on conflict transformation, nonviolence, peace education, and mediation in English and Spanish.

Kem Lowry is professor and former chair of Urban and Regional Planning and affiliate, Program on Conflict Resolution, University of Hawaii. He has served as a mediator in several multiparty disputes and has facilitated policy dialogues on land use and environmental issues. He has published on land use and environmental management, evaluation and planning theory, and has served as a consultant to a UN agency, USAID, the U.S. Office of Technology Assessment, and several city and state agencies.

Craig McEwen is Professor of Sociology at Bowdoin College. He has published widely on mediation and dispute resolution. He is coauthor of a widely recognized study on small claims mediation. His recent work is on the local culture of lawyering and the theory of mediation.

Sally Engle Merry, Professor of Anthropology at Wellesley College, is the author of Urban Danger: Life in a Neighborhood of Strangers (1981), and Getting Justice and Getting Even: Legal Consciousness among Working-Class Americans (1990). She has published on legal ideology, mediation, urban ethnic relations, and legal pluralism and from 1993 to 1995 will serve as President of the Law and Society Association. She is currently working on a project on the meanings of law and violence in the American colonization of Hawaii in the nineteenth and twentieth centuries.

Neil Milner is Professor of Political Science and director of the Program on Conflict Resolution, University of Hawaii. He has served as a facilitator on policies regarding mental health and the mentally disabled. His research includes work on mediation ideologies, the links between culture and dispute resolution, the role of rights discourse, and narratives of property ownership.

Laura Nader is Professor of Anthropology at the University of California at Berkeley. She is the author of numerous books and articles on social anthropology and law, dispute processing, the American dispute resolution movement, and the ethnology of the Middle East, Mexico, and the contemporary United States. Her most recent book is Harmony Ideology: Justice and Control in a Mountain Zapotec Village (1992). Other major works include Law in Culture and Society (1969), The Disputing Process—Law in Ten Societies, and No Access to Law—Alternatives to the American Judicial System (1980).

Judy H. Rothschild is a researcher for the National Jury Project in Oakland, California. She did some of the earliest research on Fredric DuBow's Community Boards assessment project and wrote a doctoral dissertation on that subject. She has also done other work in conflict resolution.

Raymond Shonholtz is the President of Partners for Democratic Change, a nonprofit corporation founded in 1989 to expand the conflict resolution capacity of the developing democracies in Central and Eastern Europe and the new Republics of the former Soviet Union. He is the founder and former president of the Community Board Program. The Community Board Program's national training institutes initiated the community and school conflict resolution movement in the United States and promoted the development of Native American Indian Tribal Community Boards.

Vicki Shook is the coordinator of volunteers at the Hospice Caring Project of Santa Cruz County and former associate director of the University of Hawaii's Program on Conflict Resolution. She has taught courses on conflict resolution and is the author of the book *Ho'oponopono,* a study of traditional Hawaiian forms of dispute resolution and their adaptation to contemporary society.

Douglas R. Thompson is Associate Professor of Sociology at Central Michigan University. He worked with Fredric DuBow on the materials on the San Francisco Community Boards. He has published in the field of criminal justice and organizational theory.

Barbara Yngvesson is Professor of Anthropology at Hampshire College. She has written widely on the politics of disputing and the cultural analysis of law, and is the author of *Virtuous Citizens, Disruptive Subjects: Order and Complaint in a New England Court* (1993) and coauthor (with Carol J. Greenhouse and David M. Engel) of *Contest and Community: The Meanings of Law in Three American Towns* (1993).

Index